The
RIVERSIDE
READER

The RIVERSIDE READER

ALTERNATE EDITION

Joseph F. Trimmer
Ball State University

Heather Milliet
Davis High School in Houston

Houghton Mifflin Company   Boston New York

Editor-in-Chief: Carrie Brandon
Senior Sponsoring Editor: Lisa Kimball
Senior Marketing Manager: Tom Ziolkowski
Senior Developmental Editor: Meg Botteon
Senior Project Editor: Jane Lee
Senior Art and Design Coordinator: Jill Haber
Cover Design Manager: Anne S. Katzeff
Senior Photo Editor: Jennifer Meyer Dare
Composition Buyer: Chuck Dutton
New Title Project Manager: Susan Brooks-Peltier
Editorial Assistant: Sarah Truax
Marketing Assistant: Bettina Chiu
Editorial Assistant: Anne Finley

Cover Image: *Tree at River's Edge,* © Steve Satushek/Getty Images

Text credits appear on pp. 556–559, which are hereby considered an extension of the copyright page.

Photo credits: p. 41: From *Persepolis: The Story of a Childhood* by Marjane Satrapi, translated by Mattias Ripa & Blake Ferris, translation copyright © 2003 by L'Association, Paris, France. Used by permission of Pantheon Books, a division of Random House, Inc.; p. 102: © The New Yorker Collection 1991, James Stevenson from cartoonbank.com. All rights reserved; p. 218: © The New Yorker Collection 2003, Roz Chast from Cartoonbank.com. All rights reserved; p. 287: © Shannon Mendes; p. 393: © Center for International Rehabilitation. Second color insert, p. 1: Printed by permission of the Norman Rockwell Family Agency, copyright © 1943 Norman Rockwell Family Entities; p. 2: © Tom Nebbia/ Corbis; p. 3: © Earl and Nazima Kowall/Corbis; p. 4: © Evanian Phillippe.

Printed in the U.S.A.

Library of Congress Control Number: 2007939711

ISBN 13: 978-0-618-94871-0
ISBN 10: 0-618-94871-6

1 2 3 4 5 6 7 8 9-EB-11 10 09 08 07

CONTENTS

PROCESS ANALYSIS   96

DIVISION AND CLASSIFICATION   213

Saying that even the best mothers cannot be good fathers, the author argues that children's need for a father is so important that men and women need to negotiate new kinds of marriage contracts to meet children's needs.

A Debate About Windmills

An environmental lawyer from a famous American family associated with Cape Cod argues that installing windmills in Nantucket Sound will create environmental and economic dangers.

A longtime resident of Cape Cod and a frequent contributor to the *Cape Cod Times* argues that the windmills will create no environmental dangers and will produce valuable economic benefits.

A Debate About Harry Potter

A well-known dance and theater critic traces the rich traditions of myth and legend that form the foundation of the enormously popular Harry Potter books, and concludes that the strength of their appeal lies partly in the author's willingness to raise universal moral questions without giving easy answers.

A distinguished professor of literature at Yale argues that the Harry Potter books are unimaginative and clichéd, inferior to children's classics of an earlier time.

Classical Arguments

THEMATIC TABLE OF CONTENTS

The Environment

The Family

The Other

Women

Heroes

Work

Teaching and Learning

Arts and Leisure

Science and Technology

Ethical Issues

PREFACE

The Riverside Reader, Alternate Edition, was designed with two goals in mind: to give AP* Language and Composition teachers the flexibility to teach the course according to their personal class goals, and at the same time to give them the confidence that they are providing an excellent AP* examination preparation program for their students. In other words, we strove to give teachers the freedom to teach the best class they can.

For almost three decades, *The Riverside Reader* has set the standard for rhetorical readers. Its explanations of purpose, audience, and strategies have enabled a generation of students to read prose models effectively and to write their own essays successfully. Indeed, its thorough coverage and thoughtful advice about the many issues and problems embedded in the reading and writing processes have established this book as one of the core texts in the college composition curriculum.

This alternate edition of *The Riverside Reader,* like its predecessors, presents essays by acknowledged masters of prose style, including Maya Angelou, E. B. White, and Flannery O'Connor, along with many newer voices such as Judith Ortiz Cofer, N. Scott Momaday, and Joan Acocella. Many of the selections in this reader have been chosen to correspond with the College Board's recommendations for preparing

students for the Advanced Placement* English Language and
Composition exam. Thirty-two of the authors are included on
the AP* representative authors list. As always, introductions,
readings, study questions, and writing assignments are clear,
creative, and cogent.

THE RIVERSIDE TRADITION

Compared to the traditional *Riverside Reader*, this alternate
edition includes substantially greater coverage of the reading
and writing processes college-level students are expected to
master, as well as discussion of analysis and synthesis as writing
strategies. The next seven sections are arranged in a sequence
familiar to most writing teachers. Beginning with narration
and description, moving through the five expository patterns,
and ending with persuasion and argument, these sections
group readings according to the traditional writing strategies
many teachers want to cover.

The readings within each section have been chosen to illustrate what the section introductions say they illustrate: there
are no strange hybrids or confusing models. Within each section, the selections are arranged in ascending order of length
and complexity. The ultimate purpose of *The Riverside Reader*
is to produce good writing. For that reason, the writing assignments in this book are presented after each selection. Four
assignments after each selection prompt students to analyze,
practice, argue, and synthesize both the rhetorical mode and
the content of the selection.

REVISIONS TO THE ENDURING
FEATURES

At the core of *The Riverside Reader* is our desire to assist students with their reading and writing by helping them to see
the interaction between the two processes:

- The **connection between the reading and writing
  process** is highlighted in the Introduction. The familiar

terminology of *purpose, audience,* and *strategies* provides a framework for the Introduction and for subsequent study questions and writing assignments.

- **Guidelines for Reading an Essay** is paired with **Guidelines for Determining Your Purpose, Guidelines for Analyzing Your Audience,** and **Guidelines for Selecting Your Strategy** to enhance and advance the students' understanding of the reading/writing connection.

- An **annotated essay** by Virginia Woolf, "Shakespeare's Sister," demonstrates how the reader responds to reading by writing.

- A **student essay** on the subject of writing—Kristie Ferguson's "The Scenic Route"—discusses the early experiences of one student writer. The essay is followed by commentary on what the student discovered about her writing.

- To demonstrate the increasing importance of visual literacy in our culture, each rhetorical section features a **visual text—** such as a cartoon, icon, or advertisement. Each of these texts is followed by an assignment that encourages students to look more closely at the image, discuss its significance to the chapter's rhetorical strategy, and write about what they have discovered. In addition, the Introduction includes four pages in full color illustrating the different kinds of visual information students are likely to encounter in the synthesis portion of the Advanced Placement* exam, along with discussion of how each visual strategy complements a specific rhetorical strategy.

- An **extended Introduction** now provides more in-depth discussions of the reading and writing processes, including coverage of purpose and audience; strategies, such as analysis and synthesis are also presented. In addition, a student paper is shown in multiple drafts, illustrating how an essay evolved from the first to the final draft.

- A new **synthesis assignment** follows each essay, asking students to research additional sources on the theme of the essay and then to use these sources to advance their own theses about the theme.

- A new **student argument essay** on family asks students to use the essays and photographs about family in the Persuasion and Argument section to respond to a writing prompt similar to those they will encounter on the AP* exam.
- A new **student synthesis essay** asks students to draw upon a group of texts and visuals about the potential of wind farms to create sustainable energy in order to craft a response to a writing prompt similar to the new synthesis activities required on the AP* exam.
- A **Points to Remember** list concludes each section introduction and provides a convenient summary of the essential tasks and techniques of each strategy.
- A **Thematic Table of Contents** is provided for teachers who wish to organize their course by themes or issues.
- A **short story** concludes each section to provide an interesting perspective on a particular writing strategy and to give students opportunities to broaden their reading skills. Most of the authors are drawn from the AP* representative authors list.
- The chapter on **using and documenting sources** provides expanded instruction on using and documenting sources in the Modern Language Association (MLA) style. Special attention is given to the problem of plagiarism and the citation of electronic sources. The chapter concludes with an annotated student paper (including an outline), Ashley Keith's "Video Games Redefining Education," that uses both print and electronic sources.

Supplements for *The Riverside Reader*

- **Fast Track to a 5: Preparing for the AP* English Language and Composition Examination** will help students achieve success on the AP* exam. It features a diagnostic test to assess prior knowledge, review of course content with questions similar to those on the AP* exam, recommended strategies and tips for taking the exam, and two full-length practice exams.

- **Teacher's Resource Guide for the Advanced Placement* Program** is a complete teaching resource developed by and for AP* teachers. The Resource Guide is intended to help high-school teachers and students make a smooth transition to the college-level work of an AP* course. It includes suggestions on how to pace the course, review for the AP* exam, and assess students' preparedness. The Guide is closely correlated to *The Riverside Reader, Alternate Edition.*

- **Classroom Practice Exercises to accompany** *The Riverside Reader, Alternate Edition* provides additional practice exercises to prepare students for the AP* exam. The booklet includes a full bank of multiple-choice questions like those found on the AP* exam; essay questions involving argument, synthesis, and other key rhetorical skills; and blackline masters of five complete practice exams in AP* format.

- **HM NewsNow powered by the Associated Press** allows teachers to bring the most current and up-to-date news stories into the classroom in order to spark discussion, engage students, and help students learn the skills necessary to analyze today's headlines. Our content experts scour the Associated Press headlines for the most thought-provoking and relevant news stories of the week. They place articles, videos, and photos into PowerPoint slides that teachers can download from our password-protected instructor website and show in class. Teachers can get a classroom discussion started or use the prompts for in-class, journal, or essay writing. And because HM NewsNow can be downloaded to the computer's hard drive beforehand, an Internet connection in the classroom is not necessary! Students have access to the same news story and accompanying video or photo on the book's free companion website, which means that teachers can ask students to read the material the night before class.

---

*AP and the Advanced Placement Program are registered trademarks of the College Board, which was not involved in the production of and does not endorse these products.

ACKNOWLEDGEMENTS

We are grateful to the following writing teachers who have provided extensive commentary on *The Riverside Reader* for this edition:

Cara Cassell, Decatur High School, Georgia
Rose Crnkovich, Trinity High School, Illinois
Brent Eldridge, Tustin High School, California
Sharon Gdaniec, Seneca High School, Pennsylvania
Rebecca Mayo, Cypress High School, Florida
Frank Meyer, Avon High School, Indiana
Cheryl Morris, Crystal River High School, Florida
Bill O'Brien, Fort Hamilton High School, New York
Pat Pelham, Union Grove High School, Georgia
Lisa Salyer, Carroll Senior High School, Texas
Regina Silvia, Bishop Feehan High School, Massachusetts

J. F. T.
M. H.

ABOUT THE AUTHORS

JOSEPH F. TRIMMER is Professor of English and Director of the Virginia B. Ball Center for Creative Inquiry at Ball State University in Muncie, Indiana. The author of numerous articles on literature, culture, and literacy, Professor Trimmer's books include *The National Book Award for Fiction: The First Twenty-five Years* (1978); *Understanding Others: Cultural and Cross-Cultural Studies and the Teaching of Literature* (1992); and *Narration As Knowledge: Tales of the Teaching Life* (1997).

His textbooks include *Writing With a Purpose*, 14th edition (2004); *The Riverside Reader*, 9th edition (2007); *eFICTIONS* (2002); and *The Sundance Introduction to Literature* (2007). Professor Trimmer has also worked on twenty documentary films for PBS—including the six-part series, *Middletown* (1982), which was nominated for ten Emmys and won first prize at the Sundance Film Festival. Each year, the Virginia Ball Center, which Professor Trimmer directs, sponsors four interdisciplinary, collaborative, community based seminars which research, design, and create projects such as theatrical productions, museum exhibits, books, and films.

HEATHER MILLIET'S nineteen years of experience as an educator have been almost exclusively in the Houston Independent School District, the seventh largest urban district in the United States, with the exception of one year teaching at Ball High School in Galveston, Texas. She has been an English teacher at Davis High School in Houston since 1989, during which time she has taught all levels of high school English, including, comprehensively, four years of AP Language and Composition and AP Literature and Composition. During her tenure as magnet coordinator, she also served as GT and AP Coordinator, working with gifted and talented students, the AP program, AP teacher certification, and on-going professional development for AP teachers.

INTRODUCTION

People who do well in college are nearly always good readers and good writers. They have to read well to absorb and evaluate the wealth of information they encounter online and in articles and books, and they have to write well to show that they are thinking and learning. In this book, we try to help you connect your reading and writing and become skillful at both crafts, for they are complementary skills, and you can master both of them through practice.

THE ACTIVE READING PROCESS

Although you have already discovered ways of reading that no doubt work for you, there is a big difference between being a passive reader—a reader who simply consumes, uncritically, another's writing—and an active reader—a reader who questions, challenges, and reflects on the way another writer addresses a subject and develops its interlocking topics.

1

By practicing the following steps in the reading process you will learn to interact effectively with a text.

- *Step one.* When you are reading a piece of writing you need to master, go over it quickly at first to get the main idea and the flavor of the piece. Just enjoy it for what you are learning. Unless you get lost or confused, don't go back to reread or stop to analyze the writer's argument.
- *Step two.* Now slow down. If you are reading from a book or magazine you don't own, photocopy the text. If you are reading on the Internet, print the document. Now go back over your paper copy, this time underlining or highlighting key points and jotting notes in the margins. You may want to develop a scheme for such annotations, such as the one illustrated in the sample annotated analysis of Virginia Woolf's essay "Shakespeare's Sister" on pages 6–10, where summaries of the main points are written in the *left* margin, and questions or objections are written in the *right* margin.
- *Step three.* On a separate piece of paper or in a separate file, jot down your responses to the reading. What appeals to you about the writer's ideas? What puzzles you? What elements in the piece remind you of some of your own experiences? How does this text relate to other texts you have read? Remember there's not necessarily one "right" reaction to what you are reading. Each reader brings different experiences to reading a piece of writing. So every response will be individual, and each reader will have a slightly different perspective. The notes you take on your reading will help you if you go on to write about the piece or discuss it in class.

READING TO BECOME A BETTER WRITER

Many people have learned to improve their performance in a sport or activity by watching a professional at work and then patterning their activity on that of the professional. In the same way, you can sharpen your reading and writing skills by paying attention to how professional writers practice their craft. This book is organized around that assumption. Thus you will find tips about what strategies to look for as you read these authors and questions that give you insight into their writing process. Here are three things to look for:

- *What is the writer's purpose?* What does he or she want to accomplish? How does the writer communicate that purpose? For instance, in "Shakespeare's Sister," Woolf's purpose is to challenge the age-old claim that women must be, inherently, less creative than men because there have been so few famous women writers, painters, or musicians.
- *Who is the writer's audience?* What assumptions does the writer make about what the audience knows or needs to know? Woolf's immediate audience—those who first read *A Room of One's Own* (1929)—were people interested in the arts and familiar with Shakespeare's plays and poems. Certainly Woolf assumed that many of her readers were women who did not need to be convinced about the significance of her argument.
- *What are the writer's strategies?* How does the writer organize his or her information? Does he or she tell stories, give examples, analyze evidence, or assert claims? Woolf creates a narrative to dramatize her points, knowing that she will arouse sympathy for her imaginary character, Judith Shakespeare. She also uses other strategies, such as comparison and contrast and cause and effect, to advance her argument.

When you get in the habit of asking questions about a writer's purpose, audience, and strategies, you'll begin to understand how writers work and begin to master some elements of their craft for your own writing.

READING *THE RIVERSIDE READER*

Before you begin to read essays from a chapter of *The Riverside Reader*, look over the introduction to that section to get a feel for what to expect. The introduction will explain the purpose, audience, and strategies employed in a particular writing pattern. It will also suggest how you might incorporate these strategies in your own writing. Each introduction concludes with a boxed list of Points to Remember.

Before each essay you will find a biographical headnote that explains the author's background and work. Following each essay is a set of questions to help you analyze the writer's *purpose, audience,* and *strategies.* After this set of questions you will find four kinds of writing assignments:

1. *Analysis:* This assignment asks you to analyze how the writer exploits the features of a particular writing pattern.
2. *Practice:* This assignment encourages you to use the strategies you have studied to write a similar kind of essay.
3. *Argument:* This assignment invites you to extend or contest the argument embedded in the essay.
4. *Synthesis:* This assignment urges you to research additional sources on the theme explored in the essay and then use them to advance your own thesis about that theme.

Each chapter concludes with a short story that evokes the writing strategy illustrated in the essays. After each story, a Comment discusses some of its main features.

Finally, each chapter concludes with a *visual text* and a series of questions and writing assignments that will enable you to see how a particular writing pattern can be represented in graphic form.

On pages 4–5 we provide you with Guidelines for Reading an Essay, and after those guidelines you will find Virginia Woolf's "Shakespeare's Sister," complete with one reader's annotations and response, a set of questions For Study and Discussion, and four assignments For Research and Writing.

Guidelines for Reading an Essay

I. READ THE ESSAY THROUGH CAREFULLY

a. Consider the title and what expectations it raises.
b. Note when the essay was written and where it was first published.
c. Look at the author information in the headnote, and consider what important leads that information gives you about what to expect from the essay.
d. Now go back over the essay, underlining or highhghting key ideas and jotting down any questions you have.

II. THINK ABOUT YOUR RESPONSE TO THE ESSAY

a. Note what you liked and/or disliked about it, and analyze why you had that reaction.
b. Decide what questions you have after reading the essay.
c. Think about the issues the essay raises for you.
d. What else have you read that suggests or refutes the issues in the essay?

III. WRITE A BRIEF STATEMENT OF WHAT SEEMS TO BE THE AUTHOR'S PURPOSE

a. Consider how the information about the author's life and experience may account for that purpose.
b. Decide to what extent you think the author achieved his or her purpose.

IV. AS FAR AS YOU CAN, IDENTIFY THE AUTHOR'S ORIGINAL AUDIENCE

a. Make a guess about what those readers' interests are.
b. Compare your interests and experiences to those of the readers the author had in mind when writing the essay, and decide how similar or different they are.

V. LOOK AT THE STRATEGIES THE WRITER USES TO ENGAGE AND HOLD THE READER'S INTEREST

a. Look at the lead the author uses to engage the reader.
b. Identify the main pattern the writer uses in the essay, and consider how that pattern helps to develop his or her main idea.
c. Pick out the descriptions, events, or anecdotes that make a particular impression, and consider why they're effective.
d. Identify passages or images that you find especially powerful, or that reveal that the author is using strategies from other patterns.

VI. REFLECT ON THE ESSAY, AND TRY TO STATE ITS CONTENT AND MAIN ARGUMENT IN TWO OR THREE SENTENCES

VIRGINIA WOOLF

Virginia Woolf (1882–1941) was born in London, England, the daughter of Victorian critic and philosopher Leslie Stephen. She educated herself in her father's magnificent library and, after his death, lived with her sister and two brothers in Bloomsbury, a district of London that later became identified with her and the group of writers and artists she entertained. In 1912 she married journalist Leonard Woolf and together they founded the Hogarth Press, which published the work of the Bloomsbury group, including Woolf's own novels. Woolf's adult life was tormented by intermittent periods of nervous depression; finally, she drowned herself in the river near her home at Rodmell. Her novels include *Mrs. Dalloway* (1925), *To the Lighthouse* (1927), and *Orlando* (1928). Woolf's essays and reviews are collected in books such as *The Common Reader* (1925). One of Woolf's most popular works is *A Room of One's Own* (1929), an extended analysis of the subject of women and creativity. In this selection, taken from that volume, Woolf creates a hypothetical argument to demonstrate the limitations encountered by women in Shakespeare's time.

Shakespeare's Sister

States problem | It is a perennial puzzle why no woman wrote a word of that extraordinary [Elizabethan] literature when every other man, it seemed, was capable of song or sonnet. What were the conditions in which women lived, I asked myself; for fiction, imaginative work that is, is not dropped like a pebble upon the ground, as science may be; fiction is like a spider's web, attached ever so lightly perhaps, but still attached to life at all four corners. Often the attachment is

(margin notes) States problem · Why didn't women write? · Description: Compares science and fiction

(line number) 1

scarcely perceptible; Shakespeare's plays, for instance, seem to hang there complete by themselves. But when the web is pulled askew, hooked up at the edge, torn in the middle, one remembers that these webs are not spun in mid-air by incorporeal creatures, but are the work of suffering human beings, and are attached to grossly material things, like health and money and the house we live in.

But what I find . . . is that nothing is known about women before the eighteenth century. I have no model in my mind to turn about this way and that. Here am I asking why women did not write poetry in the Elizabethan age, and I am not sure how they were educated; whether they were taught to write; whether they had sitting-rooms to themselves; how many women had children before they were twenty-one; what, in short, they did from eight in the morning till eight at night. They had no money evidently; according to Professor Trevelyan they were married whether they liked it or not before they were out of the nursery, at fifteen or sixteen very likely. It would have been extremely odd, even upon this showing, had one of them suddenly written the plays of Shakespeare, I concluded, and I thought of that old gentleman, who is dead now, but was a bishop, I think, who declared that it was impossible for any woman, past, present, or to come, to have the genius of Shakespeare. He wrote to the papers about it. He also told a lady who applied to him for information that cats do not as a matter of fact go to heaven, though they have, he added, souls of a sort. How much thinking those old gentlemen used to save one! How the borders of ignorance shrank back at their approach! Cats do not go to heaven. Women cannot write the plays of Shakespeare.

Be that as it may, I could not help thinking, as I looked at the works of Shakespeare on the shelf, that the bishop was right at least in this; it would have been impossible completely and entirely, for any

Margin notes:
Looks for evidence

2

Why has no one researched these questions before?

Cites authority

This is over-simplified

3

woman to have written the plays of Shakespeare in Begins narrative the age of Shakespeare. Let me imagine, since facts are so hard to come by, what would have happened Compares A. Shakespeare had Shakespeare had a wonderfully gifted sister, called Judith, let us say. Shakespeare himself went, very probably—his mother was an heiress—to the grammar school, where he may have learnt Latin— Ovid, Virgil and Horace—and the elements of grammar and logic. He was, it is well known, a wild boy who poached rabbits, perhaps shot a deer, and had, rather sooner than he should have done, to marry a woman in the neighbourhood, who bore him a child rather quicker than was right. That escapade sent him to seek his fortune in London. He had, it seemed, a taste for the theatre; he began by holding horses at the stage door. Very soon he got work in the theatre, became a successful actor, and lived at the hub of the universe, meeting everybody, knowing everybody, practising his art on the boards, exercising his wits in the streets, and even B. Shakespeare's sister getting access to the palace of the queen. Meanwhile his extraordinarily gifted sister, let us suppose, remained at home. She was as adventurous, as imaginative, as agog to see the world as he was. But she was not sent to school. She had no chance of learning grammar and logic, let alone of reading Horace and Virgil. She picked up a book now and then, one of her brother's perhaps, and read a few pages. But then her parents came in and told her to mend the stockings or mind the stew and not moon about with books and papers. They would have spoken sharply but kindly, for they were substantial people who knew the conditions of life for a woman and loved their daughter—indeed, more likely than not she was the apple of her father's eye. Perhaps she scribbled some pages up in an apple loft on the sly, but was careful to hide them or set fire to them. Soon, however, before she was out of her teens, she was to be betrothed to the son of a neighbouring

How did he know enough to write play

Why wasn't she given a chance?

wool-stapler. She cried out that marriage was hateful to her, and for that she was severely beaten by her father. Then he ceased to scold her. He begged her instead not to hurt him, not to shame him in this matter of her marriage. He would give her a chain of beads or a fine petticoat, he said; and there were tears in his eyes. How could she disobey him? How could she break his heart? The force of her own gift alone drove her to it. She made up a small parcel of her belongings, let herself down by a rope one summer's night and took the road to London. She was not seventeen. The birds that sang in the hedge were not more musical than she was. She had the quickest fancy, a gift like her brother's, for the tune of words. Like him, she had a taste for the theatre. She stood at the stage door; she wanted to act, she said. Men laughed in her face. The manager—a fat, loose-lipped man—guffawed. He bellowed something about poodles dancing and women acting—no woman, he said, could possibly be an actress. He hinted—you can imagine what. She could get no training in her craft. Could she even seek her dinner in a tavern or roam the streets at midnight? Yet her genius was for fiction and lusted to feed abundantly upon the lives of men and women and the study of their ways. At last—for she was very young, oddly like Shakespeare the poet in her face, with the same grey eyes and rounded brows—at last Nick Greene the actor-manager took pity on her; she found herself with child by that gentleman and so—who shall measure the heat and violence of the poet's heart when caught and tangled in a woman's body?—killed herself one winter's night and lies buried at some cross-roads where the omnibuses now stop outside the Elephant and Castle.

That, more or less, is how the story would run, I think, if a woman in Shakespeare's day had had Shakespeare's genius. But for my part, I agree with the deceased bishop, if such he was—it is

[margin notes:]
Is this why she left?

Compares Shakespeare and sister

Why?

4

Moves from narrative to argument

unthinkable that any woman in Shakespeare's day should have had Shakespeare's genius. For genius like Shakespeare's is not born among labouring, uneducated, servile people. It was not born in England among the Saxons and the Britons. It is not born today among the working classes. How, then, could it have been born among women whose work began, according to Professor Trevelyan, almost before they were out of the nursery, who were forced to it by their parents and held to it by all the power of law and custom?

Have laws a▸ customs cha that much?

Reader's Response

Woolf paints a realistic picture. That's a shame because in her time, Shakespeare's sister would have been treated just as she was presented—inconsequential. It makes me wonder why women weren't given the option to read and write when the head of state, Queen Elizabeth, was more capable and dynamic than most of the men of the time.

What's puzzling is why women accepted gender inequity. I know quite a few outstanding and confident women who would never have accepted that tradition.

Watching Judith's struggle to be accepted in a man's world reminds me of my own struggle to be accepted. Oftentimes I have felt small in comparison to my world, but there always seems to be a path available to me to fit into the world. Apparently the women of a few centuries ago could not find such a path.

For Study and Discussion

QUESTIONS ABOUT PURPOSE

1. What is the perennial question about women and creativity that Woolf tries to answer in this essay?

2. What connection does she seek to establish between the conditions under which a person lives and what that person can accomplish?

QUESTIONS ABOUT AUDIENCE

1. What assumptions does Woolf make about the cultural knowledge of her readers?
2. Do you think men or women would be most interested in Woolf's argument? Why?

QUESTIONS ABOUT STRATEGIES

1. To what extent does Woolf's speculative narrative about Judith Shakespeare seem constructed from verifiable evidence?
2. What is the argument that Woolf establishes in paragraph 4? Is it convincing? Why or why not?

For Research and Writing

1. *Analyze* the way Woolf mixes strategies—narrative, comparison and contrast, cause and effect—to construct her argument.
2. *Practice* Woolf's strategies by composing a speculative narrative about an imaginary author who reveals the experience that helped him or her to write a particular kind of book—for example, a cookbook, a children's book, or a romance novel.
3. *Argue* that in many ways today's laws and customs still discourage women from pursuing an active creative life.
4. *Synthesize* several sources that comment on how changes in laws and customs have made it possible for women to become the preeminent creative writers in our time.

THE WRITING PROCESS

If you are like most people, you find writing hard work. But writing is also an opportunity. It allows you to express something about yourself, to explore and explain ideas, and to assess the claims of other people. At times the tasks may seem overwhelming, but the rewards make the hard work worthwhile. By working through the four stages of the writing process, you will develop the confidence you need to become an effective writer.

- *Stage one: Planning.* Planning enables you to find and formulate information in writing. When you begin a writing project, you need to make a list to explore a variety of subjects, to experiment with alternative ways to think about a subject, and to construct a rough outline to see how to develop your information.
- *Stage two: Drafting.* Drafting enables you to organize and develop a sustained piece of writing. Once planning has helped you to identify several subjects and to gather information on those subjects from different perspectives, you need to select one subject, organize your information into meaningful clusters, and then discover links that connect those clusters.
- *Stage three: Revising.* Revising enables you to reexamine and reevaluate the choices that have created a piece of writing. After you have completed a preliminary draft, you need to stand back from your text and decide whether to embark on *global revision*—a complete recreation of the world of your writing—or begin *local revision*—a concentrated effort to perfect the smaller elements of your writing.
- *Stage four: Editing.* Editing enables you to correct spelling, mechanics, and usage. After you have revised your text, you should proofread it carefully to make sure you have not inadvertently misspelled words, mangled sentences, or created typographical errors.

WRITING WITHIN THE PROCESS

The division of the writing process into four stages is deceptive because it suggests that *planning, drafting, revising,* and *editing* proceed in a linear sequence. According to this logic, you would have to complete all the activities in one stage before you could move on to the next. But writing is a complex mental activity that usually unfolds as a more flexible and recursive sequence of tasks. You may have to repeat the activities in one stage several times before you are ready to move on to the next, or you may have to loop back to an earlier stage before you can move forward again.

Experienced writers seem to perform within the process in different ways. Some spend an enormous amount of time planning every detail before they write; others prefer to dispense with planning and discover their direction in drafting or revising. The American humorist James Thurber once acknowledged that he and one of his collaborators worked quite differently when writing a play:

> *Eliot Nugent . . . is a careful constructor. When we were working on* The Male Animal *together, he was constantly concerned with plotting the play. He could plot the thing from back to front—what was going to happen here, what sort of situation would end the first-act curtain and so forth. I can't work that way. Nugent would say, "Well, Thurber, we've got our problem, we've got all these people in the living room. Now what are we going to do with them?" I'd say that I didn't know and couldn't tell him until I'd sat down at my typewriter and found out. I don't believe the writer should know too much where he's going.*
>
> (*James Thurber,* Writers at Work:
> The Paris Review Interviews)

Even experienced writers with established routines for producing a particular kind of work admit that each project inevitably presents new problems. Virginia Woolf planned, drafted, and revised some of her novels with great speed, but she was bewildered by her inability to repeat the process with other novels:

> *. . . blundering on at* The Waves. *I write two pages of arrant nonsense, after straining; I write variations of every sentence; compromises; bad shots; possibilities; till my writing book is like a lunatic's*

> *dream. Then I trust to inspiration on re-reading;*
> *and pencil them into some sense. Still I am not*
> *satisfied . . . I press to my centre. I don't care if it all*
> *is scratched out. . . and then, if nothing comes of*
> *it—anyhow I have examined the possibilities.*
>
> (*Virginia Woolf, "Boxing Day 1929,"*
> A Writer's Diary)

Writers often discover a whole set of new problems when they are asked to write in a different context. Those writers who feel comfortable telling stories about their personal experience, for example, may encounter unexpected twists and turns in their writing process when they are asked to describe the lives of other people, explain a historical event, or analyze the arguments in an intellectual controversy. Each context requires them to make adjustments in the way they typically uncover, assess, and assert information. Calvin Trillin, an especially versatile writer, admits that he changes his writing process dramatically when he shifts from writing investigative reports to writing humorous essays or weekly columns.

> *In my reporting pieces, I worry a lot about struc-*
> *ture. Everything is there—in interviews, clippings,*
> *documents—but I don't know how to get it all in. I*
> *think that's why I do what we call around the house*
> *the vomit-out. I just start writing—to see how*
> *much I've got, how it might unfold, and what I've*
> *got to do to get through to the end. In my columns*
> *and humor pieces, I usually don't know the end or*
> *even the middle. I might start with a joke, but I*
> *don't know where it's going, so I fiddle along, pol-*
> *ishing each paragraph, hoping something will tell*
> *me what to write next. (Personal interview)*

This range of responses suggests that what appears to be a simple four-stage procedure may at times be a disorderly, contradictory procedure. But experienced writers know that disorder and contradiction are inevitable—although temporary—disturbances in the composition of most pieces of writing. Confusion occurs when you know too little about your writing project; contradiction occurs when you think too little about what you know. The secret to moving through such temporary impasses is to keep your eye on the constants in every writing situation.

MAKING DECISIONS IN THE WRITING PROCESS

As you write, you discover that you are constantly making decisions. Some of these decisions are complex, as when you are trying to shape ideas. Others are simple, as when you are trying to select words. But each decision, large or small, affects every other decision you make so that you are constantly adjusting and readjusting your writing to make sure it is consistent, coherent, and clear. You can test the effectiveness of your decisions by measuring them against this dictum: in every writing situation a writer is trying to communicate a *purpose* to an *audience* by manipulating *strategies.*

Initially, think of these three elements as *prompts,* ways to consider what you want to write and how you want to write about it. Later, as you move through planning and drafting to revising and editing, think of them as *touchstones,* ways to assess what you set out to accomplish. But mainly think of them as *guidelines,* ways to control every decision you make throughout the writing process, from formulating ideas to reformatting sentences.

DETERMINING YOUR PURPOSE

Writers write most effectively when they write with a purpose. Inexperienced writers occasionally have difficulty writing with a purpose because they see many purposes: to complete the assignment, to earn a grade, to publish their writing. These "purposes" lie *outside* the writing situation, but they certainly influence the way you think about your purpose. If you want a good grade, you will define your purpose in terms of your teacher's writing assignment. If you want to publish your essay, you will define your purpose in terms of a given publisher's statement about its editorial policies.

When *purpose* is considered as an element *inside* the writing situation, the term has a specific meaning: *Purpose is the overall design that governs what writers do in their writing.* Writers who have determined their purpose know what kind of information they need, how they want to organize and develop it, and why they think it's important. In effect, purpose directs and controls all the decisions writers make. It is both the *what* and the *how* of that process—that is, the specific subject the writer selects *and* the strategies the writer uses to communicate the subject most effectively

Forming a Working Purpose: The Hypothesis

A hypothesis is a provisional conjecture that serves as a guide to an investigation. Forming a hypothesis is a major step in determining your purpose. Sometimes you come to your writing certain of your hypothesis: you know from the outset what you want to prove and how you need to prove it. More often, you need to consider various possibilities. To convey something meaningful in your writing, something that bears your own mark, you need to keep an open mind and explore your options fully. Eventually, however, you must choose one hypothesis that you think most accurately says what you want to say about your subject and how you want to say it.

How do you know which hypothesis to choose? There is no easy answer to this question. The answer ultimately emerges from your temperament, experiences, and interests, and also from the requirements of the context—whether you are writing for yourself or as an assignment. Sometimes you can make the choice intuitively as you proceed. In thinking about your subject and audience, you see at once the perspective you want to adopt and how it will direct your writing. At other times you may find it helpful to write out various hypotheses and then consider their relative effectiveness. Which will be the most interesting to write about? Which expresses your way of looking at things? With which can you make the strongest case or most compelling assertions?

Testing Your Hypothesis: The Discovery Draft

After you have chosen your hypothesis, you need to determine whether this preliminary statement of purpose provides the direction and control you need to produce an effective piece of writing. You can test your hypothesis by writing a first, or *discovery*, draft. Sometimes your discovery draft demonstrates that your hypothesis works. More often, however, as you continue the writing process, you discover new information or unforeseen complications that cause you to modify your original hypothesis. In other cases, you discover you simply cannot prove what your hypothesis suggested you might be able to prove.

Whatever you discover about your hypothesis, you must proceed in writing. If your discovery draft reveals that your hypothesis represents what you want to prove and needs only slight modification, then change your perspective somewhat or find additional information so that you can modify it. If, on the other hand, your discovery draft demonstrates that your hypothesis lacks conviction or that you do not have (and suspect you cannot get) the information you need to make your case, then choose another hypothesis that reflects your intentions more accurately.

Purpose and Thesis

Whether you proceed with your original hypothesis, modify it, or choose another, you must eventually arrive at a final decision about your purpose. You make that decision during revision, when you know what you want to do and how you want to do it. Once you have established your purpose, you can make or refine other decisions—about your organization, examples and style. One way to express your purpose is to state your thesis. A *thesis* is a sentence that usually appears in the first paragraph of your essay and states the main idea you are going to develop. Although the thesis is often called a purpose statement, thesis and purpose are not precisely the same thing. Your purpose is both contained in and is larger than your thesis: it consists of all the strategies you will use to demonstrate your thesis in a sustained and successful piece of writing

Your thesis makes a *restricted, unified,* and *precise* assertion about your subject—an assertion that can be developed in the amount of space you have, that treats only one idea, and that is open to only one interpretation

In many ways, the difference between a hypothesis (a working purpose) and a thesis (a final assertion) explains why you can speculate about your purpose *before* you write but can specify your purpose only *after* you have written. This connection between your writing process and your writing purpose requires you to pause frequently to consult the criteria set forth in the following guidelines.

Guidelines for Determining Your Purpose

I. WHAT ARE THE REQUIREMENTS OF YOUR WRITING PROJECT?

a. If you are writing to fulfill an assignment, do you understand the assignment?

b. If you are writing on your own, do you have definite expectations of what you want to accomplish?

II. AS YOU PROCEED IN THIS PROJECT, WHAT DO YOU NEED TO KNOW?

a. Do you have a good understanding of your subject, or do you need more information?

b. Have you considered the possible audiences who might read your writing?

III. WHAT HYPOTHESIS CAN YOU USE AS A WORKING PURPOSE?

a. How many different hypotheses can you formulate about your subject?

b. Which of them seems to direct and control your information in the most effective manner?

IV. WHAT PURPOSE HAVE YOU DISCOVERED FOR THIS WRITING PROJECT?

a. Has your purpose changed as you have learned more about your subject and audience?
b. Have you discovered, by working with a hypothesis or hypotheses, what you want to do in your writing?

V. WHAT IS YOUR THESIS?

a. How can you state your main idea in a thesis sentence?
b. Does your thesis limit the scope of your writing to what you can demonstrate in the available space?
c. Does it focus your writing on one specific assertion?
d. Does it make an exact statement about what your writing intends to do?

ANALYZING YOUR AUDIENCE

Most inexperienced writers assume that their audience is their writing teacher. But writing teachers, like writing assignments, often vary in what they teach, what they assume, and what they expect. Such variation has often prompted inexperienced writers to define their writing tasks as "trying to figure out what the teacher wants." This definition is naïve and smart at the same time. Superficially, it suggests that the sole purpose of any writing assignment is to satisfy another person's whims. On a deeper level, it suggests that when writers analyze the knowledge, assumptions, and expectations of their readers, they develop a clearer perception of their purpose and strategies. To make this analysis truly effective, though, writers must remember that they are writing for multiple audiences, not for a single person.

The most immediate audience is *you*. You write not only to convey your ideas to others but also to clarify them for yourself. To think of yourself as an audience, however, you must stop thinking like a writer and begin thinking like a reader. This change in perspective offers advantages, for you are the reader you know best. You are also a fairly representative reader because you share broad concerns and interests with other people. If you feel your writing is clear, lively, and informed, other readers will probably feel that way, too. If you sense that your text is confused or incomplete, the rest of your audience is likely to be disappointed, too.

The main drawback to considering yourself as audience is your inclination to deceive yourself. You want every sentence and paragraph to be perfect, but you know how much time and energy you invested in composing them, and that effort may blur your judgment. You may accept bad writing from yourself even though you wouldn't accept it from someone else. For that reason you need a second audience. These readers—usually, friends, classmates, and teachers—are your most attentive audience. They help you choose your subject, coach you through various stages of the writing process, and counsel you about how to improve your sentences and paragraphs. As you write, you must certainly anticipate detailed advice from these readers. But you must remember that writing teachers and even peers are essentially collaborators and thus not your ultimate audience. They know what you have considered, cut, and corrected. The more they help you, the more eager they are to commend your writing as it approaches their standards of acceptability.

Your most significant audience consists of readers who do not know how much time and energy you invested in your writing or care about the many choices you considered and rejected. These readers want writing that tells them something interesting or important, and they are put off by writing that is tedious or trivial. It is this wider audience that you (and your collaborators) must consider as you work through the writing process.

At times this audience may seem like a nebulous creature, and you may wonder how you can direct your writing to it if you do not know any of its distinguishing features. In those cases, it may be helpful to imagine a single significant reader—an attentive, sensible, reasonably informed person who will give you a sympathetic reading as long as you do not waste his or her time. Imagine an important person whom you respect and whose respect you want. This reader—specifically imagined, though often termed the "general reader," the "universal reader," or the "common reader"—is essentially a fiction, but a helpful fiction. Your writing will benefit from the objectivity and sincerity with which you address this reader.

Many times, however, especially as you learn more about your subject, you discover a real-world audience for your writing. More precisely, as you consider your subject in a specific context, you may identify a number of audiences, in which case you will ultimately have to choose among them. Suppose, for example, you are about your evolution as a writer—an essay such as the student essay on pages 29–33. After some deliberation you see that you have three possible audiences: (1) those who love to talk about their development as writers; (2) those who refuse to even discuss an activity they despise; and (3) those who have not thought too much about how writers work.

Now that you have identified these three audiences, analyze the distinctive features of each group. What do they know? What do they think they know? What do they need to know? The more you know about each group, the more you will be able to direct your writing to their assumptions and expectations. If you have spent a lot of time discussing the challenges of writing, you will have little difficulty analyzing the devotees and detesters of the composing process. You have heard the devotees explain how they have discovered strategies for becoming successful writers. Similarly, you have heard the detesters complain that their failures have convinced them that they never want to think about writing again.

At first you may have difficulty with the third group because these readers have not developed any preconceptions about learning how to write. In some ways, readers in the third group are like the "general reader"—thoughtful, discerning people who are willing to read about the writing process if you can convince them that the subject is worth their attention.

Although this sort of audience analysis helps you visualize a group of readers, it does not help you decide which group is most suitable for your essay. If you target one group, you may fall into the trap of allowing its preferences to determine the direction of your writing. If you try to accommodate all three groups, you may waiver indecisively among them so that your writing never finds any direction. Your decision about audience, like your decision about purpose, has to be made in the context of the complete writing situation. For that reason, look at the guidelines for analyzing your audience.

Guidelines for Analyzing Your Audience

I. WHO ARE THE READERS WHO WILL BE MOST INTERESTED IN YOUR WRITING?

a. What are their probable age, gender, education, economic status, and social position?
b. What values, assumptions and prejudices characterize their general attitude toward life?

II. WHAT DO YOUR READERS KNOW OR THINK THEY KNOW ABOUT YOUR SUBJECT?

a. What is the probable source of their knowledge—direct experience, observation, reading, rumor?
b. Will your readers react positively or negatively toward your subject?

III. WHY WILL YOUR READERS READ YOUR WRITING?

a. If they know a great deal about your subject, what will they expect to learn from reading your writing?
b. If they know only a few things about your subject, what will they expect to be told about it?
c. Will they expect to be entertained, informed or persuaded?

IV. HOW CAN YOU INTEREST YOUR READERS IN YOUR SUBJECT?

a. If they are hostile toward it, how can you convince them to give your writing a fair reading?
b. If they are sympathetic, how can you fulfill and enhance their expectations?
c. If they are neutral, how can you catch and hold their attention?

V. HOW CAN YOU HELP YOUR READERS READ YOUR WRITING?

a. What kind of organizational pattern will help them see its purpose?
b. What kind of strategies and transitional markers will they need to follow this pattern?
c. What (and how many) examples will they need to understand your general statements?

SELECTING YOUR STRATEGY

As you work your way through the writing process, you will uncover various patterns for developing your ideas. In *planning*, these patterns often emerge as answers to the basic questions you might ask about any body of information: *What is it? How does it work? Why does it matter?* These questions are like the different lenses you attach to your camera: each lens gives you a different picture of your subject. Suppose you want to write an essay on the subject of women and science. You might begin by asking why so few women are ranked among the world's great scientists. You might continue asking questions. What historical forces have discouraged women from becoming scientists? How do women scientists define problems, analyze evidence, and formulate conclusions, and do they go about these processes differently than men? If women scientists look at the world differently than men do, does this difference have an effect on the established notions of inquiry? As you can see, each question not only shifts your perspective on your subject but also suggests a different method for developing your information about it.

If planning gives you the opportunity to envision your subject from a variety of perspectives, then *drafting* encourages you to develop the pattern (or patterns) that appear to you most effective for demonstrating your purpose. In some writing projects, a pattern may seem to emerge naturally from your planning. If you decide to write about your observation of a game of lacrosse, your choice seems obvious: to tell what happened. In attempting this, however, you may need to answer other questions about this unfamiliar sport: What do the field and equipment look like? What rules govern the way the game is played? How is it similar to or different from other sports? Developing this new information may complicate your original purpose.

You can solve this problem most effectively during *revision*. As you look over your draft, you will need to make two decisions. First, you must decide whether individual segments or patterns of information develop or distort your purpose. The history of lacrosse—its creation by Iroquois Indians, its discovery by French explorers, and its development by Canadians—is an interesting body of information, but it may need to be reshaped, relocated, or even eliminated to preserve your original purpose—to tell what happened. Second, you must decide whether your original design, a design that often mirrors the process by which you uncovered your information, is still the best method for presenting your information to your audience. Instead of telling "what happened," you may decide that you can best express your ideas by choosing a more formal structure—comparing lacrosse to games with which your readers are more familiar, such as soccer or hockey.

Whatever you decide, you need to understand the purpose, audience, and strategies of each pattern if you are going to use it successfully to develop a paragraph, a section of your essay, or your whole essay. For that reason, we have organized *The Riverside Reader* to demonstrate the most common patterns and questions encountered in the writing process:

> Narration and Description: What happened? What did it look like?

VISUAL STRATEGIES: A VISUAL ESSAY

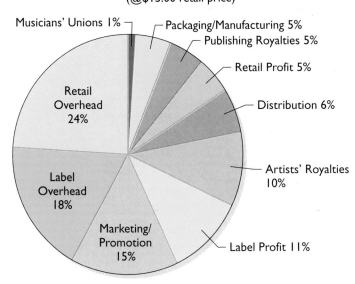

Costs: Major Record Label Release
(@$15.00 retail price)

- Musicians' Unions 1%
- Packaging/Manufacturing 5%
- Publishing Royalties 5%
- Retail Profit 5%
- Distribution 6%
- Artists' Royalties 10%
- Label Profit 11%
- Retail Overhead 24%
- Label Overhead 18%
- Marketing/Promotion 15%

Figure 1.1: Pie Chart

A pie chart is an effective way to classify *the various* subdivisions *of a subject. This pie chart subdivides the total cost of a major record label into various segments.*

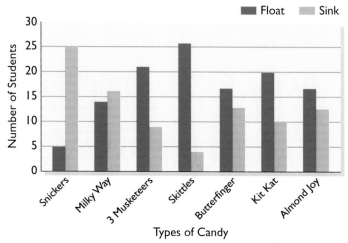

Figure 1.2: Bar Graph

A bar graph is a useful device for comparing *and* contrasting *information. This bar graph compares student opinion on whether particular candy bars will float of sink.*

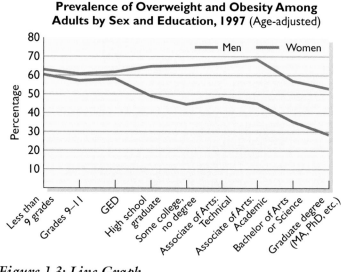

Figure 1.3: Line Graph

A line graph helps compare causes *and* effects. *This line graph documents how sex and education can be seen as contributing causes of obesity and overweight.*

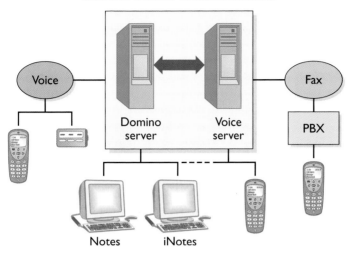

Figure 1.4: Flow Chart

A flow chart illustrates parts of a structure or steps in a process. *This flow chart displays how a communication system is connected and routed through various technological devices.*

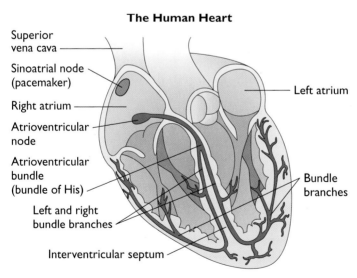

Figure 1.5: Diagram

A diagram—like a flow chart—defines the parts of a structure. This diagram identifies the chambers and arteries of the heart.

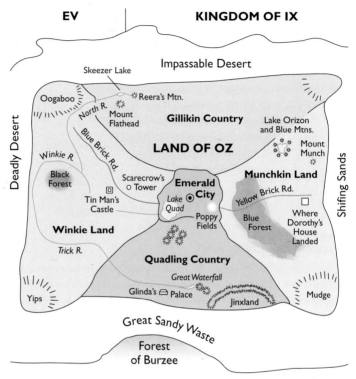

Figure 1.6: Map

A map represents the form, size and sections of an area. This map represents the various settings described *in the* narrative *of Oz.*

Process Analysis: How do you do it?

Comparison and Contrast: How is it similar or different?

Division and Classification: What kind of subdivisions does it contain?

Definition: How would you characterize it?

Cause and Effect: Why did it happen? What happened next?

Persuasion and Argument: How can you prove it?

The introductions to the chapters that feature each of these patterns of development explain its purpose, audience, and strategies. The essays in each chapter are arranged in an ascending order of complexity and are followed by questions that call your attention to how the writer has asserted his or her purpose, addressed his or her audience and used the various techniques of each strategy to develop his or her essay. If you study these essays, answer these questions and check the Points to Remember at the end of each introduction, you will see how you can adapt these common writing patterns to your writing.

By analyzing these strategies in action, you will also learn two important lessons. First, you will understand what you are expected to write when you encounter words such as *describe, compare,* and *define* in a writing assignment. Second, you will discover that you do not have to limit yourself to a single pattern for an entire piece of writing. Writers may structure their essay around one dominant strategy but use other strategies to enrich or advance their purpose.

The following guidelines will help you in selecting an appropriate strategy.

Guidelines for Selecting Your Strategy

I. WHAT STRATEGY DOES YOUR WRITING ASSIGNMENT REQUIRE?

a. What words—such as *define* or *defend*—are embedded in your writing assignment?

b. What assumptions and expectations do these words evoke?

II. WHAT STRATEGY EMERGES AS YOU PLAN YOUR ESSAY?

a. What questions naturally occur to you as you study a particular subject?
b. What patterns of development do these questions suggest?

III. WHAT OTHER STRATEGIES EMERGE AS YOU DRAFT YOUR ESSAY?

a. What new questions emerge as you draft your writing?
b. What kind of information do you need to answer these questions?

IV. HOW CAN YOU REVISE YOUR ESSAY TO INCLUDE THIS NEW INFORMATION?

a. Does this new information distort or develop your purpose?
b. Will it require you to impose a new strategy on your information to clarify your purpose to your readers?

V. HOW CAN YOU MIX STRATEGIES TO ENRICH YOUR ESSAY?

a. How does mixing strategies supplement your purpose?
b. How might such mixing confuse your readers?

Student Essay

STUDENT WRITER IN PROGRESS
Kristie Ferguson "The Scenic Route"

The following material illustrates how one student, Kristie Ferguson, responded to a writing assignment by working her way through the writing process.

Writing Assignment: Read Virginia Woolf's "Shakespeare's Sister." Then compose a narrative that describes the experiences that contributed to (or prevented) your development as a writer.

Planning (Journal Entry)

I am not sure I ever developed as a writer. My teachers all seemed to want different things.

> Never made Mrs. Scott's bulletin board
>
> Mrs. Pageant and those dumb squirrels
>
> Logan and that contest.

I could never figure out what they wanted. I suppose they wanted to teach me. But I always felt lost.

Possible Hypothesis: I should probably describe what I didn't learn. How my confusion prevented me from becoming a good writer. But then how do you explain that contest?

Drafting (Discovery Draft)

What's Wrong with This Picture?

On one of those days that convinces you certain things don't belong together, like sunshine and first grade or hot flashes in Alaska, another writing period was about to begin. At the grand old age of six, I was certain that I would never learn to write. After all I had never made the list. In the corner of our room, Mrs. Scott kept a bulletin board commending those in the class who had neat handwriting and no spelling errors. I was cursed on both counts. My handwriting looked like hieroglyphics, and my spelling always made people ask, "What's wrong with this picture."

That day Mrs. Scott surprised us. "Class, I'm cutting writing period in half so that you can go to the auditorium to see a movie." Freedom! Relief! I started to clap my hands. But wait! Something was wrong with this picture. "I am going to ask you to write a brief theme," Mrs. Scott continued. "When you are done you can go to the auditorium." I knew there must be a catch. Still, it was only a brief theme and afterward there was a movie. I grabbed my Number 2 and thumbed through my notebook looking for a clean page. "One more thing," she announced. "You must spell all words neatly and correctly. No erasers or dictionaries. I may ask for do-over's." No eraser? No dictionary? Why not cut off both my arms?

How was I ever going to make it to the auditorium? I started slowly, reminding myself to make each letter and word carefully. When I finished, I went to Mrs. Scott's desk. "Too sloppy. Misspelled words." I retreated to my desk for another try. This time she smiled. "Misspelled word. Do it over." I slumped back to my desk. The next time I looked up the room was empty. Desperate, I narrowed the culprit to one of those "ie" words. I rubbed out the letters, reprinted them, and placed a dot more or less between them. I handed my paper to Mrs. Scott. "You erased," she hissed. She was such a treasure. "No ma'am." She eyed the paper and me again, and then, finally, let me go. At last--the movie.

Collapsing near my best friend Karla, I arrived in time to watch the end of a promotion film for dental hygiene. Teeth! All that for teeth!

Revision (Revision Agenda)

1. *What is my purpose?*
   Tell a story about my early failures as a writer. Most of my grade school teachers emphasized handwriting and spelling and I was terrible at both.

2. *Who is my audience?*
   Everyone who has gone to school. They have all had a Mrs. Scott. Most remember that in

school good writing meant good handwriting and no mistakes.

3. *What strategies do I use?*
   I focused on my attempt to complete one writing assignment so I could go to a movie. I slowed the pace down and described the details of my writing process. I also used dialogue to dramatize Mrs. Scott.

4. *What revisions do I want to make in my next draft?*
   a. Include other writing experiences--fourth grade, high school.
   b. Rework introduction--state thesis--to explain why I am telling these stories.

New Hypothesis: I like the story because it tells how I tricked Mrs. Scott--and then myself. All that work for teeth. But I take too long getting there. Is learning how to write simply learning a trick? Maybe it's more like taking a trip.

Second Draft

The Scenic Route

As a writer, I always seem to take the scenic route. I don't plan it that way. My teachers provide detailed maps pointing me down the most direct road, but somehow I miss a turn or make a wrong turn and there I am--standing at some unmarked crossroads, head pounding, stomach churning, hopelessly lost. On such occasions, I used to curse my teachers, my maps, and myself. But recently, I have come to expect, even enjoy, in a perverse way, the confusion and panic of being lost. Left to my own devices, I have learned to discover my own way to my destination. And afterwards, I have a story to tell.

I did not learn this all at once. In the beginning I was confused about where I was going. One day in first grade, Mrs. Scott told us that if we wrote a brief theme we could go to a movie. I grabbed my Number 2 and listened for directions. "No erasers. No dictionaries. I may ask for do-over's." Lost! I was the worst speller in the class. My first draft was "Too sloppy. Do it over." My second, "Misspelled word. Do it over." Now I was really lost. One misspelled word. They all looked right-- and then they all looked wrong. Blind luck led me to one of those "ie" words. I rubbed out the letters, reprinted them, and placed the dot between them. "Kristie, you erased," she hissed. "No ma'am." She eyed my paper and then me again, and with a sigh waved me toward the auditorium. Collapsing next to my best friend, Karla, I arrived in time to watch a film about dental hygiene. Teeth! All that for teeth!

My next problem was trying to figure out why I was going. Mrs. Pageant, my fifth-grade teacher, was the source of my confusion. Seemingly unaware of my errors, she wrote enthusiastic notes on all my essays, suggesting on one, "Kristie, you're so creative. Why don't you write a book?" Why indeed? Why should the first-grade dummy begin such a perilous journey? "You should, Kristie. You really should. You could even write a fantasy book like the one we read today." Luckily fantasy was my forte. I used to make up stories about the family of squirrels in my backyard. And so I wrote *Squirrel Family Starts a Grocery Store*, in which, after the hoopla on page one, the squirrels run out of food on page three and close their store on page four.

As she read my book to the class, Mrs. Pageant could hardly contain herself. "What a delightful story, Kristie. You must write another immediately." My head pounded. My stomach churned. I had stumbled onto one story, but why keep going? Because Mrs. Pageant "just loved" those dumb squirrels. So there was *Squirrel Family Starts a Bank,* in which the squirrels run out of money, and *Squirrel Family Starts a Newspaper,* in which they run out of stories. By then I was looking for the nearest off-ramp. I couldn't think of another squirrel story, and Karla told me that if she had to listen to one more, she would throw up.

When I got to the eleventh grade, I knew for the first time where I was going and why. The poster on Mr. Logan's bulletin board announced a writing contest: "Threats to the Free Enterprise System." Sponsored by the Blair County Board of Realtors. First prize $200. Now my problem was how to get there. Mr. Logan took us to the school library and mapped out the first half of his strategy. Look up sources in the database. Take notes. Organize notes into an outline for first draft. It seemed like a sensible plan, but, as usual, I got lost at the first turn. I pulled a few books off the shelf, but it was pointless. I couldn't find anything on free enterprise or anybody who was threatening it.

As the deadline for the first draft approached, I was so desperate I asked my parents for directions. "Ask some local business people what they think." Not bad for parents. I borrowed my father's tape recorder and made the rounds--the grocery store, the pizza parlor, the newspaper. Most of the people seemed a lot like me--lost. They talked a lot, but they didn't focus on the question. Maybe I was asking the wrong question. I listened to the tape a couple of times and picked out some common themes. Then I rewrote my questions: "How do taxes, government regulation and foreign competition threatens your business?" The next time around people seemed to know what they were talking about. I organized their answers under my three categories, wrote out my draft, and made the deadline.

In class, Mr. Logan announced the second half of his strategy. Read draft. Listen to student and teacher responses. Revise draft. Mail essay. Karla went first. She quoted every book in the school library. Looking down at my paper, I saw myself stranded again. After a few more papers I felt better. All the papers sounded alike. I knew my quotes would be different--the guy at the pizza parlor, the newspaper editor. "You didn't do any research," Karla complained. "I bet you didn't read one article." A chorus of "yes's" came from the guys in the back row. Mr. Logan didn't say anything for a while. Then, smiling, he looked at Karla. "What is research?" Now Karla looked lost. The guys looked in their notebooks. Silence. Finally, the bell. What's the answer? What am I supposed to do? Mr. Logan never said. I thought about what I had done, considered my options, and, with a sigh, mailed my essay.

A few weeks later, I was standing not at some unmarked crossroads but in the center of town--behind the lectern in front of a room full of people. A man from the Blair County Board of Realtors handed me a trophy and an envelope and asked me to tell how I wrote the paper. I started to panic and then smiled. "Well . . ." I caught Mr. Logan's eye. "I asked a lot of people what they thought. At first they didn't know what I was talking about. Neither did I. Then I fixed my question and they helped me figure out what to say." I looked at Mr. Logan again. He just smiled. I looked at my trophy and wondered what to say next. Finally, I said "Well . . . I guess I did research."

Revision (Revision Agenda)

1. *What is my purpose?*
   Describe how I learned to trust my own judgment about writing.

2. *Who is my audience?*
   Again, anyone who has gone to school. Everybody has had to write silly stories and research papers. I bet they all tried to write something for some dumb contest. I suppose another audience might be those guys at the Blair County Board of Realtors.

3. *What strategies do I use?*
   I use brief narratives that I try to connect with my title--"The Scenic Route." I keep Karla in each episode as a kind of commentator. I also use dialogue to dramatize Mrs. Scott, Mrs. Pageant, and Mr. Logan. I try to slow the pace down at important moments-- like when I read my research paper for the first time or when I was accepting my trophy.

4. *What revisions do I want to make in my next draft?*

   Rework introduction so I can get right to my thesis---"trust your own judgment."

   Do Mrs. Scott and Mrs. Pageant fit thesis? If I cut them, I lose my funniest stuff. If I use them, I'll have to figure out a new way.

   This draft seems more organized, but I force my material into the structure--*where* I was going, *why* I was going, *how* I got there. Maybe the scenic route metaphor gets in the way.

Work more with contest. It's the one story
that makes my point.

Figure out "what's wrong with this picture?" This essay seems to be getting better
and worse at the same time.

Comment This essay takes readers on a tour of Kristie's development as a writer and highlights three memorable experiences along the way. Although the narrative focuses on
her personal experiences, it conjures up memories for many
fledgling writers: first, the autocratic teacher from second
grade who demands perfection and loves to punish mistakes;
then the sweetie-pie teacher from fifth who gushes and
lavishes praise on stuff the writer knows is junk; finally, the
practical and organized eleventh-grade teacher who outlines
a writing process and guides the students through it for a real
world audience.

NARRATION
AND
DESCRIPTION

The writer who *narrates* tells a story to make a point. The writer who *describes* evokes the senses to create a picture. Although you can use either strategy by itself, you will probably discover that they work best in combination if you want to write a detailed account of some memorable experience—your first trip alone, a last-minute political victory, a picnic in some special place. When you want to explain what happened, you will need to tell the story in some kind of chronological order, putting the most important events—I took the wrong turn, she made the right speech, we picked the perfect spot—in the most prominent position. When you want to give the texture of the experience, you will need to select words and images that help your readers see, hear, and feel what happened—the road snaked to a dead end, the crowd thundered into applause, the sunshine softened our scowls. When you show and tell in this way, you can help your readers see the meaning of the experience you want to convey.

PURPOSE

You can use narration and description for three purposes. Most simply, you can use them to introduce or illustrate a complicated subject. You might begin an analysis of the energy crisis, for example, by telling a personal anecdote that dramatizes wastefulness. Or you might conclude an argument for gun control by giving a graphic description of a shooting incident. In each case, you are using a few sentences or a detailed description to support some other strategy, such as causal analysis or argument.

Writers use narration and description most often not as isolated examples but as their primary method when they are analyzing an issue or theme. For example, you might spend a whole essay telling how you came to a new awareness of patriotism because of your experience in a foreign country. Even though your personal experience would be the center of the essay, your narrative purpose (what happened) and your descriptive purpose (what it felt like) might be linked to other purposes. You might want to *explain* what caused your new awareness (why it happened) or to *argue* that everyone needs such awareness (why everyone should reach the same conclusion you did).

The writers who use narration and description most often are those who write autobiography, history, and fiction. If you choose to write in any of these forms, your purpose will be not so much to introduce an example or tell about an experience as to throw light on your subject. You may explain why events happened as they did or argue that such events should never happen again, but you may choose to suggest your ideas subtly through telling a story or giving a description rather than stating them as direct assertions. Your primary purpose is to report the actions and describe the feelings of people entangled in the complex web of circumstance.

AUDIENCE

As you think about writing an essay using narration and description, consider how much you will need to tell your readers and how much you will need to show them. If you are writing from personal experience, few readers will know the story before you tell it. They may know similar stories or have had similar experiences, but they do not know your story. Because you can tell your story in so many different ways—adding or deleting material to fit the occasion—you need to decide how much information your readers will need. Do they need to know every detail of your story, only brief summaries of certain parts, or some mixture of detail and summary?

In order to decide what details you should provide, you need to think about how much your readers know and what they are going to expect. If your subject is unusual (a trip to see an erupting volcano), your readers will need a lot of information, much of it technical, to understand the novel experience you are going to describe. They will expect an efficient, matter-of-fact description of volcanoes but also want you to give them some sense of how it feels to see one erupting. If your subject is familiar to most people (your experience with lawn sprinklers), your readers will need few technical details to understand your subject. But they will expect you to give them new images and insights that create a fresh vision of your subject—for example, portraying lawn sprinklers as the languid pulse of summer.

STRATEGIES

The writers in this section demonstrate that you need to use certain strategies to write a successful narrative and descriptive essay. For openers, you must recognize that an experience and an essay about that experience are not the same thing. When you have any experience, no matter how long it lasts, your memory of that experience is going to be disorganized and poorly defined, but the essay you write about that experience must have a purpose and be sharply focused. When you want to transform your experience into an essay, start by locating the central **conflict.** It may be (1) between the writer and himself or herself as when E. B. White tries to recapture his summer vacations; (2) between the writer and others, as when Maya Angelou responds to Mrs. Cullinan and her friends; or (3) between the writer and the environment, as when Judith Ortiz Cofer tries to explain the difference between *individuals* and *social stereotypes.*

Once you have identified the conflict, arrange the action so that your readers know how the conflict started, how it developed, and how it was resolved. This coherent sequence of events is called a **plot.** Sometimes you may want to create a plot that sticks to a simple chronological pattern. In "My Name is Margaret," Maya Angelou begins her account of the original events at the beginning and describes them as they occur. At other times you may want to start your essay in the middle or even near the end of the events you are describing. In "The Village Watchman," Terry Tempest Williams begins at the end, after her Uncle Alan's death, and works back to the beginning as she searches for "proper instructions." The authors choose a pattern according to their purpose: Angelou wants to describe the evolution of events leading up to the broken china; Williams wants to describe the impact of a social stigma.

When you figure out what the beginning, middle, and end of your plot should be, you can establish how each event in those sections should be paced. **Pace** is the speed at which the writer recounts events. Sometimes you can narrate events quickly by omitting details, compressing time, and summarizing experience. For example, Cofer summarizes several episodes that reveal her contact with a stereotype. At other times you may want to pace events more slowly and carefully because they are vital to your purpose. You will need to include every detail, expand on time, and present the situation as a fully realized scene rather than in summary form. White creates such a scene at the conclusion of his narrative when he makes his readers see the afternoon thunderstorm and feel the cold, wet swimming suit.

You can make your scenes and summaries effective by your careful **selection of details.** Just adding more details doesn't satisfy this requirement. You must select those special details that satisfy the needs of your readers and further your purpose in the essay. For example, sometimes you will need to give *objective* or *technical* details to help your readers understand your subject. Cofer provides this kind of detail when she describes the cultural customs of Puerto Rico. At other times you will want to give *subjective* or *impressionistic* details to appeal to your readers' senses. N. Scott Momaday provides much of this sort of detail as he tries to evoke the landscape of Rainy Mountain. Finally, you may want to present your details so they form a *figurative image* or create a *dominant impression*. Williams uses both of these strategies: the first when she describes the "Wolf Pole," the second when she discusses the pattern of her uncle's seizures.

In order to identify the conflict, organize the plot, vary the pace, and select details for your essay, you need to determine your **point of view:** the person and position of the narrator (*point*) and the attitude toward the experience being presented (*view*). You choose your *person* by deciding whether you want to tell your story as "I" saw it (as Maya Angelou does in her story about her confrontation with Mrs. Cullinan) or as "he" or "she" saw it (as Williams does in her account of her uncle's last days).

You choose your *position* by deciding how close you want to be to the action in time and space. You may be involved in the action or view it from the position of an observer, or you may tell about the events as they are happening or many years after they have taken place. For example, E. B. White portrays himself as a young man in his narrative, but E. B. White the author wonders why his son does not respond to the lake as he did. You create your attitude—how you view the events you intend to present and interpret—by the person and position you choose for writing your essay. The attitudes of the narrators in the following essays might be characterized as angry (Angelou), perplexed (Cofer), reverent (Williams), mystical (Momaday), and pensive (White).

NARRATION AND DESCRIPTION

Points to Remember

1. Focus your narrative on the "story" in your story—that is, focus on the conflict that defines the plot.
2. Vary the pace of your narrative so that you can summarize some events quickly and render others as fully realized scenes.
3. Supply evocative details to help your readers experience the dramatic development of your narrative.
4. Establish a consistent point of view so that your readers know how you have positioned yourself in your story.
5. Represent the events in your narrative so that your story makes its point.

In this excerpt from her graphic novel Persepolis: The Story of a Childhood (2003), Marjane Satrapi recounts the reaction of young schoolgirls to the law requiring them to wear "the veil." Some argue that the veil debases and even erases female identity. Others argue that it provides women with safety and secret power. How do the characters in Satrapi's narrative feel about this regulation? Write a narrative describing your own reactions to some obligatory dress code.

Maya Angelou (given name, Marguerita Johnson) was born in St. Louis, Missouri, in 1928 and spent her early years in California and Arkansas. A woman of varied accomplishments, she is a novelist, poet, playwright, stage and screen performer, composer, and singer. She is perhaps best known for her auto-biographical novels: *I Know Why the Caged Bird Sings* (1970), *Gather Together in My Name* (1974), *Singin' and Swingin' and Gettin' Merry Like Christmas* (1976), *Heart of a Woman* (1981), *All God's Children Need Traveling Shoes* (1986), *Wouldn't Take Nothing for My Journey Now* (1993), *A Brave and Startling Truth* (1995), and *Oh Pray My Wings Are Gonna Fit Me Well* (1997). Angelou's poetry is equally well respected and is published in her *Complete Collected Poems* (1994). In the following selection from *I Know Why the Caged Bird Sings*, Angelou recounts how she maintained her identity in a world of prejudice.

My Name Is Margaret

RECENTLY A WHITE woman from Texas, who would quickly describe herself as a liberal, asked me about my hometown. When I told her that in Stamps my grandmother had owned the only Negro general merchandise store since the turn of the century, she exclaimed, "Why, you were a debutante." Ridiculous and even ludicrous. But Negro girls in small Southern towns, whether poverty-stricken or just munching along on a few of life's necessities, were given as extensive and irrelevant preparations for adulthood as rich white girls shown in magazines. Admittedly the training was not the same. While white girls learned to waltz and sit gracefully with a tea cup balanced on their knees, we were lagging behind, learning the mid-Victorian values with very little money to indulge them. (Come and see Edna Lomax spending the money she made picking cotton on five balls of ecru tatting thread. Her fingers are bound to snag the work and she'll have to repeat the stitches time and time again. But she knows that when she buys the thread.)

We were required to embroider and I had trunkfuls of   2
colorful dishtowels, pillowcases, runners and handkerchiefs to my credit. I mastered the art of crocheting and tatting, and there was a lifetime's supply of dainty doilies that would never be used in sacheted dresser drawers. It went without saying that all girls could iron and wash, but the finer touches around the home, like setting a table with real silver, baking roasts and cooking vegetables without meat, had to be learned elsewhere. Usually at the source of those habits. During my tenth year, a white woman's kitchen became my finishing school.

Mrs. Viola Cullinan was a plump woman who lived in a   3
three-bedroom house somewhere behind the post office. She was singularly unattractive until she smiled, and then the lines around her eyes and mouth which made her look perpetually

---

*During my tenth year, a white woman's
kitchen became my finishing school.*

---

dirty disappeared, and her face looked like the mask of an impish elf. She usually rested her smile until late afternoon when her women friends dropped in and Miss Glory, the cook, served them cold drinks on the closed-in porch.

The exactness of her house was inhuman. This glass went   4
here and only here. That cup had its place and it was an act of impudent rebellion to place it anywhere else. At twelve o'clock the table was set. At 12:15 Mrs. Cullinan sat down to

dinner (whether her husband had arrived or not). At 12:16 Miss Glory brought out the food.

It took me a week to learn the difference between a salad plate, a bread plate and a dessert plate.

Mrs. Cullinan kept up the tradition of her wealthy parents. She was from Virginia. Miss Glory, who was a descendant of slaves that had worked for the Cullinans, told me her history. She had married beneath her (according to Miss Glory). Her husband's family hadn't had their money very long and what they had "didn't 'mount to much."

As ugly as she was, I thought privately, she was lucky to get a husband above or beneath her station. But Miss Glory wouldn't let me say a thing against her mistress. She was very patient with me, however, over the housework. She explained the dishware, silverware and servants' bells. The large round bowl in which soup was served wasn't a soup bowl, it was a tureen. There were goblets, sherbet glasses, ice-cream glasses, wine glasses, green glass coffee cups with matching saucers, and water glasses. I had a glass to drink from, and it sat with Miss Glory's on a separate shelf from the others. Soup spoons, gravy boat, butter knives, salad forks and carving platter were additions to my vocabulary and in fact almost represented a new language. I was fascinated with the novelty, with the fluttering Mrs. Cullinan and her Alice-in-Wonderland house.

Her husband remains, in my memory, undefined. I lumped him with all the other white men that I had ever seen and tried not to see.

On our way home one evening, Miss Glory told me that Mrs. Cullinan couldn't have children. She said that she was too delicate-boned. It was hard to imagine bones at all under those layers of fat. Miss Glory went on to say that the doctor had taken out all her lady organs. I reasoned that a pig's organs included the lungs, heart and liver, so if Mrs. Cullinan was walking around without those essentials, it explained why she drank alcohol out of unmarked bottles. She was keeping herself embalmed.

When I spoke to Bailey about it, he agreed that I was right, but he also informed me that Mr. Cullinan had two daughters by a colored lady and that I knew them very well. He added that the girls were the spitting image of their father. I was unable to remember what he looked like, although I had just left him a few hours before, but I thought of the Coleman girls. They were very light-skinned and certainly didn't look very much like their mother (no one ever mentioned Mr. Coleman).

My pity for Mrs. Cullinan preceded me the next morning 11 like the Cheshire cat's smile. Those girls, who could have been her daughters, were beautiful. They didn't have to straighten their hair. Even when they were caught in the rain, their braids still hung down straight like tamed snakes. Their mouths were pouty little cupid's bows. Mrs. Cullinan didn't know what she missed. Or maybe she did. Poor Mrs. Cullinan.

For weeks after, I arrived early, left late and tried very hard 12 to make up for her barrenness. If she had had her own children, she wouldn't have had to ask me to run a thousand errands from her back door to the back door of her friends. Poor old Mrs. Cullinan.

Then one evening Miss Glory told me to serve the ladies 13 on the porch. After I set the tray down and turned toward the kitchen, one of the women asked, "What's your name, girl?" It was the speckled-faced one. Mrs. Cullinan said, "She doesn't talk much. Her name's Margaret."

"Is she dumb?" 14

"No. As I understand it, she can talk when she wants 15 to but she's usually quiet as a little mouse. Aren't you, Margaret?"

I smiled at her. Poor thing. No organs and couldn't even 16 pronounce my name correctly.

"She's a sweet little thing, though." 17

"Well, that may be, but the name's too long. I'd never 18 bother myself. I'd call her Mary if I was you."

I fumed into the kitchen. That horrible woman would never 19 have the chance to call me Mary because if I was starving I'd never work for her. I decided I wouldn't pee on her if her heart was on fire. Giggles drifted in off the porch and into Miss Glory's pots. I wondered what they could be laughing about.

Whitefolks were so strange. Could they be talking about   20
me? Everybody knew that they stuck together better than the
Negroes did. It was possible that Mrs. Cullinan had friends in
St. Louis who heard about a girl from Stamps being in court
and wrote to tell her. Maybe she knew about Mr. Freeman.

My lunch was in my mouth a second time and I went   21
outside and relieved myself on the bed of four-o'clocks. Miss
Glory thought I might be coming down with something and
told me to go on home, that Momma would give me some
herb tea, and she'd explain to her mistress.

I realized how foolish I was being before I reached the pond.   22
Of course Mrs. Cullinan didn't know. Otherwise she wouldn't
have given me two nice dresses that Momma cut down, and she
certainly wouldn't have called me a "sweet little thing." My
stomach felt fine, and I didn't mention anything to Momma.

That evening I decided to write a poem on being white,   23
fat, old and without children. It was going to be a tragic
ballad. I would have to watch her carefully to capture the
essence of her loneliness and pain.

The very next day, she called me by the wrong name. Miss   24
Glory and I were washing up the lunch dishes when Mrs.
Cullinan came to the doorway. "Mary?"

Miss Glory asked, "Who?"   25

Mrs. Cullinan, sagging a little, knew and I knew. "I want   26
Mary to go down to Mrs. Randall's and take her some soup.
She's not been feeling well for a few days."

Miss Glory's face was a wonder to see. "You mean   27
Margaret, ma'am. Her name's Margaret."

"That's too long. She's Mary from now on. Heat that   28
soup from last night and put it in the china tureen and, Mary,
I want you to carry it carefully."

Every person I knew had a hellish horror of being "called   29
out of his name." It was a dangerous practice to call a Negro
anything that could be loosely construed as insulting because
of the centuries of their having been called niggers, jigs,
dinges, blackbirds, crows, boots and spooks.

Miss Glory had a fleeting second of feeling sorry for me.   30
Then as she handed me the hot tureen she said, "Don't

mind, don't pay that no mind. Sticks and stones may break your bones, but words . . . You know, I been working for her for twenty years."

She held the back door open for me. "Twenty years. I 31 wasn't much older than you. My name used to be Hallelujah. That's what Ma named me, but my mistress give me 'Glory,' and it stuck. I likes it better too."

I was in the little path that ran behind the houses when 32 Miss Glory shouted, "It's shorter too."

For a few seconds it was a tossup over whether I would 33 laugh (imagine being named Hallelujah) or cry (imagine letting some white woman rename you for her convenience). My anger saved me from either outburst. I had to quit the job, but the problem was going to be how to do it. Momma wouldn't allow me to quit for just any reason.

"She's a peach. That woman is a real peach." Mrs. Randall's 34 maid was talking as she took the soup from me, and I wondered what her name used to be and what she answered to now.

For a week I looked into Mrs. Cullinan's face as she called 35 me Mary. She ignored my coming late and leaving early. Miss Glory was a little annoyed because I had begun to leave egg yolk on the dishes and wasn't putting much heart in polishing the silver. I hoped that she would complain to our boss, but she didn't.

Then Bailey solved my dilemma. He had me describe the 36 contents of the cupboard and the particular plates she liked best. Her favorite piece was a casserole shaped like a fish and the green glass coffee cups. I kept his instructions in mind, so on the next day when Miss Glory was hanging out clothes and I had again been told to serve the old biddies on the porch, I dropped the empty serving tray. When I heard Mrs. Cullinan scream, "Mary!" I picked up the casserole and two of the green glass cups in readiness. As she rounded the kitchen door I let them fall on the tiled floor.

I could never absolutely describe to Bailey what happened 37 next, because each time I got to the part where she fell on the floor and screwed up her ugly face to cry, we burst out laughing. She actually wobbled around on the floor and picked up shards of the cups and cried, "Oh, Momma. Oh, dear Gawd. It's Momma's china from Virginia. Oh, Momma, I sorry."

Miss Glory came running in from the yard and the women   38
from the porch crowded around. Miss Glory was almost as broken up as her mistress. "You mean to say she broke our Virginia dishes? What we gone do?"

Miss Cullinan cried louder, "That clumsy nigger. Clumsy   39
little black nigger."

Old speckled-face leaned down and asked, "Who did it,   40
Viola? Was it Mary? Who did it?"

Everything was happening so fast I can't remember   41
whether her action preceded her words, but I know that Mrs. Cullinan said, "Her name's Margaret, goddamn it, her name's Margaret." And she threw a wedge of the broken plate at me. It could have been the hysteria which put her aim off, but the flying crockery caught Miss Glory right over the ear and she started screaming.

I left the front door wide open so all the neighbors could   42
hear.

Mrs. Cullinan was right about one thing. My name wasn't   43
Mary.

For Study and Discussion

QUESTIONS ABOUT PURPOSE

1. In what sense does Mrs. Cullinan's kitchen serve as Angelou's "finishing school"? What is she supposed to learn there? What does she learn?
2. How does Angelou's description of Mrs. Cullinan's house as *exact* and *inhuman* support her purpose in recounting the events that take place there?

QUESTIONS ABOUT AUDIENCE

1. How does Angelou's comment about the liberal woman from Texas identify the immediate audience for her essay?
2. What assumptions does Angelou make about her other readers when she comments on the laughter of the white women on the porch?

QUESTIONS ABOUT STRATEGIES

1. How does Angelou use the three discussions of her name to organize her narrative? How does she pace the third discussion to provide an effective resolution for her essay?
2. How does Angelou's intention to write a poem about Mrs. Cullinan establish her initial attitude toward her employer? What changes her attitude toward Mrs. Cullinan's "loneliness and pain"?

For Writing and Research

1. *Analyze* the strategies Angelou uses to reveal her changing attitude toward Mrs. Cullinan.
2. *Practice* by enacting an experience in which someone mispronounces or forgets your name.
3. *Argue* Glory's versus Bailey's position about the destruction of the fish-shaped casserole.
4. *Synthesize* the advice given to girls in popular magazines. Then use this evidence to argue that such advice is an irrelevant preparation for adulthood.

Judith Ortiz Cofer was born in Hormigueros, Puerto Rico, in 1952. She emigrated to the United States in 1956 and was educated at Augusta College, Florida Atlantic University, and Oxford University. She has taught in the public schools of Palm Beach County, Florida, as well as at several universities, such as Miami University and the University of Georgia. Her poetry is collected in *Reading for the Mainland* (1987) and *Terms of Survival* (1987), and her first novel, *The Line of the Sun* (1989), was nominated for the Pulitzer Prize. Her recent books include *The Latin Deli: Prose and Poetry* (1993), *An Island like You: Stories of the Barrio* (1995), and *The Meaning of Consuelo* (2003). In "The Myth of the Latin Woman: I Just Met a Girl Named María," reprinted from *The Latin Deli,* Cofer describes several experiences that taught her about the pervasive stereotypes of Latin women.

The Myth of the Latin Woman: I Just Met a Girl Named María

O N A BUS trip to London from Oxford University where 1
I was earning some graduate credits one summer, a young man, obviously fresh from a pub, spotted me and as if struck by inspiration went down on his knees in the aisle. With both hands over his heart he broke into an Irish tenor's rendition of "María" from *West Side Story.* My politely amused fellow passengers gave his lovely voice the round of gentle applause it deserved. Though I was not quite as amused, I

managed my version of an English smile: no show of teeth, no extreme contortions of the facial muscles—I was at this time of my life practicing reserve and cool. Oh, that British control, how I coveted it. But María had followed me to London, reminding me of a prime fact of my life: you can leave the Island, master the English language, and travel as far as you can, but if you are a Latina, especially one like me who so obviously belongs to Rita Moreno's gene pool, the Island travels with you.

This is sometimes a very good thing—it may win you that extra minute of someone's attention. But with some people,   2

---

*When a Puerto Rican girl dressed in her idea of what is attractive meets a man from the mainstream culture who has been trained to react to certain types of clothing **as a sexual signal**, a clash is likely to take place.*

---

the same things can make *you* an island—not so much a tropical paradise as an Alcatraz, a place nobody wants to visit. As a Puerto Rican girl growing up in the United States and wanting like most children to "belong," I resented the stereotype that my Hispanic appearance called forth from many people I met.

Our family lived in a large urban center in New Jersey during the sixties, where life was designed as a microcosm of my parents' casas on the island. We spoke in Spanish, we ate Puerto Rican food bought at the bodega, and we practiced strict Catholicism complete with Saturday confession and Sunday mass at a church where our parents were accommodated into a one-hour Spanish mass slot, performed by a Chinese priest trained as a missionary for Latin America.

As a girl I was kept under strict surveillance, since virtue   4 and modesty were, by cultural equation, the same as family honor. As a teenager I was instructed on how to behave as a proper señorita. But it was a conflicting message girls got, since the Puerto Rican mothers also encouraged their daughters to look and act like women and to dress in clothes our Anglo friends and their mothers found too "mature" for our age. It was, and is, cultural, yet I often felt humiliated when I appeared at an American friend's party wearing a dress more suitable to a semiformal than to a playroom birthday celebration. At Puerto Rican festivities, neither the music nor the colors we wore could be too loud. I still experience a vague sense of letdown when I'm invited to a "party" and it turns out to be a marathon conversation in hushed tones rather than a fiesta with salsa, laughter, and dancing—the kind of celebration I remember from my childhood.

I remember Career Day in our high school, when teach- 5
ers told us to come dressed as if for a job interview. It quickly became obvious that to the barrio girls, "dressing up" sometimes meant wearing ornate jewelry and clothing that would be more appropriate (by mainstream standards) for the company Christmas party than as daily office attire. That morning I had agonized in front of my closet, trying to figure out what a "career girl" would wear because, essentially, except for Marlo Thomas on TV, I had no models on which to base my decision. I knew how to dress for school: at the Catholic school I attended we all wore uniforms; I knew how to dress for Sunday mass, and I knew what dresses to wear for parties at my relatives' homes. Though I do not recall the precise details of my Career Day outfit, it must have been a composite of the above choices. But I re-member a comment my friend (an Italian-American) made in later years that coalesced my impressions of that day. She said that at the business school she was attending the Puerto Rican girls always stood out for wearing "everything at once." She meant, of course, too much jewelry, too many accessories. On that day at school, we were simply made the negative models by the nuns who were themselves not cred-ible fashion experts to any of us. But it was painfully obvious to me that to the others, in their tailored skirts and silk blouses, we must have seemed "hopeless" and "vulgar."

Though I now know that most adolescents feel out of step much of the time, I also know that for the Puerto Rican girls of my generation that sense was intensified. The way our teachers and classmates looked at us that day in school was just a taste of the culture clash that awaited us in the real world, where prospective employers and men on the street would often misinterpret our tight skirts and jingling bracelets as a come-on.

Mixed cultural signals have perpetuated certain stereo- 6
types—for example, that of the Hispanic woman as the "Hot Tamale" or sexual firebrand. It is a one-dimensional view that the media have found easy to promote. In their special vocabulary, advertisers have designated "sizzling" and "smoldering" as the adjectives of choice for describing not only the foods but also the women of Latin America. From conversations in my house I recall hearing about the harassment that Puerto Rican women endured in factories where the "boss men" talked to them as if sexual innuendo was all they understood and, worse, often gave them the choice of submitting to advances or being fired.

It is custom, however, not chromosomes, that leads us to 7
choose scarlet over pale pink. As young girls, we were influenced in our decisions about clothes and colors by the women—older sisters and mothers who had grown up on a tropical island where the natural environment was a riot of primary colors, where showing your skin was one way to keep cool as well as to look sexy. Most important of all, on the island, women perhaps felt freer to dress and move more provocatively, since, in most cases, they were protected by the traditions, mores, and laws of a Spanish/Catholic system of morality and machismo whose main rule was: *You may look at my sister, but if you touch her I will kill you.* The extended family and church structure could provide a young woman with a circle of safety in her small pueblo on the island; if a man "wronged" a girl, everyone would close in to save her family honor.

This is what I have gleaned from my discussions as an adult 8
with older Puerto Rican women. They have told me about dressing in their best party clothes on Saturday nights and

going to the town's plaza to promenade with their girlfriends in front of the boys they liked. The males were thus given an opportunity to admire the women and to express their admiration in the form of *piropos:* erotically charged street poems they composed on the spot. I have been subjected to a few piropos while visiting the Island, and they can be outrageous, although custom dictates that they must never cross into obscenity. This ritual, as I understand it, also entails a show of studied indifference on the woman's part; if she is "decent," she must not acknowledge the man's impassioned words. So I do understand how things can be lost in translation. When a Puerto Rican girl dressed in her idea of what is attractive meets a man from the mainstream culture who has been trained to react to certain types of clothing as a sexual signal, a clash is likely to take place. The line I first heard based on this aspect of the myth happened when the boy who took me to my first formal dance leaned over to plant a sloppy overeager kiss painfully on my mouth, and when I didn't respond with sufficient passion said in a resentful tone: "I thought you Latin girls were supposed to mature early"—my first instance of being thought of as a fruit or vegetable—I was supposed to *ripen*, not just grow into womanhood like other girls.

It is surprising to some of my professional friends that some people, including those who should know better, still put others "in their place." Though rarer, these incidents are still commonplace in my life. It happened to me most recently during a stay at a very classy metropolitan hotel favored by young professional couples for their weddings. Late one evening after the theater, as I walked toward my room with my new colleague (a woman with whom I was coordinating an arts program), a middle-aged man in a tuxedo, a young girl in satin and lace on his arm, stepped directly into our path. With his champagne glass extended toward me, he exclaimed, "Evita!"   9

Our way blocked, my companion and I listened as the man half-recited, half-bellowed "Don't Cry for Me, Argentina." When he finished, the young girl said: "How about a round of applause for my daddy?" We complied, hoping this would   10 bring the silly spectacle to a close. I was becoming aware that our little group was attracting the attention of the other guests. "Daddy" must have perceived this too, and he once more barred the way as we tried to walk past him. He began to shout-sing a ditty to the tune of "La Bamba"—except the lyrics were about a girl named María whose exploits all rhymed with her name and gonorrhea. The girl kept saying "Oh, Daddy" and looking at me with pleading eyes. She wanted me to laugh along with the others. My companion and I stood silently waiting for the man to end his offensive song. When he finished, I looked not at him but at his daughter. I advised her calmly never to ask her father what he had done in the army. Then I walked between them and to my room. My friend complimented me on my cool handling of the situation. I confessed to her that I really had wanted to push the jerk into the swimming pool. I knew that this same man—probably a corporate executive, well educated, even worldly by most standards—would not have been likely to regale a white woman with a dirty song in public. He would perhaps have checked his impulse by assuming that she could be somebody's wife or mother, or at least *somebody* who might take offense. But to him, I was just an Evita or a María: merely a character in his cartoon-populated universe.

Because of my education and my proficiency with the English language, I have acquired many mechanisms for dealing with the anger I experience. This was not true for my parents, nor is it true for the many Latin women working at menial jobs who must put up with stereotypes about our ethnic group such as: "They make good domestics." This is another facet of the myth of the Latin woman in the United States. Its origin is simple to deduce. Work as domestics, waitressing, and factory jobs are all that's available to women with little English and few skills. The myth of the Hispanic menial has been sustained by the same media phenomenon that made "Mammy" from *Gone with the Wind* America's idea of the black woman for generations; María, the housemaid or counter girl, is now indelibly etched into the national psyche. The big and the little screens have presented us with the

11

picture of the funny Hispanic maid, mispronouncing words and cooking up a spicy storm in a shiny California kitchen.

This media-engendered image of the Latina in the United States has been documented by feminist Hispanic scholars, who claim that such portrayals are partially responsible for the denial of opportunities for upward mobility among Latinas in the professions. I have a Chicana friend working on a Ph.D. in philosophy at a major university. She says her doctor still shakes his head in puzzled amazement at all the "big words" she uses. Since I do not wear my diplomas around my neck for all to see, I too have on occasion been sent to that "kitchen," where some think I obviously belong.   12

One such incident that has stayed with me, though I recognize it as a minor offense, happened on the day of my first public poetry reading. It took place in Miami in a boat-restaurant where we were having lunch before the event. I was nervous and excited as I walked in with my notebook in my hand. An older woman motioned me to her table. Thinking (foolish me) that she wanted me to autograph a copy of my brand new slender volume of verse, I went over. She ordered a cup of coffee from me, assuming that I was the waitress. Easy enough to mistake my poems for menus, I suppose. I know that it wasn't an intentional act of cruelty, yet of all the good things that happened that day, I remember that scene most clearly, because it reminded me of what I had to overcome before anyone would take me seriously. In retrospect I understand that my anger gave my reading fire, that I have almost always taken doubts in my abilities as a challenge—and that the result is, most times, a feeling of satisfaction at having won a convert when I see the cold, appraising eyes warm to my words, the body language change, the smile that indicates that I have opened some avenue for communication. That day I read to that woman and her lowered eyes told me that she was embarrassed at her little faux pas, and when I willed her to look up at me, it was my victory, and she graciously allowed me to punish her with my full attention. We shook hands at the end of the reading, and I never saw her again. She has probably forgotten the whole thing but maybe not.   13

Yet I am one of the lucky ones. My parents made it possible for me to acquire a stronger footing in the mainstream culture by giving me the chance at an education. And books and art have saved me from the harsher forms of ethnic and racial prejudice that many of my Hispanic *compañeras* have had to endure. I travel a lot around the United States, reading from my books of poetry and my novel, and the reception I most often receive is one of positive interest by people who want to know more about my culture. There are, however, thousands of Latinas without the privilege of an education or the entrée into society that I have. For them life is a struggle against the misconceptions perpetuated by the myth of the Latina as whore, domestic or criminal. We cannot change this by legislating the way people look at us. The transformation, as I see it, has to occur at a much more individual level. My personal goal in my public life is to try to replace the old pervasive stereotypes and myths about Latinas with a much more interesting set of realities. Every time I give a reading, I hope the stories I tell, the dreams and fears I examine in my work, can achieve some universal truth which will get my audience past the particulars of my skin color, my accent, or my clothes. 14

I once wrote a poem in which I called us Latinas "God's brown daughters." This poem is really a prayer of sorts, offered upward, but also, through the human-to-human channel of art, outward. It is a prayer for communication, and for respect. In it, Latin women pray "in Spanish to an Anglo God / with a Jewish heritage," and they are "fervently hoping / that if not omnipotent, / at least He be bilingual." 15

For Study and Discussion

QUESTIONS ABOUT PURPOSE

1. Why does Cofer introduce the conflict between *custom* and *chromosomes*? How does this conflict help explain the concept of *stereotype*?

2. How does this narrative help accomplish Cofer's "personal goal in her public life"?

QUESTIONS ABOUT AUDIENCE

1. In what ways does Cofer use the references to *María* and *Evita* to identify her audience?
2. How does she use the example of the *piropos* to educate her audience?

QUESTIONS ABOUT STRATEGIES

1. How does Cofer use the details of Career Day to explain how a cultural stereotype is perpetuated?
2. How does she manipulate point of view at her "first public poetry reading" to illustrate how she intends to change that stereotype?

For Writing and Research

1. *Analyze* the way Cofer uses *Gone with the Wind* to illustrate how the media creates stereotypes.
2. *Practice* by enacting an experience in which people have misread your behavior by focusing on your clothes, your language, or your looks.
3. *Argue* that stereotypes are the result of custom or caricature.
4. *Synthesize:* Research how people respond to stereotyping. Then use this evidence to argue for the most effective way to eliminate stereotyping.

Terry Tempest Williams was born in 1955 in the Salt Valley of Utah and was educated at the University of Utah. She has taught on a Navajo reservation and in the women's studies program at the University of Utah. She currently serves as the curator of education and naturalist-in-residence at the Utah Museum of Natural History in Salt Lake City. Williams has written children's books with nature themes, including *The Secret Language of Snow* (1984); a collection of short stories set in Utah, *Coyote's Canyon* (1989); and four works of non-fiction that blend natural history and personal experience: *Pieces of White Shell: A Journey to Navajo-Land* (1984), *Refuge: An Unnatural History of Family and Place* (1991), *An Unspoken Hunger: Stories from the Field* (1994), and *Red* (2001). In "The Village Watchman," reprinted from *An Unspoken Hunger,* Williams describes the remarkable lessons she learned from her Uncle Alan.

The Village Watchman

S TORIES CARVED IN cedar rise from the deep woods of Sitka. These totem poles are foreign to me, this vertical lineage of clans; Eagle, Raven, Wolf, and Salmon. The Tlingit craftsmen create a genealogy of the earth, a reminder of mentors, that we come into this world in need of proper instruction. I sit on the soft floor of this Alaskan forest and feel the presence of Other.

The totem before me is called "Wolf Pole" by locals. The Village Watchman sits on top of Wolf's head with his knees drawn to his chest, his hands holding them tight against his body. He wears a red-and-black-striped hat. His eyes are direct, deep-set, painted blue. The expression on his face reminds me of a man I loved, a man who was born into this world feet first.

"Breech—"my mother told me of her brother's birth. 3 "Alan was born feet first. As a result, his brain was denied oxygen. He is special."

As a child, this information impressed me. I remember 4 thinking fish live underwater. Maybe Alan had gills, maybe he didn't need a face-first gulp of air like the rest of us. His sweet breath of initiation came in time, slowly moving up through the soles of his tiny webbed feet. The amniotic sea he had

---

Alan was wild, like a mustang in the desert and, like most wild horses, he was eventually rounded up.

---

floated in for nine months delivered him with a fluid memory. He knew something. Other.

Wolf, who resides in the center of this totem, holds the tail 5 of Salmon with his feet. The tongue of Wolf hangs down, blood-red, as do his front paws, black. Salmon, a sockeye, is poised downriver—a swish of a tail and he could be gone, but the clasp of Wolf is strong.

There is a story of a boy who was kidnapped from his 6 village by the Salmon People. He was taken from his family to learn the ways of water. When he returned many years later to his home, he was recognized by his own as a Holy Man privy to the mysteries of the unseen world. Twenty years after my uncle's death, I wonder if Alan could have been that boy.

But our culture tells a different story, more alien than those 7 of Tlingit or Haida. My culture calls people of sole-births retarded, handicapped, mentally disabled or challenged. We see them for who they are not, rather than for who they are.

My grandmother, Lettie Romney Dixon, wrote in her jour- 8 nal, "It wasn't until Alan was sixteen months old that a busy doctor cruelly broke the news to us. Others may have suspected our son's limitations but to those of us who loved him so unquestionably, lightning struck without warning. I hugged my sorrow to myself. I felt abandoned and lost. I wouldn't accept the verdict. Then we started the trips to a multitude of doctors. Most of them were kind and explained that our child was like a car without brakes, like an electric wire without insulation. They gave us no hope for a normal life."

Normal. Latin: *normalis; norma,* a rule; conforming with or constituting an accepted standard, model, or pattern, especially corresponding to the median or average of a large group in type, appearance, achievement, function, or development. 9

Alan was not normal. He was unique; one and only; single; sole; unusual; extraordinary; rare. His emotions were not measured, his curiosity not bridled. In a sense, he was wild like a mustang in the desert and, like most wild horses, he was eventually rounded up. 10

He was unpredictable. He created his own rules and they changed from moment to moment. Alan was twelve years old, hyperactive, mischievous, easily frustrated, and unable to learn in traditional ways. The situation was intensified by his seizures. Suddenly, without warning, he would stiffen like a rake, fall forward and crash to the ground, hitting his head. My grandparents could not keep him home any longer. They needed professional guidance and help. In 1957 they reluctantly placed their youngest child in an institution for handicapped children called the American Fork Training School. My grandmother's heart broke for the second time. 11

Once again, from her journal: "Many a night my pillow is wet from tears of sorrow and senseless dreamings of 'if things had only been different,' or wondering if he is tucked in snug and warm, if he is well and happy, if the wind still bothers him. . . ." 12

The wind may have continued to bother Alan, certainly the conditions he was living under were less than ideal, but as a family there was much about his private life we never knew. What we did know was that Alan had an enormous capacity for adaptation. We had no choice but to follow him. 13

I followed him for years.   14

Alan was ten years my senior. In my mind, growing up, he   15
was mythic. Everything I was taught not to do, Alan did. We
were taught to be polite, to not express displeasure or anger in
public. Alan was sheer, physical expression. Whatever was on
his mind was vocalized and usually punctuated with colorful
speech. We would go bowling as a family on Sundays. Each of
us would take our turn, hold the black ball to our chest, take a
few steps, swing our arm back, forward, glide, and release—the
ball would roll down the alley, hit a few pins, we would wait for
the ball to return, and then take our second run. Little emotion was shown. When it was Alan's turn, it was an event.
Nothing subtle. His style was Herculean. Big man. Big ball.
Big roll. Big bang. Whether it was a strike or a gutter, he
clapped his hands, spun around in the floor, slapped his thighs
and cried, "God-damn! Did you see that one? Send me another ball, sweet Jesus!" And the ball was always returned.

I could always count on my uncle for a straight answer. He   16
was my mentor in understanding that one of the remarkable
aspects of being human was to hold opposing views in our
mind at once.

"How are you doing?" I would ask.   17
"Ask me how I am feeling?" he answered.   18
"Okay, how are you feeling?"   19
"Today? Right now?"   20
"Yes."   21
"I am very happy and very sad."   22
"How can you be both at the same time?" I asked in all   23
seriousness, a girl of nine or ten.

"Because both require each other's company. They live in   24
the same house. Didn't you know?"

We would laugh and then go on to another topic. Talking   25
to my uncle was always like entering a maze of riddles. Ask a
question. Answer with a question and see where it leads you.

My younger brother Steve and I spent a lot of time with   26
Alan. He offered us shelter from the conventionality of a
Mormon family. At our home during Christmas, he would
direct us in his own nativity plays. "More"—he would say to
us, making wide gestures with his hands. "Give me more of

yourself." He was not like anyone we knew. In a culture where we were taught socially to be seen not heard, Alan was our mirror. We could be different too. His unquestioning belief in us as children, as human beings, was in startling contrast to the way we saw the public react to him. It hurt us. What we could never tell was if it hurt him.

Each week, Steve and I would accompany our grandparents south to visit Alan. It was an hour's drive to the training school from Salt Lake City, mostly through farmlands. 27

We would enter the grounds, pull into the parking lot of the institution where a playground filled with huge papier-mâché storybook figures stood (a twenty-foot pied piper, a pumpkin carriage with Cinderella inside, the old woman who lived in a shoe), and nine out of ten times, Alan would be standing outside his dormitory waiting for us. We would get out of the car and he would run toward us, throwing his powerful arms around us. His hugs cracked my back and at times I had to fight for my breath. My grandfather would calm him down by simply saying, "We're here, son. You can relax now." 28

Alan was a formidable man, now in his early twenties, stocky and strong. His head was large with a protruding forehead that bore many scars, a line-by-line history of seizures. He always had on someone else's clothes—a tweed jacket too small, brown pants too big, a striped golf shirt that didn't match. He showed us appearances didn't matter, personality did. If you didn't know him, he could look frightening. It was an unspoken rule in our family that the character of others was gauged in how they treated him. The only thing consistent about his attire was that he always wore a silver football helmet from Olympus High School where my grandfather was coach. It was a loving, practical solution to protect Alan when he fell. Quite simply, the helmet cradled his head and absorbed the shock of the seizures. 29

"Part of the team," my grandfather Sanky would say as he slapped him affectionately on the back. "You're a Titan, son, and I love you—you're a real player on our team." 30

The windows to the dormitory were dark, reflecting Mount Timpanogos to the east. It was hard to see inside, but I knew what the interior held. It looked like an abandoned 31 gymnasium without bleachers, filled with hospital beds. The stained white walls and yellow-waxed floors offered no warmth to its residents. The stench was nauseating, sweat and urine trapped in the oppression of stale air. I recall the dirty sheets, the lack of privacy, and the almond-eyed children who never rose from their beds. And then I would turn around and face Alan's cheerfulness, the open and loving manner in which he would introduce me to his friends, the pride he exhibited as he showed me around his home. I kept thinking, Doesn't he see how bad this is, how poorly they are being treated? His words would return to me, "I am very happy and I am very sad."

For my brother and me, Alan was our guide, our elder. He was fearless. But neither one of us will ever be able to escape the image of Alan kissing his parents good-bye after an afternoon with family and slowly walking back to his dormitory. Before we drove away, he would turn toward us, take off his silver helmet, and wave. The look on his face haunts me still. Alan walked point for all of us.

Alan liked to talk about God. Perhaps it was in these private conversations that our real friendship was forged.

"I know Him," he would say when all the adults were gone.

"You do?" I asked.

"I talk to Him every day."

"How so?"

"I talk to Him in my prayers. I listen and then I hear His voice."

"What does He tell you?"

"He tells me to be patient. He tells me to be kind. He tells me that He loves me."

In Mormon culture, children are baptized a member of the Church of Jesus Christ of Latter-Day Saints when they turn eight years old. Alan had never been baptized because my grandparents believed it should be his choice, not something simply taken for granted. When he turned twenty-two, he expressed a sincere desire to join the Church. A date was set immediately.

The entire Dixon clan convened in the Lehi Chapel, a few miles north of the group home where Alan was now living.

We were there to support and witness his conversion. As we walked toward the meetinghouse where this sacred rite was to be performed, Alan had a violent seizure. My grandfather and Uncle Don, Alan's elder brother, dropped down with him, holding his head and body as every muscle thrashed on the pavement like a school of netted fish brought on deck. I didn't want to look, but to walk away would have been worse. We stayed with him, all of us.

"Talk to God," I heard myself saying under my breath. "I 43 love you, Alan."

"Can you hear me, darling?" It was my grandmother's 44 voice, her hand holding her son's hand.

By now, many of us were gathered on our knees around 45 him, our trembling hands on his rigid body.

> *And we, who have always thought*
> *Of happiness as rising, would feel*
> *The emotion that almost overwhelms us*
> *Whenever a happy thing falls.*
> *—Rainer Maria Rilke*

Alan opened his eyes. "I want to be baptized," he said. 46 The men helped him to his feet. The gash on his left temple was deep. Blood dripped down the side of his face. He would forgo stitches once again. My mother had her arm around my grandmother's waist. Shaken, we all followed him inside.

Alan's father and brother ministered to him, stopped the 47 bleeding and bandaged the pressure wound, then helped him change into the designated white garments for baptism. He entered the room with great dignity and sat on the front pew with a dozen or more eight-year-old children seated on either side. Row after row of family sat behind him.

"Alan Romney Dixon." His name was called by the presiding 48 bishop. Alan rose from the pew and met his brother Don, also dressed in white, who took his hand and led him down the blue-tiled stairs into the baptismal font filled with water. They faced the congregation. Don raised his right arm to the square in the gesture of a holy oath as Alan placed his hands on his brother's left forearm. The sacred prayer was offered in the name of the Father, the Son, and the Holy Ghost, after which my uncle put his right hand behind Alan's shoulder and gently lowered him into the water for a complete baptism by immersion.

Alan emerged from the holy waters like an angel.   49

> *The breaking away of childhood*
> *Left you intact. In a moment,*
> *You stood there, as if completed*
> *In a miracle, all at once.*
> *—Rainer Maria Rilke*

Six years later, I found myself sitting in a chair across from   50
my uncle at the University Hospital, where he was being treated for a severe ear infection. I was eighteen. He was twenty-eight.

"Alan," I asked. "What is it really like to be inside your   51
body?"

He crossed his legs and placed both hands on the arms of   52
the chair. His brown eyes were piercing.

"I can't tell you what it's like except to say I feel pain for   53
not being seen as the person I am."

A few days later, Alan died alone; unique; one and only;   54
single; in American Fork, Utah.

The Village Watchman sits on top of his totem with Wolf and   55
Salmon—it is beginning to rain in the forest. I find it curious that this spot in southeast Alaska has brought me back into relation with my uncle, this man of sole-birth who came into the world feet first. He reminds me of what it means to live and love with a broken heart; how nothing is sacred, how everything is sacred. He was a weather vane—a storm and a clearing at once.

Shortly after his death, Alan appeared to me in a dream.   56
We were standing in my grandmother's kitchen. He was lean-ing against the white stove with his arms folded.

"Look at me, now, Terry," he said smiling. "I'm normal—   57
perfectly normal." And then he laughed. We both laughed.

He handed me his silver football helmet that was resting 58
on the counter, kissed me, and opened the back door.

"Do you recognize who I am?" 59

On this day in Sitka, I remember. 60

For Study and Discussion

QUESTIONS ABOUT PURPOSE

1. How does Williams's title suggest the purpose of her description of her Uncle Alan's life?
2. How does Williams's description of the Wolf Pole present the purpose of her narrative?

QUESTIONS ABOUT AUDIENCE

1. How does Williams's use of the pronoun *our* in the following phrase identify her audience: "our culture tells a different story, more alien"?
2. How does the following sentence separate Williams's family from her audience: "His unquestioning belief in us . . . was in startling contrast to the way we saw the public react to him"?

QUESTIONS ABOUT STRATEGIES

1. How does Williams use the quotations from Rilke's poetry to interpret Alan's baptism?
2. How does she use the visits at the school, and particularly her last visit at the hospital, to slow the pace of her narrative?

For Writing and Research

1. *Analyze* the strategies Williams uses to correct or enrich your understanding of "special" people.
2. *Practice* by enacting your reactions and reflections on your encounter with a "special" person.
3. *Argue* that the words normal and special are used or misused in our culture.
4. *Synthesize:* Research the way the media (television, movies) portray "special" people. Then use this evidence to demonstrate that such people are denigrated or celebrated.

N. Scott Momaday, a Kiowa, was born in Lawton, Oklahoma, in 1934 and was educated at the University of New Mexico and Stanford University. Although he has taught English and comparative literature at several universities, his vital interests are Native American art, history, and literature. His books include *House Made of Dawn* (1968), winner of the Pulitzer Prize for fiction, and *The Ancient Child* (1989); two collections of poetry, *Angle of Geese and Other Poems* (1974) and *The Gourd Dancer* (1976); two memoirs, *The Way to Rainy Mountain* (1969) and *The Names: A Memoir* (1976); and two collections of poetry and prose, *In the Presence of the Sun* (1998) and *In the Bear's House* (1999). In this excerpt from *The Way to Rainy Mountain*, Momaday evokes the landscapes, the legends, and the people that created the Kiowa culture.

The Way to Rainy Mountain

A SINGLE KNOLL rises out of the plain in Oklahoma, north and west of the Wichita Range. For my people, the Kiowas, it is an old landmark, and they gave it the name Rainy Mountain. The hardest weather in the world is there. Winter brings blizzards, hot tornadic winds arise in the spring, and in summer the prairie is an anvil's edge. The grass turns brittle and brown, and it cracks beneath your feet. There are green belts along the rivers and creeks, linear groves of hickory and pecan, willow and witch hazel. At a distance in July or August the steaming foliage seems almost to writhe in fire. Great green and yellow grasshoppers are everywhere in the tall grass, popping up like corn to sting the flesh, and tortoises crawl about on the red earth, going nowhere in the plenty of time. Loneliness is an aspect of the land. All things in the plain are isolate; there is no confusion of objects in the eye, but *one* hill or *one* tree or *one* man. To look upon that landscape in the early morning, with the sun at your back, is to lose the sense of proportion. Your imagination comes to life, and this, you think, is where Creation was begun.

I returned to Rainy Mountain in July. My grandmother   2
had died in the spring, and I wanted to be at her grave. She had lived to be very old and at last infirm. Her only living daughter was with her when she died, and I was told that in death her face was that of a child.

I like to think of her as a child. When she was born, the   3
Kiowas were living the last great moment of their history. For more than a hundred years they had controlled the open range from the Smoky Hill River to the Red, from the headwaters of the Canadian to the fork of the Arkansas and Cimarron. In alliance with the Comanches, they had ruled the whole of the southern Plains. War was their sacred business, and they were among the finest horsemen the world has ever known. But warfare for the Kiowas was preeminently a matter of disposition rather than of survival, and they never understood the grim, unrelenting advance of the U.S. Cavalry. When at last, divided and ill-provisioned, they were driven onto the Staked Plains in the cold rains of autumn, they fell into panic. In Palo Duro Canyon they abandoned their crucial stores to pillage and had nothing then but their lives. In order to save themselves, they surrendered to the soldiers at Fort Sill and were imprisoned in the old stone corral that now stands as a military museum. My grandmother was spared the humiliation of those high gray walls by eight or ten years, but she must have known from birth the affliction of defeat, the dark brooding of old warriors.

Her name was Aho, and she belonged to the last culture to   4
evolve in North America. Her forebears came down from the high country in western Montana nearly three centuries ago. They were a mountain people, a mysterious tribe of hunters

whose language has never been positively classified in any major group. In the late seventeenth century they began a long migration to the south and east. It was a journey toward the dawn, and it led to a golden age. Along the way the Kiowas were befriended by the Crows, who gave them the culture and religion of the Plains. They acquired horses, and their ancient nomadic spirit was suddenly free of the ground. They acquired Tai-me, the sacred Sun Dance doll, from that moment the object and symbol of their worship, and so shared in the divinity of the sun. Not least, they acquired the sense of destiny, therefore courage and pride. When they entered upon the southern Plains they had been transformed. No longer were they slaves to the simple necessity of survival; they were a lordly and dangerous society of fighters and thieves, hunters and priests of the sun. According to their origin myth, they entered the world through a hollow log. From one point of view, their migration was the fruit of an old prophecy, for indeed they emerged from a sunless world.

Although my grandmother lived out her long life in the ⁵ shadow of Rainy Mountain, the immense landscape of the continental interior lay like memory in her blood. She could tell of the Crows, whom she had never seen, and of the Black Hills, where she had never been. I wanted to see in reality what she had seen more perfectly in the mind's eye, and traveled fifteen hundred miles to begin my pilgrimage.

Yellowstone, it seemed to me, was the top of the world, a ⁶ region of deep lakes and dark timber, canyons and waterfalls. But, beautiful as it is, one might have the sense of confinement there. The skyline in all directions is close at hand, the high wall of the woods and deep cleavages of shade. There is a perfect freedom in the mountains, but it belongs to the eagle and the elk, the badger and the bear. The Kiowas reckoned their stature by the distance they could see, and they were bent and blind in the wilderness.

Descending eastward, the highland meadows are a stairway ⁷ to the plain. In July the inland slope of the Rockies is luxuriant with flax and the buckwheat, stonecrop and larkspur. The earth unfolds and the limit of the land recedes. Clusters of trees, and animals grazing far in the distance, cause the vision to reach away and wonder to build upon the mind. The sun follows a longer course in the day, and the sky is immense beyond all comparison. The great billowing clouds that sail upon it are shadows that move upon the grain like water, dividing light. Farther down, in the land of the Crows and Blackfeet, the plain is yellow. Sweet clover takes hold of the hills and bends upon itself to cover and seal the soil. There the Kiowas paused on their way; they had come to the place where they must change their lives. The sun is at home on the plains. Precisely there does it have the certain character of a god. When the Kiowas came to the land of the Crows, they could see the dark lees of the hills at dawn across the Bighorn River, the profusion of light on the grain shelves, the oldest deity ranging after the solstices. Not yet would they veer southward to the caldron of the land that lay below; they must wean their blood from the northern winter and hold the mountains a while longer in their view. They bore Tai-me in procession to the east.

A dark mist lay over the Black Hills, and the land was like iron. At the top of a ridge I caught sight of Devil's Tower upthrust against the gray sky as if in the birth of time the core of the earth had broken through its crust and the motion of the world was begun. There are things in nature that engender an awful quiet in the heart of man; Devil's Tower is one of them. Two centuries ago, because they could not do otherwise, the Kiowas made a legend at the base of the rock. My grandmother said:

> *Eight children were there at play, seven sisters and their brother. Suddenly the boy was struck dumb; he trembled and began to run upon his hands and feet. His fingers became claws, and his body was covered with fur. Directly there was a bear where the boy had been. The sisters were terrified; they ran, and the bear after them. They came to the stump of a great tree, and the tree spoke to them. It bade them climb upon it, and as they did so it began to rise into the*

air. The bear came to kill them, but they were just be-
yond its reach. It reared against the tree and scored
the bark all around with its claws. The seven sisters
were borne into the sky, and they became the stars of
the Big Dipper.

From that moment, and so long as the legend lives, the
Kiowas have kinsmen in the night sky. Whatever they were in
the mountains, they could be no more. However tenuous
their well-being, however much they had suffered and would
suffer again, they had found a way out of the wilderness.

My grandmother had a reverence for the sun, a holy re-   10
gard that now is all but gone out of mankind. There was a
wariness in her, and an ancient awe. She was a Christian in
her later years, but she had come a long way about, and she
never forgot her birthright. As a child she had been to the
Sun Dances; she had taken part in those annual rites, and by
them she had learned the restoration of her people in the
presence of Tai-me. She was about seven when the last Kiowa
Sun Dance was held in 1887 on the Washita River above
Rainy Mountain Creek. The buffalo were gone. In order to
consummate the ancient sacrifice—to impale the head of a
buffalo bull upon the medicine tree—a delegation of old men
journeyed into Texas, there to beg and barter for an animal
from the Goodnight herd. She was ten when the Kiowas
came together for the last time as a living Sun Dance culture.
They could find no buffalo; they had to hang an old hide
from the sacred tree. Before the dance could begin, a company of soldiers rode out from Fort Sill under orders to dis-
perse the tribe. Forbidden without cause the essential act of
their faith, having seen the wild herds slaughtered and left to
rot upon the ground, the Kiowas backed away forever from
the medicine tree. That was July 20, 1890, at the great bend
of the Washita. My grandmother was there. Without bitterness, and for as long as she lived, she bore a vision of deicide.

Now that I can have her only in memory, I see my grand-   11
mother in the several postures that were peculiar to her:
standing at the wood stove on a winter morning and turning

meat in a great iron skillet; sitting at the south window, bent above her beadwork, and afterwards, when her vision failed, looking down for a long time into the fold of her hands; going out upon a cane, very slowly as she did when the weight of age came upon her; praying. I remember her most often at prayer. She made long, rambling prayers out of suffering and hope, having seen many things. I was never sure that I had the right to hear, so exclusive were they of all mere custom and company. The last time I saw her she prayed standing by the side of her bed at night, naked to the waist, the light of a kerosene lamp moving upon her dark skin. Her long, black hair, always drawn and braided in the day, lay upon her shoulders and against her breasts like a shawl. I do not speak Kiowa, and I never understood her prayers, but there was something inherently sad in the sound, some merest hesitation upon the syllables of sorrow. She began in a high and descending pitch, exhausting her breath to silence; then again and again—and always the same intensity of effort, of something that is, and is not, like urgency in the human voice. Transported so in the dancing light among the shadows of her room, she seemed beyond the reach of time. But that was illusion; I think I knew then that I should not see her again.

For Study and Discussion

QUESTIONS ABOUT PURPOSE

1. How does Momaday's title provide an explanation of his purpose? How do paragraphs 2 and 5 clarify that purpose?
2. What is the purpose of Momaday's detailed description in paragraph 1? How does he use the concluding sentence to connect this description to the larger issues of his essay?

QUESTIONS ABOUT AUDIENCE

1. What audience does Momaday presume he is addressing throughout the essay? How do you know?
2. Why is the historical information (for example, paragraph 9) necessary for that audience?

QUESTIONS ABOUT STRATEGIES

1. How does Momaday arrange the events in his narrative to distinguish between the Kiowas and his own journey to the continental interior?
2 Momaday remembers his grandmother in several significant
   poses. What does each one of these "pictures" tell us about her?

For Writing and Research

1. *Analyze* the strategies Momaday uses to describe various Native
   American cultures.
2. *Practice* by creating an experience that reveals the importance of
   storytelling in your family.
3. *Argue* that "seeing" leads to "believing."
4. *Synthesize:* Research sources that help you explain a particular
   landscape. Then use this evidence to portray a landscape that impressed you as scary or serene.

E(lwyn) B(rooks) White was born in 1899 in Mt. Vernon, New York. He was educated at Cornell University, where he was taught English composition by William Strunk Jr., whose textbook, the legendary *Elements of Style,* White later revised for trade publication. In 1927 White began his career in journalism, working on the staff of *The New Yorker,* contributing a column ("One Man's Meat") to *Harper's* (1938–1943), and developing the prose style that earned him the reputation as America's finest essayist. His books include *The Second Tree from the Corner* (1954), *The Points of My Compass* (1962), and three classic children's stories, *Stuart Little* (1945), *Charlotte's Web* (1952), and *The Trumpet of the Swan* (1970). "Once More to the Lake," reprinted from *The Essays of E. B. White* (1977), is a narrative reverie about White's trip with his son to the site of his own childhood vacations.

Once More to the Lake

August 19

ONE SUMMER, ALONG about 1904, my father rented a cabin on a lake in Maine and took us all there for the month of August. We all got ringworm from some kittens and had to rub Pond's Extract on our arms and legs night and morning, and my father rolled over in a canoe with all his clothes on; but outside of that the vacation was a success and from then on none of us ever thought there was any place in the world like that lake in Maine. We returned summer after summer—always on August 1 for one month. I have since become a salt-water man, but sometimes in summer there are days when the restlessness of the tides and the fearful cold of the sea water and the incessant wind that blows across the afternoon and into the evening make me wish for the placidity of a lake in the woods. A few weeks ago this feeling got so strong I bought myself a couple of bass hooks and a spinner and returned to the lake where we used to go, for a week's fishing and to revisit old haunts.

I took along my son, who had never had any fresh water up his nose and who had seen lily pads only from train windows. On the journey over to the lake I began to wonder what it would be like. I wondered how time would have marred this unique, this holy spot—the coves and streams, the hills that the sun set behind, the camps and the paths behind the camps. I was sure that the tarred road would have found it out, and I wondered in what other ways it would be desolated. It is strange how much you can remember about places like that once you allow your mind to return into the grooves that lead back. You remember one thing, and that suddenly reminds you of another thing. I guess I remembered clearest of all the early mornings, when the lake was cool and motionless, remembered how the bedroom smelled of the lumber it was made of and of the wet woods whose scent entered through the screen. The partitions in the camp were thin and did not extend clear to the top of the rooms, and as I was always the first up I would dress softly so as not to wake the others, and sneak out into the sweet outdoors and start out in the canoe, keeping close along the shore in the long shadows of the pines. I remembered being very careful never to rub my paddle against the gunwale for fear of disturbing the stillness of the cathedral.

The lake had never been what you would call a wild lake. There were cottages sprinkled around the shores, and it was in farming country although the shores of the lake were quite heavily wooded. Some of the cottages were owned by nearby farmers, and you would live at the shore and eat your meals at the farmhouse. That's what our family did. But although it wasn't wild, it was a fairly large and undisturbed lake and there were places in it that, to a child at least, seemed infinitely remote and primeval.

I was right about the tar: it led to within half a mile of the shore. But when I got back there, with my boy, and we settled into a camp near a farmhouse and into the kind of summertime I had known, I could tell that it was going to be pretty much the same as it had been before—I knew it, lying in bed the first morning, smelling the bedroom and hearing the boy sneak quietly out and go off along the shore in a boat. I began to sustain the illusion that he was I, and therefore, by simple transposition, that I was my father. This sensation persisted, kept cropping up all the time we were there. It was not an entirely new feeling, but in this setting it grew much stronger. I seemed to be living a dual existence. I would be in the middle of some simple act, I would be picking up a bait box or laying down a table fork, or I would be saying something, and suddenly it would be not I but my father who was saying the words or making the gesture. It gave me a creepy sensation.

We went fishing the first morning. I felt the same damp moss covering the worms in the bait can, and saw the dragonfly alight on the tip of my rod as it hovered a few inches from the surface of the water. It was the arrival of this fly that convinced me beyond any doubt that everything was as it always had been, that the years were a mirage and that there had been no years. The small waves were the same, chucking the rowboat under the chin as we fished at anchor, and the boat was the same boat, the same color green and the ribs broken in the same places, and under the floorboards the same fresh-water leavings and debris—the dead helgramite, the wisps of moss, the rusty discarded fishhook, the dried blood from yesterday's catch. We stared silently at the tips of our rods, at the dragonflies that came and went. I lowered the tip of mine into the water, tentatively, pensively dislodging the fly, which darted two feet away, poised, darted two feet back, and came to rest again a little farther up the rod. There had been no years between the ducking of this dragonfly and the other one—the one that was part of memory.

I looked at the boy, who was silently watching his fly, and it was my hands that held his rod, my eyes watching. I felt dizzy and didn't know which rod I was at the end of.

We caught two bass, hauling them in briskly as though   6
they were mackerel, pulling them over the side of the boat in a businesslike manner without any landing net, and stunning them with a blow on the back of the head. When we got back for a swim before lunch, the lake was exactly where we had left it, the same number of inches from the dock, and there was only the merest suggestion of a breeze. This seemed an utterly enchanted sea, this lake you could leave to its own de- vices for a few hours and come back to, and find that it had not stirred, this constant and trustworthy body of water. In the shallows, the dark, water-soaked sticks and twigs, smooth and old, were undulating in clusters on the bottom against the clean ribbed sand, and the track of the mussel was plain. A school of minnows swam by, each minnow with its small individual shadow, doubling the attendance, so clear and sharp in the sunlight. Some of the other campers were in swimming, along the shore, one of them with a cake of soap, and the water felt thin and clear and unsubstantial. Over the years there had been this person with the cake of soap, this cultist, and here he was. There had been no years.

Up to the farmhouse to dinner through the teeming, dusty   7
field, the road under our sneakers was only a two-track road. The middle track was missing, the one with the marks of the hooves and the splotches of dried, flaky manure. There had always been three tracks to choose from in choosing which track to walk in; now the choice was narrowed down to two. For a moment I missed terribly the middle alternative. But the way led past the tennis court, and something about the way it lay there in the sun reassured me; the tape had loosened along the backline, the alleys were green with plantains and other weeds, and the net (installed in June and removed in Septem- ber) sagged in the dry noon, and the whole place steamed with midday heat and hunger and emptiness. There was a choice of pie for dessert, and one was blueberry and one was apple, and the waitresses were the same country girls, there having been

no passage of time, only the illusion of it as in a dropped curtain—the waitresses were still fifteen, their hair had been washed, that was the only difference—they had been to the movies and seen the pretty girls with the clean hair.

Summertime, oh, summertime, pattern of life indelible, the fade-proof lake, the woods unshatterable, the pasture with the sweetfern and the juniper forever and ever, summer without end; this was the background, and the life along the shore was the design, the cottages with their innocent and tranquil design, their tiny docks with the flagpole and the American flag floating against the white clouds in the blue sky, the little paths over the roots of the trees leading from camp to camp and the paths leading back to the outhouses and the can of lime for sprinkling and at the souvenir counters at the store the miniature birch-bark canoes and the postcards that showed things looking a little better than they looked. This was the American family at play, escaping the city heat, wondering whether the newcomers in the camp at the head of the cove were "common" or "nice," wondering whether it was true that the people who drove up for Sunday dinner at the farmhouse were turned away because there wasn't enough chicken.

It seemed to me, as I kept remembering all this, that those times and those summers had been infinitely precious and worth saving. There had been jollity and peace and goodness. The arriving (at the beginning of August) had been so big a business in itself, at the railway station the farm wagon drawn up, the first smell of the pine-laden air, the first glimpse of the smiling farmer, and the great importance of the trunks and your father's enormous authority in such matters, and the feel of the wagon under you for the long ten-mile haul, and at the top of the last long hill catching the first view of the lake after eleven months of not seeing this cherished body of water. The shouts and cries of the other campers when they saw you, and the trunks to be unpacked, to give up their rich burden. (Arriving was less exciting nowadays, when you sneaked up in your car and parked it under a tree near the camp and took out the bags and in five minutes it was all over, no fuss, no loud wonderful fuss about trunks.)

Peace and goodness and jollity. The only thing that was   10
wrong now, really, was the sound of the place, an unfamiliar
nervous sound of the outboard motors. This was the note
that jarred, the one thing that would sometimes break the illusion and set the years moving. In those other summertimes
all motors were inboard; and when they were at a little distance, the noise they made was a sedative, an ingredient of
summer sleep. They were one-cylinder and two-cylinder engines, and some were make-and-break and some were jump-
spark, but they all made a sleepy sound across the lake. The
one-lungers throbbed and fluttered, and the twin-cylinder
ones purred and purred, and that was a quiet sound, too. But
now the campers all had outboards. In the daytime, in the hot
mornings, these motors made a petulant, irritable sound; at
night, in the still evening when the afterglow lit the water,
they whined about one's ears like mosquitoes. My boy loved
our rented outboard, and his great desire was to achieve single-handed mastery over it, and authority, and he soon
learned the trick of choking it a little (but not too much), and
the adjustment of the needle valve. Watching him I would remember the things you could do with the old one-cylinder
engine with the heavy flywheel, how you could have it eating
out of your hand if you got really close to it spiritually.
Motorboats in those days didn't have clutches, and you would
make a landing by shutting off the motor at the proper time
and coasting in with a dead rudder. But there was a way of reversing them, if you learned the trick, by cutting the switch
and putting it on again exactly on the final dying revolution of
the flywheel, so that it would kick back against compression
and begin reversing. Approaching a dock in a strong following breeze, it was difficult to slow up sufficiently by the
ordinary coasting method, and if a boy felt he had complete
mastery over his motor, he was tempted to keep it running
beyond its time and then reverse it a few feet from the dock.
It took a cool nerve, because if you threw the switch a twen-
tieth of a second too soon you would catch the flywheel when
it still had speed enough to go up past center, and the boat
would leap ahead, charging bull-fashion at the dock.

We had a good week at the camp. The bass were biting well   11
and the sun shone endlessly, day after day. We would be tired
at night and lie down in the accumulated heat of the little
bedrooms after the long hot day and the breeze would stir almost imperceptibly outside and the smell of the swamp drift
in through the rusty screens. Sleep would come easily and in
the morning the red squirrel would be on the roof, tapping
out his gay routine. I kept remembering everything, lying in
bed in the mornings—the small steamboat that had a long
rounded stern like the lip of a Ubangi, and how quietly she
ran on the moonlight sails when the older boys played their
mandolins and the girls sang and we ate doughnuts dipped in
sugar, and how sweet the music was on the water in the shining night and what it had felt like to think about girls then.
After breakfast we would go up to the store and the things
were in the same place—the minnows in a bottle, the plugs
and spinners disarranged and pawed over by the youngsters
from the boys' camp, the Fig Newtons and the Beeman's
gum. Outside, the road was tarred and cars stood in front of
the store. Inside, all was just as it had always been except there
was more Coca-Cola and not so much Moxie and root beer
and birch beer and sarsaparilla. We would walk out with the
bottle of pop apiece and sometimes the pop would backfire up
our noses and hurt. We explored the streams, quietly, where
the turtles slid off the sunny logs and dug their way into the
soft bottom; and we lay on the town wharf and fed worms to
the tame bass. Everywhere we went I had trouble making out
which was I, the one walking at my side, the one walking in
my pants.

One afternoon while we were there at that lake a thunder-   12
storm came up. It was like the revival of an old melodrama
that I had seen long ago with childish awe. The second-act
climax of the drama of the electrical disturbance over a lake
in America had not changed in any important respect. This
was the big scene, still the big scene. The whole thing was
so familiar, the first feeling of oppression and heat and a general air around camp of not wanting to go very far away. In
midafternoon (it was all the same) a curious darkening of the

sky, and a lull in everything that had made life tick; and then the way the boats suddenly swung the other way at their moorings with the coming of a breeze out of the new quarter, and the premonitory rumble. Then the kettle drum, then the snare, then the bass drum and cymbals, then crackling light against the dark, and the gods grinning and licking their chops in the hills. Afterward the calm, the rain steadily rustling in the calm lake, the return of light and hope and spirits, and the campers running out in joy and relief to go swimming in the rain, their bright cries perpetuating the deathless joke about how they were getting simply drenched, and the children screaming with delight at the new sensation of bathing in the rain, and the joke about getting drenched linking the generations in a strong indestructible chain. And the comedian who waded in carrying an umbrella.

When the others went swimming, my son said he was   13
going in, too. He pulled his dripping trunks from the line where they had hung all through the shower and wrung them out. Languidly, and with no thought of going in, I watched him, his hard little body, skinny and bare, saw him wince slightly as he pulled up around his vitals the small, soggy, icy garment. As he buckled the swollen belt, suddenly my groin felt the chill of death.

For Study and Discussion

QUESTIONS ABOUT PURPOSE

1. Why does White return to the lake? What difference does he see between the lake and the seashore?
2. What theory about the pattern of summer life does White propose to illustrate with his narrative?

QUESTIONS ABOUT AUDIENCE

1. What kinds of common experiences does White assume he shares with his readers?
2. To what extent would people who have never spent a summer on a lake or been parents appreciate this essay?

QUESTIONS ABOUT STRATEGIES

1. How much space does White devote to the lake as it is now and how much to the lake as it used to be? How does this decision emphasize his purpose?
2. How does White pace paragraph 5 or 8? What kind of mood does he create with this pacing?

For Writing and Research

1. *Analyze* the problems White has with point of view throughout his story at the lake.
2. *Practice* by recapturing your memories of a place that held special fondness for you—visiting your elementary school, your old hometown, a group of former friends.
3. *Argue* that differences in age (or gender) affect the way people remember a certain place or event.
4. *Synthesize:* Research the problems people have with memory. Then use this evidence to argue that memory will always play "tricks" on people.

KATHERINE ANNE PORTER

Katherine Anne Porter (1890–1980) was born in Indian Creek, Texas, and was educated at a Catholic convent and a series of private schools in Texas and Louisiana. She married at the age of sixteen, but left her husband five years later to pursue a career in journalism, working on newspapers in Chicago, San Antonio, and Denver. Surviving a near-fatal attack of influenza in 1919, she worked as a ghost writer in Greenwich Village, where she became acquainted with Mexican artists. In 1920, she went to Mexico to study art and became involved in revolutionary political movements. It was during this period that she began publishing short stories in various national magazines. In 1930, she collected those stories in *Flowering Judas*. The success of this volume enabled her to take a boat from Vera Cruz, Mexico, to Bremerhaven, Germany, a cruise that became the basis of her best-selling novel, *Ship of Fools* (1962). After several years abroad and a second marriage, Porter returned to the United States in 1937 and soon thereafter published three novellas in *Pale Horse, Pale Rider* (1939). During her third marriage, to a professor at Louisiana State University, she wrote the stories that were collected in *The Leaning Tower* (1944). In the 1950s, Porter was a lecturer at Stanford, the University of Michigan, and other universities while she worked on *Ship of Fools*. In the 1960s, Porter published her *Collected Stories* (1965), which won both the Pulitzer Prize and the National Book Award. Her later books are *Collected Essays* (1970) and an account of her participation in the protest over the Sacco-Vanzetti trial in the 1920s, *The Never Ending Wrong* (1977). "The Jilting of Granny Weatherall," reprinted from *Flowering Judas*, describes an old woman's deathbed memories.

The Jilting of Granny Weatherall

S HE FLICKED HER wrist neatly out of Doctor Harry's pudgy careful fingers and pulled the sheet up to her chin. The brat ought to be in knee breeches. Doctoring around the country with spectacles on his nose! "Get along now, take your schoolbooks and go. There's nothing wrong with me." 1

Doctor Harry spread a warm paw like a cushion on her forehead where the forked green vein danced and made her eyelids twitch. "Now, now, be a good girl, and we'll have you up in no time." 2

"That's no way to speak to a woman nearly eighty years old just because she's down. I'd have you respect your elders, young man." 3

"Well, Missy, excuse me." Doctor Harry patted her cheek. "But I've got to warn you, haven't I? You're a marvel, but you must be careful or you're going to be good and sorry." 4

"Don't tell me what I'm going to be. I'm on my feet now, morally speaking. It's Cornelia. I had to go to bed to get rid of her." 5

Her bones felt loose, and floated around in her skin, and Doctor Harry floated like a balloon around the foot of the bed. He floated and pulled down his waistcoat and swung his glasses on a cord. "Well, stay where you are, it certainly can't hurt you." 6

"Get along and doctor your sick," said Granny Weatherall. "Leave a well woman alone. I'll call for you when I want you. . . . Where were you forty years ago when I pulled through milk-leg and double pneumonia? You weren't even born. Don't let Cornelia lead you on," she shouted, because Doctor Harry appeared to float up to the ceiling and out. "I pay my own bills, and I don't throw my money away on nonsense!" 7

She meant to wave good-by, but it was too much trouble. Her eyes closed of themselves, it was like a dark curtain drawn around the bed. The pillow rose and floated under her, pleasant as a hammock in a light wind. She listened to 8 the leaves rustling outside the window. No, somebody was swishing newspapers: no, Cornelia and Doctor Harry were whispering together. She leaped broad awake, thinking they whispered in her ear.

"She was never like this, *never* like this!" "Well, what can we expect?" "Yes, eighty years old. . . ."   9

Well, and what if she was? She still had ears. It was like Cornelia to whisper around doors. She always kept things secret in such a public way. She was always being tactful and kind. Cornelia was dutiful; that was the trouble with her. Dutiful and good: "So good and dutiful," said Granny, "that I'd like to spank her." She saw herself spanking Cornelia and making a fine job of it.   10

"What'd you say, Mother?"   11

Granny felt her face tying up in hard knots.   12

"Can't a body think, I'd like to know?"   13

"I thought you might want something."   14

"I do. I want a lot of things. First off, go away and don't whisper."   15

She lay and drowsed, hoping in her sleep that the children would keep out and let her rest a minute. It had been a long day. Not that she was tired. It was always pleasant to snatch a minute now and then. There was always so much to be done, let me see: tomorrow.   16

Tomorrow was far away and there was nothing to trouble about. Things were finished somehow when the time came; thank God there was always a little margin over for peace: then a person could spread out the plan of life and tuck in the edges orderly. It was good to have everything clean and folded away, with the hair brushes and tonic bottles sitting straight on the white embroidered linen: the day started without fuss and the pantry shelves laid out with rows of jelly glasses and brown jugs and white stone-china jars with blue whirligigs and words painted on them: coffee, tea, sugar, ginger, cinnamon, allspice: and the bronze clock with the lion on top nicely dusted off. The dust that lion could collect in twenty-four hours! The box in the attic with all those letters tied up, well, she'd have to go through that   17

tomorrow. All those letters—George's letters and John's letters and her letters to them both—lying around for the children to find afterwards made her uneasy. Yes, that would be
tomorrow's business. No use to let them know how silly she
had been once.

While she was rummaging around she found death in her   18
mind and it felt clammy and unfamiliar. She had spent so
much time preparing for death there was no need for bringing it up again. Let it take care of itself now. When she was
sixty she had felt very old, finished, and went around making
farewell trips to see her children and grandchildren, with a secret in her mind: This is the very last of your mother, children! Then she made her will and came down with a long
fever. That was all just a notion like a lot of other things, but
it was lucky too, for she had once for all got over the idea of
dying for a long time. Now she couldn't be worried. She
hoped she had better sense now. Her father had lived to be
one hundred and two years old and had drunk a noggin of
strong hot toddy on his last birthday. He told the reporters it
was his daily habit, and he owed his long life to that. He had
made quite a scandal and was very pleased about it. She believed she'd just plague Cornelia a little.

"Cornelia! Cornelia!" No footsteps, but a sudden hand on   19
her cheek. "Bless you, where have you been?"

"Here, Mother."   20

"Well, Cornelia, I want a noggin of hot toddy."   21

"Are you cold, darling?"   22

"I'm chilly, Cornelia. Lying in bed stops the circulation. I 23
must have told you that a thousand times."

Well, she could just hear Cornelia telling her husband that   24
Mother was getting a little childish and they'd have to humor
her. The thing that most annoyed her was that Cornelia
thought she was deaf, dumb, and blind. Little hasty glances
and tiny gestures tossed around her and over her head saying.
"Don't cross her, let her have her way, she's eighty years
old," and she sitting there as if she lived in a thin glass cage.
Sometimes Granny almost made up her mind to pack up and
move back to her own house where nobody could remind

her every minute that she was old. Wait, wait, Cornelia, till
your own children whisper behind your back!

In her day she had kept a better house and had got more   25
work done. She wasn't too old yet for Lydia to be driving
eighty miles for advice when one of the children jumped the
track, and Jimmy still dropped in and talked things over:
"Now, Mammy, you've a good business head, I want to
know what you think of this? . . ." Old. Cornelia couldn't
change the furniture around without asking. Little things,
little things! They had been so sweet when they were little.
Granny wished the old days were back again with the children young and everything to be done over. It had been a
hard pull, but not too much for her. When she thought of all
the food she had cooked, and all the clothes she had cut and
sewed, and all the gardens she had made—well, the children
showed it. There they were, made out of her, and they couldn't
get away from that. Sometimes she wanted to see John again
and point to them and say, Well, I didn't do so badly, did I?
But that would have to wait. That was for tomorrow. She
used to think of him as a man, but now all the children were
older than their father, and he would be a child beside her if
she saw him now. It seemed strange and there was something
wrong in the idea. Why, he couldn't possibly recognize her.
She had fenced in a hundred acres once, digging the post
holes herself and clamping the wires with just a negro boy to
help. That changed a woman. John would be looking for a
young woman with the peaked Spanish comb in her hair and
the painted fan. Digging post holes changed a woman. Riding country roads in the winter when women had their babies
was another thing: sitting up nights with sick horses and sick
negroes and sick children and hardly ever losing one. John, I
hardly ever lost one of them! John would see that in a
minute, that would be something he could understand, she
wouldn't have to explain anything!

It made her feel like rolling up her sleeves and putting the   26
whole place to rights again. No matter if Cornelia was determined to be everywhere at once, there were a great many
things left undone on this place. She would start tomorrow

and do them. It was good to be strong enough for everything, even if all you made melted and changed and slipped
under your hands, so that by the time you finished you almost forgot what you were working for. What was it I set out
to do? she asked herself intently, but she could not remember. A fog rose over the valley, she saw it marching across the
creek swallowing the trees and moving up the hill like an
army of ghosts. Soon it would be at the near edge of the or-
chard, and then it was time to go in and light the lamps.
Come in, children, don't stay out in the night air.

Lighting the lamps had been beautiful. The children hud- 27
dled up to her and breathed like little calves waiting at the
bars in the twilight. Their eyes followed the match and
watched the flame rise and settle in a blue curve, then they
moved away from her. The lamp was lit, they didn't have to
be scared and hang on to mother any more. Never, never,
never more. God, for all my life I thank Thee. Without Thee,
my God, I could never have done it. Hail, Mary, full of grace.

I want you to pick all the fruit this year and see that noth- 28
ing is wasted. There's always someone who can use it. Don't
let good things rot for want of using. You waste life when you
waste good food. Don't let things get lost. It's bitter to lose
things. Now, don't let me get to thinking, not when I am
tired and taking a little nap before supper. . . .

The pillow rose about her shoulders and pressed against 29
her heart and the memory was being squeezed out of it: oh,
push down the pillow, somebody: it would smother her if she
tried to hold it. Such a fresh breeze blowing and such a green
day with no threats in it. But he had not come, just the same.
What does a woman do when she has put on the white veil
and set out the white cake for a man and he doesn't come?
She tried to remember. No, I swear he never harmed me but
in that. He never harmed me but in that . . . and what if he
did? There was the day, the day, but a whirl of dark smoke
rose and covered it, crept up and over into the bright field
where everything was planted so carefully in orderly rows.
That was hell, she knew hell when she saw it. For sixty years
she had prayed against remembering him and against losing

her soul in the deep pit of hell, and now the two things were mingled in one and the thought of him was a smoky cloud from hell that moved and crept in her head when she had just got rid of Doctor Harry and was trying to rest a minute. Wounded vanity, Ellen, said a sharp voice in the top of her mind. Don't let your wounded vanity get the upper hand of you. Plenty of girls get jilted. You were jilted, weren't you? Then stand up to it. Her eyelids wavered and let in streamers of blue-gray light like tissue paper over her eyes. She must get up and pull the shades down or she'd never sleep. She was in bed again and the shades were not down. How could that happen? Better turn over, hide from the light, sleeping in the light gave you nightmares. "Mother, how do you feel now?" and a stinging wetness on her forehead. But I don't like having my face washed in cold water!

Hapsy? George? Lydia? Jimmy? No, Cornelia, and her features were swollen and full of little puddles "They're coming, darling, they'll all be here soon." Go wash your face, child, you look funny. [30]

Instead of obeying, Cornelia knelt down and put her head on the pillow. She seemed to be talking but there was no sound. "Well, are you tongue-tied? Whose birthday is it? Are you going to give a party?" [31]

Cornelia's mouth moved urgently in strange shapes. "Don't do that, you bother me, daughter." [32]

"Oh, no, Mother. Oh, no. . . ." [33]

Nonsense. It was strange about children. They disputed your every word. "No what, Cornelia?" [34]

"Here's Doctor Harry." [35]

"I won't see that boy again. He just left five minutes ago." [36]

"That was this morning, Mother. It's night now. Here's the nurse." [37]

"This is Doctor Harry, Mrs. Weatherall. I never saw you look so young and happy!" [38]

"Ah, I'll never be young again—but I'd be happy if they'd let me lie in peace and get rested." [39]

She thought she spoke up loudly, but no one answered. A warm weight on her forehead, a warm bracelet on her wrist, [40] and a breeze went on whispering, trying to tell her something. A shuffle of leaves in the everlasting hand of God, He blew on them and they danced and rattled. "Mother, don't mind, we're going to give you a little hypodermic." "Look here, daughter, how do ants get in this bed? I saw sugar ants yesterday." Did you send for Hapsy too?

It was Hapsy she really wanted. She had to go a long way back through a great many rooms to find Hapsy standing with a baby on her arm. She seemed to herself to be Hapsy also, and the baby on Hapsy's arm was Hapsy and himself and herself, all at once, and there was no surprise in the meeting. Then Hapsy melted from within and turned flimsy as gray gauze and the baby was a gauzy shadow, and Hapsy came up close and said, "I thought you'd never come," and looked at her very searchingly and said, "You haven't changed a bit!" They leaned forward to kiss, when Cornelia began whispering from a long way off, "Oh, is there anything you want to tell me? Is there anything I can do for you?"

Yes, she had changed her mind after sixty years and she would like to see George. I want you to find George. Find him and be sure to tell him I forgot him. I want him to know I had my husband just the same and my children and my house like any other woman. A good house too and a good husband that I loved and fine children out of him. Better than I hoped for even. Tell him I was given back everything he took away and more. Oh, no, oh, God, no, there was something else besides the house and the man and the children. Oh, surely they were not all? What was it? Something not given back. . . . Her breath crowded down under her ribs and grew into a monstrous frightening shape with cutting edges; it bored up into her head, and the agony was unbelievable: Yes, John, get the Doctor now, no more talk my time has come.

When this one was born it should be the last. The last. It should have been born first, for it was the one she had truly wanted. Everything came in good time. Nothing left out, left over. She was strong, in three days she would be as well as ever. Better. A woman needed milk in her to have her full health.

"Mother, do you hear me?"   44

"I've been telling you—"   45

"Mother, Father Connolly's here."   46

"I went to Holy Communion only last week. Tell him I'm   47
not so sinful as all that."

"Father just wants to speak to you."   48

He could speak as much as he pleased. It was like him to   49
drop in and inquire about her soul as if it were a teething
baby, and then stay on for a cup of tea and a round of cards
and gossip. He always had a funny story of some sort, usually
about an Irishman who made his little mistakes and confessed
them, and the point lay in some absurd thing he would blurt
out in the confessional showing his struggles between native
piety and original sin. Granny felt easy about her soul.
Cornelia, where are your manners? Give Father Connolly a
chair. She had her secret comfortable understanding with a
few favorite saints who cleared a straight road to God for her.
All as surely signed and sealed as the papers for the new Forty
Acres. Forever . . . heirs and assigns forever. Since the day the
wedding cake was not cut, but thrown out and wasted. The
whole bottom dropped out of the world, and there she was
blind and sweating with nothing under her feet and the walls
falling away. His hand had caught her under the breast, she
had not fallen, there was the freshly polished floor with the
green rug on it, just as before. He had cursed like a sailor's
parrot and said, "I'll kill him for you." Don't lay a hand on
him, for my sake leave something to God. "Now, Ellen, you
must believe what I tell you. . ."

So there was nothing, nothing to worry about any more,   50
except sometimes in the night one of the children screamed
in a nightmare, and they both hustled out shaking and
hunting for the matches and calling, "There, wait a minute,
here we are!" John, get the doctor now, Hapsy's time has
come. But there was Hapsy standing by the bed in a white
cap. "Cornelia, tell Hapsy to take off her cap. I can't see her
plain."

Her eyes opened very wide and the room stood out like   51
a picture she had seen somewhere. Dark colors with the

shadows rising towards the ceiling in long angles. The tall black dresser gleamed with nothing on it but John's picture, enlarged from a little one, with John's eyes very black when they should have been blue. You never saw him, so how do you know how he looked? But the man insisted the copy was perfect, it was very rich and handsome. For a picture, yes, but it's not my husband. The table by the bed had a linen cover and a candle and a crucifix. The light was blue from Cornelia's silk lampshades. No sort of light at all, just frippery. You had to live forty years with kerosene lamps to appreciate honest electricity. She felt very strong and she saw Doctor Harry with a rosy nimbus around him.

"You look like a saint, Doctor Harry, and I vow that's as 52
near as you'll ever come to it."

"She's saying something."   53

"I heard you, Cornelia. What's all this carrying-on?"   54

"Father Connolly's saying—"   55

Cornelia's voice staggered and bumped like a cart in a   56
bad road. It rounded corners and turned back again and arrived nowhere. Granny stepped up in the cart very lightly and reached for the reins, but a man sat beside her and she knew him by his hands, driving the cart. She did not look in his face, for she knew without seeing, but looked instead down the road where the trees leaned over and bowed to each other and a thousand birds were singing a Mass. She felt like singing too, but she put her hand in the bosom of her dress and pulled out a rosary, and Father Connolly murmured Latin in a very solemn voice and tickled her feet. My God, will you stop that nonsense? I'm a married woman. What if he did run away and leave me to face the priest by myself? I found another a whole world better. I wouldn't have exchanged my husband for anybody except St. Michael himself, and you may tell him that for me with a thank you in the bargain.

Light flashed on her closed eyelids, and a deep roaring   57
shook her. Cornelia, is that lightning? I hear thunder. There's going to be a storm. Close all the windows. Call the children in. . . . "Mother, here we are, all of us." "Is that you, Hapsy?"

"Oh, no, I'm Lydia. We drove as fast as we could." Their faces drifted above her, drifted away. The rosary fell out of her hands and Lydia put it back. Jimmy tried to help, their hands fumbled together, and Granny closed two fingers around Jimmy's thumb. Beads wouldn't do, it must be something alive. She was so amazed her thoughts ran round and round. So, my dear Lord, this is my death and I wasn't even thinking about it. My children have come to see me die. But I can't, it's not time. Oh, I always hated surprises. I wanted to give Cornelia the amethyst set—Cornelia, you're to have the amethyst set, but Hapsy's to wear it when she wants, and, Doctor Harry, do shut up. Nobody sent for you. Oh, my dear Lord, do wait a minute. I meant to do something about the Forty Acres, Jimmy doesn't need it and Lydia will later on, with that worthless husband of hers. I meant to finish the altar cloth and send six bottles of wine to Sister Borgia for her dyspepsia. I want to send six bottles of wine to Sister Borgia, Father Connolly, now don't let me forget.

Cornelia's voice made short turns and tilted over and crashed. "Oh, Mother, oh, Mother, oh, Mother. . . ."   58

"I'm not going, Cornelia. I'm taken by surprise. I can't go."   59

You'll see Hapsy again. What about her? "I thought you'd never come." Granny made a long journey outward, looking for Hapsy. What if I don't find her? What then? Her heart sank down and down, there was no bottom to death, she couldn't come to the end of it. The blue light from Cornelia's lampshade drew into a tiny point in the center of her brain, it flickered and winked liked an eye, quietly it fluttered and dwindled. Granny lay curled down within herself, amazed and watchful, staring at the point of light that was herself; her body was now only a deeper mass of shadow in an endless darkness and this darkness would curl around the light and swallow it up. God, give a sign!   60

For a second time there was no sign. Again no bridegroom   61
and the priest in the house. She could not remember any other sorrow because this grief wiped them all away. Oh, no, there's nothing more cruel than this—I'll never forgive it. She stretched herself with a deep breath and blew out the light.

COMMENT ON "THE JILTING OF GRANNY WEATHERALL"

Katherine Anne Porter's "The Jilting of Granny Weatherall" follows the mind of a dying woman through her last day and through the most important moments of her life. The third-person narrator presents Granny thoughts in stream of consciousness, and the reader is privy to all the insights and confusions of the resilient Ellen Weatherall. Granny's reflections are often puzzling and obviously distorted but they rehearse the main events of her life, the most haunting of which is her experience at being left at the altar by George, a man whom she would never see again. Although she eventually married a good man who fathered her children, Ellen struggles until the moment of her death with the grief associated with her "jilting." When at the end of the story she dies, she is still trying unsuccessfully to forgive the wrong done to her so many years ago.

PROCESS ANALYSIS

A **process** is an operation that moves through a series of steps to bring about a desired result. You can call almost any procedure a process, whether it is getting out of bed in the morning or completing a transaction on the stock exchange. A useful way to identify a particular kind of process is by its principal function. A process can be *natural* (the birth of a baby), *mechanical* (starting a car engine), *physical* (dancing), or *mental* (reading).

Analysis is an operation that divides something into its parts in order to understand the whole more clearly. For example, poetry readers analyze the lines of a poem to find meaning. Doctors analyze a patient's symptoms to prescribe treatment. Politicians analyze the opinions of individual voters and groups of voters to plan campaigns.

If you want to write a process-analysis essay, you need to go through three steps: (1) divide the process you are going to explain into its individual steps; (2) show the movement of the process, step by step, from beginning to end; and (3) explain how each step works, how it ties into other steps in the sequence, and how it brings about the desired result.

PURPOSE

Usually you will write a process analysis to accomplish two purposes: *to give directions* and *to provide information*. Sometimes you might find it difficult to separate the two purposes. After all, when you give directions about how to do something (hit a baseball), you also have to provide information on how the whole process works (rules of the game—strike zone, walks, hits, base running, outs, scoring). But usually you can separate the two because you're trying to accomplish different goals. When you give directions, you want to help your readers do something (change a tire). When you give information, you want to satisfy your readers' curiosity about some process they'd like to know about but are unlikely to perform (pilot a space shuttle).

You might also write a process analysis to demonstrate that (1) a task that looks difficult is really easy or (2) a task that looks easy is really quite complex. For instance, you might want to show that selecting a specific tool can simplify a complex process (using a microwave oven to cook a six-course dinner). You might also want to show why it's important to have a prearranged plan to make a process seem simple (explaining the preparations for an informal television interview).

AUDIENCE

When you write a process-analysis essay, you must think carefully about who your audience will be. First, you need to decide whether you're writing *to* an audience (giving directions) or writing *for* an audience (providing information). If you are writing *to* an audience, you can address directly readers who are already interested in your subject: "If you want to plant a successful garden, you must follow these seven steps." If you are writing *for* an audience, you can write from a more detached point of view, but you have to find a way to catch the interest of more casual readers: "Although many Americans say they are concerned about nuclear power, few understand how a nuclear power plant works."

Second, you have to determine how wide the knowledge gap is between you and your readers. Writing about a process suggests you are something of an expert in that area. If you can be sure your readers are also experts, you can make certain assumptions as you write your analysis. For instance, if you're outlining courtroom procedure to a group of fellow law students, you can assume you don't have to define the special meaning of the word *brief.*

On the other hand, if you feel sure your intended audience knows almost nothing about a process (or has only general knowledge), you can take nothing for granted. If you are explaining how to operate a Blackberry to readers who have never used one, you will have to define special terms and explain all procedures. If you assume your readers are experts when they are not, you will confuse or annoy them. If you assume they need to be told everything when they don't, you will bore or antagonize them. And, finally, remember that to analyze a process effectively, you must either research it carefully or have firsthand knowledge of its operation. It's risky to try to explain something you don't really understand.

STRATEGIES

The best way to write a process analysis is to organize your essay according to five parts:

> Overview
> Special terms
> Sequence of steps
> Examples
> Results

The first two parts help your readers understand the process, the next two show the process in action, and the last one evaluates the worth of the completed process.

Begin your analysis with an *overview* of the whole process. To make such an overview, you take these four steps:

1. Define the objective of the process
2. Identify (and number) the steps in the sequence
3. Group some small steps into larger units
4. Call attention to the most important steps or units

For example, Edward Hoagland begins his analysis of the jury system by pointing out that the jurists' objective was to be fair, "to be better than themselves." Nikki Giovanni makes her recommendations for black students in sequence and then goes on to illustrate some of the common problems that occur with each recommendation.

Each process has its own *special terms* to describe tools, tasks, and methods, and you will have to define those terms for your readers. You can define them at the beginning so your readers will understand the terms when you use them, but often you do better to define them as you use them. Your readers may have trouble remembering specialized language out of context, so it's often practical to define your terms throughout the course of the essay, pausing to explain their special meaning or use the first time you introduce them. Gretel Ehrlich follows this strategy as she explains the rules of the rodeo.

When you write a process-analysis essay, you must present the *sequence of steps* clearly and carefully. As you do so, give the reason for each step and, where appropriate, provide these reminders:

1. *Do not omit any steps.* A sequence is a sequence because all steps depend on one another. Nikki Giovanni explains the importance of going to class to establish "a consistent presence in the classroom."
2. *Do not reverse steps.* A sequence is a sequence because each step must be performed according to a necessary and logical

pattern. Lars Eighner reminds readers that if they start eating something before they have inspected it, they are likely to discern moldy bread or sour milk after they have put it into their mouth.

3. *Suspend certain steps.* Occasionally, a whole series of steps must be suspended and another process completed before the sequence can resume. Gretel Ehrlich suggests that a whole process—a honeymoon—can be momentarily suspended to focus on another process—the rodeo.

4. *Do not overlook steps within steps.* Each sequence is likely to have a series of smaller steps buried within each step. Edward Hoagland reminds his readers that selecting a jury may involve another procedure—agreeing to plea bargain.

5. *Avoid certain steps.* It is often tempting to insert steps that are not recommended but that appear "logical." Richard Selzer suggests that following such an impulse in the operating room can produce tragic results.

You may want to use several kinds of examples to explain the steps in a sequence.

1. *Pictures.* You can use graphs, charts, and diagrams to illustrate the operation of the process. Although none of the writers in this section uses pictures, Selzer creates colorful images to analyze the surgical process.

2. *Anecdotes.* Because you're claiming some level of expertise by writing a process analysis, you can clarify your explanation by using examples from your own experience. Eighner uses this method when he describes his experience selecting discarded pizzas.

3. *Variants.* You can mention alternative steps to show that the process may not be as rigid or simplistic as it often appears. Giovanni uses sample questions and answers to illustrate different ways to participate in class.

4. *Comparisons.* You can use comparisons to help your readers see that a complex process is similar to a process they already know. Hoagland uses this strategy when he compares jury duty to other universal experiences "like getting married or having a child, like voting."

Although you focus on the movement of the process when you write a process-analysis essay, finally you should also try to evaluate the *results* of that process. You can move to this last part by asking two questions: How do you know it's done? How do you know it's good? Sometimes the answer is simple: the car starts; the trunk opens. At other times, the answer is not so clear: the jury may have difficulty reaching a decision; a successful surgery may still result in death.

PROCESS ANALYSIS

Points to Remember

1. Arrange the steps in your process in an orderly sequence.
2. Identify and explain the purpose of each of the steps in the process.
3. Describe the special tools, terms, and tasks needed to complete the process.
4. Provide warnings, where appropriate, about the consequences of omitting, reversing, or overlooking certain steps.
5. Supply illustrations and personal anecdotes to help clarify aspects of the process.

HOW MANY IT TAKES

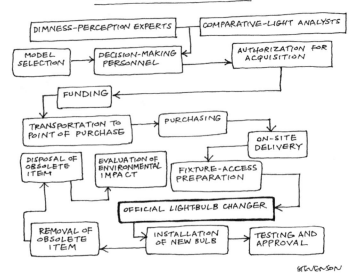

In this comic drawing, James Stevenson offers yet another variation on the old joke "How many [fill in the blank] does it take to change a light bulb?" Trace the various steps in this overwrought flow chart. Has Stevenson missed a step or placed steps out of sequence? Construct your own flow chart for a simple process such as making an ATM transaction or hitting a golf ball. Then write an analysis of your chart demonstrating why this simple process contains hidden steps or must be explained in a larger context.

LARS EIGHNER

Lars Eighner was born in 1948 in Corpus Christi, Texas, and attended the University of Texas at Austin. He held a series of jobs, including work as an attendant at the state mental hospital in Austin, before he became homeless. For five years he drifted between Austin and Hollywood, living on the streets and in abandoned buildings. Then he began to contribute essays to the *Threepenny Review;* these writings are collected in his memoir, *Travels with Lizabeth* (1993). His other writing includes a collection of short stories, *Bayou Boy and Other Stories* (1993), and a novel, *Pawn to Queen Four* (1995). In "My Daily Dives in the Dumpster," reprinted from *The Threepenny Review* (Fall: 1988), Eighner analyzes the "predictable series of stages that a person goes through in learning to scavenge."

My Daily Dives in the Dumpster

I BEGAN DUMPSTER diving about a year before I became homeless. 1

I prefer the term "scavenging" and use the word "scrounging" when I mean to be obscure. I have heard people, evidently meaning to be polite, use the word "foraging," but I prefer to reserve that word for gathering nuts and berries and such which I do also, according to the season and opportunity. 2

I like the frankness of the word "scavenging." I live from the refuse of others. I am a scavenger. I think it a sound and honorable niche, although if I could I would naturally prefer to live the comfortable consumer life, perhaps—and only perhaps—as a slightly less wasteful consumer owing to what I have learned as a scavenger. 3

Except for jeans, all my clothes come from Dumpsters.   4
Boom boxes, candles, bedding, toilet paper, medicine, books,
a typewriter, a virgin male love doll, change sometimes amount-
ing to many dollars: All came from Dumpsters. And, yes, I eat
from Dumpsters too.

There are a predictable series of stages that a person goes   5
through in learning to scavenge. At first the new scavenger is
filled with disgust and self-loathing. He is ashamed of being
seen and may lurk around trying to duck behind things,

Scavenging, more than most other pursuits,
tends to yield returns in some proportion to
the effort and the intelligence brought
to bear.

---

or he may try to dive at night. (In fact, this is unnecessary,
since most people instinctively look away from scavengers.)

Every grain of rice seems to be a maggot. Everything seems   6
to stink. The scavenger can wipe the egg yolk off the found can,
but he cannot erase the stigma of eating garbage from his mind.

This stage passes with experience. The scavenger finds a   7
pair of running shoes that fit and look and smell brand-new.
He finds a pocket calculator in perfect working order. He
finds pristine ice cream, still frozen, more than he can eat
or keep. He begins to understand: People do throw away
perfectly good stuff, a lot of perfectly good stuff.

At this stage he may become lost and never recover. All the   8
Dumpster divers I have known come to the point of trying to
acquire everything they touch. Why not take it, they reason,
it is all free. This is, of course, hopeless, and most divers come
to realize that they must restrict themselves to items of
relatively immediate utility.

The finding of objects is becoming something of an urban   9
art. Even respectable, employed people will sometimes find

something tempting sticking out of a Dumpster or standing beside one. Quite a number of people, not all of them of the bohemian type, are willing to brag that they found this or that piece in the trash.

But eating from Dumpsters is the thing that separates   10
the dilettanti from the professionals. Eating safely involves three principles: using the senses and common sense to evaluate the condition of the found materials; knowing the Dumpsters of a given area and checking them regularly; and seeking always to answer the question, Why was this discarded?

Perhaps everyone who has a kitchen and a regular supply   11
of groceries has, at one time or another, eaten half a sandwich before discovering mold on the bread, or has gotten a mouthful of milk before realizing the milk had turned. Nothing of the sort is likely to happen to a Dumpster diver because he is constantly reminded that most food is discarded for a reason.

Yet perfectly good food can be found in Dumpsters.   12
Canned goods, for example, turn up fairly often in the Dumpsters I frequent. All except the most phobic people would be willing to eat from a can even if it came from a Dumpster. I have few qualms about dry foods such as crackers, cookies, cereal, chips, and pasta if they are free of visible contaminants and still dry and crisp. Raw fruits and vegetables with intact skins seem perfectly safe to me, excluding, of course, the obviously rotten. Many are discarded for minor imperfections that can be pared away. Chocolate is often discarded only because it has become discolored as the cocoa butter de-emulsified.

I began scavenging by pulling pizzas out of the Dumpster   13
behind a pizza delivery shop. In general, prepared food requires caution, but in this case I knew what time the shop closed and went to the Dumpster as soon as the last of the help left.

Because the workers at these places are usually inexperi-   14
enced, pizzas are often made with the wrong topping, baked incorrectly, or refused on delivery for being cold. The products to be discarded are boxed up because inventory is kept

by counting boxes: A boxed pizza can be written off; an un-boxed pizza does not exist. So I had a steady supply of fresh, sometimes warm pizza.

The area I frequent is inhabited by many affluent college   15
students. I am not here by chance; the Dumpsters are very rich. Students throw out many good things, including food, particularly at the end of the semester and before and after breaks. I find it advantageous to keep an eye on the academic calendar.

A typical discard is a half jar of peanut butter—though   16
non-organic peanut butter does not require refrigeration and is unlikely to spoil in any reasonable time. Occasionally I find a cheese with a spot of mold, which, of course, I just pare off, and because it is obvious why the cheese was discarded, I treat it with less suspicion than an apparently perfect cheese found in similar circumstances. One of my favorite finds is yogurt—often discarded, still sealed, when the expiration date has passed—because it will keep for several days, even in warm weather.

I avoid ethnic foods I am unfamiliar with. If I do not know   17
what it is supposed to look or smell like when it is good, I cannot be certain I will be able to tell if it is bad.

No matter how careful I am I still get dysentery at least   18
once a month, oftener in warm weather. I do not want to paint too romantic a picture. Dumpster diving has serious drawbacks as a way of life.

Though I have a proprietary feeling about my Dumpsters,   19
I don't mind my direct competitors, other scavengers, as much as I hate the soda-can scroungers.

I have tried scrounging aluminum cans with an able-   20
bodied companion, and afoot we could make no more than a few dollars a day. I can extract the necessities of life from the Dumpsters directly with far less effort than would be required to accumulate the equivalent value in aluminum. Can scroungers, then, are people who *must* have small amounts of cash—mostly drug addicts and winos.

I do not begrudge them the cans, but can scroungers tend   21
to tear up the Dumpsters, littering the area and mixing the

contents. There are precious few courtesies among scavengers, but it is a common practice to set aside surplus items: pairs of shoes, clothing, canned goods, and such. A true scavenger hates to see good stuff go to waste, and what he cannot use he leaves in good condition in plain sight. Can scroungers lay waste to everything in their path and will stir one of a pair of good shoes to the bottom of a Dumpster to be lost or ruined in the muck. They become so specialized that they can see only cans and earn my contempt by passing up change, canned goods, and readily hockable items.

Can scroungers will even go through individual garbage cans, something I have never seen a scavenger do. Going through individual garbage cans without spreading litter is almost impossible, and litter is likely to reduce the public's tolerance of scavenging. But my strongest reservation about going through individual garbage cans is that this seems to me a very personal kind of invasion, one to which I would object if I were a homeowner. 22

Though Dumpsters seem somehow less personal than garbage cans, they still contain bank statements, bills, correspondence, pill bottles, and other sensitive information. I avoid trying to draw conclusions about the people who dump in the Dumpsters I frequent. I think it would be unethical to do so, although I know many people will find the idea of scavenger ethics too funny for words. 23

Occasionally a find tells a story. I once found a small paper bag containing some unused condoms, several partial tubes of flavored sexual lubricant, a partially used compact of birth control pills, and the torn pieces of a picture of a young man. Clearly, the woman was through with him and planning to give up sex altogether. 24

Dumpster things are often sad—abandoned teddy bears, shredded wedding albums, despaired-of sales kits. I find diaries and journals. College students also discard their papers; I am horrified to discover the kind of paper that now merits an A in an undergraduate course. 25

Dumpster diving is outdoor work, often surprisingly pleasant. It is not entirely predictable; things of interest turn 26 up every day, and some days there are finds of great value. I am always very pleased when I can turn up exactly the thing I most wanted to find. Yet in spite of the element of chance, scavenging, more than most other pursuits, tends to yield returns in some proportion to the effort and intelligence brought to bear.

I think of scavenging as a modern form of self-reliance. 27 After ten years of government service, where everything is geared to the lowest common denominator, I find work that rewards initiative and effort refreshing. Certainly I would be happy to have a sinecure again, but I am not heartbroken to be without one.

I find from the experience of scavenging two rather deep 28 lessons. The first is to take what I can use and let the rest go. I have come to think that there is no value in the abstract. A thing I cannot use or make useful, perhaps by trading, has no value, however fine or rare it may be. (I mean useful in the broad sense—some art, for example, I would think valuable.)

The second lesson is the transience of material being. I do 29 not suppose that ideas are immortal, but certainly they are longer-lived than material objects.

The things I find in Dumpsters, the love letters and rag 30 dolls of so many lives, remind me of this lesson. Many times in my travels I have lost everything but the clothes on my back. Now I hardly pick up a thing without envisioning the time I will cast it away. This, I think, is a healthy state of mind. Almost everything I have now has already been cast out at least once, proving that what I own is valueless to someone.

I find that my desire to grab for the gaudy bauble has been 31 largely sated. I think this is an attitude I share with the very wealthy—we both know there is plenty more where whatever we have came from. Between us are the rat-race millions who have confounded their selves with the objects they grasp and who nightly scavenge the cable channels looking for they know not what.

I am sorry for them. 32

For Study and Discussion

QUESTIONS ABOUT PURPOSE

1. Why does Eighner prefer the term *scavenging* to *scrounging* or *foraging* to characterize the process he analyzes?
2. In what ways does Eighner's analysis demonstrate that Dumpster diving is "a sound and honorable niche"?

QUESTIONS ABOUT AUDIENCE

1. How does Eighner anticipate his audience's reaction to his subject by presenting the "predictable series of stages that a person goes through in learning to scavenge"?
2. How do Eighner's "scavenger ethics" enhance his standing with his readers?

QUESTIONS ABOUT STRATEGIES

1. How does Eighner use the example of pizza to illustrate the three principles of eating from a Dumpster?
2. How does Eighner's analysis of the process of "soda-can scrounging" help distinguish that process from "scavenging"?

For Writing and Research

1. *Analyze* how Eighner uses anecdotes to illustrate the various steps in learning to scavenge.
2. *Practice* by listing the steps by which your readers can become a conscientious consumer.
3. *Argue* that Eighner's attitudes toward consumption and waste are similar to those of the very wealthy.
4. *Synthesize* the current research on the solutions to homelessness. Then construct an argument for the most effective method for solving the problem.

Nikki Giovanni was born in 1943 in Knoxville, Tennessee, and was educated at Fisk University, the University of Pennsylvania, and Columbia University. She has taught creative writing at Rutgers University and Virginia Tech and worked for the Ohio Humanities Council and the Appalachian Community Fund. Her poems have appeared in the collections *My House* (1972), *The Women and the Men* (1975), *Those Who Ride the Night Winds* (1983), and *The Collected Poetry of Nikki Giovanni: 1968–1998* (2003). Her nonfiction work appears in books such as *Gemini: An Extended Autobiographical Statement on My First Twenty-five Years Being a Black Poet* (1971), *Sacred Cows . . . and Other Edibles* (1988), *Racism 101* (1994), and *Prosaic Soul of Nikki Giovanni* (2003). In "Campus Racism 101," reprinted from *Racism 101,* Giovanni tells black students how to succeed at predominantly white colleges.

Campus Racism 101

THERE IS A bumper sticker that reads: TOO BAD IGNORANCE ISN'T PAINFUL. I like that. But ignorance is. We just seldom attribute the pain to it or even recognize it when we see it. Like the postcard on my corkboard. It shows a young man in a very hip jacket smoking a cigarette. In the background is a high school with the American flag waving. The caption says: "Too cool for school. Yet too stupid for the real world." Out of the mouth of the young man is a bubble enclosing the words "Maybe I'll start a band." There could be a postcard showing a jock in a uniform saying, "I don't need school. I'm going to the NFL or NBA." Or one showing a young man or woman studying and a group of young people saying, "So you want to be white." Or something equally demeaning. We need to quit it.

I am a professor of English at Virginia Tech. I've been here   2
for four years, though for only two years with academic rank. I am tenured, which means I have a teaching position for life, a rarity on a predominantly white campus. Whether from malice or ignorance, people who think I should be at a predominantly Black institution will ask, "Why are you at Tech?" Because it's here. And so are Black students. But even if Black students weren't here, it's painfully obvious that this nation and this world cannot allow white students to go through higher education without interacting with Blacks in authoritative positions. It is equally clear that predominantly Black

---

*Your job is not to educate white people; it is
to obtain an education.*

---

colleges cannot accommodate the numbers of Black students who want and need an education.

Is it difficult to attend a predominantly white college?   3
Compared with what? Being passed over for promotion because you lack credentials? Being turned down for jobs because you are not college-educated? Joining the armed forces or going to jail because you cannot find an alternative to the streets? Let's have a little perspective here. Where can you go and what can you do that frees you from interacting with the white American mentality? You're going to interact; the only question is, will you be in some control of yourself and your actions, or will you be controlled by others? I'm going to recommend self-control.

What's the difference between prison and college? They   4
both prescribe your behavior for a given period of time. They both allow you to read books and develop your writing.

They both give you time alone to think and time with your peers to talk about issues. But four years of prison doesn't give you a passport to greater opportunities. Most likely that time only gives you greater knowledge of how to get back in. Four years of college gives you an opportunity not only to lift yourself but to serve your people effectively. What's the difference when you are called nigger in college from when you are called nigger in prison? In college you can, though I admit with effort, follow procedures to have those students who called you nigger kicked out or suspended. You can bring issues to public attention without risking your life. But mostly, college is and always has been the future. We, neither less nor more than other people, need knowledge. There are discomforts attached to attending predominantly white colleges, though no more so than living in a racist world. Here are some rules to follow that may help:

Go to class. No matter how you feel. No matter how you think the professor feels about you. It's important to have a consistent presence in the classroom. If nothing else, the professor will know you care enough and are serious enough to be there.   5

Meet your professors. Extend your hand (give a firm handshake) and tell them your name. Ask them what you need to do to make an A. You may never make an A, but you have put them on notice that you are serious about getting good grades.   6

Do assignments on time. Typed or computer-generated. You have the syllabus. Follow it, and turn those papers in. If for some reason you can't complete an assignment on time, let your professor know before it is due and work out a new due date—then meet it.   7

Go back to see your professor. Tell him or her your name again. If an assignment received less than an A, ask why, and find out what you need to do to improve the next assignment.   8

Yes, your professor is busy. So are you. So are your parents who are working to pay or help with your tuition. Ask early what you need to do if you feel you are starting to get into academic trouble. Do not wait until you are failing.   9

Understand that there will be professors who do not like you; 10
there may even be professors who are racist or sexist or both.
You must discriminate among your professors to see who will
give you the help you need. You may not simply say, "They are
all against me." They aren't. They mostly don't care. Since you
are the one who wants to be educated, find the people who
want to help.

Don't defeat yourself. Cultivate your friends. Know your en- 11
emies. You cannot undo hundreds of years of prejudicial thinking. Think for yourself and speak up. Raise your hand in class.
Say what you believe no matter how awkward you may think it
sounds. You will improve in your articulation and confidence.

Participate in some campus activity. Join the newspaper 12
staff. Run for office. Join a dorm council. Do something that
involves you on campus. You are going to be there for four
years, so let your presence be known, if not felt.

You will inevitably run into some white classmates who are 13
troubling because they often say stupid things, ask stupid
questions—and expect an answer. Here are some comebacks
to some of the most common inquiries and comments:

Q: What's it like to grow up in a ghetto?   14
A: I don't know.   15

Q: (from the teacher): Can you give us the Black perspective 16
on Toni Morrison, Huck Finn, slavery, Martin Luther King,
Jr., and others?
A: I can give you *my* perspective. (Do not take the burden of 17
22 million people on your shoulders. Remind everyone that
you are an individual, and don't speak for the race or any
other individual within it.)

Q: Why do all the Black people sit together in the dining hall? 18
A: Why do all the white students sit together?   19

Q: Why should there be an African-American studies course? 20
A: Because white Americans have not adequately studied 21
the contributions of Africans and African-Americans. Both

Black and white students need to know our total common history.

Q: Why are there so many scholarships for "minority" students?   22
A: Because they wouldn't give my great-grandparents their forty acres and the mule.   23

Q: How can whites understand Black history, culture, literature, and so forth?   24
A: The same way we understand white history, culture, literature, and so forth. That is why we're in school: to learn.   25

Q: Should whites take African-American studies courses?   26
A: Of course. We take white-studies courses, though the universities don't call them that.   27

Comment: When I see groups of Black people on campus, it's really intimidating.   28
Comeback: I understand what you mean. I'm frightened when I see white students congregating.   29

Comment: It's not fair. It's easier for you guys to get into college than for other people.   30
Comeback: If it's so easy, why aren't there more of us?   31

Comment: It's not our fault that America is the way it is.   32
Comeback: It's not our fault, either, but both of us have a responsibility to make changes.   33

It's really very simple. Educational progress is a national concern; education is a private one. Your job is not to educate white people; it is to obtain an education. If you take the racial world on your shoulders, you will not get the job done. Deal with yourself as an individual worthy of respect, and make everyone else deal with you the same way. College is a little like playing grown-up. Practice what you want to be. You have been telling your parents you are grown. Now is your chance to act like it.   34

For Study and Discussion

QUESTIONS ABOUT PURPOSE

1. How does Giovanni explain her reasons for teaching at a predominantly white school?
2. In what ways does the issue of control, particularly self-control, explain the purpose of her advice?

QUESTIONS ABOUT AUDIENCE

1. How do the examples in the first paragraph and the advice in the last paragraph identify Giovanni's primary audience?
2. How does Giovanni's status as professor at a predominantly white college establish her authority to address her audience on "Racism 101"?

QUESTIONS ABOUT STRATEGIES

1. How does Giovanni arrange her advice? Why is her first suggestion—"Go to class"—her *first* suggestion? Why is her last suggestion—"Participate in some campus activity"—her *last* suggestion?
2. How does she use sample questions and answers to illustrate the experience of learning on a white campus?

For Writing and Research

1. *Analyze* how Giovanni uses comparisons—for example, college and prison—to explain the process of acquiring an education.
2. *Practice* by analyzing the process by which students can respond to teachers who do not "like" them.
3. *Argue* that, in a way, it is the job of black students to educate white people.
4. *Synthesize* the current research on America's educational progress. Then analyze the process by which the country can improve its status.

Gretel Ehrlich was born and raised in California and was educated at Bennington College, UCLA Film School, and the New School for Social Research. She now lives on a ranch in Wyoming, where she first went as a documentary filmmaker. She has also been a ranch worker—lambing, branding, herding sheep, and calving. A full-time writer since 1979, she has published prose pieces in the *New York Times,* the *Atlantic, Harper's,* and *New Age Journal. The Solace of Open Spaces,* a collection of her prose, was published in 1985. She has also published three books of poetry and a story collection (with Edward Hoagland) titled *City Tales/ Wyoming Stories* (1986); a novel, *Heart Mountain* (1988); and *The Horse Whisperer: An Illustrated Companion to the Major Motion Picture* (1998). In this essay, reprinted from *The Solace of Open Spaces,* Ehrlich describes the traditional events in a rodeo and then analyzes their relationship to life in the West.

Rules of the Game: Rodeo

INSTEAD OF HONEYMOONING in Paris, Patagonia, or the Sahara as we had planned, my new husband and I drove through a series of blizzards to Oklahoma City. Each December the National Finals Rodeo is held in a modern, multistoried colosseum next to buildings that house banks and petroleum companies in a state whose flatness resembles a swimming pool filled not with water but with oil.

The National Finals is the "World Series of Professional Rodeo," where not only the best cowboys but also the most athletic horses and bucking stock compete. All year, rodeo cowboys have been vying for the honor to ride here. They've been to Houston, Las Vegas, Pendleton, Tucson, Cheyenne, San Francisco, Calgary; to as many as eighty rodeos in one season, sometimes making two or three on a day like the Fourth of July, and when the results are tallied up (in money won, not points) the top fifteen riders in each event are invited to Oklahoma City.

We climbed to our peanut gallery seats just as Miss Rodeo 3 America, a lanky brunette swaddled in a lavender pantsuit, gloves, and cowboy hat, loped across the arena. There was a hush in the audience; all the hats swimming down in front of us, like buoys, steadied and turned toward the chutes. "Out of chute number three, Pat Linger, a young cowboy from Miles City, Montana, making his first appearance here on a little horse named Dillinger." And as fast as these words sailed across the colosseum, the first bareback horse bumped into the lights.

There's a traditional order to the four timed and three 4 rough stock events that make up a rodeo program. Bareback riders are first, then steer wrestlers, team ropers, saddle bronc riders, barrel racers, and finally, the bull riders.

After Pat Linger came Steve Dunham, J. C. Trujillo, 5 Mickey Young, and the defending champ, Bruce Ford, on a horse named Denver. Bareback riders do just that: they ride a horse with no saddle, no halter, no rein, clutching only a handhold riveted into a girth that goes around the horse's belly. A bareback rider's loose style suggests a drunken, comic bout of lovemaking: he lies back on the horse and, with each jump and jolt, flops delightfully, like a libidinous Raggedy Andy, toes turned our, knees flexed, legs spread and pumping, back arched, the back of his hat bumping the horse's rump as if nodding, "Yes, let's do 'er again." My husband, who rode saddle broncs in amateur rodeos, explains it differently: "It's like riding a runaway bicycle down a steep hill and lying on your back; you can't see where you're going or what's going to happen next."

Now the steer wrestlers shoot out of the box on their own 6 well-trained horses: there is a hazer on the right to keep the steer running straight, the wrestler on the left, and the steer between them. When the wrestler is neck and neck with the animal, he slides sideways out of his saddle as if he'd been stabbed in the ribs and reaches for the horns. He's airborne for a second; then his heels swing into the dirt, and with his arms around the horns, he skids to a stop twisting the steer's head to one side so the animal loses his balance and falls to the ground. It's a fast-paced game of catch with a thousand-pound ball of horned flesh.

The team ropers are next. Most of them hail from the hilly, oak-strewn valleys of California where dally roping originated.[1] Ropers are the graceful technicians, performing their pas de deux (plus steer) with a precision that begins to resemble a larger clarity—an erudition. Header and heeler come out of the box at the same time, steer between them, but the header acts first: he ropes the horns of the steer, dallies up, turns off, and tries to position the steer for the heeler who's been tagging behind this duo, loop clasped in his armpit as if it were a hen. Then the heeler sets his generous, unsweeping loop free and double-hocks the steer. It's a complicated act which takes about six seconds. Concomitant with this speed and skill is a feminine grace: they don't clutch their stiff loop or throw it at the steer like a bag of dirty laundry the way I do, but hold it gently, delicately, as if it were a hoop of silk. One or two cranks and both arm and loop vault forward, one becoming an appendage of the other, as if the tendons and pulse that travel through the wrist had lengthened and spun forward like fishing line until the loop sails down on the twin horns, then up under the hocks like a repeated embrace that tightens at the end before it releases.

The classic event at rodeo is saddle bronc riding. The young men look as serious as academicians: they perch spryly on their high-kicking mounts, their legs flicking forward and back, "charging the point," "going back to the cantle" in a rapid, staccato rhythm. When the horse is at the high point of his buck and the cowboy is stretched out, legs spurring above

7

8

[1] The word dally is a corruption of the Spanish *da la vuelta,* meaning to take a turn, as with a rope around the saddle horn.

the horse's shoulder, rein-holding arm straight as a board in front, and free hand lifted behind, horse and man look like a propeller. Even their dismounts can look aeronautical: springing off the back of the horse, they land on their feet with a flourish—hat still on—as if they had been ejected mechanically from a burning plane long before the crash.

Barrel racing is the one women's event. Where the men are tender in their movements, as elegant as if Balanchine had been their coach, the women are prodigies of Wayne Gretsky, all speed, bully, and grit. When they charge into the arena, their hats fly off; they ride brazenly, elbows, knees, feet fluttering, and by the time they've careened around the second of three barrels, the whip they've had clenched between their teeth is passed to a hand, and on the home stretch they urge the horse to the finish line. 9

Calf ropers are the whiz kids of rodeo: they're expert on the horse and on the ground, and their horses are as quick-witted. The cowboy emerges from the box with a loop in his hand, a piggin' string in his mouth, coils and reins in the other, and a network of slack line strewn so thickly over horse and rider, they look as if they'd run through a tangle of kudzu before arriving in the arena. After roping the calf and jerking the slack in the rope, he jumps off the horse, sprints down the length of nylon, which the horse keeps taut, throws the calf down, and ties three legs together with the piggin' string. It's said of Roy Cooper, the defending calf-roping champion, that "even with pins and metal plates in his arm, he's known for the fastest groundwork in the business; when he springs down his rope to flank the calf, the resulting action is pure rodeo poetry." The six or seven separate movements he makes are so fluid they look like one continual unfolding. 10

Bull riding is last, and of all the events it's the only one truly dangerous. Bulls are difficult to ride: they're broad-backed, loose-skinned, and powerful. They don't jump balletically the way a horse does; they jerk and spin, and if you fall off, they'll try to gore you with a horn, kick, or trample you. Bull riders are built like the animals they ride: low to the ground and hefty. They're the tough men on the rodeo circuit, and the flirts. Two 11 of the current champs are city men: Charlie Samson is a small, shy black from Watts, and Bobby Del Vecchio, a brash Italian from the Bronx who always throws the audience a kiss after a ride with a Catskill-like showmanship not usually seen here. What a bull rider lacks in technical virtuosity—you won't see the fast spurring action of a saddle bronc rider in this event— he makes up for in personal flamboyance, and because it's a deadlier game they're playing, you can see the belligerence rise up their necks and settle into their faces as the bull starts his first spin. Besides the bull and the cowboy, there are three other men in the ring—the rodeo clowns—who aren't there to make children laugh but to divert the bull from some of his deadlier tricks, and, when the rider bucks off, jump between the two— like secret service men—to save the cowboy's life.

Rodeo, like baseball, is an American sport and has been 12 around almost as long. While Henry Chadwick was writing his first book of rules for the fledgling ball clubs in 1858, ranch hands were paying $25 a dare to a kid who would ride five outlaw horses from the rough string in a makeshift arena of wagons and cars. The first commercial rodeo in Wyoming was held in Lander in 1895, just nineteen years after the National League was formed. Baseball was just as popular as bucking and roping contests in the West, but no one in Cooperstown, New York, was riding broncs. And that's been part of the problem. After 124 years, rodeo is still misunderstood. Unlike baseball, it's a regional sport (although they do have rodeos in New Jersey, Florida, and other eastern states); it's derived from and stands for the western way of life and the western spirit. It doesn't have the universal appeal of a sport contrived solely for the competition and winning; there is no ball bandied about between opposing players.

Rodeo is the wild child of ranch work and embodies some of 13 what ranching is all about. Horsemanship—not gunslinging— was the pride of western men, and the chivalrous ethics they formulated, known as the western code, became the ground rules for every human game. Two great partnerships are celebrated in this Oklahoma arena: the indispensable one between man and animal that any rancher or cowboy takes on, enduring the joys and punishments of the alliance; and the one between man and man, cowboy and cowboy.

Though rodeo is an individualist's sport, it has everything to do with teamwork. The cowboy who "covers" his bronc (stays on the full eight seconds) has become a team with that animal. The cowboys' competitive feelings amongst each other are so mixed with western tact as to appear ambivalent. When Bruce Ford, the bareback rider, won a go-round he said, "The hardest part of winning this year was taking it away from one of my best friends, Mickey Young, after he'd worked so hard all year." Stan Williamson, who'd just won the steer wrestling, said, "I just drew a better steer. I didn't want Butch to get a bad one. I just got lucky, I guess."   14

Ranchers, when working together, can be just as diplomatic. They'll apologize if they cut in front of someone while cutting out a calf, and their thanks to each other at the end of the day has a formal sound. Like those westerners who still help each other out during branding and roundup, rodeo cowboys help each other in the chutes. A bull rider will steady the saddle bronc rider's horse, help measure out the rein or set the saddle, and a bareback rider might help the bull rider set his rigging and pull his rope. Ropers lend each other horses, as do barrel racers and steer wrestlers. This isn't a show they put on; they offer their help with the utmost goodwill and good-naturedness. Once, when a bucking horse fell over backward in the chute with my husband, his friend H.A., who rode bulls, jumped into the chute and pulled him out safely.   15

Another part of the "westernness" rodeo represents is the drifting cowboys do. They're on the road much of their lives the way turn-of-the-century cowboys were on the trail, but these cowboys travel in style if they can—driving pink Lincolns and new pickups with a dozen fresh shirts hanging behind the driver, and the radio on.   16

Some ranchers look down on the sport of rodeo; they don't want these "drugstore cowboys" getting all the attention and glory. Besides, rodeo seems to have less and less to   17 do with real ranch work. Who ever heard of gathering cows on a bareback horse with no bridle, or climbing on a herd bull? Ranchers are generalists—they have to know how to do many things—from juggling the futures market to overhauling a tractor or curing viral scours (diarrhea) in calves—while rodeo athletes are specialists. Deep down, they probably feel envious of each other: the rancher for the praise and big money; the rodeo cowboy for the stay-at-home life among animals to which their sport only alludes.

People with no ranching background have even more difficulty with the sport. Every ride goes so fast, it's hard to see just what happened, and perhaps because of the Hollywood mythologizing of the West which distorted rather than distilled western rituals, rodeo is often considered corny, anachronistic, and cruel to animals. Quite the opposite is true. Rodeo cowboys are as sophisticated athletically as Bjorn Borg or Fernando Valenzuela. That's why they don't need to be from a ranch anymore, or to have grown up riding horses. And to undo another myth, rodeo is not cruel to animals. Compared to the arduous life of any "using horse" on a cattle or dude ranch, a bucking horse leads the life of Riley. His actual work load for an entire year, i.e., the amount of time he spends in the arena, totals approximately 4.6 minutes, and nothing done to him in the arena or out could in any way be called cruel. These animals aren't bludgeoned into bucking; they love to buck. They're bred to behave this way, they're athletes whose ability has been nurtured and encouraged. Like the cowboys who compete at the National Finals, the best bulls and horses from all the bucking strings in the country are nominated to appear in Oklahoma, winning money along with their riders to pay their own way. [18]

The National Finals run ten nights. Every contestant rides every night, so it is easy to follow their progress and setbacks. One evening we abandoned our rooftop seats and sat behind the chutes to watch the saddle broncs ride. Behind the chutes two cowboys are rubbing rosin—part of their staying power— behind the saddle swells and on their Easter-egg-colored chaps which are pink, blue, and light green with white fringe. Up [19] above, standing on the chute rungs, the stock contractors direct horse traffic: "Velvet Drums" in chute #3, "Angel Sings" in #5, "Rusty" in #1. Rick Smith, Monty Henson, Bobby Berger, Brad Gjermudson, Mel Coleman, and friends climb the chutes. From where I'm sitting, it looks like a field hospital with five separate operating theaters, the cowboys, like surgeons, bent over their patients with sweaty brows and looks of concern. Horses are being haltered; cowboys are measuring out the long, braided reins, saddles are set: one cowboy pulls up on the swells again and again, repositioning his hornless saddle until it sits just right. When the chute boss nods to him and says, "Pull 'em up, boys," the ground crew tightens front and back cinches on the first horse to go, but very slowly so he won't panic in the chute as the cowboy eases himself down over the saddle, not sitting on it, just hovering there. "Okay, you're on." The chute boss nods to him again. Now he sits on the saddle, taking the rein in one hand, holding the top of the chute with the other. He flips the loose bottoms of his chaps over his shins, puts a foot in each stirrup, takes a breath, and nods. The chute gate swings open releasing a flood—not of water, but of flesh, groans, legs kicking. The horse lunges up and out in the first big jump like a wave breaking whose crest the cowboy rides, "marking out the horse," spurs well above the bronc's shoulders. In that first second under the lights, he finds what will be the rhythm of the ride. Once again he "charges the point," his legs pumping forward, then so far back his heels touch behind the cantle. For a moment he looks as though he were kneeling on air, then he's stretched out again, his whole body taut but released, free hand waving in back of his head like a palm frond, rein-holding hand thrust forward: *"En garde!"* he seems to be saying, but he's airborne; he looks like a wing that has sprouted suddenly from the horse's broad back. Eight seconds. The whistle blows. He's covered the horse. Now two gentlemen dressed in white chaps and satin shirts gallop beside the bucking horse. The cowboy hands the rein to one and grabs the waist of the other—the flank strap on the bronc has been undone, so all three horses move at a run—and the pickup man from whom the cowboy is now dangling slows almost to a stop, letting him slide to his feet on the ground.

Rick Smith from Wyoming rides, looking pale and nervous   20
in his white shirt. He's bucked off and so are the brash Monty "Hawkeye" Henson, and Butch Knowles, and Bud Pauley, but with such grace and aplomb, there is no shame. Bobby Berger, an Oklahoma cowboy, wins the go-round with a score of 83.

By the end of the evening we're tired, but in no way as   21
exhausted as these young men who have ridden night after night. "I've never been so sore and had so much fun in my life," one first-time bull rider exclaims breathlessly. When the performance is over we walk across the street to the chic lobby of a hotel chock full of cowboys. Wives hurry through the crowd with freshly ironed shirts for tomorrow's ride, ropers carry their rope bags with them into the coffee shop, which is now filled with contestants, eating mild midnight suppers of scrambled eggs, their numbers hanging crookedly on their backs, their faces powdered with dust, and looking at this late hour prematurely old.

We drive back to the motel, where, the first night, they'd   22
"never heard of us" even though we'd had reservations for a month. "Hey, it's our honeymoon," I told the night clerk and showed him the white ribbons my mother had tied around our duffel bag. He looked embarrassed, then surrendered another latecomer's room.

The rodeo finals in Oklahoma may be a better place to   23
honeymoon than Paris. All week, we've observed some important rules of the game. A good rodeo, like a good marriage, or a musical instrument when played to the pitch of perfection, becomes more than what it started out to be. It is effort transformed into effortlessness; a balance becomes grace, the way love goes deep into friendship.

In the rough stock events such as the one we watched   24
tonight, there is no victory over the horse or bull. The point of the match is not conquest but communion: the rhythm of two beings becoming one. Rodeo is not a sport of opposition; there is no scrimmage line here. No one bears malice—neither the animals, the stock contractors, nor the contestants; no one

wants to get hurt. In this match of equal talents, it is only acceptance, surrender, respect, and spiritedness that make for the midair union of cowboy and horse. Not a bad thought when starting out fresh in a marriage.

For Study and Discussion

QUESTIONS ABOUT PURPOSE

1. What is Ehrlich's purpose in the first part of this essay? Look particularly at paragraphs 4–11.
2. What is her purpose in the second part of the essay? For example, how does this sentence establish her purpose for this section: "After 124 years, rodeo is still misunderstood"?

QUESTIONS ABOUT AUDIENCE

1. What assumptions does Ehrlich make about her readers' knowldge of rodeos? How does her husband help establish her expertise?
2. What does she anticipate are her readers' most common misconceptions about rodeos? What is the source of those misconceptions?

QUESTIONS ABOUT STRATEGIES

1. Ehrlich begins her formal analysis by outlining the traditional order of the rodeo program. Which of the seven events does she omit from her list?
2. How does Ehrlich analyze the multiple stages contained in a short process such as saddle bronc riding? See paragraphs 8 and 19.

For Writing and Research

1. *Analyze* how Ehrlich illustrates that the rodeo exhibits competition and cooperation.
2. *Practice* by explaining the steps you follow when you do not know the "rules of the game."
3. *Argue* that the rodeo, while it embodies ranch life, has less and less to do with real ranch work.
4. *Synthesize* the demographic information on the people who attend the National Finals. Then use this information to argue that the rodeo is/is not a major sport.

Edward Hoagland was born in New York City in 1932 and was educated at Harvard University. Although he has written several novels and books on travel, Hoagland considers himself a personal essayist, a writer who is concerned with expressing "what I think" and "what I am." He has published essays in *Commentary, Newsweek,* the *Village Voice,* and the *New York Times* on an intriguing range of subjects such as tugboats, turtles, circuses, city life in Cairo, and his own stutter. His nonfiction has been collected in books such as *The Courage of Turtles* (1971), *The Edward Hoagland Reader* (1979), *Notes from the Century Before: A Journal from British Columbia* (1982), *Balancing Acts* (1992), and *Compass Points: How I Lived* (2001). His short stories appear in *City Tales/Wyoming Stories* (1986), with Gretel Ehrlich, and *The Final Fate of the Alligators* (1992). In "In the Toils of the Law," reprinted from *Walking the Dead Diamond River* (1973), Hoagland uses his own experience to explain the process of being selected for and serving on a jury.

In the Toils of the Law

L ATELY PEOPLE SEEM to want to pigeonhole themselves ("I'm 'into' this," "I'm 'into' that"), and the anciently universal experiences like getting married or having a child, like voting or jury duty, acquire a kind of poignancy. We hardly believe that our vote will count, we wonder whether the world will wind up uninhabitable for the child, but still we do vote with a rueful fervor and look at new babies with undimmed tenderness, because who knows what will become of these old humane responsibilities? . . .

Jury duty. Here one sits listening to evidence: thumbs up   2
for a witness or thumbs down. It's unexpectedly moving;
everybody tries so hard to be fair. For their two weeks of
service people really try to be better than themselves. In
Manhattan eighteen hundred are called each week from the
voters' rolls, a third of whom show up and qualify. Later this
third is divided into three groups of two hundred, one for the
State Supreme Court of New York County, one for the Criminal Court, and one for the Civil Court. At Civil Court, 111
Centre Street, right across from the Tombs, there are jury
rooms on the third and eleventh floors, and every Monday a
new pool goes to one or the other. The building is relatively
modern, the chairs upholstered as in an airport lounge, and
the two hundred people sit facing forward like a school of

---

*Jury duty is unexpectedly moving; everybody
tries so hard to be fair.*

---

fish until the roll is called. It's like waiting six or seven hours
a day for an unscheduled flight to leave. They read and watch
the clock, go to the drinking fountain, strike up a conversation, dictate business letters into the pay telephones. When I
served, one man in a booth was shouting, "I'll knock your
teeth down your throat! I don't want to hear, I don't want to
know!"

. . . There are lots of retired men and institutional employ-   3
ees from banks, the Post Office or the Transit Authority whose
bosses won't miss them, as well as people at loose ends who
welcome the change. But some look extremely busy, rushing
back to the office when given a chance or sitting at the tables
at the front of the room, trying to keep up with their work.
They'll write payroll checks, glancing to see if you notice how
important they are, or pore over statistical charts or contact
sheets with a magnifying glass, if they are in public relations or

advertising. Once in a while a clerk emerges to rotate a lottery box and draw the names of jurors, who go into one of the challenge rooms—six jurors, six alternates—to be interviewed by the plaintiff's and defendant's lawyers. Unless the damages asked are large, in civil cases the jury has six members, only five of whom must agree on a decision, and since no one is going to be sentenced to jail, the evidence for a decision need merely seem preponderant, not "beyond a reasonable doubt."

The legal fiction is maintained that the man or woman you   4
see as defendant is actually going to have to pay, but the defense attorneys are generally insurance lawyers from a regular battery which each big company keeps at the courthouse to handle these matters, or from the legal corps of the City of New York, Con Edison, Hertz Rent A Car, or whoever. If so, they act interchangeably and you may see a different face in court than you saw in the challenge room, and still another during the judge's charge. During my stint most cases I heard about went back four or five years, and the knottiest problem for either side was producing witnesses who were still willing to testify. In negligence cases, so many of which involve automobiles, there are several reasons why the insurers haven't settled earlier. They've waited for the plaintiff to lose hope or greed, and to see what cards each contestant will finally hold in his hands when the five years have passed. More significantly, it's a financial matter. The straight-arrow companies that do right by a sufferer and promptly pay him off lose the use as capital of that three thousand dollars or so meanwhile—multiplied perhaps eighty thousand times, for all the similar cases they have.

Selecting a jury is the last little battle of nerves between   5
the two sides. By now the opposing attorneys know who will testify and have obtained pretrial depositions; this completes the hand each of them holds. Generally they think they know what will happen, so to save time and costs they settle the case either before the hearing starts or out of the jury's earshot during the hearing with the judge's help. Seeing a good sober jury waiting to hear them attempt to justify a bad case greases the wheels.

In the challenge room, though, the momentum of con-   6
frontation goes on. With a crowded court calendar, the judge
in these civil cases is not present, as a rule. It's a small room,
and there's an opportunity for the lawyers to be folksy or
emotional in ways not permitted them later on. For example,
in asking the jurors repeatedly if they will "be able to convert
pain and suffering into dollars and cents" the plaintiff's
attorney is preparing the ground for his more closely super-
vised presentation in court. By asking them if they own any
stock in an insurance company he can get across the intelligence, which is otherwise *verboten,* that not the humble
"defendant" but some corporation is going to have to pay
the tab. His opponent will object if he tells too many jokes
and wins too many friends, but both seek not so much a
sympathetic jury as a jury that is free of nuts and grudge-
holders, a jury dependably ready to give everybody "his day
in court"—a phrase one hears over and over. The questioning
we were subjected to was so polite as to be almost apologetic,
however, because of the danger of unwittingly offending any
of the jurors who remained. Having to size up a series of
strangers, on the basis of some monosyllabic answers and
each fellow's face, profession and address, was hard work for
these lawyers. Everybody was on his best behavior, the jurors
too, because the procedure so much resembled a job interview, and no one wanted to be considered less than
fair-minded, unfit to participate in the case; there was a vague
sense of shame about being excused.

The six alternates sat listening. The lawyers could look at   7
them and draw any conclusions they wished, but they could
neither question them until a sitting juror had been challenged, nor know in advance which one of the alternates
would be substituted first. Each person was asked about his
work, about any honest bias or special knowledge he might
have concerning cases of the same kind, or any lawsuits he
himself might have been involved in at one time. Some questions were probably partly designed to educate us in the
disciplines of objectivity, lest we think it was all too easy, and
one or two lawyers actually made an effort to educate us in

the majesty of the law, since, as they said, the judges some-times are "dingbats" and don't. We were told there should be no opprobrium attached to being excused, that we must not simply assume a perfect impartiality in ourselves but should help them to examine us. Jailhouse advocates, or Spartan types who might secretly believe that the injured party should swallow his misfortune and grin and bear a stroke of bad luck, were to be avoided, of course, along with the mingy, the flippant, the grieved and the wronged, as well as men who might want to redistribute the wealth of the world by finding for the plaintiff, or who might not limit their deliberations to the facts of the case, accepting the judge's interpretation of the law as law. We were told that our common sense and experience of life was what was wanted to sift out the likelihood of the testimony we heard.

Most dismissals were caused just by a lawyer's hunch—or figuring the percentages as baseball managers do. After the first day's waiting in the airport lounge, there wasn't anybody who didn't want to get on a case; even listening as an alter-nate in the challenge room was a relief. I dressed in a suit and tie and shined my shoes. I'd been afraid that when I said I was a novelist no lawyer would have me, on the theory that novelists favor the underdog. On the contrary, I was accepted every time; apparently a novelist was considered ideal, having no allegiances at all, no expertise, no professional link to the workaday world. I stutter and had supposed that this too might disqualify me [but] these lawyers did not think it so. What they seemed to want was simply a balanced group, because when a jury gets down to arguing there's no telling where its leadership will arise. The rich man from Sutton Place whom the plaintiff's lawyer almost dismissed, fearing he'd favor the powers that be, may turn out to be a fighting liberal whose idea of what constitutes proper damages is much higher than what the machinist who sits next to him has in mind. In one case I heard about, a woman was clonked by a Christmas tree in a department store and the juror whose salary was lowest suggested an award of fifty dollars, and the man who earned the most, fifty thousand dollars

8

(they rounded it off to fifteen hundred dollars). These were the kind of cases Sancho Panza did so well on when he was governor of Isle Barataria, and as I was questioned about my prejudices, and solemnly looking into each lawyer's eyes, shook my head—murmuring, No, I had no prejudices—all the time my true unreliable quirkiness filled my head. All I could do was resolve to try to be fair.

By the third day, we'd struck up shipboard friendships. There was a babbling camaraderie in the jury pool, and for lunch we plunged into that old, eclipsed, ethnic New York near City Hall—Chinese roast ducks hanging in the butcher's windows on Mulberry Street next door to an Italian store selling religious candles. We ate at Cucina Luna and Giambone's. Eating at Ping Ching's, we saw whole pigs, blanched white, delivered at the door. We watched an Oriental funeral with Madame Nhu the director waving the limousines on. The deceased's picture, heaped with flowers, was in the lead car, and all his beautiful daughters wept with faces disordered and long black hair streaming down. One of the Italian bands which plays on feast days was mourning over a single refrain—two trumpets, a clarinet, a mellophone and a drum.

As an alternate I sat in on the arguments for a rent-a-car crash case, with four lawyers, each of whom liked to hear himself talk, representing the different parties. The theme was that we were New Yorkers and therefore streetwise and no fools. The senior fellow seemed to think that all his years of trying these penny-ante negligence affairs had made him very good indeed, whereas my impression was that the reason he was still trying them was because he was rather bad. The same afternoon I got on a jury to hear the case of a cleaning woman, sixty-four, who had slipped on the floor of a Harlem ballroom in 1967 and broken her ankle. She claimed the floor was overwaxed. She'd obviously been passed from hand to hand within the firm that had taken her case and had wound up with an attractive young man who was here cutting his teeth. What I liked about her was her abusive manner, which expected no justice and made no distinction at all between her own lawyer and that of the ballroom owner, though she was confused by the fact that the judge was black. He was from the Supreme Court, assigned to help cut through this backlog, had a clerk with an Afro, and was exceedingly brisk and effective.

The porter who had waxed the floor testified—a man of 11 good will, long since at another job. The ballroom owner had operated the hall for more than thirty years, and his face was fastidious, Jewish, sensitive, sad, like that of a concertgoer who is not unduly pleased with his life. He testified, and it was not *his* fault. Nevertheless the lady had hurt her ankle and been out of pocket and out of work. It was a wedding reception, and she'd just stepped forward, saying, "Here comes the bride!"

The proceedings were interrupted while motions were 12 heard in another case, and we sat alone in a jury room, trading reading material, obeying the injunction not to discuss the case, until after several hours we were called back and thanked by the judge. "They also serve who stand and wait." He said that our presence next door as a deliberative body, passive though we were, had pressured a settlement. It was for seven hundred and fifty dollars, a low figure to me (the court attendant told me that there had been a legal flaw in the plaintiff's case), but some of the other jurors thought she'd deserved no money; they were trying to be fair to the ballroom man. Almost always that's what the disputes boiled down to: one juror trying to be fair to one person, another to another.

On Friday of my first week I got on a jury to hear the plight 13 of a woman who had been standing at the front of a bus and had been thrown forward and injured when she stooped to pick up some change that had spilled from her purse. The bus company's lawyer was a ruddy, jovial sort. "Anybody here have a bone to pick with our New York City buses?" We laughed and said, no, we were capable of sending her away without any award if she couldn't prove negligence. Nevertheless, he settled with her attorney immediately after we left the challenge room. (These attorneys did not necessarily run to type. There was a Transit Authority man who shouted like William Kunstler; five times the judge had an officer make him sit down, and once threatened to have the chap bound to his chair.)

I was an alternate for another car crash. With cases in 14 progress all over the building, the jury pool had thinned out, so that no sooner were we dropped back into it than our names were called again. Even one noteworthy white-haired fellow who was wearing a red velvet jump suit, a dragon-colored coat and a dangling gold talisman had some experiences to talk about. I was tabbed for a panel that was to hear from a soft-looking, tired, blond widow of fifty-seven who, while walking home at night five years before from the shop where she worked, had tripped into an excavation only six inches deep but ten feet long and three feet wide. She claimed that the twists and bumps of this had kept her in pain and out of work for five months. She seemed natural and truthful on the witness stand, yet her testimony was so brief and flat that one needed to bear in mind how much time had passed. As we'd first filed into the courtroom she had watched us with the ironic gravity that a person inevitably would feel who has waited five years for a hearing and now sees the cast of characters who will decide her case. This was a woeful low point of her life, but the memory of how badly she'd felt was stale.

The four attorneys on the case were straightforward 15 youngsters getting their training here. The woman's was properly aggressive; Con Edison's asked humorously if we had ever quarreled with Con Edison over a bill; the city's, who was an idealist with shoulder-length hair, asked with another laugh if we disliked New York; and the realty company's, whether we fought with our landlords. Of course, fair-minded folk that we were, we told them no. They pointed out that just as the code of the law provides that a lone woman, fifty-seven, earning a hundred dollars a week, must receive the same consideration in court as a great city, so must the city be granted an equal measure of justice as that lone woman was.

Our panel included a bank guard, a lady loan officer, a 16 young black Sing Sing guard, a pale, slim middle-aged executive from Coca-Cola, a hale fellow who sold package tours from an airline and looked like the Great Gildersleeve, and me. If her attorney had successfully eliminated Spartans

from the jury, we'd surely award her something; the question
was how much. I wondered about the five months. No bones
broken—let's say, being rather generous, maybe two months
of rest. But couldn't the remainder be one of those dead-still
intermissions that each of us must stop and take once or
twice in a life, not from any single blow but from the accumulating knocks and scabby disappointments that pile up,
the harshness of winning a living, and the rest of it—for
which the government in its blundering wisdom already
makes some provision through unemployment insurance?

But there were no arguments. The judge had allowed the   17
woman to testify about her injuries on the condition that her
physician appear. When, the next day, he didn't, a mistrial
was declared.

For Study and Discussion

QUESTIONS ABOUT PURPOSE

1. Does Hoagland's analysis suggest that jury duty is a simple or a
   complex process? What do the first few sentences in paragraph 2
   suggest about the process? What does the rest of the essay
   demonstrate?
2. In what ways does Hoagland's analysis support or contradict
   his theories about contemporary attitudes toward "anciently
   universal experiences"?

QUESTIONS ABOUT AUDIENCE

1. How does Hoagland use the pronoun *we* in the first paragraph
   to identify his audience?
2. How does Hoagland's description of his fellow jurors show his
   readers the difficulties a jury faces when it tries to arrive at a fair
   decision?

QUESTIONS ABOUT STRATEGIES

1. How does Hoagland use the lawyers' questions to illustrate the
   selection process? What kind of people are these questions
   designed to eliminate?

2. How does Hoagland use the cases he heard as examples to illustrate different problems with the jury process? For example, what problem does the jury face in the last case?

For Writing and Research

1. *Analyze* how Hoagland illustrates that selecting a jury is "the last battle of nerves between the two sides."
2. *Practice* by explaining the steps you would follow to avoid serving on a jury.
3. *Argue* that the lawsuits and plea bargains in our civil courts demonstrate that America does/does not have an effective legal system.
4. *Synthesize* the confessions of various jurors on a major trial. Then argue that the group did/did not "try to be better than themselves."

RICHARD SELZER

Richard Selzer was born in Troy, New York, in 1928 and was educated at Union College and Albany Medical College. In 1960, after his internship and postdoctoral study, Selzer established a private practice in general surgery and became an associate professor of surgery at the Yale University medical school. His articles on various aspects of medicine have appeared in magazines such as *Harper's, Esquire, Redbook,* and *Mademoiselle,* and his books include a volume of short stories, *Rituals of Surgery* (1974); several collections of essays, including *Mortal Lessons: Notes on the Art of Surgery* (1977), *Letters to a Young Doctor* (1983), *Taking the World in for Repairs* (1986), and *The Exact Location of the Soul* (2001); and two memoirs, *Down from Troy: A Doctor Comes of Age* (1992), and *Raising the Dead: A Doctor's Encounter with His Own Mortality* (1993). In "The Knife," reprinted from *Mortal Lessons,* Selzer uses a language of poetic intensity to describe the steps of the surgical process.

The Knife

ONE HOLDS THE knife as one holds the bow of a cello or a   1
tulip—by the stem. Not palmed nor gripped nor grasped, but lightly, with the tips of the fingers. The knife is not for pressing. It is for drawing across the field of skin. Like a slender fish, it waits, at the ready, then, go! It darts, followed by a fine wake of red. The flesh parts, falling away to yellow globules of fat. Even now, after so many times, I still marvel at its power—cold, gleaming, silent. More, I am still struck with a kind of dread that it is I in whose hand the blade

travels, that my hand is its vehicle, that yet again this terrible steel-bellied thing and I have conspired for a most unnatural purpose, the laying open of the body of a human being.

A stillness settles in my heart and is carried to my hand. It is the quietude of resolve layered over fear. And it is this resolve that lowers us, my knife and me, deeper and deeper into the person beneath. It is an entry into the body that is nothing like a caress; still, it is among the gentlest of acts. Then stroke and stroke again, and we are joined by other instruments, hemostats and forceps, until the wound blooms with strange flowers whose looped handles fall to the sides in steely array.

There is sound, the tight click of clamps fixing teeth into severed blood vessels, the snuffle and gargle of the suction machine clearing the field of blood for the next stroke, the litany of monosyllables with which one prays his way down and in: *clamp, sponge, suture, tie, cut.* And there is color. The green of the cloth, the white of the sponges, the red and yellow of the body. Beneath the fat lies the fascia, the tough fibrous sheet encasing the muscles. It must be sliced and the red beef of the muscles separated. Now there are retractors to hold apart the wound. Hands move together, part, weave. We are fully engaged, like children absorbed in a game or the craftsmen of some place like Damascus.

Deeper still. The peritoneum, pink and gleaming and membranous, bulges into the wound. It is grasped with forceps, and opened. For the first time we can see into the cavity of the abdomen. Such a primitive place. One expects to find drawings of buffalo on the walls. The sense of trespassing is keener now, heightened by the world's light illuminating the organs, their secret colors revealed—maroon and salmon and yellow. The vista is sweetly vulnerable at this moment, a kind of welcoming. An arc of the liver shines high and on the right, like a dark sun. It laps over the pink sweep of the stomach, from whose lower border the gauzy omentum is draped, and through which veil one sees, sinuous, slow as just-fed snakes, the indolent coils of the intestine.

You turn aside to wash your gloves. It is a ritual cleansing. One enters this temple doubly washed. Here is man as microcosm, representing in all his parts the earth, perhaps the universe.

I must confess that the priestliness of my profession has ever 6 been impressed on me. In the beginning there are vows, taken with all solemnity. Then there is the endless harsh novitiate of training, much fatigue, much sacrifice. At last one emerges as celebrant, standing close to the truth lying curtained in the Ark of the body. Not surplice and cassock but mask and gown are your regalia. You hold no chalice, but a knife. There is no wine, no wafer. There are only the facts of blood and flesh.

And if the surgeon is like a poet, then the scars you have 7 made on countless bodies are like verses into the fashioning of which you have poured your soul. I think that if years later I were to see the trace from an old incision of mine, I should know it at once, as one recognizes his pet expressions.

But mostly you are a traveler in a dangerous country, 8 advancing into the moist and jungly cleft your hands have made. Eyes and ears are shuttered from the land you left behind; mind empties itself of all other thought. You are the root of groping fingers. It is a fine hour for the fingers, their sense of touch so enhanced. The blind must know this feeling. Oh, there is risk everywhere. One goes lightly. The spleen. No! No! Do not touch the spleen that lurks below the left leaf of the diaphragm, a manta ray in a coral cave, its bloody tongue protruding. One poke and it might rupture, exploding with sudden hemorrhage. The filmy omentum must not be torn, the intestine scraped or denuded. The hand finds the liver, palms it, fingers running along its sharp lower edge, admiring. Here are the twin mounds of the kidneys, the apron of the omentum hanging in front of the intestinal coils. One lifts it aside and the fingers dip among the loops, searching, mapping territory, establishing boundaries. Deeper still, and the womb is touched, then held like a small muscular bottle—the womb and its earlike appendages, the ovaries. How they do nestle in the cup of a man's hand, their power all dormant. They are frailty itself.

There is a hush in the room. Speech stops. The hands of 9 the others, assistants and nurses, are still. Only the voice of the patient's respiration remains. It is the rhythm of a quiet sea, the sound of waiting. Then you speak, slowly, the terse entries of a Himalayan climber reporting back.

"The stomach is okay. Greater curvature clean. No sign of ulcer. Pylorus, duodenum fine. Now comes the gallbladder. No stones. Right kidney, left, all right. Liver . . . uh-oh." 10

Your speech lowers to a whisper, falters, stops for a long, long moment, then picks up again at the end of a sigh that comes through your mask like a last exhalation. 11

"Three big hard ones in the left lobe, one on the right. Metastatic deposits. Bad, bad. Where's the primary? Got to be coming from somewhere." 12

The arm shifts direction and the fingers drop lower and lower into the pelvis—the body impaled now upon the arm of the surgeon to the hilt of the elbow. 13

"Here it is." 14

The voice goes flat, all business now. 15

"Tumor in the sigmoid colon, wrapped all around it, pretty tight. We'll take out a sleeve of the bowel. No colostomy. Not that, anyway. But, God, there's a lot of it down there. Here, you take a feel." 16

You step back from the table, and lean into a sterile basin of water, resting on stiff arms, while the others locate the cancer. . . . 17

What is it, then, this thing, the knife, whose shape is virtually the same as it was three thousand years ago, but now with its head grown detachable? Before steel, it was bronze. Before bronze, stone—then back into unremembered time. Did man invent it or did the knife precede him here, hidden under ages of vegetation and hoofprints, lying in wait to be discovered, picked up, used? 18

The scalpel is in two parts, the handle and the blade. Joined, it is six inches from tip to tip. At one end of the handle is a narrow notched prong upon which the blade is slid, then snapped into place. Without the blade, the handle has a blind, decapitated look. It is helpless as a trussed maniac. But slide on the blade, click it home, and the knife springs 19 instantly to life. It is headed now, edgy, leaping to mount the fingers for the gallop to its feast.

Now is the moment from which you have turned aside, from which you have averted your gaze, yet toward which you have been hastened. Now the scalpel sings along the flesh again, its brute run unimpeded by germs or other frictions. It is a slick slide home, a barracuda spurt, a rip of embedded talon. One listens, and almost hears the whine—nasal, high, delivered through that gleaming metallic snout. The flesh splits with its own kind of moan. It is like the penetration of rape. 20

The breasts of women are cut off, arms and legs sliced to the bone to make ready for the saw, eyes freed from sockets, intestines lopped. The hand of the surgeon rebels. Tension boils through his pores, like sweat. The flesh of the patient retaliates with hemorrhage, and the blood chases the knife wherever it is withdrawn. 21

Within the belly a tumor squats, toadish, fungoid. A gray mother and her brood. The only thing it does not do is croak. It too is hacked from its bed as the carnivore knife lips the blood, turning in it in a kind of ecstasy of plenty, a gluttony after the long fast. It is just for this that the knife was created, tempered, heated, its violence beaten into paper-thin force. 22

At last a little thread is passed into the wound and tied. The monstrous booming fury is stilled by a tiny thread. The tempest is silenced. The operation is over. On the table, the knife lies spent, on its side, the bloody meal smear-dried upon its flanks. The knife rests. 23

And waits. 24

For Study and Discussion

QUESTIONS ABOUT PURPOSE

1. How do you know that Selzer does not intend to give directions on how to perform surgery?
2. Selzer calls surgery "unnatural," but he also calls it "among the gentlest of acts." How do both assertions clarify his purpose in writing the essay?

QUESTIONS ABOUT AUDIENCE

1. The surgeon may be *the* expert in our culture. What effect does Selzer anticipate when he admits to his readers that his "quietude of resolve [is] layered over fear"?
2. Although Selzer does not expect his readers to retrace his steps, he does seem to address them directly on several occasions. To whom is he speaking when he says, "No! No! Do not touch the spleen . . ."?

QUESTIONS ABOUT STRATEGIES

1. Which of the principal steps in the surgical procedure does Selzer describe? How does he use color to make the transition from step to step?
2. On numerous occasions, Selzer uses comparisons to illustrate the process he is analyzing. What characteristics do these comparisons have in common?

For Writing and Research

1. *Analyze* how Selzer compares the act of surgery to the process of traveling in a dangerous country.
2. *Practice* by recreating the steps you had to follow to cure yourself from an illness.
3. *Argue* that the skilled hands of a successful surgeon are the result of natural ability or rigorous training.
4. *Synthesize* the research on a controversial procedure—for example, bypass surgery. Then use this research to argue for or against its effectiveness.

EUDORA WELTY

Eudora Welty (1909–2001) was born in Jackson, Mississippi, and was educated at Mississippi State College for Women, the University of Wisconsin, and, for a brief period, the School of Business at Columbia University. During the Depression, Welty returned to Mississippi to write for newspapers and radio stations and to photograph and interview local residents for the Works Progress Administration, Welty's photographs were exhibited in New York City in 1936. During the 1930s Welty also began to publish her short stories in magazines such as *The Southern Review, The New Yorker,* and *The Atlantic Monthly,* winning the 1941 O. Henry Award for "A Worn Path." Welty remained in Jackson, where she wrote an impressive body of fiction that evokes a strong sense of her "place." Her stories have been collected in *A Curtain of Green and Other Stories* (1941), *The Wide Net and Other Stories* (1943), *The Golden Apples* (1949), *The Bride of the Innisfallen and Other Stories* (1955), and *The Collected Stories of Eudora Welty* (1980). Welty is also the author of three longer works of fiction, *The Ponder Heart* (1954), *Losing Battles* (1970), and *The Optimist's Daughter* (1972), which was awarded the Pulitzer Prize. Welty's collection of essays and reviews, *The Eye of the Story,* appeared in 1977. In *One Writer's Beginnings* (1984) Welty discussed the origins of her craft. "A Worn Path," reprinted from *A Curtain of Green,* documents an old woman's arduous journey to accomplish an important mission.

A Worn Path

I T WAS DECEMBER—a bright frozen day in the early morning. Far out in the country there was an old Negro woman with her head tied in a red rag, coming along a path through the pinewoods. Her name was Phoenix Jackson. She was very old and small and she walked slowly in the dark pine shadows, moving a little from side to side in her steps, with the balanced heaviness and lightness of a pendulum in a grandfather clock. She carried a thin, small cane made from an umbrella, and with this she kept tapping the frozen earth in front of her. This made a grave and persistent noise in the still air, that seemed meditative like the chirping of a solitary little bird.

She wore a dark striped dress reaching down to her shoe tops, and an equally long apron of bleached sugar sacks, with a full pocket: all neat and tidy, but every time she took a step she might have fallen over her shoelaces, which dragged from her unlaced shoes. She looked straight ahead. Her eyes were blue with age. Her skin had a pattern all its own of numberless branching wrinkles and as though a whole little tree stood in the middle of her forehead, but a golden color ran underneath, and the two knobs of her cheeks were illuminated by a yellow burning under the dark. Under the red rag her hair came down on her neck in the frailest of ringlets, still black, and with an odor like copper.

Now and then there was a quivering in the thicket. Old Phoenix said, "Out of my way, all you foxes, owls, beetles, jack rabbits, coons and wild animals! . . . Keep out from under these feet, little bob-whites. . . . Keep the big wild hogs out of my path. Don't let none of those come running my direction. I got a long way." Under her small black-freckled hand her cane, limber as a buggy whip, would switch at the brush as if to rouse up any hiding things.

On she went. The woods were deep and still. The sun made the pine needles almost too bright to look at, up where the wind rocked. The cones dropped as light as feathers.

Down in the hollow was the mourning dove—it was not too late for him.

The path ran up a hill. "Seem like there is chains about my feet, time I get this far," she said, in the voice of argument old people keep to use with themselves. "Something always take a hold of me on this hill—pleads I should stay." 5

After she got to the top she turned and gave a full, severe look behind her where she had come. "Up through pines," she said at length. "Now down through oaks." 6

Her eyes opened their widest, and she started down gently. But before she got to the bottom of the hill a bush caught her dress. 7

Her fingers were busy and intent, but her skirts were full and long, so that before she could pull them free in one place they were caught in another. It was not possible to allow the dress to tear. "I in the thorny bush," she said. "Thorns, you doing your appointed work. Never want to let folks pass, no sir. Old eyes thought you was a pretty little *green* bush." 8

Finally, trembling all over, she stood free, and after a moment dared to stoop for her cane. 9

"Sun so high!" she cried, leaning back and looking, while the thick tears went over her eyes. "The time getting all gone here." 10

At the foot of this hill was a place where a log was laid across the creek. 11

"Now comes the trial," said Phoenix. 12

Putting her right foot out, she mounted the log and shut her eyes. Lifting her skirt, leveling her cane fiercely before her, like a festival figure in some parade, she began to march across. Then she opened her eyes and she was safe on the other side. 13

"I wasn't as old as I thought," she said. 14

But she sat down to rest. She spread her skirts on the bank around her and folded her hands over her knees. Up above her was a tree in a pearly cloud of mistletoe. She did not dare to close her eyes, and when a little boy brought her a plate with a slice of marble-cake on it she spoke to him. "That would be acceptable," she said. But when she went to take it there was just her own hand in the air. 15

So she left that tree, and had to go through a barbed-wire 16
fence. There she had to creep and crawl, spreading her knees
and stretching her fingers like a baby trying to climb the
steps. But she talked loudly to herself: she could not let her
dress be torn now, so late in the day, and she could not pay
for having her arm or her leg sawed off if she got caught fast
where she was.

At last she was safe through the fence and risen up out in 17
the clearing. Big dead trees, like black men with one arm,
were standing in the purple stalks of the withered cotton
field. There sat a buzzard.

"Who you watching?" 18

In the furrow she made her way along. 19

"Glad this not the season for bulls," she said, looking side- 20
ways, "and the good Lord made his snakes to curl up and
sleep in the winter. A pleasure I don't see no two-headed
snake coming around that tree, where it come once. It took
a while to get by him, back in the summer."

She passed through the old cotton and went into a field of 21
dead corn. It whispered and shook and was taller than her
head. "Through the maze now," she said, for there was no
path.

Then there was something tall, black, and skinny there, 22
moving before her.

At first she took it for a man. It could have been a man 23
dancing in the field. But she stood still and listened, and it
did not make a sound. It was as silent as a ghost.

"Ghost," she said sharply, "who be you the ghost of? For 24
I have heard of nary death close by."

But there was no answer—only the ragged dancing in the 25
wind.

She shut her eyes, reached out her hand, and touched a 26
sleeve. She found a coat and inside that an emptiness, cold
as ice.

"You scarecrow," she said. Her face lighted. "I ought to 27
be shut up for good," she said with laughter. "My senses is
gone. I too old. I the oldest people I ever know. Dance, old
scarecrow," she said, "while I dancing with you."

She kicked her foot over the furrow, and with mouth 28
drawn down, shook her head once or twice in a little strut-
ting way. Some husks blew down and whirled in streamers
about her skirts.

Then she went on, parting her way from side to side with 29
the cane, through the whispering field. At last she came to the
end, to a wagon track where the silver grass blew between the
red nuts. The quail were walking around like pullets, seeming
all dainty and unseen.

"Walk pretty," she said. "This the easy place. This the easy 30
going."

She followed the track, swaying through the quiet bare 31
fields, through the little strings of trees silver in their dead
leaves, past cabins silver from weather, with the doors and
windows boarded shut, all like old women under a spell
sitting there. "I walking in their sleep," she said, nodding her
head vigorously.

In a ravine she went where a spring was silent flowing 32
through a hollow log. Old Phoenix bent and drank. "Sweet-
gum makes the water sweet," she said, and drank more. "Nobody know who made this well, for it was here when I was
born."

The track crossed a swampy part where the moss hung as 33
white as lace from every limb. "Sleep on, alligators, and blow
your bubbles." Then the track went into the road.

Deep, deep the road went down between the high green- 34
colored banks. Overhead the live-oaks met, and it was as dark
as a cave.

A black dog with a lolling tongue came up out of the 35
weeds by the ditch. She was meditating, and not ready, and
when he came at her she only hit him a little with her cane.
Over she went in the ditch, like a little puff of milkweed.

Down there, her senses drifted away. A dream visited her, 36
and she reached her hand up, but nothing reached down and
gave her a pull. So she lay there and presently went to talking.
"Old woman," she said to herself, "that black dog come up
out of the weeds to stall you off, and now there he sitting on
his fine tail, smiling at you."

A white man finally came along and found her—a hunter, 37
a young man, with his dog on a chain.

"Well, Granny!" he laughed. "What are you doing there?" 38

"Lying on my back like a June-bug waiting to be turned 39
over, mister," she said, reaching up her hand.

He lifted her up, gave her a swing in the air, and set her 40
down. "Anything broken, Granny?"

"No, sir, them old dead weeds is springy enough," said 41
Phoenix, when she had got her breath. "I thank you for your
trouble."

"Where do you live, Granny?" he asked, while the two 42
dogs were growling at each other.

"Away back yonder, sir, behind the ridge. You can't even 43
see it from here."

"On your way home?" 44

"No sir, I going to town." 45

"Why, that's too far! That's as far as I walk when I come 46
out myself, and I get something for my trouble." He patted
the stuffed bag he carried, and there hung down a little closed
claw. It was one of the bob-whites, and its beak hooked
bitterly to show it was dead. "Now you go home, Granny!"

"I bound to go to town, mister," said Phoenix. "The time 47
come around."

He gave another laugh, filling the whole landscape. "I 48
know you old colored people! Wouldn't miss going to town
to see Santa Claus!"

But something held old Phoenix very still. The deep lines 49
in her face went into a fierce and different radiation. Without
warning, she had seen with her own eyes a flashing nickel fall
out of the man's pocket onto the ground.

"How old are you, Granny?" he was saying. 50

"There is no telling, mister," she said, "no telling." 51

Then she gave a little cry and clapped her hands and said, 52
"Git on away from here, dog! Look! Look at that dog!" She
laughed as if in admiration. "He ain't scared of nobody. He a
big black dog." She whispered, "Sic him!"

"Watch me get rid of that cur," said the man. "Sic him, 53
Pete! Sic him!"

Phoenix heard the dogs fighting, and heard the man run-   54
ning and throwing sticks. She even heard a gunshot. But she
was slowly bending forward by that time, further and further
forward, the lids stretched down over her eyes, as if she were
doing this in her sleep. Her chin was lowered almost to her
knees. The yellow palm of her hand came out from the fold
of her apron. Her fingers slid down and along the ground
under the piece of money with the grace and care they would
have in lifting an egg from under a setting hen. Then she
slowly straightened up, she stood erect, and the nickel was in
her apron pocket. A bird flew by. Her lips moved. "God
watching me the whole time. I come to stealing."

The man came back, and his own dog panted about them.   55
"Well, I scared him off that time," he said, and then he
laughed and lifted his gun and pointed it at Phoenix.

She stood straight and faced him.   56

"Doesn't the gun scare you?" he said, still pointing it.   57

"No, sir, I seen plenty go off closer by, in my day, and for   58
less than what I done," she said, holding utterly still.

He smiled, and shouldered the gun. "Well, Granny," he   59
said, "you must be a hundred years old, and scared of nothing.
I'd give you a dime if I had any money with me. But you take
my advice and stay home, and nothing will happen to you."

"I bound to go on my way, mister," said Phoenix. She   60
inclined her head in the red rag. Then they went in different
directions, but she could hear the gun shooting again and
again over the hill.

She walked on. The shadows hung from the oak trees to   61
the road like curtains. Then she smelled wood-smoke, and
smelled the river, and she saw a steeple and the cabins on their
steep steps. Dozens of little black children whirled around her.
There ahead was Natchez shining. Bells were ringing. She
walked on.

In the paved city it was Christmas time. There were red   62
and green electric lights strung and criss-crossed everywhere,
and all turned on in the daytime. Old Phoenix would have
been lost if she had not distrusted her eyesight and depended
on her feet to know where to take her.

She paused quietly on the sidewalk where people were 63
passing by. A lady came along in the crowd, carrying an armful
of red-, green- and silver-wrapped presents; she gave off per-
fume like the red roses in hot summer, and Phoenix stopped her.

"Please, missy, will you lace up my shoe?" She held up her 64
foot.

"What do you want, Grandma?" 65

"See my shoe," said Phoenix. "Do all right for out in the 66
country, but wouldn't look right to go in a big building."

"Stand still then, Grandma," said the lady. She put her 67
packages down on the sidewalk beside her and laced and tied
both shoes tightly.

"Can't lace 'em with a cane," said Phoenix. "Thank you, 68
missy. I doesn't mind asking a nice lady to tie up my shoe,
when I gets out on the street."

Moving slowly and from side to side, she went into the big 69
building, and into a tower of steps, where she walked up and
around and around until her feet knew to stop.

She entered a door, and there she saw nailed up on the 70
wall the document that had been stamped with the gold seal
and framed in the gold frame, which matched the dream that
was hung up in her head.

"Here I be," she said. There was a fixed and ceremonial 71
stiffness over her body.

"A charity case, I suppose," said an attendant who sat at 72
the desk before her.

But Phoenix only looked above her head. There was sweat 73
on her face, the wrinkles in her skin shone like a bright net.

"Speak up, Grandma," the woman said. "What's your 74
name? We must have your history, you know. Have you been
here before? What seems to be the trouble with you?"

Old Phoenix only gave a twitch to her face as if a fly were 75
bothering her.

"Are you deaf?" cried the attendant. 76

But then the nurse came in. 77

"Oh, that's just old Aunt Phoenix," she said. "She doesn't 78
come for herself—she has a little grandson. She makes these
trips just as regular as clockwork. She lives away back off the

Old Natchez Trace." She bent down. "Well, Aunt Phoenix, why don't you just take a seat? We won't keep you standing after your long trip." She pointed.

The old woman sat down, bolt upright in the chair. 79

"Now, how is the boy?" asked the nurse. 80

Old Phoenix did not speak. 81

"I said, how is the boy?" 82

But Phoenix only waited and stared straight ahead, her 83
face very solemn and withdrawn into rigidity.

"Is his throat any better?" asked the nurse. "Aunt Phoenix, 84
don't you hear me? Is your grandson's throat any better since
the last time you came for the medicine?"

With her hands on her knees, the old woman waited, 85
silent, erect and motionless, just as if she were in armor.

"You mustn't take up our time this way, Aunt Phoenix," 86
the nurse said. "Tell us quickly about your grandson, and get
it over. He isn't dead, is he?"

At last there came a flicker and then a flame of comprehen- 87
sion across her face, and she spoke.

"My grandson. It was my memory had left me. There I sat 88
and forgot why I made my long trip."

"Forgot?" The nurse frowned. "After you came so far?" 89

Then Phoenix was like an old woman begging a dignified 90
forgiveness for waking up frightened in the night. "I never
did go to school, I was too old at the Surrender," she said in
a soft voice. "I'm an old woman without an education. It was
my memory fail me. My little grandson, he is just the same,
and I forgot it in the coming."

"Throat never heals, does it?" said the nurse, speaking in a 91
loud, sure voice to old Phoenix. By now she had a card with
something written on it, a little list. "Yes. Swallowed lye.
When was it?—January—two-three years ago—"

Phoenix spoke unasked now. "No, missy, he not dead, he 92
just the same. Every little while his throat begin to close up
again, and he not able to swallow. He not get his breath. He
not able to help himself. So the time come around, and I go
on another trip for the soothing medicine."

"All right. The doctor said as long as you came to get it, 93
you could have it," said the nurse. "But it's an obstinate case."

"My little grandson, he sit up there in the house all 94
wrapped up, waiting by himself," Phoenix went on. "We is
the only two left in the world. He suffer and it don't seem to
put him back at all. He got a sweet look. He going to last. He
wear a little patch quilt and peep out holding his mouth open
like a little bird. I remembers so plain now. I not going to
forget him again, no, the whole enduring time. I could tell
him from all the others in creation."

"All right." The nurse was trying to hush her now. She 95
brought her a bottle of medicine. "Charity," she said, making
a check mark in a book.

Old Phoenix held the bottle close to her eyes, and then 96
carefully put it into her pocket.

"I thank you," she said. 97

"It's Christmas time, Grandma," said the attendant. 98
"Could I give you a few pennies out of my purse?"

"Five pennies is a nickel," said Phoenix stiffly. 99

"Here's a nickel," said the attendant. 100

Phoenix rose carefully and held out her hand. She received 101
the nickel and then fished the other nickel out of her pocket
and laid it beside the new one. She stared at her palm closely,
with her head on one side.

Then she gave a tap with her cane on the floor. 102

"This is what come to me to do," she said. "I going to the 103
store and buy my child a little windmill they sells, made out
of paper. He going to find it hard to believe there such a
thing in the world. I'll march myself back where he waiting,
holding it straight up in his hand."

She lifted her free hand, gave a little nod, turned around, 104
and walked out of the doctor's office. Then her slow step
began on the stairs, going down.

COMMENT ON "A WORN PATH"

In Eudora Welty's "A Worn Path," a black woman, Phoenix
Jackson, too old to remember her age, makes her way deter-
minedly, but rather fearfully across the Mississippi landscape
to the city of Natchez. She has made this trip many times, but
each time the steps get more difficult: she is deteriorating

physically and prone to forget important things. She almost forgets the reason for her trip once she gets there: to retrieve medicine for her grandson who sometime earlier swallowed lye and for whom the medicine provides only temporary relief. After she gets the medicine, the nurse who dispenses it gives her a nickel, and Phoenix puts it with the nickel she has "stolen" from a white man in the course of her journey. She buys her grandson a windmill, knowing he will "find it hard to believe there is such a thing in the world."

COMPARISON AND CONTRAST

Technically speaking, when you **compare** two or more things, you're looking for similarities; when you **contrast** them, you're looking for differences. In practice, of course, the operations are opposite sides of the same coin, and one implies the other. When you look for what's similar, you will also notice what is different. You can compare things at all levels, from the trivial (plaid shoelaces and plain ones) to the really serious (the differences between a career in medicine and one in advertising). Often when you compare things at a serious level, you do so to make a choice. That's why it's helpful to know how to organize your thinking so that you can analyze similarities and differences in a systematic, useful way that brings out significant differences. It's particularly helpful to have such a system when you are going to write a comparison-and-contrast essay.

PURPOSE

You can take two approaches to writing comparison-and-contrast essays; each has a different purpose. You can make a *strict* comparison, exploring the relationship between things in the same class, or you can do a *fanciful* comparison, looking at the relationship among things from different classes.

When you write a *strict* comparison, you compare only things that are truly alike—actors with actors, musicians with musicians, but *not* actors with musicians. You're trying to find similar information about both your subjects. For instance, what are the characteristics of actors, whether they are movie or stage actors? How are jazz musicians and classical musicians alike, even if their music is quite different? In a strict comparison, you probably also want to show how two things in the same class are different in important ways. Often when you focus your comparison on differences, you do so in order to make a judgment and, finally, a choice. That's one of the main reasons people make comparisons, whether they're shopping or writing.

When you write a *fanciful* comparison, you try to set up an imaginative, illuminating comparison between two things that don't seem at all alike, and you do it for a definite reason: to help explain and clarify a complex idea. For instance, the human heart is often compared to a pump—a fanciful and useful comparison that enables one to envision the heart at work. You can use similar fanciful comparisons to help your readers see new dimensions to events. For instance, you can compare the astronauts landing on the moon to Columbus discovering the New World, or you can compare the increased drug use among young people to an epidemic spreading through part of our culture.

You may find it difficult to construct an entire essay around a fanciful comparison—such attempts tax the most creative energy and can quickly break down. Probably you can use this method of comparison most effectively as a device for enlivening your writing and highlighting dramatic similarities. When you're drawing fanciful comparisons, you're not very likely to be comparing to make judgments or recommend choices. Instead, your purpose in writing a fanciful comparison is to catch your readers' attention and show new connections between unlike things.

AUDIENCE

As you plan a comparison-and-contrast essay, think ahead about what your readers already know and what they're going to expect. First, ask yourself what they know about the items or ideas you're going to compare. Do they know a good deal about both—for instance, two popular television programs? Do they know very little about either item—for instance, Buddhism and Shintoism? Or do they know quite a bit about one but little about the other—for instance, football and rugby?

If you're confident that your readers know a lot about both items (the television programs), you can spend a little time pointing out similarities and concentrate on your reasons for making the comparison. When readers know little about either (Eastern religions), you'll have to define each, using concepts they are familiar with, before you can point out important contrasts. If readers know only one item in a pair (football and rugby), then use the known to explain the unknown. Emphasize what is familiar to them about football, and explain how rugby is like it but also how it is different.

As you think about what your readers need, remember that they want your essay to be fairly balanced, not 90 percent about Buddhism and 10 percent about Shintoism, or two paragraphs about football and nine or ten about rugby. When your focus seems so unevenly divided, you appear to be using one element in the comparison only as a springboard to talk about the other. Such an imbalance can disappoint your readers, who expect to learn about both.

STRATEGIES

You can use two basic strategies for organizing a comparison-and-contrast essay. The first is the *divided,* or *subject-by-subject,* pattern. The second is the *alternating,* or *point-by-point,* pattern.

When you use the *divided* pattern, you present all your information on one topic before you bring in information on the other topic. Mark Twain uses this method in "Two Views of the River." First he gives an apprentice's poetic view, emphasizing the beauty of the river; then he gives the pilot's practical view, emphasizing the technical problems the river poses.

When you use the *alternating* pattern, you work your way through the comparison point by point, giving information first on one aspect of the topic, then on the other. If Mark Twain had used an alternating pattern, he would have given the apprentice's poetic view of a particular feature of the river, then the pilot's pragmatic view of that same feature. He would have followed that pattern throughout, commenting on each feature—the wind, the surface of the river, the sunset, the color of the water—by alternating between the apprentice's and the pilot's points of view.

Although both methods are useful, you'll find that each has benefits and drawbacks. The divided pattern lets you present each part of your essay as a satisfying whole. It works especially well in short essays, such as Twain's, where you're presenting only two facets of a topic and your reader can easily keep track of the points you want to make. Its drawback is that sometimes you slip into writing what seems like two separate essays. When you're writing a long comparison essay about a complex topic, you may have trouble organizing your material clearly enough to keep your readers on track.

The alternating pattern works well when you want to show the two subjects you're comparing side by side, emphasizing the points you're comparing. You'll find it particularly good for longer essays, such as Laura Bohannan's "Shakespeare in the Bush," when you want to show many complex points of comparison and need to help your readers see how those points match up. The drawback of the alternating pattern is that you may reduce your analysis to an exercise. If you use it for making only a few points of comparison in a short essay on a simple topic, your essay sounds choppy and disconnected, like a simple list.

Often you can make the best of both worlds by *combining strategies*. For example, you can start out using a divided pattern to give an overall, unified view of the topics you're going to compare. Then you can shift to an alternating pattern to show how many points of comparison you've found between your subjects. Deborah Tannen uses a version of this strategy in "Rapport-Talk and Report-Talk." She begins by establishing the difference between private and public speaking; then she uses an alternating pattern within each category to demonstrate the contrasts between the speaking styles of men and women.

When you want to write a good comparison-and-contrast analysis, keep three guidelines in mind: (1) *balance parts,* (2) *include reminders,* and (3) *supply reasons.* Look, for example, at how Bruce Catton balances his analysis of Grant and Lee. Barry Lopez uses similar strategies in his comparison of the raven and the crow.

COMPARISON AND CONTRAST

Points to Remember

1. Decide whether you want the pattern of your comparison to focus on complete units (*divided*) or specific features (*alternating*).
2. Consider the possibility of combining the two patterns.
3. Determine which subject should be placed in the first position and why.
4. Arrange the points of your comparison in a logical, balanced, and dramatic sequence.
5. Make sure you introduce and clarify the reasons for making your comparison.

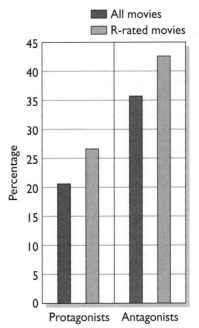

**Smoking Prevalence in
American Cinema**

This bar graph, based on data from the American College of Chest Physicians, illustrates that villains smoke more than heroes in the movies. How do these data challenge the idea that smoking is glamorous? Compare the way smoking was presented in older, black-and-white movies with the way it is presented in contemporary films.

Mark Twain (the pen name of Samuel Clemens, 1835–1910) was born in Florida, Missouri, and grew up in the river town of Hannibal, Missouri, where he watched the comings and goings of the steamboats he would eventually pilot. Twain spent his young adult life working as a printer, a pilot on the Mississippi, and a frontier journalist. After the Civil War, he began a career as a humorist and storyteller, writing such classics as *The Adventures of Tom Sawyer* (1876), *Life on the Mississippi* (1883), *The Adventures of Huckleberry Finn* (1885), and *A Connecticut Yankee in King Arthur's Court* (1889). His place in American writing was best characterized by editor William Dean Howells, who called Twain the "Lincoln of our literature." In "Two Views of the River," taken from *Life on the Mississippi*, Twain compares the way he saw the river as an innocent apprentice to the way he saw it as an experienced pilot.

Two Views of the River

N OW WHEN I had mastered the language of this water, and had come to know every trifling feature that bordered the great river as familiarly as I knew the letters of the alphabet, I had made a valuable acquisition. But I had lost something, too. I had lost something which could never be restored to me while I lived. All the grace, the beauty, the poetry, had gone out of the majestic river! I still keep in mind a certain wonderful sunset which I witnessed when steamboating was new to me. A broad expanse of the river was turned to blood; in the middle distance the red hue brightened into gold, through which a solitary log came floating black and

1

conspicuous; in one place a long, slanting mark lay sparkling upon the water; in another the surface was broken by boiling, tumbling rings that were as many-tinted as an opal; where the ruddy flush was faintest, was a smooth spot that was covered with graceful circles and radiating lines, ever so delicately traced; the shore on our left was densely wooded, and the somber shadow that fell from this forest was broken in one place by a long, ruffled trail that shone like silver; and high above the forest wall a clean-stemmed dead tree waved a single leafy bough that glowed like a flame in the unobstructed

---

When I mastered the language of this water, . . . I had made a valuable acquisition. But I had lost something too.

---

splendor that was flowing from the sun. There were graceful curves, reflected images, woody heights, soft distances; and over the whole scene, far and near, the dissolving lights drifted steadily, enriching it every passing moment with new marvels of coloring.

I stood like one bewitched. I drank it in, in a speechless rapture. The world was new to me, and I had never seen anything like this at home. But as I have said, a day came when I began to cease from noting the glories and the charms which the moon and the sun and the twilight wrought upon the river's face; another day came when I ceased altogether to note them. Then, if that sunset scene had been repeated, I should have looked upon it without rapture, and should have commented upon it, inwardly, after this fashion: "This sun means that we are going to have wind to-morrow; that floating log means that the river is rising, small thanks to it; that slanting mark on the water refers to a bluff reef which is going to kill somebody's steamboat one of these nights, if it keeps on stretching out like that; those tumbling 'boils' show a dissolving bar and a changing channel there; the lines and circles in the slick water over yonder are a warning that that troublesome place is shoaling up dangerously; that silver streak in the shadow of the forest is the 'break' from a new snag, and he has located himself in the very best place he could have found to fish for steamboats; that tall dead tree, with a single living branch, is not going to last long, and then how is a body ever going to get through this blind place at night without the friendly old landmark?"

No, the romance and beauty were all gone from the river. 3 All the value any feature of it had for me now was the amount of usefulness it could furnish toward compassing the safe piloting of a steamboat. Since those days, I have pitied doctors from my heart. What does the lovely flush in a beauty's cheek mean to a doctor but a "break" that ripples above some deadly disease? Are not all her visible charms sown thick with what are to him the signs and symbols of hidden decay? Does he ever see her beauty at all, or doesn't he simply view her professionally, and comment upon her unwholesome condition all to himself? And doesn't he sometimes wonder whether he has gained most or lost most by learning his trade?

For Study and Discussion

QUESTIONS ABOUT PURPOSE

1. What does Twain think he has gained and lost by learning the river?
2. What does Twain accomplish by *dividing* the two views of the river rather than *alternating* them beneath several headings?

QUESTIONS ABOUT AUDIENCE

1. Which attitude—poetic or pragmatic—does Twain anticipate his readers have toward the river? Explain your answer.
2. How does he expect his readers to answer the questions he raises in paragraph 3?

QUESTIONS ABOUT STRATEGIES

1. What sequence does Twain use to arrange the points of his comparison?
2. Where does Twain use transitional phrases and sentences to match up the parts of his comparison?

For Writing and Research

1. *Analyze* the strategies Twain uses to compose and contrast his two views of the river.
2. *Practice* by describing your reactions to a special place in your childhood and then comparing the way you respond to it now.
3. *Argue* that learning too much about the technical details of a process—such as painting or singing—destroys one's ability to appreciate its beauty.
4. *Synthesize* your knowledge of Mark Twain's life and writing. Then use this evidence to argue that creative achievement depends on the willingness to take risks.

BARRY LOPEZ

Barry Lopez was born in 1945 in Port Chester, New York, and was educated at the University of Notre Dame and the University of Oregon. For the last ten years he has lived near the Willamette Forest in Oregon and worked as a full-time writer and free-lance photographer. His articles and photographs on various aspects of the natural environment have appeared in *National Wildlife, American Forests, Audubon,* and other magazines. His works include *Desert Notes: Reflections in the Eye of the Raven* (1976), *River Notes: The Dance of the Herons* (1979), *Of Wolves and Men* (1978), *About This Life: Journeys on the Threshold of Memory* (1998), and *Light Action in the Caribbean* (2000). Lopez is regarded as a superb naturalist who possesses the imagination and voice of a poet. In "The Raven," from *Desert Notes,* he contrasts two birds that the casual observer may see as quite similar.

The Raven

I AM GOING to have to start at the other end by telling you this: there are no crows in the desert. What appear to be crows are ravens. You must examine the crow, however, before you can understand the raven. To forget the crow completely, as some have tried to do, would be like trying to understand the one who stayed without talking to the one who left. It is important to make note of who has left the desert.

To begin with, the crow does nothing alone. He cannot abide silence and he is prone to stealing things, twigs and bits of straw, from the nests of his neighbors. It is a game with him. He enjoys tricks. If he cannot make up his mind the crow will take two or three wives, but this is not a game. The crow is very accommodating and he admires compulsiveness.

Crows will live in street trees in the residential areas of great cities. They will walk at night on the roofs of parked cars and peck at the grit; they will scrape the pinpoints of their talons across the steel and, with their necks out-thrust, watch for frightened children listening in their beds.

Put all this to the raven: he will open his mouth as if to say something. Then he will look the other way and say nothing. Later, when you have forgotten, he will tell you he admires the crow.

The raven is larger than the crow and has a beard of black feathers at his throat. He is careful to kill only what he needs. Crows, on the other hand, will search out the great horned owl, kick and punch him awake, and then, for roosting too close to their nests, they will kill him. They will come out of the sky on a fat, hot afternoon and slam into the head of a dozing rabbit and go away laughing. They will tear out a whole row of planted corn and eat only a few kernels. They will defecate on scarecrows and go home and sleep with 200,000 of their friends in an atmosphere of congratulation. Again, it is only a game; this should not be taken to mean that they are evil.

There is however this: when too many crows come together on a roost there is a lot of shoving and noise and a white film begins to descend over the crows' eyes and they go blind. They fall from their perches and lie on the ground and starve to death. When confronted with this information, crows will look past you and warn you vacantly that it is easy to be misled.

The crow flies like a pigeon. The raven flies like a hawk. He is seen only at a great distance and then not very clearly. This is true of the crow too, but if you are very clever you can trap the crow. The only way to be sure what you have seen is a raven is to follow him until he dies of old age, and then examine the body.

Once there were many crows in the desert. I am told it was 8
like this: you could sit back in the rocks and watch a pack of
crows working over the carcass of a coyote. Some would eat,
the others would try to squeeze out the vultures. The raven
would never be seen. He would be at a distance, alone, perhaps eating a scorpion.

There was, at this time, a small alkaline water hole at the 9
desert's edge. Its waters were bitter. No one but crows would
drink there, although they drank sparingly, just one or two
sips at a time. One day a raven warned someone about the
dangers of drinking the bitter water and was overheard by a
crow. When word of this passed among the crows they felt
insulted. They jeered and raised insulting gestures to the
ravens. They bullied each other into drinking the alkaline
water until they had drunk the hole dry and gone blind.

The crows flew into canyon walls and dove straight into 10
the ground at forty miles an hour and broke their necks. The
worst of it was their cartwheeling across the desert floor, stiff
wings outstretched, beaks agape, white eyes ballooning, surprising rattlesnakes hidden under sage bushes out of the
noonday sun. The snakes awoke, struck and held. The wheel-
ing birds strew them across the desert like sprung traps.

When all the crows were finally dead, the desert bacteria 11
and fungi bored into them, burrowed through bone and
muscle, through aqueous humor and feathers until they had
reduced the stiff limbs of soft black to blue dust.

After that, there were no more crows in the desert. The few 12
who watched from a distance took it as a sign and moved away.

Finally there is this: one morning four ravens sat at the 13
edge of the desert waiting for the sun to rise. They had been
there all night and the dew was like beads of quicksilver on
their wings. Their eyes were closed and they were as still as the
cracks in the desert floor.

The wind came off the snow-capped peaks to the north 14
and ruffled their breast feathers. Their talons arched in the
white earth and they smoothed their wings with sleek dark
bills. At first light their bodies swelled and their eyes flashed
purple. When the dew dried on their wings they lifted off

from the desert floor and flew away in four directions. Crows would never have had the patience for this.

If you want to know more about the raven: bury yourself 15 in the desert so that you have a commanding view of the high basalt cliffs where he lives. Let only your eyes protrude. Do not blink—the movement will alert the raven to your continued presence. Wait until a generation of ravens has passed away. Of the new generation there will be at least one bird who will find you. He will see your eyes staring up out of the desert floor. The raven is cautious, but he is thorough. He will sense your peaceful intentions. Let him have the first word. Be careful: he will tell you he knows nothing.

If you do not have the time for this, scour the weathered 16 desert shacks for some sign of the raven's body. Look under old mattresses and beneath loose floorboards. Look behind the walls. Sooner or later you will find a severed foot. It will be his and it will be well preserved.

Take it out in the sunlight and examine it closely. Notice 17 that there are three fingers that face forward, and a fourth, the longest and like a thumb, that faces to the rear. The instrument will be black but no longer shiny, the back of it sheathed in armor plate and the underside padded like a wolf's foot.

At the end of each digit you will find a black, curved talon. 18 You will see that the talons are not as sharp as you might have suspected. They are made to grasp and hold fast, not to puncture. They are more like the jaws of a trap than a fistful of ice picks. The subtle difference serves the raven well in the desert. He can weather a storm on a barren juniper limb; he can pick up and examine the crow's eye without breaking it.

For Study and Discussion

QUESTIONS ABOUT PURPOSE

1. What is Lopez's primary purpose—to explain the difference between the raven and the crow or to demonstrate why the raven is superior to the crow? Explain your answer.
2. According to Lopez, why did the crow leave the desert?

QUESTIONS ABOUT AUDIENCE

1. Throughout the essay Lopez uses direct address, as in "you must examine the crow," "if you want to know more about the raven." What advantages does this give him in establishing a relationship with his readers?
2. In choosing to discuss the crow first, what assumptions does Lopez make about his readers' experience?

QUESTIONS ABOUT STRATEGIES

1. Where does Lopez use the divided pattern? Where does he use the alternating pattern? What aspect of his subject causes him to combine the two strategies?
2. How does he use the story of the water hole to characterize the difference between the two birds?

For Writing and Research

1. *Analyze* how Lopez uses comparisons to other birds—pigeon, hawk, vulture—to distinguish between the raven and the crow.
2. *Practice* by comparing the behavior and personalities of two domestic pets—for example, dogs and cats.
3. *Argue* that animals who live in a domestic setting develop different or similar personalities to animals who live in the wild.
4. *Synthesize* the research on animals who inhabit the same wild territory. Then use this evidence to compare and contrast their hunting strategies and feeding habits.

Bruce Catton (1899–1978) was born in Petosky, Michigan, and attended Oberlin College. After a career as a reporter for newspapers in Boston and Cleveland, he served as a director of information for various government agencies in Washington, D.C., before accepting the position of editor of *American Heritage* magazine. His fourth book, *A Stillness at Appomattox* (1953), earned him the Pulitzer Prize, the National Book Award, and the unofficial title of America's most popular historian of the Civil War. In addition to his many books on that subject— such as *Mr. Lincoln's Army* (1951), *The Coming Fury* (1961), and *Grant Takes Command* (1964)— Catton wrote a memorable account of his own boyhood in Michigan, *Waiting for the Morning Train: An American Boyhood* (1974). "Grant and Lee: A Study in Contrasts" first appeared in *The American Story* (1956), a collection of essays by eminent historians, and has been cited often as one of the classic examples of the comparison-and-contrast essay. In his analysis, Catton considers both the differences in background and similarities in character in these two great Civil War generals.

Grant and Lee:
A Study in Contrasts

WHEN ULYSSES S. GRANT and Robert E. Lee met in the parlor of a modest house at Appomattox Court House, Virginia, on April 9, 1865, to work out the terms for the surrender of Lee's Army of Northern Virginia, a great chapter in American life came to a close, and a great new chapter began.

These men were bringing the Civil War to its virtual finish. 2
To be sure, other armies had yet to surrender, and for a few
days the fugitive Confederate government would struggle desperately and vainly, trying to find some way to go on living
now that its chief support was gone. But in effect it was all
over when Grant and Lee signed the papers. And the little
room where they wrote out the terms was the scene of one of
the poignant, dramatic contrasts in American history.

They were two strong men, these oddly different generals, 3
and they represented the strengths of two conflicting cur-
rents that, through them, had come into final collision.

Back of Robert E. Lee was the notion that the old aristo- 4
cratic concept might somehow survive and be dominant in
American life.

Lee was tidewater Virginia, and in his background were 5
family, culture, and tradition . . . the age of chivalry transplanted to a New World which was making its own legends
and its own myths. He embodied a way of life that had come
down through the age of knighthood and the English country squire. America was a land that was beginning all over
again, dedicated to nothing much more complicated than the
rather hazy belief that all men had equal rights, and should
have an equal chance in the world. In such a land Lee stood
for the feeling that it was somehow of advantage to human society to have a pronounced inequality in the social structure.
There should be a leisure class, backed by ownership of land;
in turn, society itself should be keyed to the land as the chief
source of wealth and influence. It would bring forth (according to this ideal) a class of men with a strong sense of obligation to the community; men who lived not to gain advantage
for themselves, but to meet the solemn obligations which had
been laid on them by the very fact that they were privileged.
From them the country would get its leadership; to them it
could look for the higher values—of thought, of conduct, of
personal deportment—to give it strength and virtue.

Lee embodied the noblest elements of this aristocratic 6
ideal. Through him, the landed nobility justified itself. For
four years, the Southern states had fought a desperate war

to uphold the ideals for which Lee stood. In the end, it almost seemed as if the Confederacy fought for Lee; as if he himself was the Confederacy . . . the best thing that the way of life for which the Confederacy stood could ever have to offer. He had passed into legend before Appomattox. Thousands of tired, underfed, poorly clothed Confederate soldiers, long since past the simple enthusiasm of the early days of the struggle, somehow considered Lee the symbol of everything for which they had been willing to die. But they could not quite put this feeling into words. If the Lost Cause, sanctified by so much heroism and so many deaths, had a living justification, its justification was General Lee.

Grant, the son of a tanner on the Western frontier, was everything Lee was not. He had come up the hard way, and embodied nothing in particular except the eternal toughness and sinewy fiber of the men who grew up beyond the mountains. He was one of a body of men who owed reverence and obeisance to no one, who were self-reliant to a fault, who cared hardly anything for the past but who had a sharp eye for the future. 7

These frontier men were the precise opposites of the tidewater aristocrats. Back of them, in the great surge that had taken people over the Alleghenies and into the opening Western country, there was a deep, implicit dissatisfaction with a past that had settled into grooves. They stood for democracy, not from any reasoned conclusion about the proper ordering of human society, but simply because they had grown up in the middle of democracy and knew how it worked. Their society might have privileges, but they would be privileges each man had won for himself. Forms and patterns meant nothing. No man was born to anything, except perhaps to a chance to show how far he could rise. Life was competition. 8

Yet along with this feeling had come a deep sense of belonging to a national community. The Westerner who developed a farm, opened a shop or set up in business as a trader, could hope to prosper only as his own community prospered—and his community ran from the Atlantic to the Pacific and from Canada down to Mexico. If the land was settled, with towns 9 and highways and accessible markets, he could better himself. He saw his fate in terms of the nation's own destiny. As its horizons expanded, so did his. He had, in other words, an acute dollars-and-cents stake in the continued growth and development of his country.

And that, perhaps, is where the contrast between Grant and Lee becomes most striking. The Virginia aristocrat, inevitably, saw himself in relation to his own region. He lived in a static society which could endure almost anything except change. Instinctively, his first loyalty would go to the locality in which that society existed. He would fight to the limit of endurance to defend it, because in defending it he was defending everything that gave his own life its deepest meaning.   10

The Westerner, on the other hand, would fight with an equal tenacity for the broader concept of society. He fought so because everything he lived by was tied to growth, expansion, and a constantly widening horizon. What he lived by would survive or fall with the nation itself. He could not possibly stand by unmoved in the face of an attempt to destroy the Union. He would combat it with everything he had, because he could only see it as an effort to cut the ground out from under his feet.   11

So Grant and Lee were in complete contrast, representing two diametrically opposed elements in American life. Grant was the modern man emerging; beyond him, ready to come on the stage, was the great age of steel and machinery, of crowded cities and a restless, burgeoning vitality. Lee might have ridden down from the old age of chivalry, lance in hand, silken banner fluttering over his head. Each man was the perfect champion of his cause, drawing both his strengths and his weaknesses from the people he led.   12

Yet it was not all contrast, after all. Different as they were— in background, in personality, in underlying aspiration—these two great soldiers had much in common. Under everything else, they were marvelous fighters. Furthermore, their fighting qualities were really very much alike.   13

Each man had, to begin with, the great virtue of utter tenacity and fidelity. Grant fought his way down the Mississippi   14

Valley in spite of acute personal discouragement and profound military handicaps. Lee hung on in the trenches at Petersburg after hope itself had died. In each man there was an indomitable quality . . . the born fighter's refusal to give us as long as he can still remain on his feet and lift his two fists.

Daring and resourcefulness they had, too; the ability to think faster and move faster than the enemy. These were the qualities which gave Lee the dazzling campaigns of Second Manassas and Chancellorsville and won Vicksburg for Grant. 15

Lastly, and perhaps greatest of all, there was the ability, at the end, to turn quickly from war to peace once the fighting was over. Out of the way these two men behaved at Appomattox came the possibility of a peace of reconciliation. It was a possibility not wholly realized, in the years to come, but which did, in the end, help the two sections to become one nation again . . . after a war whose bitterness might have seemed to make such a reunion wholly impossible. No part of either man's life became him more than the part he played in their brief meeting in the McLean house at Appomattox. Their behavior there put all succeeding generations of Americans in their debt. Two great Americans, Grant and Lee—very different, yet under everything very much alike. Their encounter at Appomattox was one of the great moments of American history. 16

For Study and Discussion

QUESTIONS ABOUT PURPOSE

1. Catton's title identifies his essay as a strict comparison of two men—opposing military generals in the same war. What is his primary purpose in comparing them—to compare their biographies, their values, their military abilities, or their causes?
2. Catton's subtitle suggests that his purpose is to study contrasts. Does his analysis suggest that one man was superior to the other? Explain your answer.

QUESTIONS ABOUT AUDIENCE

1. How much knowledge does Catton assume his readers have about the Civil War? Do they need to know the specific details of

the battles of Second Manassas, Chancellorsville, and Vicksburg to understand this essay? Explain your answer.

2. Although Catton's title is "Grant and Lee," he presents Lee first and Grant second. Why? Does he assume his readers know more about Lee, are more fascinated by Lee, or prefer to read about the loser first and the winner second?

QUESTIONS ABOUT STRATEGIES

1. How does Catton arrange the points of his contrast? To what extent does he provide equal treatment of each point?
2. One strategy Catton uses to characterize his two subjects is to compare their values to the values of people in other times and places. If Lee embodies the values of chivalry, knighthood, and aristocracy, what values does Grant embody?

For Writing and Research

1. *Analyze* the strategies Catton uses to illustrate how Grant was a good winner and Lee was a good loser.
2. *Practice* by comparing two people who share many experiences and characteristics. Consider such points as dress, behavior, education, work, and style as you try to contrast the values each character embodies.
3. *Argue* that in the final analysis military leaders show more similarities than differences.
4. *Synthesize* the research on Grant and Lee's attitudes toward slavery. Then use this evidence to explain their position on what most historians consider the major cause of the Civil War.

DEBORAH TANNEN

Deborah Tannen was born in 1945 in Brooklyn, New York, and was educated at the State University of New York at Binghamton, Wayne State University, and the University of California at Berkeley. She has taught English at the Hellenic American Union in Athens, Greece; Herbert H. Lehman College of the City University of New York; and Georgetown University. She has contributed articles on language to numerous scholarly books, including *Language and Social Identity* (1982) and *Languages and Linguistics in Context* (1986), and she has written several books on language and gender, including *Gender and Discourse* (1994), *Talking from 9 to 5* (1994), and *You're Wearing That? Understanding Mothers and Daughters in Conversation* (2005). Tannen's *That's Not What I Meant! How Conversational Style Makes or Breaks Your Relations with Others* (1986) attracted national attention because of its engaging study of the breakdown of communication between the sexes. In "Rapport-Talk and Report-Talk," excerpted from *You Just Don't Understand* (1989), Tannen compares the public and private conversational styles of men and women.

Rapport-Talk and Report-Talk

WHO TALKS MORE, then, women or men? The seemingly   1
contradictory evidence is reconciled by the difference between what I call *public* and *private speaking*. More men feel comfortable doing "public speaking," while more women feel comfortable doing "private" speaking. Another way of capturing these differences is by using the terms *report-talk* and *rapport-talk*.

For most women, the language of conversation is primarily   2
a language of rapport: a way of establishing connections and
negotiating relationships. Emphasis is placed on displaying
similarities and matching experiences. From childhood, girls
criticize peers who try to stand out or appear better than
others. People feel their closest connections at home, or in
settings where they *feel* at home—with one or a few people
they feel close to and comfortable with—in other words,

---

*To men, talk is for information. To women,
talk is for interaction.*

---

during private speaking. But even the most public situations
can be approached like private speaking.

For most men, talk is primarily a means to preserve inde-   3
pendence and negotiate and maintain status in a hierarchical
social order. This is done by exhibiting knowledge and skill,
and by holding center stage through verbal performance
such as story-telling, joking, or imparting information. From
childhood, men learn to use talking as a way to get and keep
attention. So they are more comfortable speaking in larger
groups made up of people they know less well—in the broadest sense, "public speaking." But even the most private situations can be approached like public speaking, more like
giving a report than establishing rapport.

PRIVATE SPEAKING: THE WORDY WOMAN AND THE MUTE MAN

What is the source of the stereotype that women talk a lot?   4
Dale Spender suggests that most people feel instinctively (if
not consciously) that women, like children, should be seen
and not heard, so any amount of talk from them seems like
too much. Studies have shown that if women and men talk
equally in a group, people think the women talked more. So
there is truth to Spender's view. But another explanation is

that men think women talk a lot because they hear women talking in situations where men would not: on the telephone; or in social situations with friends, when they are not discussing topics that men find inherently interesting; or, like the couple at the women's group, at home alone—in other words, in private speaking.

Home is the setting for an American icon that features the   5
silent man and the talkative woman. And this icon, which grows out of the different goals and habits I have been describing, explains why the complaint most often voiced by women about the men with whom they are intimate is "He doesn't talk to me"—and the second most frequent is "He doesn't listen to me."

A woman who wrote to Ann Landers is typical: 6

> *My husband never speaks to me when he comes home from work. When I ask, "How did everything go today?" he says, "Rough . . ." or "It's a jungle out there." (We live in Jersey and he works in New York City.)*
>
> *It's a different story when we have guests or go visiting. Paul is the gabbiest guy in the crowd—a real spellbinder. He comes up with the most interesting stories. People hang on every word. I think to myself, "Why doesn't he ever tell me these things?"*
>
> *This has been going on for 38 years. Paul started to go quiet on me after 10 years of marriage. I could never figure out why. Can you solve the mystery?*
>   *—The Invisible Woman*

Ann Landers suggests that the husband may not want to talk because he is tired when he comes home from work. Yet women who work come home tired too, and they are nonetheless eager to tell their partners or friends everything that happened to them during the day and what these fleeting, daily dramas made them think and feel.

Sources as lofty as studies conducted by psychologists, as   7
down to earth as letters written to advice columnists, and as sophisticated as movies and plays come up with the same insight: Men's silence at home is a disappointment to women.

Again and again, women complain, "He seems to have everything to say to everyone else, and nothing to say to me."

The film *Divorce American Style* opens with a conversation in which Debbie Reynolds is claiming that she and Dick Van Dyke don't communicate, and he is protesting that he tells her everything that's on his mind. The doorbell interrupts their quarrel, and husband and wife compose themselves before opening the door to greet their guests with cheerful smiles. 8

Behind closed doors, many couples are having conversations like this. Like the character played by Debbie Reynolds, women feel men don't communicate. Like the husband played by Dick Van Dyke, men feel wrongly accused. How can she be convinced that he doesn't tell her anything, while he is equally convinced he tells her everything that's on his mind? How can women and men have such different ideas about the same conversations? 9

When something goes wrong, people look around for a source to blame: either the person they are trying to communicate with ("You're demanding, stubborn, self-centered") or the group that the other person belongs to ("All women are demanding"; "All men are self-centered"). Some generous-minded people blame the relationship ("We just can't communicate"). But underneath, or overlaid on these types of blame cast outward, most people believe that something is wrong with them. 10

If individual people or particular relationships were to blame, there wouldn't be so many different people having the same problems. The real problem is conversational style. Women and men have different ways of talking. Even with the best intentions, trying to settle the problem through talk can only make things worse if it is ways of talking that are causing trouble in the first place. 11

BEST FRIENDS

Once again, the seeds of women's and men's styles are sown in the ways they learn to use language while growing up. In our culture, most people, but especially women, look to their 12 closest relationships as havens in a hostile world. The center of a little girl's social life is her best friend. Girls' friendships are made and maintained by telling secrets. For grown women too, the essence of friendship is talk, telling each other what they're thinking and feeling, and what happened that day: who was at the bus stop, who called, what they said, how that made them feel. When asked who their best friends are, most women name other women they talk to regularly. When asked the same question, most men will say it's their wives. After that, many men name other men with whom they do things such as play tennis or baseball (but never just sit and talk) or a chum from high school whom they haven't spoken to in a year.

When Debbie Reynolds complained that Dick Van Dyke   13 didn't tell her anything, and he protested that he did, both were right. She felt he didn't tell her anything because he didn't tell her the fleeting thoughts and feelings he experienced throughout the day—the kind of talk she would have with her best friend. He didn't tell her these things because to him they didn't seem like anything to tell. He told her anything that seemed important—anything he would tell his friends.

Men and women often have very different ideas of what's   14 important—and at what point "important" topics should be raised. A woman told me, with lingering incredulity, of a conversation with her boyfriend. Knowing he had seen his friend Oliver, she asked, "What's new with Oliver?" He replied, "Nothing." But later in the conversation it came out that Oliver and his girlfriend had decided to get married. "That's nothing?" the woman gasped in frustration and disbelief.

For men, "Nothing" may be a ritual response at the start of   15 a conversation. A college woman missed her brother but rarely called him because she found it difficult to get talk going. A typical conversation began with her asking, "What's up with you?" and his replying, "Nothing." Hearing his "Nothing" as meaning "There is nothing personal I want to talk about," she supplied talk by filling him in on her news and eventually hung up in frustration. But when she thought back, she remembered that later in the conversation he had mumbled, "Christie

and I got into another fight." This came so late and so low that
she didn't pick up on it. And he was probably equally frustrated
that she didn't.

Many men honestly do not know what women want, and   16
women honestly do not know why men find what they want
so hard to comprehend and deliver.

"TALK TO ME!"

Women's dissatisfaction with men's silence at home is cap-   17
tured in the stock cartoon setting of a breakfast table at
which a husband and wife are sitting: He's reading a newspaper; she's glaring at the back of the newspaper. In a Dagwood
strip, Blondie complains, "Every morning all he sees is the
newspaper! I'll bet you don't even know I'm here!" Dagwood
reassures her, "Of course I know you're here. You're my
wonderful wife and I love you very much." With this, he un-
seeingly pats the paw of the family dog, which the wife has
put in her place before leaving the room. The cartoon strip
shows that Blondie is justified in feeling like the woman who
wrote to Ann Landers: invisible.

Another cartoon shows a husband opening a newspaper   18
and asking his wife, "Is there anything you would like to say
to me before I begin reading the newspaper?" The reader
knows that there isn't—but that as soon as he begins reading
the paper, she will think of something. The cartoon highlights the difference in what women and men think talk is for:
To him, talk is for information. So when his wife interrupts
his reading, it must be to inform him of something that he
needs to know. This being the case, she might as well tell him
what she thinks he needs to know before he starts reading.
But to her, talk is for interaction. Telling things is a way to
show involvement, and listening is a way to show interest and
caring. It is not an odd coincidence that she always thinks of
things to tell him when he is reading. She feels the need for
verbal interaction most keenly when he is (unaccountably,
from her point of view) buried in the newspaper instead of
talking to her.

Yet another cartoon shows a wedding cake that has, on   19
top, in place of the plastic statues of bride and groom in
tuxedo and gown, a breakfast scene in which an unshaven
husband reads a newspaper across the table from his disgrun-
tled wife. The cartoon reflects the enormous gulf between
the romantic expectations of marriage represented by the
plastic couple in traditional wedding costume, and the often
disappointing reality represented by the two sides of the
newspaper at the breakfast table—the front, which he is reading, and the back, at which she is glaring.

These cartoons, and many others on the same theme, are   20
funny because people recognize their own experience in
them. What's not funny is that many women are deeply hurt
when men don't talk to them at home, and many men are
deeply frustrated by feeling they have disappointed their
partners, without understanding how they failed or how else
they could have behaved.

Some men are further frustrated because, as one put it,   21
"When in the world am I supposed to read the morning
paper?" If many women are incredulous that many men do not
exchange personal information with their friends, this man is
incredulous that many women do not bother to read the
morning paper. To him, reading the paper is an essential part
of his morning ritual, and his whole day is awry if he doesn't
get to read it. In his words, reading the newspaper in the
morning is as important to him as putting on makeup in the
morning is to many women he knows. Yet many women,
he observed, either don't subscribe to a paper or don't read it
until they get home in the evening. "I find this very puzzling,"
he said. "I can't tell you how often I have picked up a woman's
morning newspaper from her front door in the evening and
handed it to her when she opened the door for me."

To this man (and I am sure many others), a woman who ob-   22
jects to his reading the morning paper is trying to keep him
from doing something essential and harmless. It's a violation of
his independence—his freedom of action. But when a woman
who expects her partner to talk to her is disappointed that he
doesn't, she perceives his behavior as a failure of intimacy: He's

keeping things from her; he's lost interest in her; he's pulling away. A woman I will call Rebecca, who is generally quite happily married, told me that this is the one source of serious dissatisfaction with her husband, Stuart. Her term for his taciturnity is *stinginess of spirit*. She tells him what she is thinking, and he listens silently. She asks him what he is thinking, and he takes a long time to answer, "I don't know." In frustration she challenges, "Is there nothing on your mind?"

For Rebecca, who is accustomed to expressing her fleeting   23
thoughts and opinions as they come to her, *saying* nothing means *thinking* nothing. But Stuart does not assume that his passing thoughts are worthy of utterance. He is not in the habit of uttering his fleeting ruminations, so just as Rebecca "naturally" speaks her thoughts, he "naturally" dismisses his as soon as they occur to him. Speaking them would give them more weight and significance than he feels they merit. All her life she has had practice in verbalizing her thoughts and feelings in private conversations with people she is close to; all his life he has had practice in dismissing his and keeping them to himself. . . .

PUBLIC SPEAKING: THE TALKATIVE MAN AND THE SILENT WOMAN

So far I have been discussing the private scenes in which   24
many men are silent and many women are talkative. But there are other scenes in which the roles are reversed. Returning to Rebecca and Stuart, we saw that when they are home alone, Rebecca's thoughts find their way into words effortlessly, whereas Stuart finds he can't come up with anything to say. The reverse happens when they are in other situations. For example, at a meeting of the neighborhood council or the parents' association at their children's school, it is Stuart who stands up and speaks. In that situation, it is Rebecca who is silent, her tongue tied by an acute awareness of all the negative reactions people could have to what she might say, all the mistakes she might make in trying to express her ideas. If she musters her courage and prepares to say something, she

needs time to formulate it and then waits to be recognized by the chair. She cannot just jump up and start talking the way Stuart and some other men can.

Eleanor Smeal, president of the Fund for the Feminist Majority, was a guest on a call-in radio talk show, discussing abortion. No subject could be of more direct concern to women, yet during the hour-long show, all the callers except two were men. Diane Rehm, host of a radio talk show, expresses puzzlement that although the audience for her show is evenly split between women and men, 90 percent of the callers to the show are men. I am convinced that the reason is not that women are uninterested in the subjects discussed on the show. I would wager that women listeners are bringing up the subjects they heard on *The Diane Rehm Show* to their friends and family over lunch, tea, and dinner. But fewer of them call in because to do so would be putting themselves on display, claiming public attention for what they have to say, catapulting themselves onto center stage.

I myself have been the guest on innumerable radio and television talk shows. Perhaps I am unusual in being completely at ease in this mode of display. But perhaps I am not unusual at all, because, although I am comfortable in the role of invited expert, I have never called in to a talk show I was listening to, although I have often had ideas to contribute. When I am the guest, my position of authority is granted before I begin to speak. Were I to call in, I would be claiming that right on my own. I would have to establish my credibility by explaining who I am, which might seem self-aggrandizing, or not explain who I am and risk having my comments ignored or not valued. For similar reasons, though I am comfortable lecturing to groups numbering in the thousands, I rarely ask questions following another lecturer's talk, unless I know both the subject and the group very well.

My own experience and that of talk show hosts seems to hold a clue to the difference in women's and men's attitudes toward talk: Many men are more comfortable than most women in using talk to claim attention. And this difference lies at the heart of the distinction between report-talk and rapport-talk.

REPORT-TALK IN PRIVATE

Report-talk, or what I am calling public speaking, does not arise only in the literally public situation of formal speeches delivered to a listening audience. The more people there are in a conversation, the less well you know them, and the more status differences among them, the more a conversation is *like* public speaking or report-talk. The fewer the people, the more intimately you know them, and the more equal their status, the more it is like private speaking or rapport-talk. Furthermore, women feel a situation is more "public"—in the sense that they have to be on good behavior—if there are men present, except perhaps for family members. Yet even in families, the mother and children may feel their home to be "backstage" when Father is not home, "on-stage" when he is: Many children are instructed to be on good behavior when Daddy is home. This may be because he is not home often, or because Mother—or Father—doesn't want the children to disturb him when he is. 28

The difference between public and private speaking also explains the stereotype that women don't tell jokes. Although some women are great raconteurs who can keep a group spellbound by recounting jokes and funny stories, there are fewer such personalities among women than among men. Many women who do tell jokes to large groups of people come from ethnic backgrounds in which verbal performance is highly valued. For example, many of the great women stand-up comics, such as Fanny Brice and Joan Rivers, came from Jewish backgrounds. 29

Although it's not true that women don't tell jokes, it is true that many women are less likely than men to tell jokes in large groups, especially groups including men. So it's not surprising that men get the impression that women never tell jokes at all. Folklorist Carol Mitchell studied joke telling on a college campus. She found that men told most of their jokes to other men, but they also told many jokes to mixed groups and to women. Women, however, told most of their jokes to other women, fewer to men, and very few to groups that included men as well as women. Men preferred and were more 30 likely to tell jokes when they had an audience: at least two, often four or more. Women preferred a small audience of one or two, rarely more than three. Unlike men, they were reluctant to tell jokes in front of people they didn't know well. Many women flatly refused to tell jokes they knew if there were four or more in the group, promising to tell them later in private. Men never refused the invitation to tell jokes.

All of Mitchell's results fit in with the picture I have been   31
drawing of public and private speaking. In a situation in which there are more people in the audience, more men, or more strangers, joke telling, like any other form of verbal performance, requires speakers to claim center stage and prove their abilities. These are the situations in which many women are reluctant to talk. In a situation that is more private, because the audience is small, familiar, and perceived to be members of a community (for example, other women), they are more likely to talk.

The idea that telling jokes is a kind of self-display does not   32
imply that it is selfish or self-centered. The situation of joke telling illustrates that status and connection entail each other. Entertaining others is a way of establishing connections with them, and telling jokes can be a kind of gift giving, where the joke is a gift that brings pleasure to receivers. The key issue is asymmetry: One person is the teller and the others are the audience. If these roles are later exchanged—for example, if the joke telling becomes a round in which one person after another takes the role of teller—then there is symmetry on the broad scale, if not in the individual act. However, if women habitually take the role of appreciative audience and never take the role of joke teller, the asymmetry of the individual joke telling is diffused through the larger interaction as well. This is a hazard for women. A hazard for men is that continually telling jokes can be distancing. This is the effect felt by a man who complained that when he talks to his father on the phone, all his father does is tell him jokes. An extreme instance of a similar phenomenon is the class clown, who, according to teachers, is nearly always a boy.

RAPPORT-TALK IN PUBLIC

Just as conversations that take place at home among friends 33
can be like public speaking, even a public address can be like
private speaking: for example, by giving a lecture full of personal examples and stories.

At the executive committee of a fledgling professional 34
organization, the outgoing president, Fran, suggested that
the organization adopt the policy of having presidents deliver
a presidential address. To explain and support her proposal,
she told a personal anecdote: Her cousin was the president of
a more established professional organization at the time that
Fran held the same position in this one. Fran's mother had
been talking to her cousin's mother on the telephone. Her
cousin's mother told Fran's mother that her daughter was
preparing her presidential address, and she asked when Fran's
presidential address was scheduled to be. Fran was embarrassed to admit to her mother that she was not giving one.
This made her wonder whether the organization's professional identity might not be enhanced if it emulated the more
established organizations.

Several men on the committee were embarrassed by Fran's 35
reference to her personal situation and were not convinced
by her argument. It seemed to them not only irrelevant but
unseemly to talk about her mother's telephone conversations
at an executive committee meeting. Fran had approached the
meeting—a relatively public context—as an extension of the
private kind. Many women's tendency to use personal experience and examples, rather than abstract argumentation, can
be understood from the perspective of their orientation to
language as it is used in private speaking.

A study by Celia Roberts and Tom Jupp of a faculty meeting 36
at a secondary school in England found that the women's arguments did not carry weight with their male colleagues because
they tended to use their own experience as evidence, or argue
about the effect of policy on individual students. The men at
the meeting argued from a completely different perspective,
making categorical statements about right and wrong.

The same discussion is found in discussions at home. A man   37
told me that he felt critical of what he perceived as his wife's
lack of logic. For example, he recalled a conversation in which
he had mentioned an article he had read in *The New York
Times* claiming that today's college students are not as idealistic as students were in the 1960s. He was inclined to accept
this claim. His wife questioned it, supporting her argument
with the observation that her niece and her niece's friends were
very idealistic indeed. He was incredulous and scornful of her
faulty reasoning; it was obvious to him that a single personal
example is neither evidence nor argumentation—it's just anecdote. It did not occur to him that he was dealing with a different logical system, rather than a lack of logic.

The logic this woman was employing was making sense of   38
the world as a more private endeavor—observing and inte-
grating her personal experience and drawing connections to
the experiences of others. The logic the husband took for
granted was a more public endeavor—more like gathering information, conducting a survey, or devising arguments by
rules of formal logic as one might in doing research.

Another man complained about what he and his friends call   39
women's "shifting sands" approach to discussion. These men
feel that whereas they try to pursue an argument logically, step
by step, until it is settled, women continually change course in
mid-stream. He pointed to the short excerpt from *Divorce
American Style* quoted above as a case in point. It seemed to
him that when Debbie Reynolds said, "I can't argue now. I
have to take the French bread out of the oven," she was evad-
ing the argument because she had made an accusation—"All
you do is criticize"—that she could not support.

This man also offered an example from his own experi-   40
ence. His girlfriend had told him of a problem she had
because her boss wanted her to do one thing and she wanted
to do another. Taking the boss's view for the sake of argumentation, he pointed out a negative consequence that
would result if she did what she wanted. She countered that
the same negative consequence would result if she did what
the boss wanted. He complained that she was shifting over to

the other field of battle—what would happen if she followed her boss's will—before they had made headway with the first—what would happen if she followed her own.

For Study and Discussion

QUESTIONS ABOUT PURPOSE

1. What does Tannen want to demonstrate about the relationship between communication failure and conversational style?
2. How do size (the number of people) and status (those people claiming authority) contribute to Tannen's comparison of rapport-talk and report-talk?

QUESTIONS ABOUT AUDIENCE

1. What assumptions does Tannen make about the probable gender of most of her readers?
2. How does Tannen assume her audience can benefit from her analysis?

QUESTIONS ABOUT STRATEGIES

1. How does Tannen use advice columns, movies, and cartoons to illustrate the problems of domestic communication?
2. How does Tannen use her own experience as a lecturer to compare the way men and women talk in public?

For Writing and Research

1. *Analyze* how Tannen combines the divided and alternating patterns to develop her comparison of conversational styles.
2. *Practice* by comparing the way you talk—diction, tone, and style—in private and in public.
3. *Argue* that it is difficult, if not impossible, to change conversational styles because they depend on individual skill (personality) rather than social behavior (learned habits).
4. *Synthesize* some of the other research Tannen has published. Then use this evidence to demonstrate that men use personal experience and women make categorical assertions in conversation.

LAURA BOHANNAN

Laura Bohannan was born in New York City in 1922 and was educated at Smith College, the University of Arizona, and Oxford University. She has taught anthropology at Northwestern University, the University of Chicago, and the University of Illinois, Chicago Circle. She has held several fellowships to conduct research in East Africa that has resulted in books such as *The Tiv of Central Nigeria* (1953) and *A Sourcebook on Tiv Religion* (1972). In "Shakespeare in the Bush," reprinted from *Ants, Indians and Little Dinosaurs,* edited by A. Ternes (1975), Bohannan compares her version of *Hamlet* with the interpretation of the elders of an African tribe.

Shakespeare in the Bush
An American Anthropologist Set Out to Study the Tiv of West Africa and Was Taught the True Meaning of Hamlet

JUST BEFORE I left Oxford for the Tiv in West Africa, conversation turned to the season at Stratford. "You Americans," said a friend, "often have difficulty with Shakespeare. He was, after all, a very English poet, and one can easily misinterpret the universal by misunderstanding the particular."   1

I protested that human nature is pretty much the same the whole world over; at least the general plot and motivation of the greater tragedies would always be clear—everywhere— although some details of custom might have to be explained and difficulties of translation might produce other slight changes. To end an argument we could not conclude, my friend gave me a copy of *Hamlet* to study in the African   2 bush: it would, he hoped, lift my mind above its primitive surroundings, and possibly I might, by prolonged meditation, achieve the grace of correct interpretation.

It was my second field trip to that African tribe, and I thought   3
myself ready to live in one of its remote sections—an area difficult to cross even on foot. I eventually settled on the hillock of a very knowledgeable old man, the head of a homestead

---

*Before the end of the second month, grace
descended on me. I was quite sure that*
Hamlet *had only one possible interpretation,
and that one universally obvious.*

---

of some hundred and forty people, all of whom were either his close relatives or their wives and children. Like the other elders of the vicinity, the old man spent most of his time performing ceremonies seldom seen these days in the more accessible parts of the tribe. I was delighted. Soon there would be three months of enforced isolation and leisure, between the harvest that takes place just before the rising of the swamps and the clearing of new farms when the water goes down. Then, I thought, they would have even more time to perform ceremonies and explain them to me.

I was quite mistaken. Most of the ceremonies demanded   4
the presence of elders from several homesteads. As the swamps rose, the old men found it too difficult to walk from one homestead to the next, and the ceremonies gradually ceased. As the swamps rose even higher, all activities from one came to an end. The women brewed beer from maize and millet. Men, women, and children sat on their hillocks and drank it.

People began to drink at dawn. By midmorning the whole   5
homestead was singing, dancing, and drumming. When it rained, people had to sit inside their huts: there they drank and sang or they drank and told stories. In any case, by noon

or before, I either had to join the party or retire to my own hut and my books. "One does not discuss serious matters when there is beer. Come, drink with us." Since I lacked their capacity for the thick native beer, I spent more and more time with *Hamlet*. Before the end of the second month, grace descended on me. I was quite sure that *Hamlet* had only one possible interpretation, and that one universally obvious.

Early every morning, in the hope of having some serious talk before the beer party, I used to call on the old man at his reception hut—a circle of posts supporting a thatched roof above a low mud wall to keep out wind and rain. One day I crawled through the low doorway and found most of the men of the homestead sitting huddled in their ragged cloths on stools, low plank beds, and reclining chairs, warming themselves against the chill of the rain around a smoky fire. In the center were three pots of beer. The party had started. 6

The old man greeted me cordially. "Sit down and drink." I accepted a large calabash full of beer, poured some into a small drinking gourd, and tossed it down. Then I poured some more into the same gourd for the man second in seniority to my host before I handed my calabash over to a young man for further distribution. Important people shouldn't ladle beer themselves. 7

"It is better like this," the old man said, looking at me approvingly and plucking at the thatch that had caught in my hair. "You should sit and drink with us more often. Your servants tell me that when you are not with us, you sit inside your hut looking at a paper." 8

The old man was acquainted with four kinds of "papers": tax receipts, bride price receipts, court fee receipts, and letters. The messenger who brought him letters from the chief used them mainly as a badge of office, for he always knew what was in them and told the old man. Personal letters for the few who had relatives in the government or mission stations were kept until someone went to a large market where there was a letter writer and reader. Since my arrival, letters were brought to me to be read. A few men also brought me bride price receipts, privately, with requests to change the 9 figures to a higher sum. I found moral arguments were of no avail, since in-laws are fair game, and the technical hazards of forgery difficult to explain to an illiterate people. I did not wish them to think me silly enough to look at any such papers for days on end, and I hastily explained that my "paper" was one of the "things of long ago" of my country.

"Ah," said the old man. "Tell us." 10

I protested that I was not a storyteller. Storytelling is a 11 skilled art among them; their standards are high, and the audiences critical—and vocal in their criticism. I protested in vain. This morning they wanted to hear a story while they drank. They threatened to tell me no more stories until I told them one of mine. Finally, the old man promised that no one would criticize my style "for we know you are struggling with our language." "But," put in one of the elders, "you must explain what we do not understand, as we do when we tell you our stories." Realizing that here was my chance to prove *Hamlet* universally intelligible, I agreed.

The old man handed me some more beer to help me on 12 with my storytelling. Men filled their long wooden pipes and knocked coals from the fire to place in the pipe bowls; then, puffing contentedly, they sat back to listen. I began in the proper style, "Not yesterday, not yesterday, but long ago, a thing occurred. One night three men were keeping watch outside the homestead of the great chief, when suddenly they saw the former chief approach them."

"Why was he no longer their chief?" 13

"He was dead," I explained. "That is why they were trou- 14 bled and afraid when they saw him."

"Impossible," began one of the elders, handing his pipe 15 on to his neighbor, who interrupted, "Of course it wasn't the dead chief. It was an omen sent by a witch. Go on."

Slightly shaken, I continued. "One of these three was a 16 man who knew things"—the closest translation for scholar, but unfortunately it also meant witch. The second elder looked triumphantly at the first. "So we spoke to the dead chief saying, 'Tell us what we must do so you may rest in your grave,' but the dead chief did not answer. He vanished, and they could see him no more. Then the man who knew things—his name was Horatio—said this event was the affair of the dead chief's son, Hamlet."

There was a general shaking of heads round the circle. "Had the dead chief no living brothers? Or was this son the chief?" 17

"No," I replied. "That is, he had one living brother who became the chief when the elder brother died." 18

The old men muttered: such omens were matters for chiefs and elders, not for youngsters; no good could come of going behind a chief's back; clearly Horatio was not a man who knew things. 19

"Yes, he was," I insisted, shooing a chicken away from my beer. "In our country the son is next to the father. The dead chief's younger brother had become the great chief. He had also married his elder brother's widow only about a month after the funeral." 20

"He did well," the old man beamed and announced to the others, "I told you that if we knew more about Europeans, we would find they really were very like us. In our country also," he added to me, "the younger brother marries the elder brother's widow and becomes the father of his children. Now, if your uncle, who married your widowed mother, is your father's full brother, then he will be a real father to you. Did Hamlet's father and uncle have one mother?" 21

His question barely penetrated my mind; I was too upset and thrown too far off balance by having one of the most important elements of *Hamlet* knocked straight out of the picture. Rather uncertainly I said that I thought they had the same mother, but I wasn't sure—the story didn't say. The old man told me severely that these genealogical details made all the difference and that when I got home I must ask the elders about it. He shouted out the door to one of his younger wives to bring his goatskin bag. 22

Determined to save what I could of the mother motif, I took a deep breath and began again. "The son Hamlet was very sad because his mother had married again so quickly. 23

There was no need for her to do so, and it is our custom for a widow not to go to her next husband until she has mourned for two years."

"Two years is too long," objected the wife, who had ap- 24 peared with the old man's battered goatskin bag. "Who will hoe your farms for you while you have no husband?"

"Hamlet," I retorted without thinking, "was old enough 25 to hoe his mother's farms himself. There was no need for her to remarry." No one looked convinced. I gave up. "His mother and the great chief told Hamlet not to be sad, for the great chief himself would be a father to Hamlet. Furthermore, Hamlet would be the next chief: therefore he must stay to learn the things of a chief. Hamlet agreed to remain, and all the rest went off to drink beer."

While I paused, perplexed at how to render Hamlet's 26 disgusted soliloquy to an audience convinced that Claudius and Gertrude had behaved in the best possible manner, one of the younger men asked me who had married the other wives of the dead chief.

"He had no other wives," I told him. 27

"But a chief must have many wives! How else can he brew 28 beer and prepare food for all his guests?"

I said firmly that in our country even chiefs had only one 29 wife, that they had servants to do their work, and that they paid them from tax money.

It was better, they returned, for a chief to have many wives 30 and sons who would help him hoe his farms and feed his people; then everyone loved the chief who gave much and took nothing—taxes were a bad thing.

I agreed with the last comment, but for the rest fell back 31 on their favorite way of fobbing off my questions: "That is the way it is done, so that is how we do it."

I decided to skip the soliloquy. Even if Claudius was here 32 thought quite right to marry his brother's widow, there remained the poison motif, and I knew they would disapprove of fratricide. More hopefully I resumed, "That night Hamlet kept watch with the three who had seen his dead father. The dead chief again appeared, and although the others were afraid, Hamlet followed his dead father off to one side. When they were alone, Hamlet's dead father spoke."

"Omens can't talk!" The old man was emphatic.   33

"Hamlet's dead father wasn't an omen. Seeing him might   34
have been an omen, but he was not." My audience looked as confused as I sounded. "It *was* Hamlet's dead father. It was a thing we call a 'ghost.'" I had to use the English word, for unlike many of the neighboring tribes, these people didn't believe in the survival after death of any individuating part of the personality.

"What is a 'ghost'? An omen?"   35

"No, a 'ghost' is someone who is dead but who walks   36
around and can talk, and people can hear him and see him but not touch him."

They objected. "One can touch zombis."   37

"No, no! It was not a dead body the witches had animated   38
to sacrifice and eat. No one else made Hamlet's dead father walk. He did it himself."

"Dead men can't walk," protested my audience as one man.   39

I was quite willing to compromise. "A 'ghost' is the dead   40
man's shadow."

But again they objected. "Dead men cast no shadows."   41

"They do in my country," I snapped.   42

The old man quelled the babble of disbelief that arose   43
immediately and told me with that insincere, but courteous, agreement one extends to the fancies of the young, ignorant, and superstitious, "No doubt in your country the dead can also walk without being zombis." From the depths of his bag he produced a withered fragment of kola nut, bit off one end to show it wasn't poisoned, and handed me the rest as a peace offering.

"Anyhow," I resumed, "Hamlet's dead father said that his   44
own brother, the one who became chief, had poisoned him. He wanted Hamlet to avenge him. Hamlet believed this in his heart, for he did not like his father's brother." I took another swallow of beer. "In the country of the great chief, living in the same homestead, for it was a very large one, was an important elder who was often with the chief to advise and

help him. His name was Polonius. Hamlet was courting his daughter, but her father and her brother . . . [I cast hastily about for some tribal analogy] warned her not to let Hamlet visit her when she was alone on her farm, for he would be a great chief and so could not marry her."

"Why not?" asked the wife, who had settled down on the edge of the old man's chair. He frowned at her for asking stupid questions and growled, "They lived in the same homestead." 45

"That was not the reason," I informed them. "Polonius was a stranger who lived in the homestead because he helped the chief, not because he was a relative." 46

"Then why couldn't Hamlet marry her?" 47

"He could have," I explained, "but Polonius didn't think he would. After all, Hamlet was a man of great importance who ought to marry a chief's daughter, for in his country a man could have only one wife. Polonius was afraid that if Hamlet made love to his daughter, then no one else would give a high price for her." 48

"That might be true," remarked one of the shrewder elders, "but a chief's son would give his mistress's father enough presents and patronage to more than make up the difference. Polonius sounds like a fool to me." 49

"Many people think he was," I agreed. "Meanwhile Polonius sent his son Laertes off to Paris to learn the things of that country, for it was the homestead of a very great chief indeed. Because he was afraid that Laertes might waste a lot of money on beer and women and gambling, or get into trouble by fighting, he sent one of his servants to Paris secretly, to spy out what Laertes was doing. One day Hamlet came upon Polonius's daughter Ophelia. He behaved so oddly he frightened her. Indeed"—I was fumbling for words to express the dubious quality of Hamlet's madness—"the chief and many others had also noticed that when Hamlet talked one could understand the words but not what they meant. Many people thought that he had become mad." My audience suddenly became much more attentive. "The great chief wanted to know what was wrong with Hamlet, so he sent for two of Hamlet's age mates [school friends would 50 have taken long explanation] to talk to Hamlet and find out what troubled his heart. Hamlet, seeing that they had been bribed by the chief to betray him, told them nothing. Polonius, however, insisted that Hamlet was mad because he had been forbidden to see Ophelia, whom he loved."

"Why," inquired a bewildered voice, "should anyone   51
bewitch Hamlet on that account?"

"Bewitch him?"   52

"Yes, only witchcraft can make anyone mad, unless, of 53
course, one sees the beings that lurk in the forest."

I stopped being a storyteller, took out my notebook and 54
demanded to be told more about these two causes of madness. Even while they spoke and I jotted notes, I tried to calculate the effect of this new factor on the plot. Hamlet had not been exposed to the beings that lurk in the forests. Only his relatives in the male line could bewitch him. Barring relatives not mentioned by Shakespeare, it had to be Claudius who was attempting to harm him. And, of course, it was.

For the moment I staved off questions by saying that the 55
great chief also refused to believe that Hamlet was mad for the love of Ophelia and nothing else. "He was sure that something much more important was troubling Hamlet's heart."

"Now Hamlet's age mates," I continued, "had brought   56
with them a famous storyteller. Hamlet decided to have this man tell the chief and all his homestead a story about a man who had poisoned his brother because he desired his brother's wife and wished to be chief himself. Hamlet was sure the great chief could not hear the story without making a sign if he was indeed guilty, and then he would discover whether his dead father had told him the truth."

The old man interrupted, with deep cunning, "Why   57
should a father lie to his son?" he asked.

I hedged: "Hamlet wasn't sure that it really was his dead 58
father." It was impossible to say anything, in that language, about devil-inspired visions.

"You mean," he said, "it actually was an omen, and he   59
knew witches sometimes send false ones. Hamlet was a fool

not to go to one skilled in reading omens and divining the truth in the first place. A man-who-sees-the-truth could have told him how his father died, if he really had been poisoned, and if there was witchcraft in it; then Hamlet could have called the elders to settle the matter."

The shrewd elder ventured to disagree. "Because his fa- 60 ther's brother was a great chief, one-who-sees-the-truth might therefore have been afraid to tell it. I think it was for that reason that a friend of Hamlet's father—a witch and an elder—sent an omen so his friend's son would know. Was the omen true?"

"Yes," I said, abandoning ghosts and the devil; a witch- 61 sent omen it would have to be. "It was true, for when the storyteller was telling his tale before all the homestead, the great chief rose in fear. Afraid that Hamlet knew his secret he planned to have him killed."

The stage set of the next bit presented some difficulties of 62 translation. I began cautiously. "The great chief told Hamlet's mother to find out from her son what he knew. But because a woman's children are always first in her heart, he had the important elder Polonius hide behind a cloth that hung against the wall of Hamlet's mother's sleeping hut. Hamlet started to scold his mother for what she had done."

There was a shocked murmur from everyone. A man 63 should never scold his mother.

"She called out in fear, and Polonius moved behind the 64 cloth. Shouting, 'A rat!' Hamlet took his machete and slashed through the cloth." I paused for dramatic effect. "He had killed Polonius!"

The old men looked at each other in supreme disgust. 65 "That Polonius truly was a fool and a man who knew nothing! What child would not know enough to shout, 'It's me!'" With a pang, I remembered that these people are ardent hunters, always armed with bow, arrow, and machete; at the first rustle in the grass an arrow is aimed and ready, and the hunter shouts "Game!" If no human voice answers immediately, the arrow speeds on its way. Like a good hunter Hamlet had shouted, "A rat!"

I rushed in to save Polonius's reputation. "Polonius did   66
speak. Hamlet heard him. But he thought it was the chief and
wished to kill him to avenge his father. He had meant to kill
him earlier that evening. . . ." I broke down, unable to describe to these pagans, who had no belief in individual after-
life, the difference between dying at one's prayers and dying
"unhousell'd, disappointed, unaneled."

This time I had shocked my audience seriously. "For a man   67
to raise his hand against his father's brother and the one who
has become his father—that is a terrible thing. The elders
ought to let such a man be bewitched."

I nibbled at my kola nut in some perplexity, then pointed   68
out that after all the man had killed Hamlet's father.

"No," pronounced the old man, speaking less to me than   69
to the young men sitting behind the elders. "If your father's
brother has killed your father, you must appeal to your father's age mates; *they* may avenge him. No man may use violence against his senior relatives." Another thought struck
him. "But if his father's brother had indeed been wicked
enough to bewitch Hamlet and make him mad that would be
a good story indeed, for it would be his fault that Hamlet,
being mad, no longer had any sense and thus was ready to kill
his father's brother."

There was a murmur of applause. *Hamlet* was again a   70
good story to them, but it no longer seemed quite the same
story to me. As I thought over the coming complications of
plot and motive, I lost courage and decided to skim over dangerous ground quickly.

"The great chief," I went on, "was not sorry that Hamlet   71
had killed Polonius. It gave him a reason to send Hamlet
away, with his two treacherous age mates, with letters to a
chief of a far country, saying that Hamlet should be killed.
But Hamlet changed the writing on their papers, so that the
chief killed his age mates instead." I encountered a reproachful glare from one of the men whom I had told undetectable
forgery was not merely immoral but beyond human skill. I
looked the other way.

"Before Hamlet could return, Laertes came back for his 72 father's funeral. The great chief told him Hamlet had killed Polonius. Laertes swore to kill Hamlet because of this, and because his sister Ophelia, hearing her father had been killed by the man she loved, went mad and drowned in the river."

"Have you already forgotten what we told you?" The old 73 man was reproachful. "One cannot take vengeance on a madman; Hamlet killed Polonius in his madness. As for the girl, she not only went mad, she was drowned. Only witches can make people drown. Water itself can't hurt anything. It is merely something one drinks and bathes in."

I began to get cross. "If you don't like the story, I'll stop." 74

The old man made soothing noises and himself poured me 75 some more beer. "You tell the story well, and we are listening. But it is clear that the elders of your country have never told you what the story really means. No, don't interrupt! We believe you when you say your marriage customs are different, or your clothes and weapons. But people are the same everywhere; therefore, there are always witches and it is we, the elders, who know how witches work. We told you it was the great chief who wished to kill Hamlet, and now your own words have proved us right. Who were Ophelia's male relatives?"

"There were only her father and her brother." Hamlet was 76 clearly out of my hands.

"There must have been many more; this also you must ask of 77 your elders when you get back to your country. From what you tell us, since Polonius was dead, it must have been Laertes who killed Ophelia, although I do not see the reason for it."

We had emptied one pot of beer, and the old men argued the 78 point with slightly tipsy interest. Finally one of them demanded of me, "What did the servant of Polonius say on his return?"

With difficulty I recollected Reynaldo and his mission. "I 79 don't think he did return before Polonius was killed."

"Listen," said the elder, "and I will tell you how it was and 80 how your story will go, then you may tell me if I am right. Polonius knew his son would get into trouble, and so he did. He had many fines to pay for fighting, and debts from gambling. But he had only two ways of getting money quickly.

One was to marry off his sister at once, but it is difficult to find a man who will marry a woman desired by the son of a chief. For if the chief's heir commits adultery with your wife, what can you do? Only a fool calls a case against a man who will someday be his judge. Therefore Laertes had to take the second way: he killed his sister by witchcraft, drowning her so he could secretly sell her body to the witches."

I raised an objection. "They found her body and buried it. 81
Indeed Laertes jumped into the grave to see his sister once more—so, you see, the body was truly there. Hamlet, who had just come back, jumped in after him."

"What did I tell you?" The elder appealed to the others. 82
"Laertes was up to no good with his sister's body. Hamlet prevented him, because the chief's heir, like a chief, does not wish any other man to grow rich and powerful. Laertes would be angry, because he would have killed his sister without benefit to himself. In our country he would try to kill Hamlet for that reason. Is this not what happened?"

"More or less," I admitted. "When the great chief found 83
Hamlet was still alive, he encouraged Laertes to try to kill Hamlet and arranged a fight with machetes between them. In the fight both the young men were wounded to death. Hamlet's mother drank the poisoned beer that the chief meant for Hamlet in case he won the fight. When he saw his mother die of poison, Hamlet, dying, managed to kill his father's brother with his machete."

"You see, I was right!" exclaimed the elder. 84

"That was a very good story," added the old man, "and 85
you told it with very few mistakes. There was just one more error, at the very end. The poison Hamlet's mother drank was obviously meant for the survivor of the fight, whichever it was. If Laertes had won, the great chief would have poisoned him, for no one would know that he arranged Hamlet's death. Then, too, he need not fear Laertes' witchcraft; it takes a strong heart to kill one's only sister by witchcraft.

"Sometime," concluded the old man, gathering his ragged 86
toga about him, "you must tell us some more stories of your

country. We, who are elders, will instruct you in their true meaning, so that when you return to your own land your elders will see that you have not been sitting in the bush, but among those who know things and who have taught you wisdom."

For Study and Discussion

QUESTIONS ABOUT PURPOSE

1. What belief convinces Bohannan that *Hamlet* is universally intelligible?
2. How does her attempt to tell Hamlet's story prove that her friend was right: "one can easily misinterpret the universal by misunderstanding the particular"?

QUESTIONS ABOUT AUDIENCE

1. How does Bohannan translate concepts—*chief* for *king, farm* for *castle*—to help her African audience understand her story?
2. How does she reveal her frustration and anger in trying to tell her audience what she thought was a simple story?

QUESTIONS ABOUT STRATEGIES

1. How does Bohannan's discussion of Hamlet's *madness* reveal differences in the English and African culture?
2. Ironically, what feature of her version of Hamlet's story convinces her African audience that "people are the same everywhere"?

For Writing and Research

1. *Analyze* how Bohannan combines strategies to interpret Hamlet's story to his audience.
2. *Practice* by comparing the story you wanted to tell to the story you were forced to tell by an audience who keep interrupting and misunderstanding you.
3. *Argue* the elders' position on how Hamlet should have resolved his conflict with Claudius.
4. *Synthesize* several major interpretations of Hamlet. Then use this evidence to defend or challenge the presumed superiority of English culture.

ALICE WALKER

Alice Walker was born in 1944 in Eatonton, Georgia, attended Spelman College in Atlanta, and graduated from Sarah Lawrence College. She then became active in the civil rights movement, helping to register voters in Georgia, teaching in the Head Start program in Mississippi, and working on the staff of the New York City welfare department. In subsequent years, she began her own writing career while teaching at Wellesley College, the University of California at Berkeley, and Brandeis University. Her writing reveals her interest in the themes of sexism and racism, themes she embodies in her widely acclaimed novels: *The Third Life of Grange Copeland* (1970), *Meridian* (1976), *The Color Purple* (1982), *Possessing the Secret of Joy* (1992), and *Now Is the Time to Open Your Heart* (2004). Her stories, collected in *In Love and Trouble: Stories of Black Women* (1973) and *You Can't Keep a Good Woman Down* (1981), and essays, found in *Living by the Word* (1988) and *The Same River Twice* (1996), examine the complex experiences of black women. "Everyday Use," reprinted from *In Love and Trouble,* focuses on a reunion that reveals two contrasting attitudes toward the meaning of family heritage.

Everyday Use
For Your Grandmama

I WILL WAIT for her in the yard that Maggie and I made so 1
clean and wavy yesterday afternoon. A yard like this is more comfortable than most people know. It is not just a yard. It is like an extended living room. When the hard clay is

swept clean as a floor and the fine sand around the edges lined with tiny, irregular grooves anyone can come and sit and look up into the elm tree and wait for the breezes that never come inside the house.

Maggie will be nervous until after her sister goes: she will stand hopelessly in corners homely and ashamed of the burn scars down her arms and legs, eyeing her sister with a mixture of envy and awe. She thinks her sister has held life always in the palm of one hand, that "no" is a word the world never learned to say to her. 2

You've no doubt seen those TV shows where the child who has "made it" is confronted, as a surprise, by her own mother and father, tottering in weakly from backstage. (A pleasant surprise, of course: What would they do if parent and child came on the show only to curse out and insult each other?) On TV mother and child embrace and smile into each other's faces. Sometimes the mother and father weep, the child wraps them in her arms and leans across the table to tell how she would not have made it without their help. I have seen these programs. 3

Sometimes I dream a dream in which Dee and I are sud- denly brought together on a TV program of this sort. Out of a dark and soft-seated limousine I am ushered into a bright room filled with many people. There I meet a smiling, gray, sporty man like Johnny Carson who shakes my hand and tells me what a fine girl I have. Then we are on the stage and Dee is embracing me with tears in her eyes. She pins on my dress a large orchid, even though she has told me once that she thinks orchids are tacky flowers. 4

In real life I am a large, big-boned woman with rough, man-working hands. In the winter I wear flannel nightgowns to bed and overalls during the day. I can kill and clean a hog as mercilessly as a man. My fat keeps me hot in zero weather. I can work all day, breaking ice to get water for washing. I can eat pork liver cooked over the open fire minutes after it comes steaming from the hog. One winter I knocked a bull calf straight in the brain between the eyes with a sledge hammer 5 and had the meat hung up to chill before nightfall. But of course all this does not show on television. I am the way my daughter would want me to be: a hundred pounds lighter, my skin like an uncooked barley pancake. My hair glistens in the hot bright lights. Johnny Carson has much to do to keep up with my quick and witty tongue.

But that is a mistake. I know even before I wake up. Who   6
ever knew a Johnson with a quick tongue? Who can even imagine me looking a strange white man in the eye? It seems to me I have talked to them always with one foot raised in flight, with my head turned in whichever way is farthest from them. Dee, though. She would always look anyone in the eye. Hesitation was no part of her nature.

"How do I look, Mama?" Maggie says, showing just enough   7
of her thin body enveloped in pink skirt and red blouse for me to know she's there, almost hidden by the door.

"Come out into the yard," I say.   8

Have you ever seen a lame animal, perhaps a dog run over   9
by some careless person rich enough to own a car, sidle up to someone who is ignorant enough to be kind to him? That is the way my Maggie walks. She has been like this, chin on chest, eyes on ground, feet in shuffle, ever since the fire that burned the other house to the ground.

Dee is lighter than Maggie, with nicer hair and a fuller   10
figure. She's a woman now, though sometimes I forget. How long ago was it that the other house burned? Ten, twelve years? Sometimes I can still hear the flames and feel Maggie's arm sticking to me, her hair smoking and her dress falling off her in little black papery flakes. Her eyes seemed stretched open, blazed open by the flames reflected in them. And Dee. I see her standing off under the sweet gum tree she used to dig gum out of; a look of concentration on her face as she watched the last dingy gray board of the house fall in toward the red-hot brick chimney. Why don't you do a dance around the ashes? I'd wanted to ask her. She had hated the house that much.

I used to think she hated Maggie, too. But that was before   11
we raised the money, the church and me, to send her to Augusta to school. She used to read to us without pity;

forcing words, lies, other folks' habits, whole lives upon us two, sitting trapped and ignorant underneath her voice. She washed us in a river of make-believe, burned us with a lot of knowledge we didn't necessarily need to know. Pressed us to her with the serious way she read, to shove us away at just the moment, like dimwits, we seemed about to understand.

Dee wanted nice things. A yellow organdy dress to wear to her graduation from high school; black pumps to match a green suit she'd made from an old suit somebody gave me. She was determined to stare down any disaster in her efforts. Her eyelids would not flicker for minutes at a time. Often I fought off the temptation to shake her. At sixteen she had a style of her own: and knew what style was. 12

I never had an education myself. After second grade the school was closed down. Don't ask me why: in 1927 colored asked fewer questions than they do now. Sometimes Maggie reads to me. She stumbles along good-naturedly but can't see well. She knows she is not bright. Like good looks and money, quickness passed her by. She will marry John Thomas (who has mossy teeth in an earnest face) and then I'll be free to sit here and I guess just sing church songs to myself. Although I never was a good singer. Never could carry a tune. I was always better at a man's job. I used to love to milk till I was hoofed in the side in '49. Cows are soothing and slow and don't bother you, unless you try to milk them the wrong way. 13

I have deliberately turned my back on the house. It is three rooms, just like the one that burned, except the roof is tin; they don't make shingle roofs any more. There are no real windows, just some holes cut in the sides, like the portholes in a ship, but not round and not square, with rawhide holding the shutters up on the outside. This house is in a pasture, too, like the other one. No doubt when Dee sees it she will want to tear it down. She wrote me once that no matter where we "choose" to live, she will manage to come see us. But she will never bring her friends. Maggie and I thought about this and Maggie asked me, "Mama, when did Dee ever *have* any friends?" 14

She had a few. Furtive boys in pink shirts hanging about   15
on washday after school. Nervous girls who never laughed.
Impressed with her they worshiped the well-turned phrase,
the cute shape, the scalding humor that erupted like bubbles
in lye. She read to them.

When she was courting Jimmy T she didn't have much   16
time to pay to us, but turned all her faultfinding power on
him. He *flew* to marry a cheap gal from a family of ignorant
flashy people. She hardly had time to recompose herself.

When she comes I will meet—but there they are!   17

Maggie attempts to make a dash for the house, in her   18
shuffling way, but I stay her with my hand. "Come back here,"
I say. And she stops and tries to dig a well in the sand with
her toe.

It is hard to see them clearly through the strong sun. But   19
even the first glimpse of leg out of the car tells me it is Dee.
Her feet were always neat-looking, as if God himself had
shaped them with a certain style. From the other side of the
car comes a short, stocky man. Hair is all over his head a foot
long and hanging from his chin like a kinky mule tail. I hear
Maggie suck in her breath. "Uhnnnh," is what it sounds like.
Like when you see the wriggling end of a snake just in front
of your foot on the road. "Uhnnnh."

Dee next. A dress down to the ground, in this hot weather.   20
A dress so loud it hurts my eyes. There are yellows and oranges
enough to throw back the light of the sun. I feel my whole
face warming from the heat waves it throws out. Earrings, too,
gold and hanging down to her shoulders. Bracelets dangling
and making noises when she moves her arm up to shake the
folds of the dress out of her armpits. The dress is loose and
flows, and as she walks closer, I like it. I hear Maggie go
"Uhnnnh" again. It is her sister's hair. It stands straight up like
the wool on a sheep. It is black as night and around the edges
are two long pigtails that rope about like small lizards disappearing behind her ears.

"Wa-su-zo-Tean-o!" she says, coming on in that gliding   21
way the dress makes her move. The short stocky fellow with
the hair to his navel is all grinning and he follows up with

"Asalamalakim, my mother and sister!" He moves to hug Maggie but she falls back, right up against the back of my chair. I feel her trembling there and when I look up I see the perspiration falling off her chin.

"Don't get up," says Dee. Since I am stout it takes something of a push. You can see me trying to move a second or two before I make it. She turns, showing white heels through her sandals, and goes back to the car. Out she peeks next with a Polaroid. She stoops down quickly and lines up picture after picture of me sitting there in front of the house with Maggie cowering behind me. She never takes a shot without making sure the house is included. When a cow comes nibbling around the edge of the yard she snaps it and me and Maggie *and* the house. Then she puts the Polaroid in the back seat of the car, and comes up and kisses me on the forehead.   22

Meanwhile Asalamalakim is going through the motions with Maggie's hand. Maggie's hand is limp as a fish, and probably as cold, despite the sweat, and she keeps trying to pull it back. It looks like Asalamalakim wants to shake hands but wants to do it fancy. Or maybe he don't know how people shake hands. Anyhow, he soon gives up on Maggie.   23

"Well," I say. "Dee."   24

"No, Mama," she says. "Not 'Dee,' Wangero Leewanika Kemanjo!"   25

"What happened to 'Dee'?" I wanted to know.   26

"She's dead," Wangero said. "I couldn't bear it any longer being named after the people who oppress me."   27

"You know as well as me you was named after your aunt Dicie," I said. Dicie is my sister. She named Dee. We called her "Big Dee" after Dee was born.   28

"But who was *she* named after?" asked Wangero.   29

"I guess after Grandma Dee," I said.   30

"And who was she named after?" asked Wangero.   31

"Her mother," I said, and saw Wangero getting tired. "That's about as far back as I can trace it," I said. Though, in fact, I probably could have carried it back beyond the Civil War through the branches.   32

"Well," said Asalamalakim, "there you are."   33

"Uhnnnh," I heard Maggie say.   34

"There I was not," I said, "before 'Dicie' cropped up in   35
our family, so why should I try to trace it that far back?"

He just stood there grinning, looking down on me like   36
somebody inspecting a Model A car. Every once in a while he
and Wangero sent eye signals over my head.

"How do you pronounce this name?" I asked.   37

"You don't have to call me by it if you don't want to," said   38
Wangero.

"Why shouldn't I?" I asked. "If that's what you want us to   39
call you, we'll call you."

"I know it might sound awkward at first," said Wangero.   40

"I'll get used to it," I said. "Ream it out again."   41

Well, soon we got the name out of the way. Asalamalakim   42
had a name twice as long and three times as hard. After I
tripped over it two or three times he told me to just call him
Hakim-a-barber. I wanted to ask him was he a barber, but I
didn't really think he was, so I didn't ask.

"You must belong to those beef-cattle peoples down the   43
road," I said. They said "Asalamalakim" when they met you,
too, but they didn't shake hands. Always too busy: feeding the
cattle, fixing the fences, putting up salt-lick shelters, throwing
down hay. When the white folks poisoned some of the herd
the men stayed up all night with rifles in their hands, I walked
a mile and half just to see the sight.

Hakim-a-barber said, "I accept some of their doctrines,   44
but farming and raising cattle is not my style." (They didn't
tell me, and I didn't ask, whether Wangero [Dee] had really
gone and married him.)

We sat down to eat and right away he said he didn't eat   45
collards and pork was unclean. Wangero, though, went on
through the chitlins and corn bread, the greens and everything else. She talked a blue streak over the sweet potatoes.
Everything delighted her. Even the fact that we still used the
benches her daddy made for the table when we couldn't afford to buy chairs.

"Oh, Mama!" she cried. Then turned to Hakim-a-barber.   46
"I never knew how lovely these benches are. You can feel the

rump prints," she said, running her hands underneath her and along the bench. Then she gave a sigh and her hand closed over Grandma Dee's butter dish. "That's it!" she said. "I knew there was something I wanted to ask you if I could have." She jumped up from the table and went over in the corner where the churn stood, the milk in its clabber by now. She looked at the churn and looked at it.

"This churn top is what I need," she said. "Didn't Uncle   47
Buddy whittle it out of a tree you all used to have?"

"Yes," I said.   48

"Uh huh," she said happily. "And I want the dasher, too."   49

"Uncle Buddy whittle that, too?" asked the barber.   50

Dee (Wangero) looked up at me.   51

"Aunt Dee's first husband whittled the dash," said Maggie   52
so low you almost couldn't hear her. "His name was Henry, but they called him Stash."

"Maggie's brain is like an elephant's," Wangero said,   53
laughing. "I can use the churn top as a centerpiece for the alcove table," she said, sliding a plate over the churn, "and I'll think of something artistic to do with the dasher."

When she finished wrapping the dasher the handle stuck   54
out. I took it for a moment in my hands. You didn't even have to look close to see where hands pushing the dasher up and down to make butter had left a kind of sink in the wood. In fact, there were a lot of small sinks; you could see where thumbs and fingers had sunk into the wood. It was beautiful light yellow wood, from a tree that grew in the yard where Big Dee and Stash had lived.

After dinner Dee (Wangero) went to the trunk at the foot   55
of my bed and started rifling through it. Maggie hung back in the kitchen over the dishpan. Out came Wangero with two quilts. They had been pieced by Grandma Dee and then Big Dee and me had hung them on the quilt frames on the front porch and quilted them. One was in the Lone Star pattern. The other was Walk Around the Mountain. In both of them were scraps of dresses Grandma Dee had worn fifty and more years ago. Bits and pieces of Grandpa Jarrell's Paisley shirts. And one teeny faded blue piece, about the size of a penny

matchbox, that was from Great Grandpa Ezra's uniform that he wore in the Civil War.

"Mama," Wangero said sweet as a bird. "Can I have these old quilts?"   56

I heard something fall in the kitchen, and a minute later the kitchen door slammed.   57

"Why don't you take one or two of the others?" I asked. "These old things was just done by me and Big Dee from some tops your grandma pieced before she died."   58

"No," said Wangero. "I don't want those. They are stitched around the borders by machine."   59

"That'll make them last better," I said.   60

"That's not the point," said Wangero. "These are all pieces of dresses Grandma used to wear. She did all this stitching by hand. Imagine!" She held the quilts securely in her arms, stroking them.   61

"Some of the pieces, like those lavender ones, come from old clothes her mother handed down to her," I said, moving up to touch the quilts. Dee (Wangero) moved back just enough so that I couldn't reach the quilts. They already belonged to her.   62

"Imagine!" she breathed again, clutching them closely to her bosom.   63

"The truth is," I said, "I promised to give them quilts to Maggie, for when she marries John Thomas."   64

She gasped like a bee had stung her.   65

"Maggie can't appreciate these quilts!" she said. "She'd probably be backward enough to put them to everyday use."   66

"I reckon she would," I said. "God knows I been saving 'em for long enough with nobody using 'em. I hope she will!" I didn't want to bring up how I had offered Dee (Wangero) a quilt when she went away to college. Then she had told me they were old-fashioned, out of style.   67

"But they're *priceless!*" she was saying now, furiously; for she has a temper. "Maggie would put them on the bed and in five years they'd be in rags. Less than that!"   68

"She can always make some more," I said. "Maggie knows how to quilt."   69

Dee (Wangero) looked at me with hatred. "You just will   70
not understand. The point is these quilts, *these* quilts!"

"Well," I said, stumped. "What would *you* do with them?"   71

"Hang them," she said. As if that was the only thing you   72
could do with quilts.

Maggie by now was standing in the door. I could almost   73
hear the sound her feet made as they scraped over each other.

"She can have them, Mama," she said, like somebody used   74
to never winning anything, or having anything reserved for
her. "I can 'member Grandma Dee without the quilts."

I looked at her hard. She had filled her bottom lip with   75
checkerberry snuff and it gave her face a kind of dopey,
hangdog look. It was Grandma Dee and Big Dee who taught
her how to quilt herself. She stood there with her scarred
hands hidden in the folds of her skirt. She looked at her
sister with something like fear but she wasn't mad at her.
This was Maggie's portion. This was the way she knew God
to work.

When I looked at her like that something hit me in the top   76
of my head and ran down to the soles of my feet. Just like
when I'm in church and the spirit of God touches me and
I get happy and shout. I did something I never had done
before: hugged Maggie to me, then dragged her on into the
room, snatched the quilts out of Miss Wangero's hands and
dumped them into Maggie's lap. Maggie just sat there on my
bed with her mouth open.

"Take one or two of the others," I said to Dee.   77

But she turned without a word and went out to Hakim-a-   78
barber.

"You just don't understand," she said, as Maggie and I   79
came out to the car.

"What don't I understand?" I wanted to know.   80

"Your heritage," she said. And then she turned to Maggie,   81
kissed her and said, "You ought to try to make something of
yourself, too, Maggie. It's really a new day for us. But from
the way you and Mama still live you'd never know it."

She put on some sunglasses that hid everything above the   82
tip of her nose and her chin.

Maggie smiled; maybe at the sunglasses. But a real smile,   83
not scared. After we watched the car dust settle I asked Maggie
to bring me a dip of snuff. And then the two of us sat there
just enjoying, until it was time to go in the house and go to
bed.

COMMENT ON "EVERYDAY USE"

Alice Walker's "Everyday Use" describes a difference between a mother's and her visiting daughter's understanding
of the word *heritage*. For Mama and her daughter Maggie,
heritage is a matter of everyday living, of "everyday use."
For Mama's other daughter, Dee (Wangero), however, heritage is a matter of style, a fashionable obsession with one's
roots. These comparisons are revealed first in Walker's description of the physical appearance of the characters. Mama
is fat and manly, and Maggie bears the scars from a fire. By
contrast, Dee (Wangero) is beautiful and striking in her
brightly colored African dress, earrings, sunglasses, and
Afro hairstyle. Next, Walker compares the characters' skills.
Mama can butcher a hog or break ice to get water, and
Maggie is able to make beautiful quilts. Dee (Wangero), on
the other hand, thinks of herself as outside this domestic
world, educated by books to understand the cultural significance of her heritage. The problem posed by the debate over
family possessions is whether heritage is an object to be preserved, like a priceless painting, or a process, to be learned,
like the creation of a quilt.

DIVISION
AND
CLASSIFICATION

Division and **classification** are mental processes that often work together. When you *divide,* you separate something (a college, a city) into sections (departments, neighborhoods). When you *classify,* you place examples of something (restaurants, jobs) into categories or classes (restaurants: moderately expensive, very expensive; jobs: unskilled, semiskilled, and skilled).

When you divide, you move downward from a concept to the subunits of that concept. When you classify, you move upward from specific examples to classes or categories that share a common characteristic. For example, you could

213

divide a television news program into subunits such as news, features, editorials, sports, and weather. And you could *classify* some element of that program—such as the editorial commentator on the six o'clock news—according to his or her style, knowledge, and trustworthiness. You can use either division or classification singly, depending on your purpose, but most of the time you will probably use them together when you are writing a classification essay. First you might identify the subunits in a college sports program—football, basketball, hockey, volleyball, tennis; then you could classify them according to their budgets—most money budgeted for football, the least budgeted for volleyball.

PURPOSE

When you write a classification essay, your chief purpose is to *explain*. You might want to explain an established method for organizing information, such as the Library of Congress system, or a new plan for arranging data, such as the Internal Revenue Service's latest schedule for itemizing tax deductions. On one level, your purpose in such an essay is simply to show how the system works. At a deeper level, your purpose is to define, analyze, and justify the organizing principle that underlies the system.

You can also write a classification essay to *entertain* or to *persuade*. If you classify to entertain, you have an opportunity to be clever and witty. If you classify to persuade, you have a chance to be cogent and forceful. If you want to entertain, you might concoct an elaborate scheme for classifying fools, pointing out the distinguishing features of each category and giving particularly striking examples of each type. But if you want to persuade, you could explain how some new or controversial plan, such as the metric system or congressional redistricting, is organized, pointing out how the schemes use new principles to identify and organize information. Again, although you may give your readers a great deal of information in such an essay, your main purpose is to persuade them that the new plan is better than the old one.

AUDIENCE

As with any writing assignment, when you write a classification essay, you need to think carefully about what your readers already know and what they need to get from your writing. If you're writing on a new topic (social patterns in a primitive society) or if you're explaining a specialized system of classification (the botanist's procedure for identifying plants), your readers need precise definitions and plenty of illustrations for each subcategory. If your readers already know about your subject and the system it uses for classification (the movies' G, PG, PG-13, R, and NC-17 rating codes), then you don't need to give them an extensive demonstration. In that kind of writing situation, you might want to sketch the system briefly to refresh your readers' memories but then move on, using examples of specific movies to analyze whether the system really works.

You also need to think about how your readers might use the classification system that you explain in your essay. If you're classifying rock musicians, your readers are probably going to regard the system you create as something self-enclosed—interesting and amusing, perhaps something to quibble about, but not something they're likely to use in their everyday lives. On the other hand, if you write an essay classifying digital video equipment, your readers may want to use your system when they shop. For the first audience, you can use an informal approach to classification, dividing your subject into interesting subcategories and illustrating them with vivid examples. For the other audience, you need to be careful and strict in your approach, making sure you divide your topic into all its possible classes and illustrating each class with concrete examples.

STRATEGIES

When you write a classification essay, your basic strategy for organization should be to *divide your subject* into major categories that exhibit a common trait, then subdivide those categories into smaller units. Next, *arrange your categories* into a sequence that shows a logical or a dramatic progression. Finally, *define each of your categories.* First, show how each category is different from the others; then discuss its most vivid examples.

To make this strategy succeed, you must be sure that your classification system is *consistent, complete, emphatic,* and *significant.* Here is a method for achieving this goal. First, when you divide your subject into categories, *apply the same principle of selection to each class.* You may find this hard to do if you're trying to explain a system that someone else has already established but that is actually inconsistent. You have undoubtedly discovered that record stores use overlapping and inconsistent categories. CDs by Shania Twain, for example, may be found in sections labeled *country, pop,* and *female vocal.* You can avoid such tangles if you create and control your own classification system.

For instance, Calvin Trillin classifies people who take food off other people's plates, Russell Baker classifies inanimate objects, James Austin classifies different kinds of chance, and Lewis Thomas classifies different types of medical technology.

After you have divided your subject into separate and consistent categories, *make sure your division is complete.* The simplest kind of division separates a subject into two categories: A and Not-A (for example, conformists and nonconformists). This kind of division, however, is rarely encouraged. It allows you to tell your readers about category A (conformists), but you won't tell them much about Not-A (nonconformists). For this reason, you should try to exhaust your subject by finding at least three separate categories and by acknowledging any examples that don't fit into the system. When an author writes a formal classification essay, such as George Orwell's "Politics and the English Language," he or she tries to be definitive—to include everything significant. Even when writers are writing less formal classification essays, such as Trillin's "The Extendable Fork," they try to set up a reasonably complete system.

Once you have completed your process of division, *arrange your categories and examples in an emphatic order.* Austin arranges his classification of chance from blind luck to personal sensibility. Thomas arranges his categories of medical technology dramatically, from least effective to most effective. The authors of these essays reveal the principal purpose underlying their classification schemes: to show variety in similarity, to challenge the arbitrariness of an established system, and to point out how concepts change.

Finally, *you need to show the significance of your system of classification.* The strength of the classification process is that you can use it to analyze a subject in any number of ways. Its weakness is that you can use it to subdivide a subject into all kinds of trivial or pointless categories. You can classify people by their educational backgrounds, their work experience, or their significant achievements. You can also classify them by their shoe size, the kind of socks they wear, or their tastes in ice cream. Notice that, when writers such as Lewis Thomas or George Orwell classify a subject according to a particular system, they assert that the system is significant. Even if writers such as Calvin Trillin or Russell Baker choose a subject that doesn't seem particularly significant, they still must convince readers that the system counts in some way, if only because it lays out and demonstrates, consistently and completely, the significant subdivisions of the subject.

DIVISION AND CLASSIFICATION

Points to Remember

1. Determine whether you want to (a) explain an existing system of classification or (b) create your own system.
2. Divide your subject into smaller categories by applying the same principle of selection to each category.
3. Make sure that your division is complete by establishing separate and consistent types of categories.
4. Arrange your categories (and the examples you use to illustrate each category) in a logical and emphatic sequence.
5. Demonstrate the significance of your system by calling your readers' attention to its significance.

CLOUD CHART

LONERS

Single clouds that like to hang out in an otherwise cloudless sky.

SHEEP

Little clouds that always appear in bunches.

SPEEDY GONZALI

Clouds in a huge hurry to get to the next sky.

BLOCKERS

Mischievous clouds with a fondness for popping up just as one decides to go in the ocean.

GRAY BLANKET

One vast gray cloud that usually covers several states at once.

INDUSTRIOS

Beautiful clouds that are most often seen over large manufacturing plants.

SIGMUNDS

Clouds with an uncanny ability to make you feel anxious or depressed.

DUHS

No-name, generic clouds having no meteorological significance whatsoever.

R. Chst

In this quirky cartoon Roz Chast classifies the different kinds of clouds one can see in the sky. Examine the various categories in her "Cloud Chart." Reflect on your own experience watching clouds. What categories has she omitted or mislabeled? Write an essay that explains how meteorologists classify clouds or, alternatively, how clouds figure metaphorically in expressions ("his face clouded over"), literature (including song lyrics), or art.

CALVIN TRILLIN

Calvin Trillin was born in Kansas City, Missouri, in 1935 and was educated at Yale University. He began his career by working as a reporter for *Time* magazine, then as a columnist for *The New Yorker.* In recent years, he has written a national newspaper column and staged a one-man show off-Broadway. His writing includes three novels, *Runestruck* (1977), *Floater* (1980), and *Tepper Isn't Going Out* (2001); books of poetry, including *Deadline Poet; or, My Life as a Doggerelist* (1994) and *Obliviously on He Sails: The Bush Administration in Rhyme* (2004); collections of reporting, including *U.S. Journal* (1971), *Killings* (1982), and *American Stories* (1991); a best-selling memoir, *Remembering Denny* (1993); numerous books of humor, such as *Family Man* (1998); and a portrait of his late wife, *About Alice* (2006). In "The Extendable Fork" (1995), reprinted from his syndicated column, Trillin classifies eaters by how they eat off other people's plates.

The Extendable Fork

IN OUR HOUSE, news that the extendable fork had been invented was greeted with varying degrees of enthusiasm. I think it's fair to say that I was the most enthusiastic of all. I eat off of other people's plates. My wife was mildly enthusiastic. She figures that if I use an extendable fork I'm less likely to come away from the table with gravy on my cuff.

People who eat off of other people's plates can be categorized in four types—The Finisher, The Waif, The Researcher and The Simple Thief. I might as well admit right here at the beginning that I am all four.

The Finisher demonstrates concern that food may be left   3
uneaten even though the starving children your mother told
you about are still hungry. Once the pace of eating begins to
slacken off a bit, he reaches across to spear a roast potato off
of someone's plate a nanosecond after saying, "If you're not
planning to finish these . . ."

The long-reach eater I think of as The Waif often doesn't   4
order much himself at a restaurant, claiming that he's not terribly hungry or that he's trying to lose weight. Then, he
gazes at his dinner companions' plates, like a hungry urchin
who has his nose pressed up against the window of a restaurant where enormously fat rich people are slurping oysters
and shoveling down mounds of boeuf bourguignon. Occasionally, he murmurs something like, "That looks delicious."
Answering "Actually, it's not all that good" does not affect

> *People who eat off other people's plates come*
> *in four categories: The Finisher, The Waif,*
> *The Researcher, and The Simple Thief.*

him—although it may slow down The Researcher, who, as he
extends his fork usually says something like, "I'm curious
how they do these fried onions."

The Simple Thief simply waits for his dining companions   5
to glance away, then confidently grabs what he wants. If he's
desperate, he may actually take measures to distract them,
saying something like, "Is it my imagination, or could that be
Michael Jackson and Lisa Marie Presley at the table over by
the door?"

That sort of subterfuge is not necessary, by the way, if the   6
plate I have singled out as a target is my wife's. She does not
object to my sampling—a reflection, I've always thought, of
her generous heart. In fact, I have said in the past that if a
young groom on his honeymoon reaches over for the first

time to sample his bride's fettuccine only to be told "Don't you like what you're having?" or "There really isn't that much of this," he knows he's in for a long haul.

Actually, my wife might be called a Finisher herself. If we're having fried chicken, she will stare at what's on my plate after I have indeed finished. "Look at all the chicken you left," she'll say. Or "There's a ton of meat still on that chicken." 7

Oddly enough, this is precisely the sort of thing that I heard from my mother, who was also fond of saying that I didn't "do a good job" on the chicken. The way my wife eats chicken is to eat every speck of meat off the bones, so that the chicken looks as if it had been staked out on an anthill by a tribe of crazed chicken torturers. She treats a lobster the same way. 8

I eat more the way a shark eats—tearing off whatever seems exposed and easy to get at. I have suggested, in fact, that in fried-chicken or lobster restaurants we could economize by getting only one order, which I could start and my wife could finish. 9

My wife's approach to finishing does not, of course, require an extendable fork, but I intend to be an early customer myself. According to an item in the *New York Times,* the fork is nearly two feet long when fully opened. It's being marketed under the name of Alan's X-Tenda Fork. 10

I might have chosen another name, but this one is, I'll admit, evocative. For me, it conjures up visions of a Limbaugh-sized man named Alan sitting in a restaurant with friends and family. He seems to be engaging in normal conversation, but his tiny eyes dart from plate to plate; occasionally, with a fork as quick as the strike of an adder, he helps with the finishing. 11

In fact, I can imagine Alan inventing other needed implements—a sort of vacuum tube, for instance, that can suck up french fries from three feet away. I can see him improving on Alan's X-Tenda Fork. He might install a tiny tape recorder in it, so when you pulled it out to its full length and moved it quickly across the table a voice said, "If you're not planning to finish these . . ." 12

For Study and Discussion

QUESTIONS ABOUT PURPOSE

1. How does Trillin use the news of the invention of the "extend-able fork" to justify his classification of eaters?
2. What purpose does Trillin accomplish by admitting that he fits into all four categories?

QUESTIONS ABOUT AUDIENCE

1. What assumptions does Trillin make about the eating habits of his readers?
2. How do his comments about his wife's and mother's behavior clarify his attitude toward his readers?

QUESTIONS ABOUT STRATEGIES

1. What principle does Trillin use to divide and identify his four types of eaters?
2. How does he use dialogue to illustrate the strategies of each eater?

For Writing and Research

1. *Analyze* how Trillin uses special names to define the subcate-gories in his classification.
2. *Practice* by classifying the types of reasons you give for sampling food off someone's plate or for not finishing what's on your plate.
3. *Argue* that the concept of *finishing* fits into our cultural attitudes of efficiency and economy.
4. *Synthesize* the advice provided by books of etiquette about the practice of eating from another's plate. Then use this evidence to explain why Americans appear to waste food.

Russell Baker was born in 1925 in rural Loudoun County, Virginia, graduated from Johns Hopkins University, and served in the navy during World War II. He began his newspaper career in 1947, covering the State Department, White House, and Congress for the *New York Times* until, as he re- counts, "I just got bored. I had done enough reporting." The *Times* offered him a thrice-weekly column, which came to be called "Observer" and which Baker continues to write today. Many of his columns have been collected in book form: *Poor Russell's Almanac* (1972), *So This Is Depravity* (1980), *The Rescue of Miss Yaskell and Other Pipe Dreams* (1983), and *There's a Country in My Cellar* (1990). His autobiography, *Growing Up* (1982), was awarded the Pulitzer Prize. *The Good Times* (1989) and *Looking Back* (2002) continue his reminiscences. In "The Plot Against People," *The New York Times* (1968) Baker employs his wry humor to classify inanimate objects into three categories.

The Plot Against People

I NANIMATE OBJECTS ARE classified into three major categories—those that don't work, those that break down and those that get lost.   1

The goal of all inanimate objects is to resist man and ultimately to defeat him, and the three major classifications are based on the method each object uses to achieve its purpose. As a general rule, any object capable of breaking down at the moment when it is most needed will do so. The automobile is typical of the category.   2

With the cunning typical of its breed, the automobile never breaks down while entering a filling station with a large   3 staff of idle mechanics. It waits until it reaches a downtown intersection in the middle of the rush hour, or until it is fully loaded with family and luggage on the Ohio Turnpike.

Thus it creates maximum misery, inconvenience, frustra- 4 tion and irritability among its human cargo, thereby reducing its owner's life span.

Washing machines, garbage disposals, lawn mowers, light 5 bulbs, automatic laundry dryers, water pipes, furnaces, electrical fuses, television tubes, hose nozzles, tape recorders, slide projectors—all are in league with the automobile to take

---

The goal of all inanimate objects is to defeat man; their strategies are to break down, not work, or get lost.

---

their turn at breaking down whenever life threatens to flow smoothly for their human enemies.

Many inanimate objects, of course, find it extremely diffi- 6 cult to break down. Pliers, for example, and gloves and keys are almost totally incapable of breaking down. Therefore, they have had to evolve a different technique for resisting man.

They get lost. Science has still not solved the mystery of 7 how they do it, and no man has ever caught one of them in the act of getting lost. The most plausible theory is that they have developed a secret method of locomotion which they are able to conceal the instant a human eye falls upon them.

It is not uncommon for a pair of pliers to climb all the way 8 from the cellar to the attic in its single-minded determination to raise its owner's blood pressure. Keys have been known to burrow three feet under mattresses. Women's purses, despite their great weight, frequently travel through six or seven rooms to find hiding space under a couch.

Scientists have been struck by the fact that things that 9 break down virtually never get lost, while things that get lost hardly ever break down.

A furnace, for example, will invariably break down at the depth of the first winter cold wave, but it will never get lost. A woman's purse, which after all does have some inherent capacity for breaking down, hardly ever does; it almost invariably chooses to get lost.

Some persons believe this constitutes evidence that inanimate objects are not entirely hostile to man, and that a negotiated peace is possible. After all, they point out, a furnace could infuriate a man even more thoroughly by getting lost than by breaking down, just as a glove could upset him far more by breaking down than by getting lost.

Not everyone agrees, however, that this indicates a conciliatory attitude among inanimate objects. Many say it merely proves that furnaces, gloves and pliers are incredibly stupid.

The third class of objects—those that don't work—is the most curious of all. These include such objects as barometers, car clocks, cigarette lighters, flashlights and toy-train locomotives. It is inaccurate, of course, to say that they never work. They work once, usually for the first few hours after being brought home, and then quit. Thereafter, they never work again.

In fact, it is widely assumed that they are built for the purpose of not working. Some people have reached advanced ages without ever seeing some of these objects—barometers, for example—in working order.

Science is utterly baffled by the entire category. There are many theories about it. The most interesting holds that the things that don't work have attained the highest state possible for an inanimate object, the estate to which things that break down and things that get lost can still only aspire.

They have truly defeated man by conditioning him never to expect anything of them, and in return they have given man the only peace he receives from inanimate society. He does not expect his barometer to work, his electric locomotive to run, his cigarette lighter to light or his flashlight to illuminate, and when they don't, it does not raise his blood pressure.

He cannot attain that peace with furnaces and keys and cars and women's purses as long as he demands that they work for their keep.

For Study and Discussion

QUESTIONS ABOUT PURPOSE

1. How do Baker's introduction of his first category (paragraph 2) and his illustrative example (paragraph 3) demonstrate that his primary purpose is to entertain?
2. In what ways do Baker's repeated references to science reinforce or alter his purpose?

QUESTIONS ABOUT AUDIENCE

1. How does Baker's use of examples reveal his assumptions about the common experience of his audience?
2. How does Baker expect his readers to use his classification system? Look particularly at paragraphs 11, 12, and 16.

QUESTIONS ABOUT STRATEGIES

1. What is the principle by which Baker divides objects into three categories?
2. What does Baker accomplish by scrambling the sequence of categories he presents in his opening sentence?

For Writing and Research

1. *Analyze* the examples that Baker uses to illustrate his categories.
2. *Practice* by subdividing one of Baker's categories—for example, things that get lost—into smaller subcategories.
3. *Argue* that objects do *not* defeat people but provide them with ways to extend their creative powers.
4. *Synthesize* the research that has been conducted on product or service warranties. Then use this evidence to argue that American manufacturers make good or bad products.

JAMES H. AUSTIN

James H. Austin was born in 1925 in Cleveland, Ohio, and was educated at Brown University and Harvard University Medical School. After an internship at Boston City Hospital and a residency at the Neurological Institute of New York, Austin established a private practice in neurology, first in Portland, Oregon, and then in Denver, Colorado. He currently serves as professor and head of the Department of Neurology at the University of Colorado Medical School. His major publication, *Chase, Chance, and Creativity: The Lucky Art of Novelty* (1978), addresses the issue of how "chance and creativity interact in biomedical research." His most recent book is *Zen and the Brain: Toward an Understanding of Meditation and Consciousness* (1999). In this essay, published originally in *Saturday Review* (November 2, 1972), Austin distinguishes four kinds of chance by the way humans react to their environment.

Four Kinds of Chance

W HAT IS CHANCE? Dictionaries define it as something 1 fortuitous that happens unpredictably without discernible human intention. Chance is unintentional and capricious, but we needn't conclude that chance is immune from human intervention. Indeed, chance plays several distinct roles when humans react creatively with one another and with their environment.

We can readily distinguish four varieties of chance if we 2 consider that they each involve a different kind of motor activity and a special kind of sensory receptivity. The varieties of chance also involve distinctive personality traits and differ in the way one particular individual influences them.

Chance I is the pure blind luck that comes with no effort   3
on your part. If, for example, you are sitting at a bridge table of four, it's "in the cards" for you to receive a hand of all 13 spades, but it will come up only once in every 6.3 trillion deals. You will ultimately draw this lucky hand—with no intervention on your part—but it does involve a longer wait than most of us have time for.

Chance II evokes the kind of luck Charles Kettering had in   4
mind when he said: "Keep on going and the chances are you

The term serendipity *describes the facility for encountering unexpected good luck, as the result of accident, general exploratory behavior, or sagacity.*

---

will stumble on something, perhaps when you are least ex-pecting it. I have never heard of anyone stumbling on some-thing sitting down."

In the sense referred to here, Chance II is not passive, but   5
springs from an energetic, generalized motor activity. A cer-tain basal level of action "stirs up the pot," brings in random ideas that will collide and stick together in fresh combina-tions, lets chance operate. When someone, *anyone,* does swing into motion and keeps on going, he will increase the number of collisions between events. When a few events are linked together, they can then be exploited to have a fortuitous outcome, but many others, of course, cannot. Kettering was right. Press on. Something will turn up. We may term this the Kettering Principle.

In the two previous examples, a unique role of the individ-   6
ual person was either lacking or minimal. Accordingly, as we move on to Chance III, we see blind luck, but in camouflage.

Chance presents the clue, the opportunity exists, but it would be missed except by that one person uniquely equipped to observe it, visualize it conceptually, and fully grasp its significance. Chance III involves a special receptivity and discernment unique to the recipient. Louis Pasteur characterized it for all time when he said: "Chance favors only the prepared mind."

Pasteur himself had it in full measure. But the classic example of his principle occurred in 1928, when Alexander Fleming's mind instantly fused at least five elements into a conceptually unified nexus. His mental sequences went something like this: (1) I see that a mold has fallen by accident into my culture dish; (2) the staphylococcal colonies residing near it failed to grow; (3) the mold must have secreted something that killed the bacteria; (4) I recall a similar experience once before; (5) if I could separate this new "something" from the mold, it could be used to kill staphylococci that cause human infections.   7

Actually, Fleming's mind was exceptionally well prepared for the penicillin mold. Six years earlier, while he was suffering from a cold, his own nasal drippings had found their way into a culture dish, for reasons not made entirely clear. He noted that nearby bacteria were killed, and astutely followed up the lead. His observations led him to discover a bactericidal enzyme present in nasal mucus and tears, called lysozyme. Lysozyme proved too weak to be of medical use, but imagine how receptive Fleming's mind was to the penicillin mold when it later happened on the scene!   8

One word evokes the quality of the operations involved in the first three kinds of chance. It is *serendipity*. The term describes the facility for encountering unexpected good luck, as the result of: accident (Chance I), general exploratory behavior (Chance II), or sagacity (Chance III). The word itself was coined by the Englishman-of-letters Horace Walpole, in 1754. He used it with reference to the legendary tales of the Three Princes of Serendip (Ceylon), who quite unexpectedly encountered many instances of good fortune on their travels. In today's parlance, we have usually watered down *serendipity* to   9 mean the good luck that comes solely by accident. We think of it as a result, not an ability. We have tended to lose sight of the element of sagacity, by which term Walpole wished to emphasize that some distinctive personal receptivity is involved.

There remains a fourth element in good luck, an unintentional but subtle personal prompting of it. The English Prime Minister Benjamin Disraeli summed up the principle underlying Chance IV when he noted that "we make our fortunes and we call them fate." Disraeli, a politician of considerable practical experience, appreciated that we each shape our own destiny, at least to some degree. One might restate the principle as follows: *Chance favors the individualized action.* 10

In Chance IV the kind of luck is peculiar to one person, and like a personal hobby, it takes on a distinctive individual flavor. This form of chance is one-man-made, and it is as personal as a signature. . . . Chance IV has an elusive, almost miragelike, quality. Like a mirage, it is difficult to get a firm grip on, for it tends to recede as we pursue it and advance as we step back. But we still accept a mirage when we see it, because we vaguely understand the basis for the phenomenon. A strongly heated layer of air, less dense than usual, lies next to the earth, and it bends the light rays as they pass through. The resulting image may be magnified as if by a telescopic lens in the atmosphere, and real objects, ordinarily hidden far out of sight over the horizon, are brought forward and revealed to the eye. What happens in a mirage then, and in this form of chance, not only appears farfetched but indeed is farfetched. 11

About a century ago, a striking example of Chance IV took place in the Spanish cave of Altamira.* There, one day in 1879, Don Marcelino de Sautuola was engaged in his hobby of archaeology, searching Altamira for bones and stones. With him was his daughter, Maria, who had asked him if she could come along to the cave that day. The indulgent father had said 12

*The cave had first been discovered some years before by an enterprising hunting dog in search of game. Curiously, in 1932 the French cave of Lascaux was discovered by still another dog.

she could. Naturally enough, he first looked where he had always found heavy objects before, on the *floor* of the cave. But Maria, unhampered by any such preconceptions, looked not only at the floor but also all around the cave with the open-eyed wonder of a child! She looked up, exclaimed, and then he looked up, to see incredible works of art on the cave ceiling! The magnificent colored bison and other animals they saw at Altamira, painted more than 15,000 years ago, might lead one to call it "the Sistine Chapel of Prehistory." Passionately pursuing his interest in archaeology, de Sautuola, to his surprise, discovered man's first paintings. In quest of science, he happened upon Art.

Yes, a dog did "discover" the cave, and the initial receptivity was his daughter's, but the pivotal reason for the cave paintings' discovery hinged on a long sequence of prior events originating in de Sautuola himself. For when we dig into the background of this amateur excavator, we find he was an exceptional person. Few Spaniards were out probing into caves 100 years ago. The fact that he—not someone else—decided to dig that day in the cave of Altamira was the culmination of his passionate interest in his hobby. Here was a rare man whose avocation had been to educate himself from scratch, as it were, in the science of archaeology and cave exploration. This was no simple passive recognizer of blind luck when it came his way, but a man whose unique interests served as an active creative thrust—someone whose own actions and personality would focus the events that led circuitously but inexorably to the discovery of man's first paintings.

Then, too, there is a more subtle matter. How do you give full weight to the personal interests that imbue your child with your own curiosity, that inspire her to ask to join you in your own musty hobby, and that then lead you to agree to her request at the critical moment? For many reasons, at Altamira, more than the special receptivity of Chance III was required—this was a different domain, that of the personality and its actions.

A century ago no one had the remotest idea our caveman ancestors were highly creative artists. Weren't their talents rather minor and limited to crude flint chippings? But the paintings at Altamira, like a mirage, would quickly magnify this diminutive view, bring up into full focus a distant, hidden era of man's prehistory, reveal sentient minds and well-developed aesthetic sensibilities to which men of any age might aspire. And like a mirage, the events at Altamira grew out of de Sautuola's heated personal quest and out of the invisible forces of chance we know exist yet cannot touch. Accordingly, one may introduce the term *altamirage* to identify the quality underlying Chance IV. Let us define it as the facility for encountering unexpected good luck as the result of highly individualized action. *Altamirage* goes well beyond the boundaries of serendipity in its emphasis on the role of personal action in chance.

Chance IV is favored by distinctive, if not eccentric, hobbies, personal life-styles, and modes of behavior peculiar to one individual, usually invested with some passion. The farther apart these personal activities are from the area under investigation, the more novel and unexpected will be the creative product of the encounter.

For Study and Discussion

QUESTIONS ABOUT PURPOSE

1. What elements of human behavior and attitude does Austin demonstrate by dividing chance into four varieties?
2. What relationship does Austin discover between the words *luck, serendipity, sagacity, and altamirage*?

QUESTIONS ABOUT AUDIENCE

1. What assumptions does Austin make about his readers when he offers them *the best example* rather than several examples to illustrate each category?
2. How does Austin's attitude toward his audience change during the essay? For example, why does he speak directly to his readers when he explains Chance I but address them more formally in his discussion of other categories?

QUESTIONS ABOUT STRATEGIES

1. How does Austin arrange his four categories? Why doesn't he give equal treatment to each category?
2. How does Austin use transitions and summaries to clarify the differences between the major categories? In particular, see paragraphs 6 and 9.

For Writing and Research

1. *Analyze* the "best" examples Austin uses to illustrate his four kinds of chance.
2. *Practice* by classifying types of bad luck.
3. *Argue* in favor of baseball owner Branch Rickey's assertion that "luck is the residue of design."
4. *Synthesize* the research on those who make a career of gambling— for example, professional poker players. Then use this evidence to argue that skill does or does not contribute to this success.

Lewis Thomas (1913–1993) was born in Flushing, New York, and was educated at Princeton University and Harvard University Medical School. He held appointments at numerous research hospitals and medical schools before assuming the position of president of the Sloan-Kettering Cancer Center in New York City. In 1974 his collection of essays, *The Lives of a Cell: Notes of a Biology Watcher,* won the National Book Award for Arts and Letters. His other books include *The Medusa and the Snail: More Notes of a Biology Watcher* (1979), *The Youngest Science* (1983), *Late Night Thoughts on Listening to Mahler's Ninth Symphony* (1983), and *The Fragile Species* (1992). In "The Technology of Medicine" from *The Lives of a Cell,* Thomas classifies "three quite different levels of technology in medicine."

The Technology of Medicine

TECHNOLOGY ASSESSMENT HAS become a routine exercise for the scientific enterprises on which the country is obliged to spend vast sums for its needs. Brainy committees are continually evaluating the effectiveness and cost of doing various things in space, defense, energy, transportation, and the like, to give advice about prudent investments for the future. 1

Somehow medicine, for all the $80-odd billion that it is said to cost the nation, has not yet come in for much of this analytical treatment. It seems taken for granted that the technology of medicine simply exists, take it or leave it, and the only major technologic problem which policy-makers are interested in is how to deliver today's kind of health care, with equity, to all the people. 2

When, as is bound to happen sooner or later, the analysts ₃ get around to the technology of medicine itself, they will have to face the problem of measuring the relative cost and effectiveness of all the things that are done in the management of disease. They make their living at this kind of thing, and I wish them well, but I imagine they will have a bewildering

---

There are three quite different levels of technology in medicine, so unlike each other as to seem altogether different undertakings.

---

time. For one thing, our methods of managing disease are constantly changing—partly under the influence of new bits of information brought in from all corners of biologic science. At the same time, a great many things are done that are not so closely related to science, some not related at all.

In fact, there are three quite different levels of technology ₄ in medicine, so unlike each other as to seem altogether different undertakings. Practitioners of medicine and the analysts will be in trouble if they are not kept separate.

1. First of all, there is a large body of what might be termed ₅ "nontechnology," impossible to measure in terms of its capacity to alter either the natural course of disease or its eventual outcome. A great deal of money is spent on this. It is valued highly by the professionals as well as the patients. It consists of what is sometimes called "supportive therapy." It tides patients over through diseases that are not, by and large, understood. It is what is meant by the phrases "caring for" and "standing by." It is indispensable. It is not, however, a technology in any real sense, since it does not involve measures directed at the underlying mechanism of disease.

It includes the large part of any good doctor's time that is ₆ taken up with simply providing reassurance, explaining to patients who fear that they have contracted one or another lethal disease that they are, in fact, quite healthy.

It is what physicians used to be engaged in at the bedside of patients with diphtheria, meningitis, poliomyelitis, lobar pneumonia, and all the rest of the infectious diseases that have since come under control. 7

It is what physicians must now do for patients with intractable cancer, severe rheumatoid arthritis, multiple sclerosis, stroke, and advanced cirrhosis. One can think of at least twenty major diseases that require this kind of supportive medical care because of the absence of an effective technology. I would include a large amount of what is called mental disease, and most varieties of cancer, in this category. 8

The cost of this nontechnology is very high, and getting higher all the time. It requires not only a great deal of time but also very hard effort and skill on the part of physicians; only the very best of doctors are good at coping with this kind of defeat. It also involves long periods of hospitalization, lots of nursing, lots of involvement of nonmedical professionals in and out of the hospital. It represents, in short, a substantial segment of today's expenditures for health. 9

2. At the next level up is a kind of technology best termed "halfway technology." This represents the kinds of things that must be done after the fact, in efforts to compensate for the incapacitating effects of certain diseases whose course one is unable to do very much about. It is a technology designed to make up for disease, or to postpone death. 10

The outstanding examples in recent years are the transplantations of hearts, kidneys, livers, and other organs, and the equally spectacular inventions of artificial organs. In the public mind, this kind of technology has come to seem like the equivalent of the high technologies of the physical sciences. The media tend to present each new procedure as though it represented a breakthrough and therapeutic triumph, instead of the makeshift that it really is. 11

In fact, this level of technology is, by its nature, at the same time highly sophisticated and profoundly primitive. It is the kind of thing that one must continue to do until there 12 is a genuine understanding of the mechanisms involved in disease. In chronic glomerulonephritis, for example, a much clearer insight will be needed into the events leading to the destruction of glomeruli by the immunologic reactants that now appear to govern this disease, before one will know how to intervene intelligently to prevent the process, or turn it around. But when this level of understanding has been reached, the technology of kidney replacement will not be much needed and should no longer pose the huge problems of logistics, cost, and ethics that it poses today.

An extremely complex and costly technology for the man-   13
agement of coronary heart disease has evolved—involving specialized ambulances and hospital units, all kinds of electronic gadgetry, and whole platoons of new professional personnel—to deal with the end results of coronary thrombosis. Almost everything offered today for the treatment of heart disease is at this level of technology, with the transplanted and artificial hearts as ultimate examples. When enough has been learned to know what really goes wrong in heart disease, one ought to be in a position to figure out ways to prevent or reverse the process, and when this happens the current elaborate technology will probably be set to one side.

Much of what is done in the treatment of cancer, by sur-   14
gery, irradiation, and chemotherapy, represents halfway technology, in the sense that these measures are directed at the existence of already established cancer cells, but not at the mechanisms by which cells become neoplastic.

It is a characteristic of this kind of technology that it costs   15
an enormous amount of money and requires a continuing expansion of hospital facilities. There is no end to the need for new, highly trained people to run the enterprise. And there is really no way out of this, at the present state of knowledge. If the installation of specialized coronary-care units can result in the extension of life for only a few patients with coronary disease (and there is no question that this technology is effective in a few cases), it seems to me an inevitable fact of life that as many of these as can be will be put together, and as

much money as can be found will be spent. I do not see that anyone has much choice in this. The only thing that can move medicine away from this level of technology is new information, and the only imaginable source of this information is research.

3. The third type of technology is the kind that is so 16 effective that it seems to attract the least public notice; it has come to be taken for granted. This is the genuinely decisive technology of modern medicine, exemplified best by modern methods for immunization against diphtheria, pertussis, and the childhood virus diseases, and the contemporary use of antibiotics and chemotherapy for bacterial infections. The capacity to deal effectively with syphilis and tuberculosis represents a milestone in human endeavor, even though full use of this potential has not yet been made. And there are, of course, other examples: the treatment of endocrinologic disorders with appropriate hormones, the prevention of hemolytic disease of the newborn, the treatment and prevention of various nutritional disorders, and perhaps just around the corner the management of Parkinsonism and sickle-cell anemia. There are other examples, and everyone will have his favorite candidates for the list, but the truth is that there are nothing like as many as the public has been led to believe.

The point to be made about this kind of technology—the 17 real high technology of medicine—is that it comes as the result of a genuine understanding of disease mechanisms, and when it becomes available, it is relatively inexpensive, and relatively easy to deliver.

Offhand, I cannot think of any important human disease 18 for which medicine possesses the outright capacity to prevent or cure where the cost of the technology is itself a major problem. The price is never as high as the cost of managing the same diseases during the earlier stages of no-technology or halfway technology. If a case of typhoid fever had to be managed today by the best methods of 1935, it would run to a staggering expense. At, say, around fifty days of hospitalization, requiring the most demanding kind of nursing care, with the obsessive concern for details of diet that characterized the therapy of that time, with daily laboratory monitoring, and, on occasion, surgical intervention for abdominal catastrophe, I should think $10,000 would be a conservative estimate for the illness, as contrasted with today's cost of a bottle of chloramphenicol and a day or two of fever. The halfway technology that was evolving for poliomyelitis in the early 1950s, just before the emergence of the basic research that made the vaccine possible, provides another illustration of the point. Do you remember Sister Kenny, and the cost of those institutes for rehabilitation, with all those ceremonially applied hot fomentations, and the debates about whether the affected limbs should be totally immobilized or kept in passive motion as frequently as possible, and the masses of statistically tormented data mobilized to support one view or the other? It is the cost of that kind of technology, and its relative effectiveness, that must be compared with the cost and effectiveness of the vaccine.

Pulmonary tuberculosis had similar episodes in its history. [19] There was a sudden enthusiasm for the surgical removal of infected lung tissue in the early 1950s, and elaborate plans were being made for new and expensive installations for major pulmonary surgery in tuberculosis hospitals, and then INH and streptomycin came along and the hospitals themselves were closed up.

It is when physicians are bogged down by their incomplete [20] technologies, by the innumerable things they are obliged to do in medicine when they lack a clear understanding of disease mechanisms, that the deficiencies of the health-care system are most conspicuous. If I were a policy-maker, interested in saving money for health care over the long haul, I would regard it as an act of high prudence to give high priority to a lot more basic research in biologic science. This is the only way to get the full mileage that biology owes to the science of medicine, even though it seems, as used to be said in the days when the phrase still had some meaning, like asking for the moon.

For Study and Discussion

QUESTIONS ABOUT PURPOSE

1. Is Thomas's primary purpose to explain the various kinds of medical technology or to argue that certain technologies are more useful than others? Explain your answer.
2. What does Thomas demonstrate about the relationship between cost-effective technology and a genuine understanding of the disease mechanism?

QUESTIONS ABOUT AUDIENCE

1. How does Thomas's assertion that policy-makers are interested in "how to deliver today's kind of health care, with equity, to all the people," suggest that he is aware of his readers' interest in the issue he will discuss?
2. To what extent does Thomas assume that his readers are familiar with the diseases he uses to illustrate each category? How does he provide assistance to his readers when the disease may be unfamiliar? See, for example, his discussion of typhoid fever in paragraph 18.

QUESTIONS ABOUT STRATEGIES

1. How does Thomas's definition of his three categories—nontechnology, halfway technology, and effective technology—clarify the single principle he has used to establish his classification system?
2. How does Thomas's discussion of specific diseases demonstrate that his divisions are complete? What aspect of his system enables him to discuss cancer as an illustration in two categories?

For Writing and Research

1. *Analyze* use of the word *technology* to classify various medical treatments.
2. *Practice* by classifying the emotional reactions you have felt when you have had various kinds of medical tests.
3. *Argue* that the best solution to the problem of illness is wellness—that is, eating carefully, exercising regularly, and avoiding dangerous addictions such as smoking.
4. *Synthesize* the research on diseases Thomas does not mention, such as AIDS or SARS. Then explain where such a disease would fit into his classification system.

George Orwell (a pen name for Eric Blair, 1903–1950) was born in Motihari, Bengal, where his father was employed with the Bengal civil service. He was brought to England at an early age for schooling (Eton), but rather than completing his education at the university, he served with the Indian imperial police in Burma (1922–1927). He wrote about these experiences in his first novel, *Burmese Days*. Later he returned to Europe and worked at various jobs (*Down and Out in Paris and London,* 1933) before fighting on the Republican side of the Spanish Civil War (*Homage to Catalania,* 1938). Orwell's attitudes toward war and government are reflected in his most famous books, *Animal Farm* (1945) and *Nineteen Eighty-Four* (1949). In "Politics and the English Language" (from *Shooting an Elephant, and Other Essays,* 1950) Orwell characterizes those aspects of our language that have allowed politicians to defend the indefensible.

Politics and the English Language

MOST PEOPLE WHO bother with the matter at all would admit that the English language is in a bad way, but it is generally assumed that we cannot by conscious action do anything about it. Our civilization is decadent and our language—so the argument runs—must inevitably share in the general collapse. It follows that any struggle against the abuse of language is a sentimental archaism, like preferring candles to electric light or hansom cabs to aeroplanes. Underneath this lies the half-conscious belief that language is a natural growth and not an instrument which we shape for our own purposes.

Now, it is clear that the decline of a language must ² ultimately have political and economic causes: it is not due simply to the bad influence of this or that individual writer. But an effect can become a cause, reinforcing the original cause and producing the same effect in an intensified form, and so on indefinitely. A man may take to drink because he feels himself to be a failure, and then fail all the more completely because he drinks. It is rather the same thing that is happening to the English language. It becomes ugly and inaccurate because our thoughts are foolish, but the slovenliness of our language makes it easier for us to have foolish thoughts. The point is that the process is reversible. Modern English, especially written English, is full of bad habits which spread by imitation and which can be avoided if one is willing to take the necessary trouble. If one gets rid of these habits one can think more clearly, and to think clearly is a necessary first step toward political regeneration: so that the fight against bad English is not frivolous and is not the exclusive concern of professional writers. I will come back to this presently, and I hope that by that time the meaning of what I have said here will have become clearer. Meanwhile, here are five specimens of the English language as it is now habitually written.

These five passages have not been picked out because they ³ are especially bad—I could have quoted far worse if I had chosen—but because they illustrate various of the mental vices from which we now suffer. They are a little below the average, but are fairly representative samples. I number them so that I can refer back to them when necessary:

> (1) I am not, indeed, sure whether it is not true to say that the Milton who once seemed not unlike a seventeenth-century Shelley had not become out of an experience ever more bitter in each year, more alien [*sic*] to the founder of that Jesuit sect which nothing could induce him to tolerate.
>
> Professor Harold Laski
> (Essay in *Freedom of Expression*)

(2) Above all, we cannot play ducks and drakes with a native battery of idioms which prescribes such egregious collocations of vocables as the Basic *put up with* for *tolerate* or *put at a loss* for *bewilder.*

Professor Lancelot Hogben (*Interglossa*)

(3) On the one side we have the free personality: by definition it is not neurotic, for it has neither conflict nor dream. Its desires, such as they are, are transparent, for they are just what institutional approval keeps in the forefront of consciousness; another institutional pattern would alter their number and intensity; there is little in them that is natural, irreducible, or culturally dangerous. But *on the other side,* the social bond itself is nothing but the mutual reflection of these self-secure integrities. Recall the definition of love. Is not this the very picture of a small academic? Where is there a place in this hall of mirrors for either personality or fraternity?

Essay on psychology in *Politics* (New York)

(4) All the "best people" from the gentlemen's clubs, and all the frantic fascist captains, united in common hatred of Socialism and bestial horror of the rising tide of the mass revolutionary movement, have turned to acts of provocation, to foul incendiarism, to medieval legends of poisoned wells, to legalize their own destruction of proletarian organizations, and rouse the agitated petty-bourgeoisie to chauvinistic fervor on behalf of the fight against the revolutionary way out of the crisis.

Communist pamphlet

(5) If a new spirit *is* to be infused into this old country, there is one thorny and contentious reform which must be tackled, and that is the humanization and galvanization of the B.B.C. Timidity

here will bespeak canker and atrophy of the soul. The heart of Britain may be sound and of strong beat, for instance, but the British lion's roar at present is like that of Bottom in Shakespeare's *Midsummer Night's Dream*—as gentle as any sucking dove. A virile new Britain cannot continue indefinitely to be traduced in the eyes or rather ears, of the world by the effete languors of Langham Place, brazenly masquerading as "standard English." When the Voice of Britain is heard at nine o'clock, better far and infinitely less ludicrous to hear aitches honestly dropped than the present priggish, inflated, inhibited, schoolma'amish arch braying of blameless bashful mewing maidens!

Letter in *Tribune*

Each of these passages has faults of its own, but, quite apart from avoidable ugliness, two qualities are common to all of them. The first is staleness of imagery; the other is lack of precision. The writer either has a meaning and cannot express it, or he inadvertently says something else, or he is almost indifferent as to whether his words mean anything or not. This mixture of vagueness and sheer incompetence is the most marked characteristic of modern English prose, and especially of any kind of political writing. As soon as certain topics are raised, the concrete melts into the abstract and no one seems able to think of turns of speech that are not hackneyed: prose consists less and less of *words* chosen for the sake of their meaning, and more and more of *phrases* tacked together like the sections of a prefabricated henhouse. I list below, with notes and examples, various of the tricks by means of which the work of prose-construction is habitually dodged:

DYING METAPHORS

A newly invented metaphor assists thought by evoking a visual image, while on the other hand a metaphor which is technically "dead" (e.g., *iron resolution*) has in effect reverted to being an ordinary word and can generally be used without loss of vividness. But in between these two classes there is a huge dump of worn-out metaphors which have lost all evocative power and are merely used because they save people the trouble of inventing phrases for themselves. Examples are: *Ring the changes on, take up the cudgels for, toe the line, ride roughshod over, stand shoulder to shoulder with, play into the hands of, no axe to grind, grist to the mill, fishing in troubled waters, on the order of the day, Achilles' heel, swan song, hotbed.* Many of these are used without knowledge of their meaning (what is a "rift," for instance?), and incompatible metaphors are frequently mixed, a sure sign that the writer is not interested in what he is saying. Some metaphors now current have been twisted out of their original meaning without those who use them even being aware of the fact. For example, *toe the line* is sometimes written *tow the line.* Another example is *the hammer and the anvil,* now always used with the implication that the anvil gets the worst of it. In real life it is always the anvil that breaks the hammer, never the other way about: a writer who stopped to think what he was saying would be aware of this, and would avoid perverting the original phrase.

OPERATORS OR VERBAL FALSE LIMBS

These save the trouble of picking out appropriate verbs and nouns, and at the same time pad each sentence with extra syllables which give it an appearance of symmetry. Characteristic phrases are *render inoperative, militate against, make contact with, be subjected to, give rise to, give grounds for, have the effect of, play a leading part (role) in, make itself felt, take effect, exhibit a tendency to, serve the purpose of, etc., etc.* The keynote is the elimination of simple verbs. Instead of being a single word, such as *break, stop, spoil, mend, kill,* a verb becomes a *phrase,* made up of a noun or adjective tacked on to some general-purpose verb such as *prove, serve, form, play, render.* In addition, the passive voice is wherever possible used in

6

preference to the active, and noun constructions are used instead of gerunds (*by examination of* instead of *by examining*). The range of verbs is further cut down by means of the -*ize* and *de-* formations, and the banal statements are given an appearance of profundity by means of the *not un-* formation. Simple conjunctions and prepositions are replaced by such phrases as *with respect to, having regard to, the fact that, by dint of, in view of, in the interests of, on the hypothesis that;* and the ends of sentences are saved by anticlimax by such resounding commonplaces as *greatly to be desired, cannot be left out of account, a development to be expected in the near future, deserving of serious consideration, brought to a satisfactory conclusion,* and so on and so forth.

PRETENTIOUS DICTION

Words like *phenomenon, element, individual* (as noun), *objective, categorical, effective, virtual, basic, primary, promote, constitute, exhibit, exploit, utilize, eliminate, liquidate* are used to dress up simple statement and give an air of scientic impartiality to biased judgments. Adjectives like *epoch-making, epic, historic, unforgettable, triumphant, age-old, inevitable, inexorable, veritable,* are used to dignify the sordid processes of international politics; while writing that aims at glorifying war usually takes on an archaic color, its characteristic words being: *realm, throne, chariot, mailed fist, trident, sword, shield, buckler, banner, jackboot, clarion.* Foreign words and expressions such as *cul de sac, ancien régime, deus ex machina, mutatis mutandis, status quo, gleichschaltung, weltanschauung,* are used to give an air of culture and elegance. Except for the useful abbreviations *i.e., e.g.,* and *etc.,* there is no real need for any of the hundreds of foreign phrases now current in English. Bad writers, and especially scientific, political, and sociological writers, are nearly always haunted by the notion that Latin or Greek words are grander than Saxon ones, and unnecessary words like *expedite, ameliorate, predict, extraneous, deracinated, clandestine, subaqueous,* and hundreds of others constantly gain ground from their Anglo-Saxon opposite numbers.* The jargon peculiar to Marxist writing (*hyena, hangman, cannibal, petty bourgeois, these gentry, lackey, flunkey, mad dog, White Guard,* etc.) consists largely of words and phrases translated from Russian, German, or French; but the normal way of coining a new word is to use a Latin or Greek root with the appropriate affix and, where necessary, the size formation. It is often easier to make up words of this kind (*deregionalize, impermissible, extramarital, nonfragmentary* and so forth) than to think up the English words that will cover one's meaning. The result, in general, is an increase in slovenliness and vagueness.

MEANINGLESS WORDS

In certain kinds of writing, particularly in art criticism and literary criticism, it is normal to come across long passages which are almost completely lacking in meaning.** Words like *romantic, plastic, values, human, dead, sentimental, natural, vitality,* as used in art criticism, are strictly meaningless, in the sense that they not only do not point to any discoverable object, but are hardly ever expected to do so by the reader. When one critic writes, "The outstanding feature of Mr. X's work is its living quality," while another writes, "The immediately striking thing about Mr. X's work is its peculiar deadness," the reader accepts this as a simple difference of opinion. If words like *black* and *white* were involved, instead of the

8

---

*An interesting illustration of this is the way in which the English flower names which were in use till very recently are being ousted by Greek ones, *snapdragon* becoming *antirrhinum, forget-me-not* becoming *myosotis,* etc. It is hard to see any practical reason for this change of fashion: it is probably due to an instinctive turning away from the more homely word and a vague feeling that the Greek word is scientific.

**Example: "Comfort's catholicity of perception and image, strangely Whitmanesque in range, almost the exact opposite in aesthetic compulsion, continues to evoke that trembling atmospheric accumulative hinting at a cruel, an inexorably serene timelessness. . . . Wrey Gardiner scores by aiming at simple bull's-eyes with precision. Only they are not so simple, and through this contented sadness runs more than the surface bittersweet of resignation." (*Poetry Quarterly*)

jargon words *dead* and *living*, he would see at once that language was being used in an improper way. Many political words are similarly abused. The word *Fascism* has now no meaning except in so far as it signifies "something not desirable." The words *democracy, socialism, freedom, patriotic, realistic, justice,* have each of them several different meanings which cannot be reconciled with one another. In the case of a word like *democracy,* not only is there no agreed definition, but the attempt to make one is resisted from all sides. It is almost universally felt that when we call a country democratic we are praising it: consequently the defenders of every kind of régime claim that it is a democracy, and fear that they might have to stop using the word if it were tied down to any one meaning. Words of this kind are often used in a consciously dishonest way. That is, the person who uses them has his own private definition, but allows his hearer to think he means something quite different. Statements like *Marshal Pétain was a true patriot, The Soviet press is the freest in the world, The Catholic Church is opposed to persecution,* are almost always made with intent to deceive. Other words used in variable meanings, in most cases more or less dishonestly, are: *class, totalitarian, science, progressive, reactionary, bourgeois, equality.*

Now that I have made this catalogue of swindles and perversions, let me give another example of the kind of writing that they lead to. This time it must of its nature be an imaginary one. I am going to translate a passage of good English into modern English of the worst sort. Here is a well-known verse from *Ecclesiastes:*   9

> I returned and saw under the sun, that the race is not to the swift, nor the battle to the strong, neither yet bread to the wise, nor yet riches to men of understanding, nor yet favour to men of skill; but time and chance happeneth to them all.

Here it is in modern English: 10

> Objective considerations of contemporary phenomena compels the conclusion that success or

failure in competitive activities exhibits no tendency to be commensurate with innate capacity, but that a considerable element of the unpredictable must invariably be taken into account.

This is a parody, but not a very gross one. Exhibit (3), above, for instance, contains several patches of the same kind of English. It will be seen that I have not made a full translation. The beginning and ending of the sentence follow the original meaning fairly closely, but in the middle the concrete illustrations—race, battle, bread—dissolve into the vague phrase "success or failure in competitive activities." This had to be so, because no modern writer of the kind I am discussing—no one capable of using phrases like "objective consideration of contemporary phenomena"—would ever tabulate his thoughts in that precise and detailed way. The whole tendency of modern prose is away from concreteness. Now analyze these two sentences a little more closely. The first contains forty-nine words but only sixty syllables, and all its words are those of everyday life. The second contains thirty-eight words of ninety syllables: eighteen of its words are from Latin roots, and one from Greek. The first sentence contains six vivid images, and only one phrase ("time and chance") that could be called vague. The second contains not a single fresh, arresting phrase, and in spite of its ninety syllables it gives only a shortened version of the meaning contained in the first. Yet without a doubt it is the second kind of sentence that is gaining ground in modern English. I do not want to exaggerate. This kind of writing is not yet universal, and outcrops of simplicity will occur here and there in the worst-written page. Still, if you or I were told to write a few lines on the uncertainty of human fortunes, we should probably come much nearer to my imaginary sentence than to the one from *Ecclesiastes*.

As I have tried to show, modern writing at its worst does not consist in picking out words for the sake of their meaning and inventing images in order to make the meaning clearer. It consists in gumming together long strips of words which

11

12

have already been set in order by someone else, and making the results presentable by sheer humbug. The attraction of this way of writing is that it is easy. It is easier—even quicker, once you have the habit—to say *In my opinion it is not an unjustifiable assumption that* than to say *I think*. If you use ready-made phrases, you not only don't have to hunt about for words; you also don't have to bother with the rhythms of your sentences, since these phrases are generally so arranged as to be more or less euphonious. When you are composing in a hurry—when you are dictating to a stenographer, for instance, or making a public speech—it is natural to fall into a pretentious, Latinized style. Tags like *a consideration which we should do well to bear in mind* or *a conclusion to which all of us would readily assent* will save many a sentence from coming down with a bump. By using stale metaphors, similes, and idioms, you save much mental effort, at the cost of leaving your meaning vague, not only for your reader but for yourself. This is the significance of mixed metaphors. The sole aim of a metaphor is to call up a visual image. When these images clash—as in *The Fascist octopus has sung its swan song, the jackboot is thrown into the melting pot*—it can be taken as certain that the writer is not seeing a mental image of the objects he is naming; in other words he is not really thinking. Look again at the examples I gave at the beginning of this essay. Professor Laski (1) uses five negatives in fifty-three words. One of these is superfluous, making nonsense of the whole passage, and in addition there is the slip—*alien* for akin— making further nonsense, and several avoidable pieces of clumsiness which increase the general vagueness. Professor Hogben (2) plays ducks and drakes with a battery which is able to write prescriptions, and, while disapproving of the everyday phrase *put up with,* is unwilling to look *egregious* up in the dictionary and see what it means; (3), if one takes an uncharitable attitude towards it, is simply meaningless: probably one could work out its intended meaning by reading the whole of the article in which it occurs. In (4), the writer knows more or less what he wants to say, but an accumulation of stale phrases chokes him like tea leaves blocking a sink. In (5), words and meaning have almost parted company. People who write in this manner usually have a general emotional meaning—they dislike one thing and want to express solidarity with another—but they are not interested in the detail of what they are saying. A scrupulous writer, in every sentence that he writes, will ask himself at least four questions, thus: What am I trying to say? What words will express it? What image or idiom will make it clearer? Is this image fresh enough to have an effect? And he will probably ask himself two more: Could I put it more shortly? Have I said anything that is avoidably ugly? But you are not obliged to go to all this trouble. You can shirk it by simply throwing your mind open and letting the ready-made phrases come crowding in. They will construct your sentences for you—even think your thoughts for you, to a certain extent—and at need they will perform the important service of partially concealing your meaning even from yourself. It is at this point that the special connection between politics and the debasement of language becomes clear.

In our time it is broadly true that political writing is bad writing. Where it is not true, it will generally be found that the writer is some kind of rebel, expressing his private opinions and not a "party line." Orthodoxy, of whatever color, seems to demand a lifeless, imitative style. The political dialects to be found in pamphlets, leading articles, manifestoes, White Papers and the speeches of undersecretaries do, of course, vary from party to party, but they are all alike in that one almost never finds in them a fresh, vivid, homemade turn of speech. When one watches some tired hack on the platform mechanically repeating the familiar phrases—*bestial atrocities, iron heel, bloodstained tyranny, free peoples of the world, stand shoulder to shoulder*—one often has a curious feeling that one is not watching a live human being but some kind of dummy: a feeling which suddenly becomes stronger at moments when the light catches the speaker's spectacles and turns them into blank discs which seem to have no eyes behind them. And this is not altogether fanciful. A speaker who uses that kind of phraseology has gone

13

some distance toward turning himself into a machine. The appropriate noises are coming out of his larynx, but his brain is not involved as it would be if he were choosing his words for himself. If the speech he is making is one that he is accustomed to make over and over again, he may be almost unconscious of what he is saying, as one is when one utters the responses in church. And this reduced state of consciousness, if not indispensable, is at any rate favorable to political conformity.

In our time, political speech and writing are largely the defense of the indefensible. Things like the continuance of British rule in India, the Russian purges and deportations, the dropping of the atom bombs on Japan, can indeed be defended, but only by arguments which are too brutal for most people to face, and which do not square with the professed aims of political parties. Thus political language has to consist largely of euphemism, question-begging and sheer cloudy vagueness. Defenseless villages are bombarded from the air, the inhabitants driven out into the countryside, the cattle machine-gunned, the huts set on fire with incendiary bullets: this is called *pacification*. Millions of peasants are robbed of their farms and sent trudging along the roads with no more than they can carry: this is called *transfer of population* or *rectification of frontiers*. People are imprisoned for years without trial, or shot in the back of the neck or sent to die of scurvy in Arctic lumber camps: this is called *elimination of unreliable elements*. Such phraseology is needed if one wants to name things without calling up mental pictures of them. Consider for instance some comfortable English professor defending Russian totalitarianism. He cannot say outright, "1 believe in killing off your opponents when you can get good results by doing so." Probably, therefore, he will say something like this:

"While freely conceding that the Soviet régime exhibits certain features which the humanitarian may be inclined to deplore, we must, I think, agree that a certain curtailment of the right to political opposition is an unavoidable concomitmant of transitional periods, and that the rigors which the

14

15

Russian people have been called upon to undergo have been amply justified in the sphere of concrete achievement."

The inflated style is itself a kind of euphemism. A mass of Latin words falls upon the facts like soft snow, blurring the outlines and covering up all the details. The great enemy of clear language is insincerity. When there is a gap between one's real and one's declared aims, one turns as it were instinctively to long words and exhausted idioms, like a cuttle-fish squirting out ink. In our age there is no such thing as "keeping out of politics." All issues are political issues, and politics itself is a mass of lies, evasions, folly, hatred, and schizophrenia. When the general atmosphere is bad, language must suffer. I should expect to find—this is a guess which I have not sufficient knowledge to verify—that the German, Russian and Italian languages have all deteriorated in the last ten or fifteen years, as a result of dictatorship.

But if thought corrupts language, language can also corrupt thought. A bad usage can spread by tradition and imitation, even among people who should and do know better. The debased language that I have been discussing is in some ways very convenient. Phrases like *a not unjustifiable assumption, leaves much to be desired, would serve no good purpose, a consideration which we should do well to bear in mind,* are a continuous temptation, a packet of aspirins always at one's elbow. Look back through this essay, and for certain you will find that I have again and again committed the very faults I am protesting against. By this morning's post I have received a pamphlet dealing with conditions in Germany. The author tells me that he "felt impelled" to write it. I open it at random, and here is almost the first sentence that I see: "[The Allies] have an opportunity not only of achieving a radical transformation of Germany's social and political structure in such a way as to avoid a nationalistic reaction in Germany itself, but at the same time of laying the foundations of a co-operative and unified Europe." You see, he "feels impelled" to write—feels, presumably, that he has something new to say—and yet his words, like cavalry horses answering the bugle, group themselves automatically into the familiar dreary pattern.

This invasion of one's mind by ready-made phrases *(lay the foundation, achieve a radical transformation)* can only be prevented if one is constantly on guard against them, and every such phrase anaesthetizes a portion of one's brain.

I said earlier that the decadence of our language is prob- 18 ably curable. Those who deny this would argue, if they produced an argument at all, that language merely reflects existing social conditions, and that we cannot influence its development by any direct tinkering with words and con- structions. So far as the general tone or spirit of a language goes, this may be true, but it is not true in detail. Silly words and expressions have often disappeared, not through any evolutionary process but owing to the conscious action of a minority. Two recent examples were *explore every avenue* and *leave no stone unturned,* which were killed by the jeers of a few journalists. There is a long list of flyblown metaphors which could similarly be got rid of if enough people would interest themselves in the job; and it should also be possible to laugh the *not un-* formation out of existence,* to reduce the amount of Latin and Greek in the average sentence, to drive out foreign phrases and strayed scientific words, and, in general, to make pretentiousness unfashionable. But all these are minor points. The defense of the English language im- plies more than this, and perhaps it is best to start by saying what it does *not* imply.

To begin with it has nothing to do with archaism, with 19 the salvaging of obsolete words and turns of speech, or with the setting up of a "standard English" which must never be departed from. On the contrary, it is especially concerned with the scrapping of every word or idiom which has outworn its usefulness. It has nothing to do with correct grammar and syntax, which are of no importance so long as one makes one's meaning clear, or with the avoid- ance of Americanisms, or with having what is called a

---

*One can cure oneself of the *not un-* formation by memorizing this sentence: *A not unblack dog was chasing a not unsmall rabbit across a not ungreen field.*

"good prose style." On the other hand it is not concerned with fake simplicity and the attempt to make written English colloquial. Nor does it even imply in every case preferring the Saxon word to the Latin one, though it does imply using the fewest and shortest words that will cover one's meaning. What is above all needed is to let the meaning choose the word, and not the other way about. In prose, the worst thing one can do with words is to surrender to them. When you think of a concrete object, you think wordlessly, and then, if you want to describe the thing you have been visualizing you probably hunt about till you find the exact words that seem to fit it. When you think of something abstract you are more inclined to use words from the start, and unless you make a conscious effort to prevent it, the existing dialect will come rushing in and do the job for you, at the expense of blurring or even changing your meaning. Probably it is better to put off using words as long as possible and get one's meaning as clear as one can through pictures or sensations. Afterward one can choose—not simply *accept*—the phrases that will best cover the meaning, and then switch round and decide what impression one's words are likely to make on another person. This last effort of the mind cuts out all stale or mixed images, all prefabricated phrases, needless repetitions, and humbug and vagueness generally. But one can often be in doubt about the effect of a word or a phrase, and one needs rules that one can rely on when instinct fails. I think the following rules will cover most cases.

(i) Never use a metaphor, simile, or other figure of speech which you are used to seeing in print.
(ii) Never use a long word where a short one will do.
(iii) If it is possible to cut a word out, always cut it out.
(iv) Never use the passive where you can use the active.
(v) Never use a foreign phrase, a scientific word, or a jargon word if you can think of an everyday English equivalent.
(vi) Break any of these rules sooner than say anything outright barbarous.

These rules sound elementary, and so they are, but they demand a deep change of attitude in anyone who has grown used to writing in the style now fashionable. One could keep all of them and still write bad English, but one could not write the kind of stuff that I quoted in those five specimens at the beginning of this article.

I have not here been considering the literary use of language, but merely language as an instrument for expressing and not for concealing or preventing thought. Stuart Chase and others have come near to claiming that all abstract words are meaningless, and have used this as a pretext for advocating a kind of political quietism. Since you don't know what Fascism is, how can you struggle against Fascism? One need not swallow such absurdities as this, but one ought to recognize that the present political chaos is connected with the decay of language, and that one can probably bring about some improvement by starting at the verbal end. If you simplify your English, you are freed from the worst follies of orthodoxy. You cannot speak any of the necessary dialects, and when you make a stupid remark its stupidity will be obvious, even to yourself. Political language—and with variations this is true of all political parties, from Conservatives to Anarchists—is designed to make lies sound truthful and murder respectful, and to give an appearance of solidity to pure wind. One cannot change this all in a moment, but one can at least change one's own habits, and from time to time one can even, if one jeers loudly enough, send some worn-out and useless phrase—some *jackboot, Achilles' heel, hotbed, melting pot, acid test, veritable inferno,* or other lump of verbal refuse—into the dustbin where it belongs.

For Study and Discussion

QUESTIONS ABOUT PURPOSE

1. How does Orwell believe the abuse of the English language can be reversed?
2. What connection does he see between politics and the debasement of language?

QUESTIONS ABOUT AUDIENCE

1. How does Orwell expect his readers to respond to the two versions of *Ecclesiastes*?
2. What assumptions does he make about his readers' writing when he addresses them as "you"?

QUESTIONS ABOUT STRATEGIES

1. What is the guiding principle Orwell uses to classify the various "tricks" he illustrates?
2. What strategies (questions, rules) should "scrupulous writers" use as they compose each sentence?

For Writing and Research

1. *Analyze* Orwell's own writing to see if he has "committed the very faults I am protesting?
2. *Practice* by classifying various abuses of language you can find in writings about celebrities.
3. *Argue* that vague and evasive political language has convinced the public to dismiss politicians as insincere and irrelevant.
4. *Synthesize* the various speeches by presidents such as Abraham Lincoln, Franklin D. Roosevelt, John F. Kennedy, Ronald Reagan, and George W. Bush. Then use this evidence to support or correct Orwell's assertion that political speech is "the defense of the indefensible."

Flannery O'Connor (1925–1964) was born in Savannah, Georgia, and was educated at the Women's College of Georgia and the University of Iowa. She returned to her mother's farm near Milledgeville, Georgia, when she discovered that she had contracted lupus erythematosus, the systemic disease that had killed her father and of which she herself was to die. For the last fourteen years of her life, she lived a quiet, productive life on the farm—raising peacocks, painting, and writing the extraordinary stories and novels that won her worldwide acclaim. Her novels, *Wise Blood* (1952), which was adapted for film in 1979, and *The Violent Bear It Away* (1960), deal with fanatical preachers. Her thirty-one carefully crafted stories, combining grotesque comedy and violent tragedy, appear in *A Good Man Is Hard to Find* (1955), *Everything That Rises Must Converge* (1965), and *The Complete Stories* (1971), which won the National Book Award. "Revelation," reprinted from *The Complete Stories* dramatizes the ironic discoveries a woman makes about how different classes of people fit into the order of things.

Revelation

T HE DOCTOR'S WAITING room, which was very small, was almost full when the Turpins entered and Mrs. Turpin, who was very large, made it look even smaller by her presence. She stood looming at the head of the magazine table set in the center of it, a living demonstration that the room was inadequate and ridiculous. Her little bright black eyes took in all the patients as she sized up the seating situation.

1

There was one vacant chair and a place on the sofa occupied by a blond child in a dirty blue romper who should have been told to move over and make room for the lady. He was five or six, but Mrs. Turpin saw at once that no one was going to tell him to move over. He was slumped down in the seat, his arms idle at his sides and his eyes idle in his head; his nose ran unchecked.

Mrs. Turpin put a firm hand on Claud's shoulder and said   2
in a voice that included anyone who wanted to listen, "Claud, you sit in that chair there," and gave him a push down into the vacant one. Claud was florid and bald and sturdy, somewhat shorter than Mrs. Turpin, but he sat down as if he were accustomed to doing what she told him to.

Mrs. Turpin remained standing. The only man in the room   3
besides Claud was a lean stringy old fellow with a rusty hand spread out on each knee, whose eyes were closed as if he were asleep or dead or pretending to be so as not to get up and offer her his seat. Her gaze settled agreeably on a well-dressed gray-haired lady whose eyes met hers and whose expression said: if that child belonged to me, he would have some manners and move over—there's plenty of room there for you and him too.

Claud looked up with a sigh and made as if to rise.   4

"Sit down," Mrs. Turpin said. "You know you're not sup-   5
posed to stand on that leg. He has an ulcer on his leg," she explained.

Claud lifted his foot onto the magazine table and rolled his   6
trouser leg up to reveal a purple swelling on a plump marble-white calf.

"My!" the pleasant lady said. "How did you do that?"   7

"A cow kicked him," Mrs. Turpin said.   8

"Goodness!" said the lady.   9

Claud rolled his trouser leg down.   10

"Maybe the little boy would move over," the lady sug-   11
gested, but the child did not stir.

"Somebody will be leaving in a minute," Mrs. Turpin said.   12
She could not understand why a doctor—with as much money as they made charging five dollars a day to just stick their head

in the hospital door and look at you—couldn't afford a decent-sized waiting room. This one was hardly bigger than a garage. The table was cluttered with limp-looking magazines and at one end of it there was a big green glass ash tray full of cigarette butts and cotton wads with little blood spots on them. If she had had anything to do with the running of the place, that would have been emptied every so often. There were no chairs against the wall at the head of the room. It had a rectangular-shaped panel in it that permitted a view of the office where the nurse came and went and the secretary listened to the radio. A plastic fern in a gold pot sat in the opening and trailed its fronds down almost to the floor. The radio was softly playing gospel music.

Just then the inner door opened and a nurse with the high- 13
est stack of yellow hair Mrs. Turpin had ever seen put her face in the crack and called for the next patient. The woman sitting beside Claud grasped the two arms of her chair and hoisted herself up; she pulled her dress free from her legs and lumbered through the door where the nurse had disappeared.

Mrs. Turpin eased into the vacant chair, which held her 14
tight as a corset. "I wish I could reduce," she said, and rolled her eyes and gave a comic sigh.

"Oh, *you* aren't fat," the stylish lady said. 15

"Ooooo I am too," Mrs. Turpin said. "Claud he eats all he 16
wants to and never weighs over one hundred and seventy-five pounds, but me I just look at something good to eat and I gain some weight," and her stomach and shoulders shook with laughter. "You can eat all you want to, can't you, Claud?" she asked, turning to him.

Claud only grinned. 17

"Well, as long as you have such a good disposition," the 18
stylish lady said, "I don't think it makes a bit of difference what size you are. You just can't beat a good disposition."

Next to her was a fat girl of eighteen or nineteen, scowling 19
into a thick blue book which Mrs. Turpin saw was entitled *Human Development*. The girl raised her head and directed her scowl at Mrs. Turpin as if she did not like her looks. She appeared annoyed that anyone should speak while she tried

to read. The poor girl's face was blue with acne and Mrs. Turpin thought how pitiful it was to have a face like that at that age. She gave the girl a friendly smile but the girl only scowled the harder. Mrs. Turpin herself was fat but she had always had good skin, and, though she was forty-seven years old, there was not a wrinkle in her face except around her eyes from laughing too much.

Next to the ugly girl was the child, still in exactly the same position, and next to him was a thin leathery old woman in a cotton print dress. She and Claud had three sacks of chicken feed in their pump house that was in the same print. She had seen from the first that the child belonged with the old woman. She could tell by the way they sat—kind of vacant and white-trashy, as if they would sit there until Doomsday if nobody called and told them to get up. And at right angles but next to the well-dressed pleasant lady was a lank-faced woman who was certainly the child's mother. She had on a yellow sweat shirt and wine-colored slacks, both gritty-looking, and the rims of her lips were stained with snuff. Her dirty yellow hair was tied behind with a little piece of red paper ribbon. Worse than niggers any day, Mrs. Turpin thought.

The gospel hymn playing was, "When I looked up and He looked down," and Mrs. Turpin, who knew it, supplied the last line mentally, "And wona these days I know I'll weear a crown."

Without appearing to, Mrs. Turpin always noticed people's feet. The well-dressed lady had on red and gray suede shoes to match her dress. Mrs. Turpin had on her good black patent leather pumps. The ugly girl had on Girl Scout shoes and heavy socks. The old woman had on tennis shoes and the white-trashy mother had on what appeared to be bedroom slippers, black straw with gold braid threaded through them—exactly what you would have expected her to have on.

Sometimes at night when she couldn't go to sleep, Mrs. Turpin would occupy herself with the question of who she would have chosen to be if she couldn't have been herself. If Jesus had said to her before he made her, "There's only two places available for you. You can either be a nigger or white-trash," what would she have said? "Please, Jesus, please," she would have said, "just let me wait until there's another place available," and he would have said, "No, you have to go right now and I have only those two places so make up your mind." She would have wiggled and squirmed and begged and pleaded but it would have been no use and finally she would have said, "All right, make me a nigger then—but that don't mean a trashy one." And he would have made her a neat clean respectable Negro woman, herself but black.

Next to the child's mother was a red-headed youngish   24
woman, reading one of the magazines and working a piece of chewing gum, hell for leather, as Claud would say. Mrs. Turpin could not see the woman's feet. She was not white-trash, just common. Sometimes Mrs. Turpin occupied herself at night naming the classes of people. On the bottom of the heap were most colored people, not the kind she would have been if she had been one, but most of them; then next to them—not above, just away from—were the white-trash; then above them were the home-owners, and above them the home-and-land-owners, to which she and Claud belonged. Above she and Claud were people with a lot of money and much bigger houses and much more land. But here the complexity of it would begin to bear in on her, for some of the people with a lot of money were common and ought to be below she and Claud and some of the people who had good blood had lost their money and had to rent and then there were colored people who owned their homes and land as well. There was a colored dentist in town who had two red Lincolns and a swimming pool and a farm with registered white-face cattle on it. Usually by the time she had fallen asleep all the classes of people were moiling and roiling around in her head, and she would dream they were all crammed in together in a box car, being ridden off to be put in a gas oven.

"That's a beautiful clock," she said and nodded to her right.   25
It was a big wall clock, the face encased in a brass sunburst.

"Yes, it's very pretty," the stylish lady said agreeably. "And   26
right on the dot too," she added, glancing at her watch.

The ugly girl beside her cast an eye upward at the clock, smirked, then looked directly at Mrs. Turpin and smirked again. Then she returned her eyes to her book. She was obviously the lady's daughter because, although they didn't look anything alike as to disposition, they both had the same shape of face and the same blue eyes. On the lady they sparkled pleasantly but in the girl's seared face they appeared alternately to smolder and to blaze.

What if Jesus had said, "All right, you can be white-trash or a nigger or ugly"!

Mrs. Turpin felt an awful pity for the girl, though she thought it was one thing to be ugly and another to act ugly.

The woman with the snuff-stained lips turned around in her chair and looked up at the clock. Then she turned back and appeared to look a little to the side of Mrs. Turpin. There was a cast in one of her eyes. "You want to know wher you can get you one of themther clocks?" she asked in a loud voice.

"No, I already have a nice clock," Mrs. Turpin said. Once somebody like her got a leg in the conversation, she would be all over it.

"You can get you one with green stamps," the woman said. "That's most likely wher he got hisn. Save you up enough, you can get you most anythang. I got me some joo'ry."

Ought to have got you a wash rag and some soap, Mrs. Turpin thought.

"I get contour sheets with mine," the pleasant lady said.

The daughter slammed her book shut. She looked straight in front of her, directly through Mrs. Turpin and on through the yellow curtain and the plate glass window which made the wall behind her. The girl's eyes seemed lit all of a sudden with a peculiar light, an unnatural light like night road signs give. Mrs. Turpin turned her head to see if there was anything going on outside that she should see, but she could not see anything. Figures passing cast only a pale shadow through the curtain. There was no reason the girl should single her out for her ugly looks.

"Miss Finley," the nurse said, cracking the door. The gum-chewing woman got up and passed in front of her and Claud and went into the office. She had on red high-heeled shoes.

Directly across the table, the ugly girl's eyes were fixed 37
on Mrs. Turpin as if she had some very special reason for
disliking her.

"This is wonderful weather, isn't it?" the girl's mother said. 38

"It's good weather for cotton if you can get the niggers to 39
pick it," Mrs. Turpin said, "but niggers don't want to pick
cotton any more. You can't get the white folks to pick it and
now you can't get the niggers—because they got to be right
up there with the white folks."

"They gonna *try* anyways," the white-trash woman said, 40
leaning forward.

"Do you have one of the cotton-picking machines?" the 41
pleasant lady asked.

"No," Mrs. Turpin said, "they leave half the cotton in the 42
field. We don't have much cotton anyway. If you want to make
it farming now, you have to have a little of everything. We got
a couple of acres of cotton and a few hogs and chickens and just
enough white-face that Claud can look after them himself."

"One thang I don't want," the white-trash woman said, 43
wiping her mouth with the back of her hand. "Hogs. Nasty
stinking things, a-gruntin and a-rootin all over the place."

Mrs. Turpin gave her the merest edge of her attention. 44
"Our hogs are not dirty and they don't stink," she said.
"They're cleaner than some children I've seen. Their feet never
touch the ground. We have a pig-parlor—that's where you
raise them on concrete," she explained to the pleasant lady,
"and Claud scoots them down with the hose every afternoon
and washes off the floor." Cleaner by far than that child right
there, she thought. Poor nasty little thing. He had not moved
except to put the thumb of his dirty hand into his mouth.

The woman turned her face away from Mrs. Turpin. "I 45
know I wouldn't scoot down no hog with no hose," she said
to the wall.

You wouldn't have no hog to scoot down, Mrs. Turpin 46
said to herself.

"A-gruntin and a-rootin and a-groanin," the woman 47
muttered.

"We got a little of everything," Mrs. Turpin said to the pleasant lady. "It's no use in having more than you can handle yourself with help like it is. We found enough niggers to pick our cotton this year but Claud he has to go after them and take them home again in the evening. They can't walk that half a mile. No they can't. I tell you," she said and laughed merrily, "I sure am tired of buttering up niggers, but you got to love em if you want em to work for you. When they come in the morning, I run out and I say, 'Hi yawl this morning?' and when Claud drives them off to the field I just wave to beat the band and they just wave back." And she waved her hand rapidly to illustrate.

"Like you read out of the same book," the lady said, showing she understood perfectly.

"Child, yes," Mrs. Turpin said. "And when they come in from the field, I run out with a bucket of icewater. That's the way it's going to be from now on," she said. "You may as well face it."

"One thang I know," the white-trash woman said. "Two thangs I ain't going to do: love no niggers or scoot down no hog with no hose." And she let out a bark of contempt.

The look that Mrs. Turpin and the pleasant lady exchanged indicated they both understood that you had to *have* certain things before you could *know* certain things. But every time Mrs. Turpin exchanged a look with the lady, she was aware that the ugly girl's peculiar eyes were still on her, and she had trouble bringing her attention back to the conversation.

"When you got something," she said, "you got to look after it." And when you ain't got a thing but breath and britches, she added to herself, you can afford to come to town every morning and just sit on the Court House coping and spit.

A grotesque revolving shadow passed across the curtain behind her and was thrown palely on the opposite wall. Then a bicycle clattered down against the outside of the building. The door opened and a colored boy glided in with a tray from the drugstore. It had two large red and white paper cups on it with tops on them. He was a tall, very black boy in discolored white pants and a green nylon shirt. He was chewing gum slowly, as if to music. He set the tray down in the office opening next to the fern and stuck his head through to look for the secretary. She was not in there. He rested his arms on the ledge and waited, his narrow bottom stuck out, swaying to the left and right. He raised a hand over his head and scratched the base of his skull.

"You see that button there, boy?" Mrs. Turpin said. "You can punch that and she'll come. She's probably in the back somewhere." 55

"Is thas right?" the boy said agreeably, as if he had never seen the button before. He leaned to the right and put his finger on it. "She sometime out," he said and twisted around to face his audience, his elbows behind him on the counter. The nurse appeared and he twisted back again. She handed him a dollar and he rooted in his pocket and made the change and counted it out to her. She gave him fifteen cents for a tip and he went out with the empty tray. The heavy door swung too slowly and closed at length with the sound of suction. For a moment no one spoke. 56

"They ought to send all them niggers back to Africa," the white-trash woman said. "That's wher they come from in the first place." 57

"Oh, I couldn't do without my good colored friends," the pleasant lady said. 58

"There's a heap of things worse than a nigger," Mrs. Turpin agreed. "It's all kinds of them just like it's all kinds of us." 59

"Yes, and it takes all kinds to make the world go round," the lady said in her musical voice. 60

As she said it, the raw-complexioned girl snapped her teeth together. Her lower lip turned downwards and inside out, revealing the pale pink inside of her mouth. After a second it rolled back up. It was the ugliest face Mrs. Turpin had ever seen anyone make and for a moment she was certain that the girl had made it at her. She was looking at her as if she had 61 known and disliked her all her life—all of Mrs. Turpin's life, it seemed too, not just all the girl's life. Why, girl, I don't even know you, Mrs. Turpin said silently.

She forced her attention back to the discussion. "It wouldn't be practical to send them back to Africa," she said. "They wouldn't want to go. They got it too good here." 62

"Wouldn't be what they wanted—if I had anythang to do with it," the woman said. 63

"It wouldn't be a way in the world you could get all the niggers back over there," Mrs. Turpin said. "They'd be hiding out and lying down and turning sick on you and wailing and hollering and raring and pitching. It wouldn't be a way in the world to get them over there." 64

"They got over here," the trashy woman said. "Get back like they got over." 65

"It wasn't so many of them then," Mrs. Turpin explained. 66

The woman looked at Mrs. Turpin as if here was an idiot indeed but Mrs. Turpin was not bothered by the look, considering where it came from. 67

"Nooo," she said, "they're going to stay here where they can go to New York and marry white folks and improve their color. That's what they all want to do, every one of them, improve their color." 68

"You know what comes of that, don't you?" Claud asked. 69

"No, Claud, what?" Mrs. Turpin said. 70

Claud's eyes twinkled. "White-faced niggers," he said with never a smile. 71

Everybody in the office laughed except the white-trash and the ugly girl. The girl gripped the book in her lap with white fingers. The trashy woman looked around her from face to face as if she thought they were all idiots. The old woman in the feed sack dress continued to gaze expressionless across the floor at the high-top shoes of the man opposite her, the one who had been pretending to be asleep when the Turpins came in. He was laughing heartily, his hands still spread out on his knees. The child had fallen to the side and was lying now almost face down in the old woman's lap. 72

While they recovered from their laughter, the nasal chorus   73
on the radio kept the room from silence.

> *You go to blank blank*
> *And I'll go to mine*
> *But we'll all blank along*
> *To-geth-ther,*
> *And all along the blank*
> *We'll hep eachother out*
> *Smile-ling in any kind of*
> *Weath-ther!*

Mrs. Turpin didn't catch every word but she caught   74
enough to agree with the spirit of the song and it turned her
thoughts sober. To help anybody out that needed it was her
philosophy of life. She never spared herself when she found
somebody in need, whether they were white or black, trash
or decent. And of all she had to be thankful for, she was most
thankful that this was so. If Jesus had said, "You can be high
society and have all the money you want and be thin and
svelte-like, but you can't be a good woman with it," she
would have had to say, "Well don't make me that then. Make
me a good woman and it don't matter what else, how fat or
how ugly or how poor!" Her heart rose. He had not made
her a nigger or white-trash or ugly! He had made her herself
and given her a little of everything. Jesus, thank you! she said.
Thank you thank you thank you! Whenever she counted her
blessings she felt as buoyant as if she weighed one hundred
and twenty-five pounds instead of one hundred and eighty.

"What's wrong with your little boy?" the pleasant lady   75
asked the white-trashy woman.

"He has a ulcer," the woman said proudly. "He ain't give   76
me a minute's peace since he was born. Him and her are just
alike," she said, nodding at the old woman, who was running
her leathery fingers through the child's pale hair. "Look like
I can't get nothing down them two but Co' Cola and candy."

That's all you try to get down em, Mrs. Turpin said to her-   77
self. Too lazy to light the fire. There was nothing you could
tell her about people like them that she didn't know already.

And it was not just that they didn't have anything. Because if you gave them everything, in two weeks it would all be broken or filthy or they would have chopped it up for lightwood. She knew all this from her own experience. Help them you must, but help them you couldn't.

All at once the ugly girl turned her lips inside out again. Her   78
eyes fixed like two drills on Mrs. Turpin. This time there was no mistaking that there was something urgent behind them.

Girl, Mrs. Turpin exclaimed silently, I haven't done a thing   79
to you! The girl might be confusing her with somebody else. There was no need to sit by and let herself be intimidated. "You must be in college," she said boldly, looking directly at the girl. "I see you reading a book there."

The girl continued to stare and pointedly did not answer.   80

Her mother blushed at this rudeness. "The lady asked you   81
a question, Mary Grace," she said under her breath.

"I have ears," Mary Grace said.   82

The poor mother blushed again. "Mary Grace goes to   83
Wellesley College," she explained. She twisted one of the buttons on her dress. "In Massachusetts," she added with a grimace. "And in the summer she just keeps right on studying. Just reads all the time, a real book worm. She's done real well at Wellesley; she's taking English and Math and History and Psychology and Social Studies," she rattled on, "and I think it's too much. I think she ought to get out and have fun."

The girl looked as if she would like to hurl them all   84
through the plate glass window.

"Way up north," Mrs. Turpin murmured and thought,   85
well, it hasn't done much for her manners.

"I'd almost rather to have him sick," the white-trash   86
woman said, wrenching the attention back to herself. "He's so mean when he ain't. Look like some children just take natural to meanness. It's some gets bad when they get sick but he was the opposite. Took sick and turned good. He don't give me no trouble now. It's me waitin to see the doctor," she said.

If I was going to send anybody back to Africa, Mrs. Turpin   87
thought, it would be your kind, woman. "Yes, indeed," she

said aloud, but looking up at the ceiling, "it's a heap of things worse than a nigger." And dirtier than a hog, she added to herself.

"I think people with bad dispositions are more to be pitied than anyone on earth," the pleasant lady said in a voice that was decidedly thin. 88

"I thank the Lord he has blessed me with a good one," Mrs. Turpin said. "The day has never dawned that I couldn't find something to laugh at." 89

"Not since she married me anyways," Claud said with a comical straight face. 90

Everybody laughed except the girl and the white-trash. 91

Mrs. Turpin's stomach shook. "He's such a caution," she said, "that I can't help but laugh at him." 92

The girl made a loud ugly noise through her teeth. 93

Her mother's mouth grew thin and tight. "I think the worst thing in the world," she said, "is an ungrateful person. To have everything and not appreciate it. I know a girl," she said, "who has parents who would give her anything, a little brother who loves her dearly, who is getting a good education, who wears the best clothes, but who can never say a kind word to anyone, who never smiles, who just criticizes and complains all day long." 94

"Is she too old to paddle?" Claud asked. 95

The girl's face was almost purple. 96

"Yes," the lady said, "I'm afraid there's nothing to do but leave her to her folly. Some day she'll wake up and it'll be too late." 97

"It never hurt anyone to smile," Mrs. Turpin said. "It just makes you feel better all over." 98

"Of course," the lady said sadly, "but there are just some people you can't tell anything to. They can't take criticism." 99

"If it's one thing I am," Mrs. Turpin said with feeling, "it's grateful. When I think who all I could have been besides myself and what all I got, a little of everything, and a good disposition besides, I just feel like shouting, 'Thank you, Jesus, for making everything the way it is!' It could have been different!" For one thing, somebody else could have got Claud. 100

At the thought of this, she was flooded with gratitude and a terrible pang of joy ran through her. "Oh thank you, Jesus, Jesus, thank you!" she cried aloud.

The book struck her directly over her left eye. It struck almost at the same instant that she realized the girl was about to hurl it. Before she could utter a sound, the raw face came crashing across the table toward her, howling. The girl's fingers sank like clamps into the soft flesh of her neck. She heard the mother cry out and Claud shout, "Whoa!" There was an instant when she was certain that she was about to be in an earthquake.

All at once her vision narrowed and she saw everything as if it were happening in a small room far away, or as if she were looking at it through the wrong end of a telescope. Claud's face crumpled and fell out of sight. The nurse ran in, then out, then in again. Then the gangling figure of the doctor rushed out of the inner door. Magazines flew this way and that as the table turned over. The girl fell with a thud and Mrs. Turpin's vision suddenly reversed itself and she saw everything large instead of small. The eyes of the white-trashy woman were staring hugely at the floor. There the girl, held down on one side by the nurse and on the other by her mother, was wrenching and turning in their grasp. The doctor was kneeling astride her, trying to hold her arm down. He managed after a second to sink a long needle into it.

Mrs. Turpin felt entirely hollow except for her heart which swung from side to side as if it were agitated in a great empty drum of flesh.

"Somebody that's not busy call for the ambulance," the doctor said in the off-hand voice young doctors adopt for terrible occasions.

Mrs. Turpin could not have moved a finger. The old man who had been sitting next to her skipped nimbly into the office and made the call, for the secretary still seemed to be gone.

"Claud!" Mrs. Turpin called.

He was not in his chair. She knew she must jump up and find him but she felt like some one trying to catch a train in a dream, when everything moves in slow motion and the faster you try to run the slower you go.

"Here I am," a suffocated voice, very unlike Claud's, said.   108

He was doubled up in the corner on the floor, pale as   109
paper, holding his leg. She wanted to get up and go to him
but she could not move. Instead, her gaze was drawn slowly
downward to the churning face on the floor, which she could
see over the doctor's shoulder.

The girl's eyes stopped rolling and focused on her. They   110
seemed a much lighter blue than before, as if a door that had
been tightly closed behind them was now open to admit light
and air.

Mrs. Turpin's head cleared and her power of motion   111
returned. She leaned forward until she has looking directly
into the fierce brilliant eyes. There was no doubt in her mind
that the girl did know her, knew her in some intense and personal way, beyond time and place and condition. "What you
got to say to me?" she asked hoarsely and held her breath,
waiting, as for a revelation.

The girl raised her head. Her gaze locked with Mrs. Turpin's.   112
"Go back to hell where you came from, you old wart hog," she
whispered. Her voice was low but clear. Her eyes burned for a
moment as if she saw with pleasure that her message had struck
its target.

Mrs. Turpin sank back in her chair.   113

After a moment the girl's eyes closed and she turned her   114
head wearily to the side.

The doctor rose and handed the nurse the empty syringe.   115
He leaned over and put both hands for a moment on the
mother's shoulders, which were shaking. She was sitting on
the floor, her lips pressed together, holding Mary Grace's
hand in her lap. The girl's fingers were gripped like a baby's
around her thumb. "Go on to the hospital," he said. "I'll call
and make the arrangements."

"Now let's see that neck," he said in a jovial voice to   116
Mrs. Turpin. He began to inspect her neck with his first two
fingers. Two little moon-shaped lines like pink fish bones
were indented over her windpipe. There was the beginning
of an angry red swelling above her eye. His fingers passed
over this also.

"Lea' me be," she said thickly and shook him off. "See   117
about Claud. She kicked him."

"I'll see about him in a minute," he said and felt her pulse.   118
He was a thin gray-haired man, given to pleasantries. "Go
home and have yourself a vacation the rest of the day," he
said and patted her on the shoulder.

Quit your pattin me, Mrs. Turpin growled to herself.   119

"And put an ice pack over that eye," he said. Then he went   120
and squatted down beside Claud and looked at his leg. After
a moment he pulled him up and Claud limped after him into
the office.

Until the ambulance came, the only sounds in the room   121
were the tremulous moans of the girl's mother, who continued to sit on the floor. The white-trash woman did not take
her eyes off the girl. Mrs. Turpin looked straight ahead at nothing. Presently the ambulance drew up, a long dark shadow, behind the curtain. The attendants came in and set the stretcher
down beside the girl and lifted her expertly onto it and carried her out. The nurse helped the mother gather up her
things. The shadow of the ambulance moved silently away
and the nurse came back in the office.

"That ther girl is going to be a lunatic, ain't she?" the   122
white-trash woman asked the nurse, but the nurse kept on to
the back and never answered her.

"Yes, she's going to be a lunatic," the white-trash woman   123
said to the rest of them.

"Po' critter," the old woman murmured. The child's face   124
was still in her lap. His eyes looked idly out over her knees.
He had not moved during the disturbance except to draw
one leg up under him.

"I thank Gawd," the white-trash woman said fervently, "I   125
ain't a lunatic."

Claud came limping out and the Turpins went home.   126

As their pick-up truck turned into their own dirt road and   127
made the crest of the hill, Mrs. Turpin gripped the window
ledge and looked out suspiciously. The land sloped gracefully
down through a field dotted with lavender weeds and at the
start of the rise their small yellow frame house, with its little

flower beds spread out around it like a fancy apron, sat primly in its accustomed place between two giant hickory trees. She would not have been startled to see a burnt wound between two blackened chimneys.

Neither of them felt like eating so they put on their house clothes and lowered the shade in the bedroom and lay down, Claud with his leg on a pillow and herself with a damp washcloth over her eye. The instant she was flat on her back, the image of a razor-backed hog with warts on its face and horns coming out behind its ears snorted into her head. She moaned, a low quiet moan. ¹²⁸

"I am not," she said tearfully, "a wart hog. From hell." But the denial had no force. The girl's eyes and her words, even the tone of her voice, low but clear, directed only to her, brooked no repudiation. She had been singled out for the message, though there was trash in the room to whom it might justly have been applied. The full force of this fact struck her only now. There was a woman there who was neglecting her own child but she had been overlooked. The message had been given to Ruby Turpin, a respectable, hard-working, church-going woman. The tears dried. Her eyes began to burn instead with wrath. ¹²⁹

She rose on her elbow and the washcloth fell into her hand. Claud was lying on his back, snoring. She wanted to tell him what the girl had said. At the same time, she did not wish to put the image of herself as a wart hog from hell into his mind. ¹³⁰

"Hey, Claud," she muttered and pushed his shoulder. ¹³¹

Claud opened one pale baby blue eye. ¹³²

She looked into it warily. He did not think about any thing. He just went his way. ¹³³

"Wha, whasit?" he said and closed the eye again. ¹³⁴

"Nothing," she said. "Does your leg pain you?" ¹³⁵

"Hurts like hell," Claud said. ¹³⁶

"It'll quit terreckly," she said and lay back down. In a moment Claud was snoring again. For the rest of the afternoon they lay there. Claud slept. She scowled at the ceiling. Occasionally she raised her fist and made a small stabbing motion over her chest as if she was defending her innocence ¹³⁷

to invisible guests who were like the comforters of Job, reasonable-seeming but wrong.

About five-thirty Claud stirred. "Got to go after those niggers," he sighed, not moving. [138]

She was looking straight up as if there were unintelligible handwriting on the ceiling. The protuberance over her eye had turned a greenish-blue. "Listen here," she said. [139]

"What?" [140]

"Kiss me." [141]

Claud leaned over and kissed her loudly on the mouth. He pinched her side and their hands interlocked. Her expression of ferocious concentration did not change. Claud got up, groaning and growling, and limped off. She continued to study the ceiling. [142]

She did not get up until she heard the pick-up truck coming back with the Negroes. Then she rose and thrust her feet in her brown oxfords, which she did not bother to lace, and stumped out onto the back porch and got her red plastic bucket. She emptied a tray of ice cubes into it and filled it half full of water and went out into the back yard. Every afternoon after Claud brought the hands in, one of the boys helped him put out hay and the rest waited in the back of the truck until he was ready to take them home. The truck was parked in the shade under one of the hickory trees. [143]

"Hi yawl this evening?" Mrs. Turpin asked grimly, appearing with the bucket and the dipper. There were three women and a boy in the truck. [144]

"Us doin nicely," the oldest woman said. "Hi you doin?" and her gaze stuck immediately on the dark lump on Mrs. Turpin's forehead. "You done fell down, ain't you?" she asked in a solicitous voice. The old woman was dark and almost toothless. She had on an old felt hat of Claud's set back on her head. The other two women were younger and lighter and they both had new bright green sunhats. One of them had hers on her head; the other had taken hers off and the boy was grinning beneath it. [145]

Mrs. Turpin set the bucket down on the floor of the truck. "Yawl hep yourselves," she said. She looked around to make [146] sure Claud had gone. "No, I didn't fall down," she said, folding her arms. "It was something worse than that."

"Ain't nothing bad happen to you!" the old woman said.   147
She said it as if they all knew that Mrs. Turpin was protected in some special way by Divine Providence. "You just had you a little fall."

"We were in town at the doctor's office for where the cow   148
kicked Mr. Turpin," Mrs. Turpin said in a flat tone that indicated they could leave off their foolishness. "And there was this girl there. A big fat girl with her face all broke out. I could look at that girl and tell she was peculiar but I couldn't tell how. And me and her mama was just talking and going along and all of a sudden WHAM! She throws this big book she was reading at me and . . ."

"Naw!" the old woman cried out.   149

"And then she jumps over the table and commences to   150
choke me."

"Naw!" they all exclaimed, "naw!"   151

"Hi come she do that?" the old woman asked. "What ail   152
her?"

Mrs. Turpin only glared in front of her.   153

"Somethin ail her," the old woman said.   154

"They carried her off in an ambulance," Mrs. Turpin continued, "but before she went she was rolling on the floor and   155
they were trying to hold her down to give her a shot and she said something to me." She paused. "You know what she said to me?"

"What she say?" they asked.   156

"She said," Mrs. Turpin began, and stopped, her face very   157
dark and heavy. The sun was getting whiter and whiter, blanching the sky overhead so that the leaves of the hickory tree were black in the face of it. She could not bring forth the words. "Something real ugly," she muttered.

"She sho shouldn't said nothin ugly to you," the old   158
woman said. "You so sweet. You the sweetest lady I know."

"She pretty too," the one with the hat on said.   159

"And stout," the other one said. "I never knowed no   160
sweeter white lady."

"That's the truth befo' Jesus," the old woman said. "Amen! 161
You des as sweet and pretty as you can be."

Mrs. Turpin knew exactly how much Negro flattery was 162
worth and it added to her rage. "She said," she began again
and finished this time with a fierce rush of breath, "that I was
an old wart hog from hell."

There was an astounded silence. 163

"Where she at?" the youngest woman cried in a piercing 164
voice.

"Lemme see her. I'll kill her!" 165

"I'll kill her with you!" the other one cried. 166

"She b'long in the sylum," the old woman said emphati- 167
cally. "You the sweetest white lady I know."

"She pretty too," the other two said. "Stout as she can be 168
and sweet. Jesus satisfied with her!"

"Deed he is," the old woman declared. 169

Idiots! Mrs. Turpin growled to herself. You could never 170
say anything intelligent to a nigger. You could talk at them
but not with them. "Yawl ain't drunk your water," she said
shortly. "Leave the bucket in the truck when you're finished
with it. I got more to do than just stand around and pass the
time of day," and she moved off and into the house.

She stood for a moment in the middle of the kitchen. The 171
dark protuberance over her eye looked like a miniature tornado
cloud which might any moment sweep across the horizon of
her brow. Her lower lip protruded dangerously. She squared
her massive shoulders. Then she marched into the front of the
house and out the side door and started down the road to the
pig parlor. She had the look of a woman going single-handed,
weaponless, into battle.

The sun was a deep yellow now like a harvest moon and 172
was riding westward very fast over the far tree line as if it
meant to reach the hogs before she did. The road was rutted
and she kicked several good-sized stones out of her path as she
strode along. The pig parlor was on a little knoll at the end of
a lane that ran off from the side of the barn. It was a square of
concrete as large as a small room, with a board fence about
four feet high around it. The concrete floor sloped slightly so

that the hog wash could drain off into a trench where it was carried to the field for fertilizer. Claud was standing on the outside, on the edge of the concrete, hanging onto the top board, hosing down the floor inside. The hose was connected to the faucet of a water trough nearby.

Mrs. Turpin climbed up beside him and glowered down at the hogs inside. There were seven long-snouted bristly shoats in it—tan with liver-colored spots—and an old sow a few weeks off from farrowing. She was lying on her side grunting. The shoats were running about shaking themselves like idiot children, their little slit pig eyes searching the floor for anything left. She had read that pigs were the most intelligent animal. She doubted it. They were supposed to be smarter than dogs. There had even been a pig astronaut. He had performed his assignment perfectly but died of a heart attack afterwards because they left him in his electric suit, sitting upright throughout his examination when naturally a hog should be on all fours. 173

A-gruntin and a-rootin and a-groanin. 174

"Gimme that hose," she said, yanking it away from Claud. "Go on and carry them niggers home and then get off that leg." 175

"You look like you might have swallowed a mad dog," Claud observed, but he got down and limped off. He paid no attention to her humors. 176

Until he was out of earshot, Mrs. Turpin stood on the side of the pen, holding the hose and pointing the stream of water at the hind quarters of any shoat that looked as if it might try to lie down. When he had had time to get over the hill, she turned her head slightly and her wrathful eyes scanned the path. He was nowhere in sight. She turned back again and seemed to gather herself up. Her shoulders rose and she drew in her breath. 177

"What do you send me a message like that for?" she said in a low fierce voice, barely above a whisper but with the force of a shout in its concentrated fury. "How am I a hog and me both? How am I saved and from hell too?" Her free fist was knotted and with the other she gripped the hose, blindly 178 pointing the stream of water in and out of the eye of the old sow whose outraged squeal she did not hear.

The pig parlor commanded a view of the back pasture where their twenty beef cows were gathered around the haybales Claud and the boy had put out. The freshly cut pasture sloped down to the highway. Across it was their cotton field and beyond that a dark green dusty wood which they owned as well. The sun was behind the wood, very red, looking over the paling of trees like a farmer inspecting his own hogs.   179

"Why me?" she rumbled. "It's no trash around here, black or white, that I haven't given to. And break my back to the bone every day working. And do for the church."   180

She appeared to be the right size woman to command the arena before her. "How am I a hog?" she demanded. "Exactly how am I like them?" and she jabbed the stream of water at the shoats. "There was plenty of trash there. It didn't have to be me.   181

"If you like trash better, go get yourself some trash then," she railed. "You could have made me trash. Or a nigger. If trash is what you wanted why didn't you make me trash?" She shook her fist with the hose in it and a watery snake appeared momentarily in the air. "I could quit working and take it easy and be filthy," she growled. "Lounge about the sidewalks all day drinking root beer. Dip snuff and spit in every puddle and have it all over my face. I could be nasty.   182

"Or you could have made me a nigger. It's too late for me to be a nigger," she said with deep sarcasm, "but I could act like one. Lay down in the middle of the road and stop traffic. Roll on the ground."   183

In the deepening light everything was taking on a mysterious hue. The pasture was growing a peculiar glassy green and the streak of highway had turned lavender. She braced herself for a final assault and this time her voice rolled out over the pasture. "Go on," she yelled, "call me a hog! Call me a hog again. From hell. Call me a wart hog from hell. Put that bottom rail on top. There'll still be a top and bottom!"   184

A garbled echo returned to her.   185

A final surge of fury shook her and she roared, "Who do you think you are?"   186

The color of everything, field and crimson sky, burned for   187
a moment with a transparent intensity. The question carried
over the pasture and across the highway and the cotton field
and returned to her clearly like an answer from beyond the
wood.

She opened her mouth but no sound came out of it.   188

A tiny truck, Claud's, appeared on the highway, heading   189
rapidly out of sight. Its gears scraped thinly. It looked like a
child's toy. At any moment a bigger truck might smash into it
and scatter Claud's and the niggers', brains all over the road.

Mrs. Turpin stood there, her gaze fixed on the highway, all   190
her muscles rigid, until in five or six minutes the truck reap-
peared, returning. She waited until it had had time to turn
into their own road. Then like a monumental statue coming
to life, she bent her head slowly and gazed, as if through the
very heart of mystery, down into the pig parlor at the hogs.
They had settled all in one corner around the old sow who
was grunting softly. A red glow suffused them. They appeared
to pant with a secret life.

Until the sun slipped finally behind the tree line, Mrs.   191
Turpin remained there with her gaze bent to them as if she
were absorbing some abysmal life-giving knowledge. At last
she lifted her head. There was only a purple streak in the sky,
cutting through a field of crimson and leading, like an extension of the highway, into the descending dusk. She raised her
hands from the side of the pen in a gesture hieratic and profound. A visionary light settled in her eyes. She saw the streak
as a vast swinging bridge extending upward from the earth
through a field of living fire. Upon it a vast horde of souls were
rumbling toward heaven. There were whole companies of
white-trash, clean for the first time in their lives, and bands of
black niggers in white robes, and battalions of freaks and
lunatics shouting and clapping and leaping like frogs. And
bringing up the end of the procession was a tribe of people
whom she recognized at once as those who, like herself
and Claud, had always had a little of everything and the
God-given wit to use it right. She leaned forward to observe
them closer. They were marching behind the others with great

dignity, accountable as they had always been for good order and common sense and respectable behavior. They alone were on key. Yet she could see by their shocked and altered faces that even their virtues were being burned away. She lowered her hands and gripped the rail of the hog pen, her eyes small but fixed unblinkingly on what lay ahead. In a moment the vision faded but she remained where she was, immobile.

At length she got down and turned off the faucet and made her slow way on the darkening path to the house. In the woods around her the invisible cricket choruses had struck up, but what she heard were the voices of the souls climbing upward into the starry field and shouting hallelujah.

₁₉₂

COMMENT ON "REVELATION"

Ruby Turpin, the central character in Flannery O'Connor's "Revelation," is obsessed with the classification process. At night she occupies herself "naming the classes of people": most "colored people" are on the bottom; "next to them— not above, just away from—are the white trash;" and so on. Mrs. Turpin puzzles about the exceptions to her system—the black dentist who owns property and the decent white folks who have lost their money—but for the most part she is certain about her system and her place in it. In the doctor's waiting room, she sizes up the other patients, placing them in their appropriate classes. But her internal and external dialogue reveals the ironies and inconsistencies in her rigid system. Self-satisfied, pleased that Jesus is on her side, she is not prepared for the book on human development that is thrown at her or the events that follow—the transparent flattery of the black workers, her cleaning of the pig parlor, and finally her vision of the highway to heaven that reveals her real place in God's hierarchy.

DEFINITION

As a writer, both in and out of college, you're likely to spend a good deal of time writing definitions. In an astronomy class, you may be asked to explain what the Doppler effect is or what a white dwarf star is. In a literature class, you may be asked to define a sonnet and identify its different forms. If you become an engineer, you may write to define problems your company proposes to solve or to define a new product your company has developed. If you become a business executive, you may have to write a brochure to describe a new service your company offers or draft a letter that defines the company's policy on credit applications.

Writers use definitions to establish boundaries, to show the essential nature of something, and to explain the special qualities that identify a purpose, place, object, or concept and distinguish it from others similar to it. Writers often write extended definitions—definitions that go beyond the one-sentence or one-paragraph explanations that you find in a dictionary or encyclopedia—to expand on and examine the essential qualities of a policy, an event, a group, or a trend. Sometimes an extended definition becomes an entire book. Some books are written to define the good life; others are written to define the ideal university or the best kind of government. In fact, many of the books on any current nonfiction best-seller list are primarily definitions. The essays in this section of *The Riverside Reader* are all extended definitions.

PURPOSE

When you write, you can use definitions in several ways. For instance, you can define to *point out the special nature* of something. You may want to show the special flavor of San Francisco that makes it different from other major cities in the world, or you may want to describe the unique features that make the Macintosh computer different from other personal computers.

You can also define to *explain.* In an essay about cross-country skiing, you might want to show your readers what the sport is like and point out why it's less hazardous and less expensive than downhill skiing but better exercise. You might also define to *entertain*—to describe the essence of what it means to be a "good old boy," for instance. Often you define to *inform;* that is what you are doing in college papers when you write about West Virginia folk art or postmodern architecture. Often you write to *establish a standard,* perhaps for a good exercise program, a workable environmental policy, or even the ideal pair of running shoes. Notice that when you define to set a standard, you may also be defining to *persuade,* to convince your reader to accept the ideal you describe. Many definitions are essentially arguments.

Sometimes you may even write to *define yourself.* That is what you are doing when you write an autobiographical statement for a college admissions officer or a scholarship committee, or when you write a job application letter. You hope to give your readers the special information that will distinguish you from all other candidates. When that is your task, you'll profit by knowing the common strategies for defining and by recognizing how other writers have used them.

AUDIENCE

When you're going to use definition in your writing, you can benefit by thinking ahead of time about what your readers expect from you. Why are they reading, and what questions will they want you to answer? You can't anticipate all their questions, but you should plan on responding to at least two kinds of queries.

First, your readers are likely to ask, "What distinguishes what you're writing about? What's typical or different about it? How do I know when I see one?" For example, if you were writing about the Olympic games, your readers would perhaps want to know the difference between today's Olympic games and the original games in ancient Greece. With a little research, you could tell them about several major differences.

Second, for more complex topics you should expect that your readers will also ask, "What is the basic character or the essential nature of what you're writing about? What do you mean when you say 'alternative medicine,' 'Marxist theory,' or 'white-collar crime'?" Answering questions such as these is more difficult, but if you're going to use terms like these in an essay, you have an obligation to define them, using as many strategies as you need to clarify your terms. To define white-collar crime, for instance, you could specify that it is nonviolent, likely to happen within businesses, and involves illegal manipulation of funds or privileged information. You should also strengthen your definition by giving examples that your readers might be familiar with.

STRATEGIES

You can choose from several strategies for defining, using them singly or in combination. A favorite strategy we all use is *giving examples,* something we do naturally when we point to a special automobile we like or show a child a picture of a raccoon in a picture book. Writers use the same method when they describe a scene, create a visual image, or cite a specific instance of something.

Every author in this section uses an abundance of examples. But Joan Didion depends on it most heavily. Perhaps because she is a novelist, she chooses dramatic personal incidents to convey to her readers a feeling that she believes cannot be adequately expressed by adjectives alone.

You can define by *analyzing qualities* to emphasize what specific traits distinguish the person or thing you're defining. Tom Wolfe uses this as his chief strategy in "The Right Stuff," identifying and illustrating the particular qualities that a successful test pilot must have: nerve, stamina, and arrogance.

A similar strategy is *attributing characteristics*. Susan Sontag uses this strategy in her essay "Beauty" when she points out new characteristics that term has taken on now that it is applied principally to women.

Another strategy is *defining negatively*. In "A Word's Meaning Can Often Depend on Who Says It," Gloria Naylor explains how the black community has transformed a negative word into a complex word that signifies a variety of meanings.

Another way to define is by *using analogies*. Richard Rodriguez uses this strategy in "Growing Up in Los Angeles" when he says that the graffiti done by street gangs is a kind of advertising comparable to a billboard on Sunset Boulevard.

You can also define by *showing function*. Often the most important feature about an object, agency, or institution is what it does. The element of function figures centrally in Sontag's essay on beauty as she argues that often people assume that a woman's primary function is to be beautiful.

COMBINING STRATEGIES

Even when you're writing an essay that is primarily an exercise in definition, you may want to do as professional writers often do and bring in other strategies, perhaps narration or argument or process analysis. For instance, in "Stone Soup" (pages 394–403), Barbara Kingsolver provides a definition of family and then argues that we need an expanded definition.

Some writers also combine definition with narration and description. In "The Myth of the Latin Woman: I Just Met a Girl Named María" (pages 50–57), Judith Ortiz Cofer challenges stereotypes to define the true character of Hispanic women. In "Stone Soup" (pages 394–403), Barbara Kingsolver uses stories about children as a way of defining a strong family. So you can mix and mingle strategies even though one may dominate. As you read essays in this section, and especially as you reread them, try to be conscious of the strategies authors are using. You may find that you can incorporate some of them into your own writing.

DEFINITION

Points to Remember

1. Remember that you are obligated to define key terms that you use in your writing—such as *Marxism, alternative medicine,* or *nontraditional student.*
2. Understand your purpose in defining: to explain, to entertain, to persuade, to set boundaries, or to establish a standard.
3. Understand how writers construct an argument from a definition. For example, by defining the good life or good government, they argue for that kind of life or government.
4. Know the several ways of defining: giving examples, analyzing qualities, attributing characteristics, defining negatively, using analogies, and showing function.
5. Learn to use definition in combination with other strategies, as a basis on which to build an argument, or as supporting evidence.

In this photograph, reprinted from an early issue of the anticommercial, anticonsumption magazine Adbusters, *Shannon Mendes captures three high school students showing off their tattoos. In what ways do these tattoos define these students? In what ways are some of these tattoos dated? Write an essay in which you explain how your choice of some product—beverage, clothes, car—defines you.*

Gloria Naylor was born in 1950 in New York City and was educated at Brooklyn College and Yale University. For several years she worked as a missionary for the Jehovah's Witnesses, working "for better world conditions." While teaching at several universities, such as George Washington and Princeton, Naylor published numerous stories and essays and five interconnected novels: *The Women of Brewster Place* (1982), *Linden Hills* (l985), *Mamma Day* (1988), *Bailey's Café* (1992), and *The Men of Brewster Place* (1998). *The Women of Brewster Place*, which won the American Book Award for best first novel, was adapted as a television miniseries. In "A Word's Meaning Can Often Depend on Who Says It," first published in the *New York Times* (1986), Naylor explains that the meaning of a word depends on social context and community consensus.

A Word's Meaning Can Often Depend on Who Says It

L ANGUAGE IS THE subject. It is the written form with which I've managed to keep the wolf away from the door and, in diaries, to keep my sanity. In spite of this, I consider the written word inferior to the spoken, and much of the frustration experienced by novelists is the awareness that whatever we manage to capture in even the most transcendent passages falls far short of the richness of life. Dialogue achieves its power in the dynamics of a fleeting moment of sight, sound, smell, and touch.

I'm not going to enter the debate here about whether it is language that shapes reality or vice versa. That battle is doomed to be waged whenever we seek intermittent reprieve from the chicken and egg dispute. I will simply take the position that the spoken word, like the written word, amounts to a nonsensical arrangement of sounds or letters without a consensus that assigns "meaning." And building from the meanings of what we hear, we order reality. Words themselves are innocuous; it is the consensus that gives them true power.

I remember the first time I heard the word *nigger*. In my third-grade class, our math tests were being passed down the rows, and as I handed the papers to a little boy in back of me, I remarked that once again he had received a much lower mark than I did. He snatched his test from me and spit out that word. Had he called me a nymphomaniac or a necrophiliac, I couldn't have been more puzzled. I didn't know what a nigger was, but I knew that whatever it meant, it was something he shouldn't have called me. This was verified when I raised my hand, and in a loud voice repeated what he had said and watched the teacher scold him for using a "bad" word. I was later to go home and ask the inevitable question that every black parent must face—"Mommy, what does *nigger* mean?"

And what exactly did it mean? Thinking back, I realize that this could not have been the first time the word was used in my presence. I was part of a large extended family that had migrated from the rural South after World War II and formed a close-knit network that gravitated around my maternal grandparents. Their ground-floor apartment in one of the buildings they owned in Harlem was a weekend mecca for my immediate family, along with countless aunts, uncles, and cousins who brought along assorted friends. It was a bustling and open house with assorted neighbors and tenants popping in and out to exchange bits of gossip, pick up an old quarrel, or referee the ongoing checkers game in which my grandmother cheated shamelessly. They were all there to let down their hair and put up their feet after a week of labor in the factories, laundries, and shipyards of New York.

Amid the clamor, which could reach deafening proportions—two or three conversations going on simultaneously, punctuated by the sound of a baby's crying somewhere in the back rooms or out on the street—there was still a rigid set of rules about what was said and how. Older children were sent out of the living room when it was time to get into the juicy details about "you-know-who" up on the third floor who had gone and gotten herself "p-r-e-g-n-a-n-t!" But my parents, knowing that I could spell well beyond my years, always demanded that I follow the others out to play. Beyond sexual misconduct and death, everything else was considered harmless for our young ears. And so among the anecdotes of the triumphs and disappointments in the various workings of their lives, the word *nigger* was used in my presence, but it was set within contexts and inflections that caused it to register in my mind as something else.

In the singular, the word was always applied to a man who had distinguished himself in some situation that brought their approval for his strength, intelligence, or drive: 6

"Did Johnny *really* do that?"   7

I'm telling you, that nigger pulled in $6,000 of overtime   8
last year. Said he got enough for a down payment on a house."

When used with a possessive adjective by a woman—"my   9
nigger"—it became a term of endearment for her husband or boyfriend. But it could be more than just a term applied to a man. In their mouths it became the pure essence of manhood—a disembodied force that channeled their past history of struggle and present survival against the odds into a victorious statement of being: "Yeah, that old foreman found out quick enough—you don't mess with a nigger."

In the plural, it became a description of some group within   10
the community that had overstepped the bounds of decency as my family defined it. Parents who neglected their children, a drunken couple who fought in public, people who simply refused to look for work, those with excessively dirty mouths or unkempt households were all "trifling niggers." This particular circle could forgive hard times, unemployment, the occasional bout of depression—they had gone through all of that themselves—but the unforgivable sin was a lack of self-respect.

A woman could never be a "nigger" in the singular, with 11
its connotation of confirming worth. The noun *girl* was its
closest equivalent in that sense, but only when used in direct
address and regardless of the gender doing the addressing.
Girl was a token of respect for a woman. The one-syllable
word was drawn out to sound like three in recognition of the
extra ounce of wit, nerve, or daring that the woman had
shown in the situation under discussion.

"G-i-r-l, stop. You mean you said that to his face?" 12

But if the word was used in a third-person reference 13
or shortened so that it almost snapped out of the mouth,
it always involved some element of communal disapproval.
And age became an important factor in these exchanges.
It was only between individuals of the same generation,
or from any older person to a younger (but never the
other way around), that *girl* would be considered a
compliment.

I don't agree with the argument that use of the word 14
nigger at this social stratum of the black community was an
internalization of racism. The dynamics were the exact opposite: The people in my grandmother's living room took
a word that whites used to signify worthlessness or degra-
dation and rendered it impotent. Gathering there together,
they transformed *nigger* to signify the varied and complex
human beings they knew themselves to be. If the word was
to disappear totally from the mouths of even the most liberal of white society, no one in that room was naive
enough to believe it would disappear from white minds.
Meeting the word head-on, they proved it had absolutely
nothing to do with the way they were determined to live
their lives.

So there must have been dozens of times that *nigger* was 15
spoken in front of me before I reached the third grade. But I
didn't "hear" it until it was said by a small pair of lips that had
already learned it could be a way to humiliate me. That was
the word I went home and asked my mother about. And
since she knew that I had to grow up in America, she took me
in her lap and explained.

For Study and Discussion

QUESTIONS ABOUT PURPOSE

1. Why does Naylor think the written language is inferior to spoken language?
2. How does she use the word *nigger* to support her assertion?

QUESTIONS ABOUT AUDIENCE

1. What does Naylor assume about the racial identity of most of her readers?
2. What does she assume her readers think about the word *nigger*?

QUESTIONS ABOUT STRATEGIES

1. How does Naylor illustrate the difference between the way the white community and the black community use the word *nigger*?
2. How does she explain why the word could never be applied to a woman?

For Writing and Research

1. *Analyze* how Naylor illustrates the various ways the black community uses the word *nigger*.
2. *Practice* by defining a word that has special, perhaps even an opposite, meaning when it is used in your social group.
3. *Argue* that the way a word is spoken—by particular people in a particular context—gives it its true meanings.
4. *Synthesize* the explanations of the way the black community uses the word *girl*. See paragraphs 11–13 in Naylor's essay. Then use this information to explain how Jamaica Kincaid uses the word in her short story, "Girl." See pages 318–320.

JOAN DIDION

Joan Didion was born in Sacramento, California, in 1934 and was educated at the University of California at Berkeley. She worked first as an associate feature editor for *Vogue* and then later as a contributing editor for *The Saturday Evening Post, National Review,* and *Esquire.* Although she is the author of four novels—*Run, River* (1963), *Play It As It Lays* (1970), *A Book of Common Prayer* (1976), and *Democracy* (1984)—Didion is best known as a writer of essays that sometimes poignantly, sometimes pungently, and always memorably describe particular psychological and cultural conditions that seem to characterize American society. Her nonfiction includes *Slouching toward Bethlehem* (1968), *Miami* (1987), and *The Year of Magical Thinking* (2005)—which has been adapted for the stage. In this essay, taken from *The White Album* (1979), Didion defines a medical condition that torments her and perplexes most doctors—migraine headaches.

In Bed

T HREE, FOUR, SOMETIMES five times a month, I spend the day in bed with a migraine headache, insensible to the world around me. Almost every day of every month, between these attacks, I feel the sudden irrational irritation and the flush of blood into the cerebral arteries which tell me that migraine is on its way, and I take certain drugs to avert its arrival. If I did not take the drugs, I would be able to function perhaps one day in four. The physiological error called migraine is, in brief, central to the given of my life. When I was 15, 16, even 25, I used to think that I could rid myself of this error by simply denying it, character over chemistry. "Do you have headaches *sometimes? frequently? never?*" the application forms would demand. "Check one." Wary of the trap, wanting whatever it was that the successful circumnavigation of that particular form could bring (a job, a scholarship, the respect of mankind and the grace of God), I would check one. *"Sometimes,"* I would lie. That in fact I spent one or two days a week almost unconscious with pain seemed a shameful secret, evidence not merely of some chemical inferiority but of all my bad attitudes, unpleasant tempers, wrongthink.

For I had no brain tumor, no eyestrain, no high blood pressure, nothing wrong with me at all: I simply had migraine headaches, and migraine headaches were, as everyone who did not have them knew, imaginary. I fought migraine then, ignored the warnings it sent, went to school and later to work in spite of it, sat through lectures in Middle English and presentations to advertisers with involuntary tears running down the right side of my face, threw up in washrooms, stumbled home by instinct, emptied ice trays onto my bed and tried to freeze the pain in my right temple, wished only for a neurosurgeon who would do a lobotomy on house call, and cursed my imagination.

It was a long time before I began thinking mechanistically enough to accept migraine for what it was: something with which I would be living, the way some people live with diabetes. Migraine is something more than the fancy of a neurotic imagination. It is an essentially hereditary complex of symptoms, the most frequently noted but by no means the most unpleasant of which is a vascular headache of blinding severity, suffered by a surprising number of women, a fair number of men (Thomas Jefferson had migraine, and so did Ulysses S. Grant, the day he accepted Lee's surrender), and by some unfortunate children as young as two years old. (I had my first when I was eight. It came on during a fire drill at the Columbia School in Colorado Springs, Colorado. I was taken first home and then to the infirmary at Peterson Field, where my father was stationed. The Air Corps doctor prescribed an enema.) Almost anything can trigger a specific attack of migraine: stress, allergy, fatigue, an abrupt change in barometric pressure, a contretemps over a parking ticket. A flashing light. A fire drill. One inherits, of course, only the predisposition. In other words I spent yesterday in bed with a headache not merely because of my bad attitudes, unpleasant tempers and wrongthink, but because both my grandmothers had migraine, my father has migraine and my mother has migraine.

No one knows precisely what it is that is inherited. The chemistry of migraine, however, seems to have some connection with the nerve hormone named serotonin, which is naturally present in the brain. The amount of serotonin in the blood falls sharply at the onset of migraine, and one migraine drug, methysergide, or Sansert, seems to have some effect on serotonin. Methysergide is a derivative of lysergic acid (in fact Sandoz Pharmaceuticals first synthesized LSD-25 while looking for a migraine cure), and its use is hemmed about with so many contraindications and side effects that most doctors prescribe it only in the most incapacitating cases. Methysergide, when it is prescribed, is taken daily, as a preventive; another preventive which works for some people is old-fashioned ergotamine tartrate, which helps to constrict the swelling blood vessels during the "aura," the period which in most cases precedes the actual headache.

Once an attack is under way, however, no drug touches it. Migraine gives some people mild hallucinations, temporarily blinds others, shows up not only as a headache but as a gastrointestinal disturbance, a painful sensitivity to all sensory stimuli, an abrupt overpowering fatigue, a strokelike aphasia, and a crippling inability to make even the most routine connections. When I am in a migraine aura (for some people the aura lasts fifteen minutes, for others several hours), I will drive through red lights, lose the house keys, spill whatever I am holding, lose the ability to focus my eyes or frame coherent sentences, and generally give the appearance of being on drugs, or drunk. The actual headache, when it comes, brings with it chills, sweating, nausea, a debility that seems to stretch the very limits of endurance. That no one dies of migraine seems, to someone deep into an attack, an ambiguous blessing.

My husband also has migraine, which is unfortunate for him but fortunate for me: perhaps nothing so tends to prolong an attack as the accusing eye of someone who has never had a headache. "Why not take a couple of aspirin," the unafflicted will say from the doorway, or "I'd have a headache, too, spending a beautiful day like this inside with all the shades drawn." All of us who have migraine suffer not only from the attacks themselves but from this common conviction that we are perversely refusing to cure ourselves by taking a couple of aspirin, that we are making ourselves sick, that we "bring it on ourselves." And in the most immediate sense, the sense of why we have a headache this Tuesday and not last Thursday, of course we often do. There certainly is what doctors call a "migraine personality," and that personality tends to be ambitious, inward, intolerant of error, rather rigidly organized, perfectionist. "You don't look like a migraine personality," a doctor once said to me. "Your hair's messy. But I suppose you're a compulsive housekeeper." Actually my house is kept even more negligently than my hair, but the doctor was right nonetheless: perfectionism can also take the form of spending most of a week writing and rewriting and not writing a single paragraph.

But not all perfectionists have migraine, and not all migrainous people have migraine personalities. We do not escape heredity. I have tried in most of the available ways to escape my own migrainous heredity (at one point I learned to give myself two daily injections of histamine with a hypodermic needle, even though the needle so frightened me that I had to close my eyes when I did it), but I still have migraine. And I have learned now to live with it, learned when to expect it, how to outwit it, even how to regard it, when it does come, as more friend than lodger. We have reached a certain understanding, my migraine and I. It never comes when I am in real trouble. Tell me that my house is burned down, my husband has left me, that there is gunfighting in the streets and panic in the banks, and I will not respond by getting a headache. It comes instead when I am fighting not an open but a guerrilla war with my own life, during weeks of small household confusions, lost laundry, unhappy help, canceled appointments, on days when the telephone rings too much and I get no work done and the wind is coming up. On days like that my friend comes uninvited.

And once it comes, now that I am wise in its ways, I no longer fight it. I lie down and let it happen. At first every small apprehension is magnified, every anxiety a pounding terror. Then the pain comes, and I concentrate only on that. Right there is the usefulness of migraine, there in that imposed yoga, the concentration on the pain. For when the pain recedes, ten or twelve hours later, everything goes with it, all the hidden resentments, all the vain anxieties. The migraine has acted as a circuit breaker, and the fuses have emerged intact. There is a pleasant convalescent euphoria. I open the windows and feel the air, eat gratefully, sleep well. I notice the particular nature of a flower in a glass on the stair landing. I count my blessings. 8

For Study and Discussion

QUESTIONS ABOUT PURPOSE

1. What popular misconceptions about migraines does Didion want to correct?
2. What changes do you think she hopes to bring about for people who do suffer from migraine?

QUESTIONS ABOUT AUDIENCE

1. Even though many readers have never had migraines, what other experiences with ongoing pain are common enough for Didion to assume that many people can sympathize with the agony of migraines?
2. What beliefs about migraine headaches does Didion assume her audience may have that she wants to counteract in her essay?

QUESTIONS ABOUT STRATEGIES

1. Why does Didion use "I" in most of the essay but switch to the third person in paragraph 4?
2. Where in the essay do you find Didion using her novelist's skills of narration and description? What does she accomplish by those strategies?

For Writing and Research

1. *Analyze* the various examples Didion provides to define the word *migraine*.
2. *Practice* by defining a particular illness you have experienced.
3. *Argue* that it is difficult, if not impossible, to define one's pain to someone else.
4. *Synthesize* the most recent research on treating migraine headaches. Then use this evidence to help readers cope with this illness.

RICHARD RODRIGUEZ

Richard Rodriguez was born in San Francisco in 1944 and was educated at Stanford, Columbia, and the University of California at Berkeley. The son of Mexican immigrants and unable to speak English when he started school, he eventually went on to earn a master's degree and was awarded a Fulbright fellowship to study English Renaissance literature at the Warburg Institute in London. His compelling and controversial autobiography, *Hunger of Memory: The Education of Richard Rodriguez* (1982), provides details of Rodriguez's experiences in the American educational system and his alienation from his own culture. His recent books include *Days of Obligation: An Argument with My Mexican Father* (1994), and *Brown: The Last Discovery of America* (2002). In "Growing Up Old in Los Angeles" (reprinted from *U.S. News and World Report,* April 7, 1997), Rodriguez tries to define the idea of adolescence as it is acted out in southern California.

Growing Up Old in Los Angeles

A MERICA'S GREATEST CONTRIBUTION to the world of ideas is adolescence. European novels often begin with a first indelible memory—a golden poplar, or Mama standing in the kitchen. American novels begin at the moment of rebellion, the moment of appetite for distance, the moonless night Tom Sawyer pries open the back-bedroom window, shinnies down the drainpipe, drops to the ground, and runs.

America invented a space—a deferment, a patch of asphalt between childhood and adulthood, between the child's ties to family and the adult's re-creation of family. Within this space, within this boredom, American teenagers are supposed to innovate, to improvise, to rebel, to turn around three times before they harden into adults.

If you want to see the broadcasting center, the trademark   3
capital of adolescence, come to Los Angeles. The great post-war, postmodern, suburban city in Dolby sound was built by restless people who intended to give their kids an unending spring.

There are times in Los Angeles—our most American of   4
American cities—when teenagers seem the oldest people around. Many seem barely children at all—they are tough and

---

The baby boom generation transformed
youth into a lifestyle, a political manifesto,
an aesthetic, a religion.

---

cynical as ancients, beyond laughter in a city that idolizes them. Their glance, when it meets ours, is unblinking.

At a wedding in Brentwood, I watch the 17-year-old   5
daughter of my thrice-divorced friend give her mother away. The mother is dewey with liquid blush. The dry-eyed daughter has seen it all before.

I know children in Los Angeles who carry knives and guns   6
because the walk to and from school is more dangerous than their teachers or parents realize. One teenager stays home to watch her younger sister, who is being pursued by a teenage stalker. The girls have not told their parents because they say they do not know how their parents would react.

Have adults become the innocents?   7

Adults live in fear of the young. It's a movie script, a boffo   8
science-fiction thriller that has never been filmed but that might well star Jean-Claude Van Damme or Sylvester Stallone.

A friend of mine, a heavyweight amateur wrestler, wonders   9
if it's safe for us to have dinner at a Venice Beach restaurant.

(There are, he says, 12-year-old gangsters who prowl the neighborhood with guns.)

Some of the richest people in town have figured out how 10 to sell the idea of American adolescence to the world. The children with the most interesting dilemma are the children of 90210. What does adolescence mean when your father is a record producer who drives to work in a Jeep to audition rap groups? What do you do when your father—who has a drug habit and is nowhere around in the years when you are growing up—is an internationally recognizable 50-foot face on the movie screen?

On the other hand: What can it feel like to grow up a 11 teenager in South Central when your mama is on crack and you are responsible for her five kids? Teenagers who never had reliable parents or knew intimacy are having babies. There are teenagers in East L.A. who (literally) spend their young lives searching for family—"blood"—in some gang that promises what they never had.

It is every teenager's dream to "get big." In L.A. you 12 can be very big, indeed. Fame is a billboard along Sunset Boulevard. Mexican-American gangstas pass the Southern California night by writing crypto-nonsense on sides of buildings, because the biggest lesson they have taken from the city is that advertisement is existence. Los Angeles is a horizontal city of separate freeway exits, separate malls, suburb fleeing suburb. Parents keep moving their children away from what they suppose is the diseased inner city. But there is no possibility of a healthy suburb radiant from a corrupt center. *No man is an island entire of itself.* Didn't we learn that in high school?

The children of East L.A. live in the same city as Madonna 13 and Harvard-educated screenwriters who use cocaine for inspiration, selling a believably tarnished vision of the world to children of the crack mothers in Compton.

And look: There's always a TV in the houses of Watts. And 14 it is always on. In the suburbs, white kids watch black rappers on MTV. Suburbanites use TV to watch the mayhem of the inner city. But on the TV in the inner city, they watch the rest of us. The bejeweled pimp in his gold BMW parodies the Beverly Hills matron on Rodeo Drive.

Elsewhere in America, we like to tell ourselves that Los 15 Angeles is the exception. The truth is that, for all its eccentricity, Los Angeles tells us a great deal about adolescence in rural Kansas. And postmodern L.A. is linked to colonial Boston. Today's gangsta with a tattooed tear on his face is kin to young men fighting Old Man Europe's wars in the trenches of 1914 or 1941, to the young rebels who overthrew Old Man Englande rather than submit to another curfew, and to Judy Garland, who will always be a stagestruck teenager.

The earliest Americans imagined that they had fled the 16 past—motherland, fatherland—and had come upon land that was without history or meaning. By implication, the earliest Americans imagined themselves adolescent, orphans. Their task was self-creation, without benefit or burden of family. The myth that we must each create our own meaning has passed down through American generations.

Young Meriwether Lewis heads out for the territory. He 17 writes to his widowed mother, "I . . . hope therefore you will not suffer yourself to indulge any anxiety for my safety. . . ." The ellipsis is adolescence: estrangement, embarrassment, self-absorption, determination. The adolescent body plumps and furs, bleeds and craves to be known for itself. In some parts of the world, puberty is a secret, a shameful biological event, proof that you have inevitably joined the community of your gender. In America, puberty is the signal to rebel.

American teenagers invent their own tongue, meant to be 18 indecipherable to adult hearing. Every generation of adolescents does it. Adults are left wondering what they mean: *Scrilla. Juking. Woop, woop, woop.*

"Children grow up too quickly," American parents sigh. 19 And yet nothing troubles an American parent so much as the teenager who won't leave home.

Several times in this century, American teenagers have been 20 obliged to leave home to fight overseas. Nineteen-year-old fathers vowed to their unborn children that never again would the youth of the world be wasted by the Potentates of Winter.

My generation, the baby boom generation, was the refoliation of the world. We were the children of mothers who learned how to drive, dyed their hair, used Maybelline, and decorated their houses for Christmas against the knowledge that winter holds sway in the world. Fathers, having returned from blackened theaters of war, used FHA loans to move into tract houses that had no genealogy. In such suburbs, our disillusioned parents intended to ensure their children's optimism. 21

Prolonged adolescence became the point of us—so much the point of me that I couldn't give it up. One night, in the 1950s, I watched Mary Martin, a middle-aged actress, play an enchanted boy so persuasively that her rendition of "I Won't Grow Up" nurtured my adolescent suspicions of anyone over the age of 30. 22

My generation became the first in human history (only hyperbole can suggest our prophetic sense of ourselves) that imagined we might never grow old. 23

Jill, a friend of mine whose fame was an orange bikini, whose face has fallen, whose breasts have fallen, whose hair is gray, is telling me about her son who has just gone to New York and has found there the most wonderful possibilities. My friend's eyes fill with tears. She fumbles in her handbag for the pack of cigarettes she had just sworn off. 24

What's wrong? 25

"Dammit," she says, "I'm a geezer." 26

From my generation arose a culture for which America has become notorious. We transformed youth into a lifestyle, a political manifesto, an aesthetic, a religion. My generation turned adolescence into a commodity that could be sold worldwide by 45-year-old executives at Nike or Warner Bros. To that extent, we control youth. 27

But is it unreasonable for a child to expect that Mick Jagger or Michael Jackson will grow up, thicken, settle, and slow—relinquish adolescence to a new generation? 28

At the Senior Ball, teenagers in the ballroom of the Beverly Hills Hotel, beautiful teenagers in black tie and gowns, try very hard not to look like teenagers. But on the other hand, it is very important not to look like one's parents. 29

The balancing trick of American adolescence is to stand   30
in-between—neither to be a child nor an adult.

Where are you going to college?   31

The question intrudes on the ball like a gong from some   32
great clock. It is midnight, Cinderella. Adolescence must
come to an end. Life is governed by inevitabilities and
consequences—a thought never communicated in America's
rock-and-roll lyrics.

American storytellers do better with the beginning of the 33
story than the conclusion. We do not know how to mark the
end of adolescence. Mark Twain brings Huck Finn back to
Missouri, to Hannibal, and forces his young hero to bend
toward inevitability. But Huck yearns, forever, "to light out
for the territory . . . because Aunt Sally she's going to adopt
me and sivilize me, and I can't stand it."

And then comes the least convincing conclusion ever   34
written in all of American literature: THE END, YOURS TRULY,
HUCK FINN.

For Study and Discussion

QUESTIONS ABOUT PURPOSE

1. Rodriguez projects an angry tone in this article. Toward whom
   do you think the anger is directed and what does he hope to
   accomplish by stirring up anger with his readers?
2. What new information or insights about American adolescents
   did you get from this essay? What do you think Rodriguez wants
   you to do with that information?

QUESTIONS ABOUT AUDIENCE

1. This article was originally published in *U.S. News and World
   Report,* a magazine whose readers are generally well educated,
   fairly prosperous, and in their late thirties or forties. How do you
   think they view most adolescents, and what might they learn
   from Rodriguez that could help them with their own children?
2. What different experiences and attitudes about adolescents do
   readers under thirty bring to this essay? How do you think their
   experiences affect their response to the essay?

QUESTIONS ABOUT STRATEGIES

1. Probably most of Rodriguez's readers haven't been to Los Angeles. What details does he use to convey the flavor of that city to a stranger? How well do they work to help you envision Los Angeles?
2. Rodriguez uses exaggeration as a strategy. For example, he says that Los Angeles is the most American of cities, he compares a pimp in his gold BMW to a Beverly Hills matron, and he mentions Madonna and the mothers of crack babies in the same sentence. What effects does he achieve with this strategy? How effective do you find it?

For Writing and Research

1. *Analyze* the way Rodriguez uses analogies to define "adolescence."
2. *Practice* by defining the characteristics of "adulthood."
3. *Argue* that American popular culture has turned adolescence into a commercial product.
4. *Synthesize* the way various storytellers have dealt with the theme of adolescence. Then use this evidence to argue that these writers have trouble portraying adult characters.

Tom Wolfe was born in 1931 in Richmond, Virginia, and was educated at Washington and Lee University and Yale University. After working as a reporter for several newspapers, Wolfe began writing for *New York* magazine, where he developed the free-wheeling style he was later to label "the New Journalism." His essays on various aspects of American popular culture have appeared in *Esquire* and *New York* and have been collected in books with memorable titles such as *The Kandy-Kolored Tangerine-Flake Streamline Baby* (1965), *The Electric Kool-Aid Acid Test* (1968), and *Radical Chic and Mau-Mauing the Flak Catchers* (1970). Wolfe's interpretation of the origin and growth of the writing style he made famous appears in his introduction to *The New Journalism* (1973). His novels include *The Bonfire of the Vanities* (1987), *A Man in Full* (1998), and *I Am Charlotte Simmons* (2004). In this selection from *The Right Stuff* (1979) he defines that "ineffable quality" that characterizes America's test pilots and astronauts.

The Right Stuff

A YOUNG MAN might go into military flight training believing that he was entering some sort of technical school in which he was simply going to acquire a certain set of skills. Instead, he found himself all at once enclosed in a fraternity. And in this fraternity, even though it was military, men were not rated by their outward rank as ensigns, lieutenants, commanders, or whatever. No, herein the world was divided into those who had it and those who did not. This quality, this *it*, was never named, however, nor was it talked about in any way.

As to just what this ineffable quality was . . . well, it obviously involved bravery. But it was not bravery in the simple sense of being willing to risk your life. The idea seemed to be that any fool could do that, if that was all that was required, just as any fool could throw away his life in the process. No, the idea here (in the all-enclosing fraternity) seemed to be that a man should have the ability to go up in a hurtling piece of machinery and put his hide on the line and then have the moxie, the reflexes, the experience, the coolness, to pull it back in the last yawning moment—and then to go up again *the next day,* and the next day, and every next day, even if the series should prove infinite—and, ultimately, in its best expression, do so in a cause that means something to thousands, to a people, a nation, to humanity, to God. Nor was there *a test* to show whether or not a pilot had this righteous quality. There was, instead, a seemingly infinite series of tests. A career in flying was like climbing one of those ancient Babylonian pyramids made up of a dizzy progression of steps and ledges, a zigurat, a pyramid extraordinarily high and steep; and the idea was to prove at every foot of the way up that pyramid that you were one of the elected and anointed ones who had *the right stuff* and could move higher and higher and even—ultimately, God willing, one day—that you might be able to join that special few at the very top, that elite who had the capacity to bring tears to men's eyes, the very Brotherhood of the Right Stuff itself.

None of this was to be mentioned, and yet it was acted out in a way that a young man could not fail to understand. When a new flight (i.e., a class) of trainees arrived at Pensacola, they were brought into an auditorium for a little lecture. An officer would tell them: "Take a look at the man on either side of you." Quite a few actually swiveled their heads this way and that, in the interest of appearing diligent. Then the officer would say: "One of the three of you is not going to make it!"—meaning, not get his wings. That was the opening theme, the *motif* of primary training. We already know that one-third of you do not have the right stuff—it only remains to find out who.

Furthermore, that was the way it turned out. At every level   4
in one's progress up that staggeringly high pyramid, the
world was once more divided into those men who had the
right stuff to continue the climb and those who had to be *left
behind* in the most obvious way. Some were eliminated in the
course of the opening classroom work, as either not smart
enough or not hardworking enough, and were left behind.
Then came the basic flight instruction, in single-engine,
propeller-driven trainers, and a few more—even though the
military tried to make this stage easy—were washed out and
left behind. Then came more demanding levels, one after the
other, formation flying, instrument flying, jet training, all-
weather flying, gunnery, and at each level more were washed
out and left behind. By this point easily a third of the original
candidates had been, indeed, eliminated . . . from the ranks of
those who might prove to have the right stuff. . . .

Those who remained, those who qualified for carrier   5
duty—and even more so those who later on qualified for
night carrier duty—began to feel a bit like Gideon's warriors.
So many have been left behind! The young warriors were now
treated to a deathly sweet and quite unmentionable sight.
They could gaze at length upon the crushed and wilted pariahs
who had washed out. They could inspect those who did not
have that righteous stuff.

The military did not have very merciful instincts. Rather   6
than packing up these poor souls and sending them home, the
Navy, like the Air Force and the Marines, would try to make
use of them in some other role, such as flight controller. So
the washout has to keep taking classes with the rest of his
group, even though he can no longer touch an airplane. He
sits there in the classes staring at sheets of paper with cataracts
of sheer human mortification over his eyes while the rest steal
looks at him . . . this man reduced to an ant, this untouchable,
this poor sonofabitch. And in what test had he been found
wanting? Why, it seemed to be nothing less than *manhood*
itself. Naturally, this was never mentioned, either. Yet there
it was. *Manliness, manhood, manly courage* . . . there was

something ancient, primordial, irresistible about the challenge of this stuff, no matter what a sophisticated and rational age one might think he lived in. . . .

A fighter pilot soon found he wanted to associate only with other fighter pilots. Who else could understand the nature of the little proposition (right stuff/death) they were all dealing with? And what other subject could compare with it? It was riveting! To talk about it in so many words was forbidden, of course. The very words *death, danger, bravery, fear* were not to be uttered except in the occasional specific instance or for ironic effect. Nevertheless, the subject could be adumbrated in *code* or *by example*. Hence the endless evenings of pilots huddled together talking about flying. On these long and drunken evenings (the bane of their family life) certain theorems would be propounded and demonstrated—and all by *code* and *example*. One theorem was: There are no *accidents* and no fatal flaws in the machines; there are only pilots with the wrong stuff. (I.e., blind Fate can't kill me.) When Bud Jennings crashed and burned in the swamps at Jacksonville, the other pilots in Pete Conrad's squadron said: *How could he have been so stupid?* It turned out that Jennings had gone up in the SNJ with his cockpit canopy opened in a way that was expressly forbidden in the manual, and carbon monoxide had been sucked in from the exhaust, and he passed out and crashed. All agreed that Bud Jennings was a good guy and a good pilot, but his epitaph on the ziggurat was: *How could he have been so stupid?* This seemed shocking at first, but by the time Conrad had reached the end of that bad string at Pax River, he was capable of his own corollary to the theorem: viz., no single factor ever killed a pilot; there was always a chain of mistakes. But what about Ted Whelan, who fell like a rock from 8,100 feet when his parachute failed? Well, the parachute was merely part of the chain: first, someone should have caught the structural defect that resulted in the hydraulic leak that triggered the emergency; second, Whelan did not check out his seat-parachute rig, and the drogue failed to separate the main parachute from the seat; but even after those two mistakes, Whelan had fifteen or twenty seconds, as he fell, to disengage himself from the seat and open the parachute manually. Why just stare at the scenery coming up to smack you in the face! And everyone nodded. (He failed—but I wouldn't have!) Once the theorem and the corollary were understood, the Navy's statistics about one in every four Navy aviators dying meant nothing. The figures were averages, and averages applied to those with average stuff.

A riveting subject, especially if it were one's own hide that was on the line. Every evening at bases all over America, there were military pilots huddled in officers clubs eagerly cutting the right stuff up in coded slices so they could talk about it. What more compelling topic of conversation was there in the world? In the Air Force there were even pilots who would ask the tower for priority landing clearance so that they could make the beer call on time, at 4 P.M. sharp, at the Officers Club. They would come right out and state the reason. The drunken rambles began at four and sometimes went on for ten or twelve hours. Such conversations! They diced that righteous stuff up into little bits, bowed ironically to it, stumbled blindfolded around it, groped, lurched, belched, staggered, bawled, sang, roared, and feinted at it with self-deprecating humor. Nevertheless!—they never mentioned it by name. No, they used the approved codes, such as: "Like a jerk I got myself into a hell of a corner today." They told of how they "lucked out of it." To get across the extreme peril of his exploit, one would use certain oblique cues. He would say, "I looked over at Robinson"— who would be known to the listeners as a non-com who sometimes rode backseat to read radar—"and he wasn't talking any more, he was just staring at the radar, like this, giving it that *zombie* look. Then I *knew* I was in trouble!" Beautiful! Just right! For it would also be known to the listeners that the non-coms advised one another: "*Never* fly with a lieutenant. *Avoid* captains and majors. Hell, man, do yourself a favor: don't fly with anybody below colonel."

Which in turn said: "Those young bucks shoot dice with death!" And yet once in the air the non-com had his own standards. He was determined to remain as outwardly cool as the pilot, so that when the pilot did something that truly petrified him, he would say nothing; instead, he would turn silent, catatonic, like a zombie. Perfect! *Zombie.* There you had it, compressed into a single word all of the foregoing. I'm a hell of a pilot! I shoot dice with death! And now all you fellows know it! And I haven't spoken of that unspoken stuff even once!

For Study and Discussion

QUESTIONS ABOUT PURPOSE

1. What is Wolfe trying to illustrate in his stories about reckless fighter pilots?
2. What special qualities does Wolfe define as essential to the lives of fighter pilots?

QUESTIONS ABOUT AUDIENCE

1. Judging by Wolfe's word choice and sentence structure, what assumptions do you think he makes about the educational level of his audience?
2. To what extent do you think Wolfe can anticipate that his audience will be sympathetic toward the pilots he is writing about?

QUESTIONS ABOUT STRATEGIES

1. What is the effect of Wolfe's drawing an analogy between going through flight training and climbing a ziggurat pyramid? How much does the reader have to know about ziggurat pyramids to get the point?
2. What is the effect of the string of verbs Wolfe uses in paragraph 8 in the sentence that begins, "They diced that righteous stuff up into little bits. . ."?

For Writing and Research

1. *Analyze* the strategies Wolfe uses to illustrate the procedures for weeding out those who do not have "the right stuff."
2. *Practice* by defining a word that attributes positive but difficult-to-obtain qualities to someone.
3. *Argue* that having "the right stuff" is the defining characteristic of the American character.
4. *Synthesize* information on the training procedures for various professions. Then use this evidence to demonstrate how these professions define "the right stuff."

SUSAN SONTAG

Susan Sontag (1933–2004) was born in New York City and was educated at the University of California, the University of Chicago, Harvard University, and St. Anne's College of Oxford University. She worked for several years as an instructor and writer in residence at universities in the New York City area. Beginning with the publication of *Against Interpretation, and Other Essays* (1966), Sontag established herself as one of America's major social critics. She has written two novels (*The Benefactor*, 1964; *Death Kit*, 1967), numerous short stories, and several screenplays, but she is best known for her nonfiction. Some of her books—*Trip to Hanoi* (1969), *Styles of Radical Will* (1969), *Illness as Metaphor* (1977), *Under the Sign of Saturn* (1980), and *Regarding the Pain of Others* (2003)—exhibit Sontag's polemical style, her political obsessions, and some evidence for her reputation as the "Dark Lady of American Literature." But in these same books, in her articles in magazines such as *Atlantic* and *Harper's*, and most particularly in her widely praised *On Photography* (1976), Sontag reveals her extraordinary ability to understand and interpret modern art. In "Beauty," first published in *Vogue magazine* in 1975, she traces the history of a word that was once defined as *general excellence* but which has often been used to characterize *female appearance*.

Beauty

OR THE GREEKS, beauty was a virtue: a kind of excellence. Persons then were assumed to be what we now have to call—lamely, enviously—*whole* persons. If it did occur to the Greeks to distinguish between a person's "inside" and "outside," they still expected that inner beauty would be matched by beauty of the other kind. The well-born young Athenians who gathered around Socrates found it quite paradoxical that their hero was so intelligent, so brave, so honorable, so seductive—and so ugly. One of Socrates' main pedagogical acts was to be ugly—and teach those innocent, no doubt splendid-looking disciples of his how full of paradoxes life really was.

They may have resisted Socrates' lesson. We do not. Several   2 thousand years later, we are more wary of the enchantments of beauty. We not only split off—with the greatest facility— the "inside" (character, intellect) from the "outside" (looks); but we are actually surprised when someone who is beautiful is also intelligent, talented, good.

It was principally the influence of Christianity that de-   3 prived beauty of the central place it had in classical ideals of human excellence. By limiting excellence (*virtus* in Latin) *to moral* virtue only, Christianity set beauty adrift—as an alienated, arbitrary, superficial enchantment. And beauty has continued to lose prestige. For close to two centuries it has become a convention to attribute beauty to only one of the two sexes: the sex which, however Fair, is always Second. Associating beauty with women has put beauty even further on the defensive, morally.

A beautiful woman, we say in English. But a handsome man.   4 "Handsome" is the masculine equivalent of—and refusal of—a compliment which has accumulated certain demeaning overtones, by being reserved for women only. That one can call a man "beautiful" in French and in Italian suggests that Catholic countries—unlike those countries shaped by the Protestant version of Christianity—still retain some vestiges of the pagan admiration for beauty. But the difference, if one exists, is of degree only. In every modern country that is Christian or post-Christian, women *are* the beautiful sex—to the detriment of the notion of beauty as well as women.

To be called beautiful is thought to name something   5 essential to women's character and concerns. (In contrast to

men—whose essence is to be strong, or effective, or competent.) It does not take someone in the throes of advanced
feminist awareness to perceive that the way women are
taught to be involved with beauty encourages narcissism,
reinforces dependence and immaturity. Everybody (women
and men) knows that. For it is "everybody," a whole society,
that has identified being feminine with caring about how
one *looks*. (In contrast to being masculine—which is identified with caring about what one *is* and *does* and only second-
arily, if at all, about how one looks.) Given these stereotypes,
it is no wonder that beauty enjoys, at best, a rather mixed
reputation.

It is not, of course, the desire to be beautiful that is wrong   6
but the obligation to be—or to try. What is accepted by most
women as a flattering idealization of their sex is a way of making women feel inferior to what they actually are—or normally
grow to be. For the ideal of beauty is administered as a form of
self-oppression. Women are taught to see their bodies in *parts*,
and to evaluate each part separately. Breasts, feet, hips, waist-
line, neck, eyes, nose, complexion, hair, and so on—each in
turn is submitted to an anxious, fretful, often despairing
scrutiny. Even if some pass muster, some will always be found
wanting. Nothing less than perfection will do.

In men, good looks is a whole, something taken in at a   7
glance. It does not need to be confirmed by giving measure-
ments of different regions of the body, nobody encourages a
man to dissect his appearance, feature by feature. As for perfection, that is considered trivial—almost unmanly. Indeed,
in the ideally good-looking man a small imperfection or
blemish is considered positively desirable. According to one
movie critic (a woman) who is a declared Robert Redford
fan, it is having that cluster of skin-colored moles on one
cheek that saves Redford from being merely a "pretty face."
Think of the depreciation of women—as well as of beauty—
that is implied in that judgment.

"The privileges of beauty are immense," said Cocteau. To   8
be sure, beauty is a form of power. And deservedly so. What
is lamentable is that it is the only form of power that most

women are encouraged to seek. This power is always conceived in relation to men; it is not the power to do but the
power to attract. It is a power that negates itself. For this
power is not one that can be chosen freely—at least, not by
women—or renounced without social censure.

To preen, for a woman, can never be just a pleasure. It is   9
also a duty. It is her work. If a woman does real work—and
even if she has clambered up to a leading position in politics,
law, medicine, business, or whatever—she is always under
pressure to confess that she still works at being attractive. But
in so far as she is keeping up as one of the Fair Sex, she brings
under suspicion her very capacity to be objective, professional, authoritative, thoughtful. Damned if they do—
women are. And damned if they don't.

One could hardly ask for more important evidence of the   10
dangers of considering persons as split between what is
"inside" and what is "outside" than that interminable half-
comic half-tragic tale, the oppression of women. How easy
it is to start off by defining women as caretakers of their
surfaces, and then to disparage them (or find them adorable)
for being "superficial." It is a crude trap, and it has worked
for too long. But to get out of the trap requires that women
get some critical distance from that excellence and privilege
which is beauty, enough distance to see how much beauty
itself has been abridged in order to prop up the mythology of
the "feminine." There should be a way of saving beauty *from*
women—and *for* them.

For Study and Discussion

QUESTIONS ABOUT PURPOSE

1. What is the conventional attitude about beauty that Sontag seeks
   to discredit?
2. If beauty is a source of power, why does Sontag object to
   women's striving to attain it?

QUESTIONS ABOUT AUDIENCE

1. Why does Sontag assume that her male and female readers will bring significantly different attitudes to this essay? Do you agree?
2. What do you think Sontag is saying to beautiful women? How do you think they would respond?

QUESTIONS ABOUT STRATEGIES

1. Why does Sontag begin her essay by defining the Greek attitude toward beauty?
2. To what extent does Sontag use *giving functions* as her strategy for defining? To what extent does she use *drawing analogies*?

For Writing and Research

1. *Analyze* the strategies Sontag uses to define the difference between a person's "inside" and "outside" beauty.
2. *Practice* by defining the word *handsome*.
3. *Argue* that the obligation to be beautiful does or does not produce certain psychological benefits.
4. *Synthesize* the research on the relationship between beauty and success. Then use this evidence to argue that beauty—physical attractiveness—is or is not essential to professional advancement and economic achievement.

Jamaica Kincaid was born in 1949 in St. John's, Antigua, and was educated at Franconia College in New Hampshire. She began contributing stories to *Rolling Stone, The Paris Review,* and *The New Yorker.* Her first collection of stories, *At the Bottom of the River* (1983), won the Morton Dauwen Zabel Award of the American Academy and Institute of Arts and Letters. Her novels include *Annie John* (1985), *Lucy* (1990), and *Mr. Potter* (2002), and focus on the struggles of young girls to understand their heritage. She has also published two collections of essays about the West Indies, *A Small Place* (1988) and *Talk Stories* (2000). In "Girl," reprinted from *At the Bottom of the River,* a mother describes the appropriate behavior for a young woman.

Girl

WASH THE WHITE clothes on Monday and put them on the stone heap; wash the color clothes on Tuesday and put them on the clothesline to dry; don't walk barehead in the hot sun; cook pumpkin fritters in very hot sweet oil; soak your little cloths right after you take them off; when buying cotton to make yourself a nice blouse, be sure that it doesn't have gum on it, because that way it won't hold up well after a wash; soak salt fish overnight before you cook it; is it true that you sing benna in Sunday school?; always eat your food in such a way that it won't turn someone else's stomach; on Sundays try to walk like a lady and not like the slut you are so bent on becoming; don't sing benna in Sunday school; you mustn't speak to wharf-rat boys, not even to give directions; don't eat fruits on the street—flies will follow you; *but I don't sing benna on Sundays at all and never in Sunday school;* this is how to sew on a button; this is how to make a buttonhole for the button you have just sewed on; this is how to hem a dress when you see the hem coming down and so to prevent yourself from looking like the slut I know you are so bent on becoming; this is how you iron your father's khaki shirt so that it doesn't have a crease; this is how you iron your father's khaki pants so that they don't have a crease; this is how you grow okra—far from the house, because okra tree harbors red ants; when you are growing dasheen, make sure it gets plenty of water or else it makes your throat itch when you are eating it; this is how you sweep a corner; this is how you sweep a whole house; this is how you sweep a yard; this is how you smile to some-one you don't like too much; this is how you smile to some-one you don't like at all; this is how you smile to someone you like completely; this is how you set a table for tea; this is how you set a table for dinner; this is how you set a table for dinner with an important guest; this is how you set a table for lunch; this is how you set a table for breakfast; this is how you behave in the presence of men who don't know you very well, and this way they won't recognize immediately the slut I have warned you against becoming; be sure to wash every day, even if it is with your own spit; don't squat down to play marbles—you are not a boy, you know; don't pick people's flowers—you might catch something; don't throw stones at blackbirds, because it might not be a blackbird at all; this is how to make a bread pudding; this is how to make doukona; this is how to make pepper pot; this is how to make a good medicine for a cold; this is how to make a good medicine to throw away a child before it even becomes a child; this is how to catch a fish; this is how to throw back a fish you don't like, and that way something bad won't fall on you; this is how to bully a man; this is how a man bullies you; this is how to love a man, and if this doesn't work there are other ways, and if they don't work don't feel too bad about giving up; this is how to spit up in the air if you feel like it, and this is how to move quick so that it doesn't fall on you; this is

how to make ends meet; always squeeze bread to make sure
it's fresh; *but what if the baker won't let me feel the bread?;*
you mean to say that after all you are really going to be the
kind of woman who the baker won't let near the bread?

COMMENT ON "GIRL"

An unusual, nebulous point of view shapes the effect of
Kincaid's "Girl." A Caribbean mother's imperative—her
instruction list for polite living—is absorbed by a daughter,
whose voice is seldom and only faintly heard, revealing the
archetypal tension between mothers and daughters. The one-
paragraph story—both humorous and dark—is an interesting
study of the discrepancy between what a mother says and
what she means.

CAUSE
AND
EFFECT

If you are like most people, you're just naturally curious: you look at the world around you and wonder why things happen. But you're also curious because you want some control over your life and over your environment, and you can't have that control unless you can understand **causes.** That's why so much writing is cause-and-effect writing, writing that seeks to explain the causes for change and new developments. In almost every profession you will be asked to do writing that analyzes causes; that's why such writing has an important place in college composition courses.

You also want to understand effects. If A happens, will B be the effect? You want to try to predict the consequences of putting some plan into effect or look at some effect and explain what brought it about. Or you want to set a goal (the effect) and plan a strategy for reaching it. This kind of writing also prepares you for writing you're likely to do later in your career.

PURPOSE

Of the several purposes that cause-and-effect writing can serve, the most important is to *inform and educate*. Informative cause-and-effect writing is important because it helps people understand the world better, and often they can control events if they understand causes. Much writing about behavior, the environment, natural resources, or the economy is actually written to encourage control.

Another kind of causal analysis is *primarily speculative*. In this kind of writing, an author hypothesizes about what factors may be causing certain events or what the consequences of certain actions may be. Writers for newspapers and magazines often use this pattern, picking out a topic of interest, such as crime or health care, and speculating why it occurs or what problems it causes. Such writing may be informative or entertaining or both.

A third major purpose of cause-and-effect writing is to provide *the basis for argument*. Writers point out causal relationships as they try to persuade their readers to approve or disapprove of something. They can argue positively by asserting that certain courses of action will produce good results, or they can argue negatively by claiming that whatever it is they seek to change—an institution, a custom, a law—produces bad results. Much writing about politics, obviously, serves this purpose.

AUDIENCE

Writers can assume that almost everyone is interested in reading about cause and effect because most people are curious about what goes on in the world around them. Because they don't want to think that the world is chaotic and unpredictable, people seek reasons for what they see happening, and they wonder about the connections between the past and the future. Within this large audience, however, several groups have specific interests that writers of causal analysis need to consider.

One major group of readers is intellectually curious people who want to know how things work and why people behave as they do. They will read explanatory essays about the relationship between air pollutants and skin disease as readily as they will read speculative essays about the causes of voter apathy. These readers are a pleasure to write for because they enjoy expanding their store of information, but the cautious writer knows that this informed audience will be skeptical about oversimplified causal analysis.

Another group that reads about cause and effect is those who want to learn how to solve problems and thus have better control over their lives and their environment. They might be reading to find ways to improve their health through better nutrition, or to find out what kinds of child-rearing practices are most likely to promote good parent-child relationships. Authors who write to this audience must remember that these serious-minded readers want responsible answers to their questions. For them, a writer needs to present a rational and well-supported causal analysis.

A third group reads to find out more about cause-and-effect relationships in the past or to learn about past investigations. This group includes people who read history and biography and articles of social and political analysis; it also includes readers who are interested in explanations of important theories in the physical and behavioral sciences. Writers who write for this audience need to demonstrate their competence in the subject about which they are writing.

STRATEGIES

Writers may choose among a number of different strategies when they write about cause and effect. The simplest strategy is to describe an action or event and then show its consequences. You could use this strategy if you wanted to claim that a culture that glorifies competition, particularly in bruising sports such as football and hockey, should not be surprised at the prevalence of gangs and street violence among young males.

Another favorite strategy of authors who write causal analysis is to describe an event or circumstance that seems significant and then examine the probable reasons for it. Loren Eiseley uses this strategy in "How Flowers Changed the World" when he speculates about how flower seeds first became airborne.

Conversely, a writer sometimes begins by isolating an effect and then looking for plausible causes. E. M. Forster follows this strategy in "My Wood" in which he writes about the changes he noticed in himself after he bought several acres of woods. In this kind of essay, the writer must be careful to distinguish between *direct,* or *simple, causes* and *indirect,* or *complex, causes.* In his essay "Carrie Buck's Daughter," Stephen Jay Gould points out that Carrie Buck's treatment was motivated as much by prejudice and shame as it was by concern over her mental abilities.

Another approach to cause-and-effect writing is to focus on two apparently unrelated phenomena and speculate whether there might be a cause-and-effect connection between them. Such speculation is risky, and the writer who indulges in it should be prepared to back it with a strong argument. Nevertheless, this kind of hypothesizing can be fruitful and enlightening, as when Ellen Goodman speculates in "The Chem 20 Factor" on the relationship between the rigors of organic chemistry and the high price of medical bills. Similarly, Terry McMillan speculates on the relationship between her observations of her own family and neighbors and the people she sees in *The Wizard of Oz.*

There are still other ways to write about cause and effect; the ones given here are by no means the only strategies writers can use. To be effective and responsible, however, all strategies should meet the following criteria:

1. *You should not overstate your case.* When writing about a complex situation, particularly those that involve people, you do best to say, "X will probably cause Y," or "A seems to be the effect of B," rather than insist that there must be a necessary and direct causal connection between two events. Many plausible cause-and-effect relationships are difficult to prove conclusively, and the writer who does not claim too much in such instances makes the best impression.

2. *You should not oversimplify cause-and-effect relationships.* Seldom does an important effect result from a simple and direct cause. For example, if 15 percent fewer people died of heart attacks in 2007 than in 2000, a researcher should assume that many factors contributed to this decline, not that one element was the cause. Furthermore, most happenings of any significance have more than one effect, and any cause or effect may be only one link in a long chain of causes and effects. Wise writers qualify their assertions with phrases such as *a major cause, one result,* and *an immediate effect.*

3. *You should not mistake coincidence or simple sequence for a necessary cause-and-effect relationship.* The fact that the crime rate in a state rose the year after the legal drinking age was lowered does not mean that there is a direct connection between the two occurrences. An investigator who wanted to prove such a causal relationship would need many more data. The person who jumps to conclusions about cause and effect too quickly commits the *false cause,* or *after this, therefore this,* fallacy.

These cautions do not, however, mean that writers should refrain from drawing conclusions about cause and effect until they are absolutely sure of their ground. It is not always possible or wise to wait for complete certainty before writing an analysis of what has happened or a forecast of what may happen. The best any writer can do is to observe carefully and speculate intelligently.

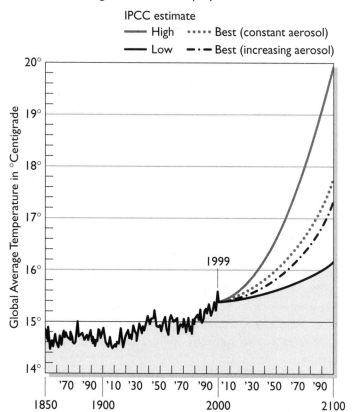

Projected Changes in Global Temperature
Global average 1856–1999 and projection estimates to 2100

Source: Temperatures 1856–1999. Climatic Research Unit, University at East Anglia, Norwich, UK Projections: IPCC report 95.

This line graph, based on data compiled by the Intergovernmental Panel on Climate Change, projects dramatic changes in global temperature. What do you think is the cause of such changes? What do you think will be their effect? Analyze the changes people will have to make to reverse (or stabilize) these projections.

CAUSE AND EFFECT

Points to Remember

1. Remember that, in human events, you can almost never prove direct, simple, cause-and-effect relationships. Qualify your claims.

2. Be careful not to oversimplify your cause-and-effect statements; be cautious about saying that a cause always produces a certain effect or that a remedy never succeeds.

3. Avoid confusing coincidence or simple sequence with cause and effect; because B follows A doesn't mean that A caused B.

4. Build your cause-and-effect argument as a trial lawyer would. Present as much evidence as you can, and argue for your hypothesis.

ELLEN GOODMAN

Ellen Goodman was born in 1941 in Newton, Massachusetts, and was educated at Radcliffe College. After graduation she worked as a researcher and reporter for *Newsweek* magazine, then as a feature writer for the *Detroit Free Press* before assuming the position of feature writer and columnist for the *Boston Globe*. Since 1976 her columns have been syndicated by the Washington Post Writers Group. In 1980 Goodman was awarded a Pulitzer Prize in journalism for distinguished commentary. Many of her columns are collected in *Close to Home* (1979), *Keeping in Touch* (1985), and *Value Judgments* (1993). In "The Chem 20 Factor," taken from *Close to Home,* Goodman argues that the atmosphere in one college chemistry course "causes" the competitive drive in the medical profession.

The Chem 20 Factor

WHEN I WAS in college, there was an infamous course 1
known as Chem 20. Organic chemistry was the sieve into which was poured every premedical student in the university. But only those who came through it with an A or B could reasonably expect to get into medical school.

Chem 20, therefore, became a psychological laboratory of 2
pre-med anxiety. Every class was a combat mission. Each grade was a life-or-death matter. It reeked of Olympian anguish and Olympic competitiveness. It taught people whose goal in life was the relief of pain and suffering that only the fittest, the most single-minded, would survive.

I remember Chem 20 whenever I read about President ³
Carter's outrage at the medical establishment, or when
someone sardonically points out yet another M.D. plate on
yet another Mercedes Benz, or when the National Council
on Wage and Price Stability points out that the median income of doctors—$63,000 in 1976—has risen faster than
any other group. In short, at times when other people talk
about the M.D. as a license to make money, I think of the
Chem 20 factor.

I know that we regard doctors as altruistic when they are ⁴
treating us and avaricious when they are billing us. But I
don't think we can understand the end result—high fees—
unless we understand the process of selection and even self-
selection by which people actually do become doctors.

On the whole, doctors made a commitment to go into ⁵
medicine when they were eighteen or nineteen years old, with
the full knowledge that they wouldn't be "practicing" until
they were thirty or older. In a "Now Society," they would
hold the record among their peers for delayed gratification.
The sort of laid-back, noncompetitive person who wants to
"live in the Moment" would drop out of Chem 20 with an
acute case of culture shock in a week.

It is the dedicated or the narrow-minded (choose one from ⁶
column A) who go through college competing for medical
school and go through medical school competing for a good
internship and go through internship competing for a good
residency.

Today, residency is not the financial hardship it was when ⁷
most practicing doctors in this country were young. The
magazine *Hospital Physician* says that the average doctor in
training earns $12,500 to $15,000. But it is still basically an
emotionalized physical-endurance contest.

It is normal for a young doctor to work an eighty-hour ⁸
week. It is normal to work every other night and every other
weekend. It is normal to be cut off for ten years from anything
approaching a rich personal life. It is normal to come to regard the world as a hierarchy and a ladder to be climbed. It is,
after all, the Chem 20 factor.

While there are thousands of others who work long   9
hours just to keep a toehold in solvency, there is no other
professional training that is comparable in terms of sheer
stress. So, many of the doctors are sustained through this
training by one vision: the Big Payoff. In this society, the Big
Payoff is traditionally translated into dollars.

The end result of the training process is doctors who are   10
often as addicted to work as patients to morphine. And doctors
who have come to genuinely believe that they are "worth"
whatever fees they can charge because they "worked for it."

I suspect that they are searching—sometimes desperately,   11
and often futilely—for a return on the real investment they
have made: their twenties.

So, the government may be right when it says that medical   12
fees are spiraling because there is no free-market economy in
doctors. The law of supply and demand doesn't work very
well in medicine.

But that is only half of the story. If they want to see the   13
psychological side, they have to go deeper, further, back to
where the system begins—back as far as Chem 20.

The course is still being given. Only these days, I hear,   14
there are pre-med students who won't even share their notes.

For Study and Discussion

QUESTIONS ABOUT PURPOSE

1. According to Goodman, what lasting effect does taking Chem
   20 have on students who complete the course successfully?
2. What sequence of causes and effects is Goodman trying to
   establish in the essay?

QUESTIONS ABOUT AUDIENCE

1. Goodman writes her syndicated column for a general newspaper-
   reading audience. What kinds of readers in that audience would
   probably respond favorably to this article?
2. What varied kinds of responses would you expect a young
   college audience to have after reading this article?

QUESTIONS ABOUT STRATEGIES

1. Why does Goodman use the phrases *combat mission, life-or-death,* and *Olympian* in paragraph 2?
2. What specific examples does Goodman use to trace the stages that a doctor goes through during the years between taking Chem 20 and becoming a highly paid specialist?

For Writing and Research

1. *Analyze* the techniques Goodman uses to enlist her readers' sympathies for medical students and doctors.
2. *Practice* by speculating on how another college course serves as a screening or testing device for students planning to go into a profession.
3. *Argue* that there is a direct correlation between the amount of time and effort professionals invest in their education and the rewards they receive.
4. *Synthesize* the kinds of data college graduates have to assemble to apply for a particular job. Then use this evidence to argue that one source of data is the most important cause of their success.

E. M. F O R S T E R

E(dward) M(organ) Forster (1879–1970) was
born in London, England, and was educated at
King's College, Cambridge. In the early decades
of this century he lived and wrote in Greece and
Italy. After World War I he moved to India to serve
as private secretary to the Maharajah of Dewas
State Senior. That experience enabled him to write
A Passage to India (1924), a novel that earned him
enough royalties to purchase a small estate in England, where he lived until his death. Forster wrote
five other novels—*Where Angels Fear to Tread*
(1905), *The Longest Journey* (1907), *A Room with
a View* (1908), *Howards End* (1910), and *Maurice*
(posthumous)—and several collections of short
fiction and literary criticism, the most famous of
which is *Aspects of the Novel* (1927). In "My
Wood" (from *Abinger Harvest,* 1936) he provides
a humorous portrait of the "effect of property
upon character."

My Wood

A FEW YEARS ago I wrote a book which dealt in part with
the difficulties of the English in India. Feeling that
they would have had no difficulties in India themselves, the
Americans read the book freely. The more they read it the
better it made them feel, and a cheque to the author was
the result. I bought a wood with the cheque. It is not a large
wood—it contains scarcely any trees, and it is intersected,
blast it, by a public footpath. Still, it is the first property that
I have owned, so it is right that other people should participate in my shame, and should ask themselves, in accents that
will vary in horror, this very important question: What is the

effect of property upon the character? Don't let's touch economics; the effect of private ownership upon the community as a whole is another question—a more important question, perhaps, but another one. Let's keep to psychology. If you own things, what's their effect on you? What's the effect on me of my wood?

In the first place, it makes me feel heavy. Property does have this effect. Property produces men of weight and it was a man of weight who failed to get into the Kingdom of Heaven. He was not wicked, that unfortunate millionaire in the parable, he was only stout; he stuck out in front, not to mention behind, and as he wedged himself this way and that in the crystalline entrance and bruised his well-fed flanks, he saw beneath him a comparatively slim camel passing through the eye of a needle and being woven into the robe of God. The Gospels all through couple stoutness and slowness. They point out what is perfectly obvious, yet seldom realized: that if you have a lot of things you cannot move about a lot, that furniture requires dusting, dusters require servants, servants require insurance stamps, and the whole tangle of them make you think twice before you accept an invitation to dinner or go for a bathe in the Jordan. Sometimes the Gospels proceed further and say with Tolstoy that property is sinful; they approach the difficult ground of asceticism here where I cannot follow them. But as to the immediate effects of property on people, they just show straightforward logic. It produces men of weight. Men of weight cannot, by definition, move like the lightning from the East unto the West, and the ascent of a fourteen-stone bishop into a pulpit is thus the exact antithesis of the coming of the Son of Man. My wood makes me feel heavy.

In the second place, it makes me feel it ought to be larger.

The other day I heard a twig snap in it. I was annoyed at first, for I thought that someone was blackberrying, and depreciating the value of the undergrowth. On coming nearer, I saw it was not a man who had trodden on the twig and snapped it, but a bird, and I felt pleased. My bird. The bird was not equally pleased. Ignoring the relation between us, it took fright as soon as it saw the shape of my face, and flew straight over the boundary hedge into a field, the property of Mrs. Henessy, where it sat down with a loud squawk. It had become Mrs. Henessy's bird. Something seemed grossly amiss here, something that would not have occurred had the wood been larger. I could not afford to buy Mrs. Henessy out, I dared not murder her, and limitations of this sort beset me on every side. . . .

In the third place, property makes its owner feel that he ought to do something to it. Yet he isn't sure what. A restlessness comes over him, a vague sense that he has a personality to express—the same sense which, without any vagueness, leads the artist to an act of creation. Sometimes I think I will cut down such trees as remain in the wood, at other times I want to fill up the gaps between them with new trees. Both impulses are pretentious and empty. They are not honest movements towards money-making or beauty. They spring from a foolish desire to express myself and from an inability to enjoy what I have got. Creation, property, enjoyment form a sinister trinity in the human mind. Creation and enjoyment are both very, very good, yet they are often unattainable without a material basis, and at such moments property pushes itself in as a substitute, saying, "Accept me instead—I'm good enough for all three." It is not enough. It is, as Shakespeare said of lust, "The expense of spirit in a waste of shame": it is "Before, a joy proposed; behind, a dream." Yet we don't know how to shun it. It is forced on us by our economic system as the alternative to starvation. It is also forced on us by an internal defect in the soul, by the feeling that in property may lie the germs of self-development and of exquisite or heroic deeds. Our life on earth is, and ought to be, material and carnal. But we have not yet learned to manage our materialism and carnality properly; they are still entangled with the desire for ownership, where (in the words of Dante) "Possession is one with loss."

And this brings us to our fourth and final point: the blackberries.

Blackberries are not plentiful in this meagre grove, but 7
they are easily seen from the public footpath which traverses
it, and all too easily gathered. Foxgloves, too—people will
pull up the foxgloves, and ladies of an educational tendency
even grub for toadstools to show them on the Monday in
class. Other ladies, less educated, roll down the bracken in
the arms of their gentlemen friends. There is paper, there are
tins. Pray, does my wood belong to me or doesn't it? And, if
it does, should I not own it best by allowing no one else to
walk there? There is a wood near Lyme Regis, also cursed by
a public footpath, where the owner has not hesitated on this
point. He had built high stone walls each side of the path,
and has spanned it by bridges, so that the public circulate like
termites while he gorges on the blackberries unseen. He
really does own his wood, this able chap. And perhaps I shall
come to this in time. I shall wall in and fence out until I really taste the sweets of property. Enormously stout, endlessly
avaricious, pseudo-creative, intensely selfish, I shall weave
upon my forehead the quadruple crown of possession until
those nasty Bolshies come and take it off again and thrust me
aside into the outer darkness.

For Study and Discussion

QUESTIONS ABOUT PURPOSE

1. Why does Forster write about the effects that buying a piece of
   land has on a person's character instead of writing about the
   effects that making money has on a person's character? How are
   the two different?
2. Why does Forster apologize for the effects of owning his woods?

QUESTIONS ABOUT AUDIENCE

1. What kind of people does Forster seem to think might criticize
   him for owning property?
2. How do you think people who own a large amount of property
   would react to this essay? Would they understand Forster's
   concerns?

QUESTIONS ABOUT STRATEGIES

1. Using his own experience as a basis, Forster generalizes about the effects on a person of owning property. Do you think he is justified in making his generalizations?
2. How does he use the bird and the blackberries to illustrate how his wood makes him feel possessive?

For Writing and Research

1. *Analyze* how Forster uses anecdotes and phrases to give his essay a lighthearted tone.
2. *Practice* by analyzing the effects that purchasing a new piece of technology, a new car, or a new home had on you.
3. *Argue* that owning a lot of "stuff" is likely to hamper a person's creativity.
4. *Synthesize* the research on how different groups of people have purchased private property. Then use this evidence to argue that such purchases have had positive or negative effects.

LOREN EISELEY

Loren Eiseley (1907–1979) was born in Lincoln, Nebraska, and was educated at the University of Nebraska and the University of Pennsylvania. He held faculty positions at the University of Kansas, Oberlin College, and the University of Pennsylvania, where he was Franklin Professor of Anthropology and History of Science. He contributed articles to scientific journals, such as *American Anthropologist* and *Scientific Monthly,* and popular magazines, such as *Holiday* and *Ladies' Home Journal.* His books include *The Immense Journey* (1957), *Darwin's Century* (1958), *The Mind as Nature* (1962), *Francis Bacon and the Modern Dilemma* (1963), and *The Unexpected Universe* (1969). In "How Flowers Changed the World," reprinted from *The Immense Journey,* Eiseley explains the sequence of events that caused a change in the earth's environment and made possible the development of man.

How Flowers Changed the World

I F IT HAD been possible to observe the Earth from the far side of the solar system over the long course of geological epochs, the watchers might have been able to discern a subtle change in the light emanating from our planet. That world of long ago would, like the red deserts of Mars, have reflected light from vast drifts of stone and gravel, the sands of wandering wastes, the blackness of naked basalt, the yellow dust of endlessly moving storms. Only the ceaseless marching of the clouds and the intermittent flashes from the restless surface of the sea would have told a different story, but still essentially a barren one. Then, as the millennia rolled away and age followed age, a new and greener light would, by degrees, have come to twinkle across those endless miles.

This is the only difference those far watchers, by the use of 2 subtle instruments, might have perceived in the whole history of the planet Earth. Yet that slowly growing green twinkle would have contained the epic march of life from the tidal oozes upward across the raw and unclothed continents. Out of the vast chemical bath of the sea—not from the deeps, but from the element-rich, light-exposed platforms of the continental shelves—wandering fingers of green had crept upward along the meanderings of river systems and fringed the gravels of forgotten lakes.

In those first ages plants clung of necessity to swamps and 3 watercourses. Their reproductive processes demanded direct access to water. Beyond the primitive ferns and mosses that enclosed the borders of swamps and streams the rocks still lay vast and bare, the winds still swirled the dust of a naked planet. The grass cover that holds our world secure in place was still millions of years in the future. The green marchers had gained a soggy foothold upon the land, but that was all. They did not reproduce by seeds but by microscopic swimming sperm that had to wriggle their way through water to fertilize the female cell. Such plants in their higher forms had clever adaptations for the use of rain water in their sexual phases, and survived with increasing success in a wet land environment. They now seem part of man's normal environment. The truth is, however, that there is nothing very "normal" about nature. Once upon a time there were no flowers at all.

A little while ago—about one hundred million years, as 4 the geologist estimates time in the history of our four-billion-year-old planet—flowers were not to be found anywhere on the five continents. Wherever one might have looked, from the poles to the equator, one would have seen only the cold dark monotonous green of a world whose plant life possessed no other color.

Somewhere, just a short time before the close of the Age 5
of Reptiles, there occurred a soundless, violent explosion. It
lasted millions of years, but it was an explosion, nevertheless.
It marked the emergence of the angiosperms—the flowering
plants. Even the great evolutionist, Charles Darwin, called
them "an abominable mystery," because they appeared so
suddenly and spread so fast.

Flowers changed the face of the planet. Without them, 6
the world we know—even man himself—would never have
existed. Francis Thompson, the English poet, once wrote
that one could not pluck a flower without troubling a star.
Intuitively he had sensed like a naturalist the enormous inter-
linked complexity of life. Today we know that the appearance
of the flowers contained also the equally mystifying emergence of man.

If we were to go back into the Age of Reptiles, its drowned 7
swamps and birdless forest would reveal to us a warmer
but, on the whole, a sleepier world than that of today. Here
and there, it is true, the serpent heads of bottom-feeding
dinosaurs might be upreared in suspicion of their huge flesh-
eating compatriots. Tyrannosaurs, enormous bipedal carica-
tures of men, would stalk mindlessly across the sites of future
cities and go their slow way down into the dark of geologic
time.

In all that world of living things nothing saw save with the 8
intense concentration of the hunt, nothing moved except
with the grave sleepwalking intentness of the instinct-driven
brain. Judged by modern standards, it was a world in slow
motion, a cold-blooded world whose occupants were most
active at noonday but torpid on chill nights, their brains
damped by a slower metabolism than any known to even the
most primitive of warm-blooded animals today.

A high metabolic rate and the maintenance of a constant 9
body temperature are supreme achievements in the evolution
of life. They enable an animal to escape, within broad limits,
from the overheating or the chilling of its immediate surroundings, and at the same time to maintain a peak mental
efficiency. Creatures without a high metabolic rate are slaves

to weather. Insects in the first frosts of autumn all run down like little clocks. Yet if you pick one up and breathe warmly upon it, it will begin to move about once more.

In a sheltered spot such creatures may sleep away the winter, but they are hopelessly immobilized. Though a few warm-blooded mammals, such as the woodchuck of our day, have evolved a way of reducing their metabolic rate in order to undergo winter hibernation, it is a survival mechanism with drawbacks, for it leaves the animal helplessly exposed if enemies discover him during his period of suspended animation. Thus bear or woodchuck, big animal or small, must seek, in this time of descending sleep, a safe refuge in some hidden den or burrow. Hibernation is, therefore, primarily a winter refuge of small, easily concealed animals rather than of large ones.

A high metabolic rate, however, means a heavy intake of energy in order to sustain body warmth and efficiency. It is for this reason that even some of these later warm-blooded mammals existing in our day have learned to descend into a slower, unconscious rate of living during the winter months when food may be difficult to obtain. On a slightly higher plane they are following the procedure of the cold-blooded frog sleeping in the mud at the bottom of a frozen pond.

The agile brain of the warm-blooded birds and mammals demands a high oxygen consumption and food in concentrated forms, or the creatures cannot long sustain themselves. It was the rise of the flowering plants that provided that energy and changed the nature of the living world. Their appearance parallels in a quite surprising manner the rise of the birds and mammals.

Slowly, toward the dawn of the Age of Reptiles, something over two hundred and fifty million years ago, the little naked sperm cells wriggling their way through dew and raindrops had given way to a kind of pollen carried by the wind. Our present-day pine forests represent plants of a pollen-disseminating variety. Once fertilization was no longer dependent on exterior water, the march over drier regions could be extended. Instead of spores simple primitive seeds carrying some nourishment for the young plant had developed, but true flowers were still scores of millions of years away. After a long period of hesitant evolutionary groping, they exploded upon the world with truly revolutionary violence.

The event occurred in Cretaceous times in the close of the 14 Age of Reptiles. Before the coming of the flowering plants our own ancestral stock, the warm-blooded mammals, consisted of a few mousy little creatures hidden in trees and underbrush. A few lizard-like birds with carnivorous teeth flapped awkwardly on ill-aimed flights among archaic shrubbery. None of these insignificant creatures gave evidence of any remarkable talents. The mammals in particular had been around for some millions of years, but had remained well lost in the shadow of the mighty reptiles. Truth to tell, man was still, like the genie in the bottle, encased in the body of a creature about the size of a rat.

As for the birds, their reptilian cousins the Pterodactyls, 15 flew farther and better. There was just one thing about the birds that paralleled the physiology of the mammals. They, too, had evolved warm blood and its accompanying temperature control. Nevertheless, if one had been seen stripped of his feathers, he would still have seemed a slightly uncanny and unsightly lizard.

Neither the birds nor the mammals, however, were quite 16 what they seemed. They were waiting for the Age of Flowers. They were waiting for what flowers, and with them the true encased seed, would bring. Fish-eating, gigantic leather-winged reptiles, twenty-eight feet from wing tip to wing tip, hovered over the coasts that one day would be swarming with gulls.

Inland the monotonous green of the pine and spruce 17 forests with their primitive wooden cone flowers stretched everywhere. No grass hindered the fall of the naked seeds to earth. Great sequoias towered to the skies. The world of that time has a certain appeal but it is a giant's world, a world moving slowly like the reptiles who stalked magnificently among the boles of its trees.

The trees themselves are ancient, slow-growing and   18
immense, like the redwood groves that have survived to our
day on the California coast. All is stiff, formal, upright and
green, monotonously green. There is no grass as yet; there
are no wide plains rolling in the sun, no tiny daisies dotting
the meadows underfoot. There is little versatility about this
scene; it is, in truth, a giant's world.

A few nights ago it was brought home vividly to me that   19
the world has changed since that far epoch. I was awakened
out of sleep by an unknown sound in my living room. Not a
small sound—not a creaking timber or a mouse's scurry—but
a sharp, rending explosion as though an unwary foot had
been put down upon a wine glass. I had come instantly out of
sleep and lay tense, unbreathing. I listened for another step.
There was none.

Unable to stand the suspense any longer, I turned on the   20
light and passed from room to room glancing uneasily behind chairs and into closets. Nothing seemed disturbed, and
I stood puzzled in the center of the living room floor. Then
a small button-shaped object upon the rug caught my eye. It
was hard and polished and glistening. Scattered over the
length of the room were several more shining up at me like
wary little eyes. A pine cone that had been lying in a dish had
been blown the length of the coffee table. The dish itself
could hardly have been the source of the explosion. Beside it
I found two ribbonlike strips of a velvety-green. I tried to
place the two strips together to make a pod. They twisted res-
olutely away from each other and would no longer fit.

I relaxed in a chair, then, for I had reached a solution of   21
the midnight disturbance. The twisted strips were wistaria
pods that I had brought in a day or two previously and placed
in the dish. They had chosen midnight to explode and dis-
tribute their multiplying fund of life down the length of the
room. A plant, a fixed, rooted thing, immobilized in a single
spot, had devised a way of propelling its offspring across open
space. Immediately there passed before my eyes the million
airy troopers of the milkweed pod and the clutching hooks of
the sandburs. Seeds on the coyote's tail, seeds on the hunter's

coat, thistledown mounting on the winds—all were somehow triumphing over life's limitations. Yet the ability to do
this had not been with them at the beginning. It was the
product of endless effort and experiment.

The seeds on my carpet were not going to lie stiffly where   22
they had dropped like their antiquated cousins, the naked
seeds on the pine-cone scales. They were travelers. Struck by
the thought, I went out next day and collected several other
varieties. I line them up now in a row on my desk—so many
little capsules of life, winged, hooked or spiked. Every one
is an angiosperm, a product of the true flowering plants.
Contained in these little boxes is the secret of that far-off
Cretaceous explosion of a hundred million years ago that
changed the face of the planet. And somewhere in here, I
think, as I poke seriously at one particularly resistant seedcase
of a wild grass, was once man himself.

For Study and Discussion

QUESTIONS ABOUT PURPOSE

1. What are the key events in the chain of cause and effect that, as
   Eiseley shows, culminated in the development of warm-blooded
   mammals?
2. What is Eiseley suggesting about the process of scientific discovery when he recounts the incident of the seed pod exploding in
   his kitchen (paragraphs 19 through 22)?

QUESTIONS ABOUT AUDIENCE

1. How much geology and biology does Eiseley assume his readers
   know?
2. What kind of language and writing style do most readers expect
   to encounter in books and articles about science? Does this essay
   confirm that expectation?

QUESTIONS ABOUT STRATEGIES

1. How does Eiseley use narrative strategies to develop his explanation about evolutionary cause and effect?
2. Why does Eiseley use the pronouns *we* and *you* in this essay and
   end his account with a narrative told in the first person?

For Writing and Research

1. *Analyze* the basic information about evolutionary theory Eiseley is trying to communicate to his readers.
2. *Practice* by speculating about how certain natural events might *cause* other natural events.
3. *Argue* that the destruction of trees, bushes, and flowers for commercial purposes has caused global warming.
4. *Synthesize* some of the research on the prehistoric world. Then use this evidence to support Eiseley's description of what life was like in those times.

STEPHEN JAY GOULD

Stephen Jay Gould (1941–2002) was born in New York City and attended Antioch College and Columbia University. Trained as a paleontologist, Gould was a professor of geology at Harvard University. Throughout his teaching and writing career he has been known for his ability to translate challenging scientific theories into understandable terms. His books include *The Panda's Thumb: More Reflections in Natural History* (1980), *Hen's Teeth and Horse's Toes: Further Reflections in Natural History* (1983), *The Flamingo's Smile: Reflections in Natural History* (1985), *An Urchin in the Storm: Essays About Books and Ideas* (1987), *Bully for Brontosaurus* (1991), *Eight Little Piggies* (1993), *The Structure of Evolutionary Theory*, (2002), and *Triumph and Tragedy in Mudville: A Lifelong Passion for Baseball* (2003). Several of these books are collections of his monthly column for *Natural History* magazine, "This View of Life." In "Carrie Buck's Daughter," reprinted from *The Flamingo's Smile,* Gould traces the tragic consequences of a simplistic assessment of the chain of cause and effect.

Carrie Buck's Daughter

THE LORD REALLY put it on the line in his preface to that prototype of all prescription, the Ten Commandments: 1

> *. . . for I, the Lord thy God, am a jealous God, visiting the iniquity of the fathers upon the children unto the third and fourth generation of them that hate me (Exod. 20:5).*

345

The terror of this statement lies in its patent unfairness— its promise to punish guiltless offspring for the misdeeds of their distant forebears.

A different form of guilt by genealogical association attempts to remove this stigma of injustice by denying a cherished premise of Western thought—human free will. If offspring are tainted not simply by the deeds of their parents but by a material form of evil transferred directly by biological inheritance, then "the iniquity of the fathers" becomes a signal or warning for probable misbehavior of their sons. Thus Plato, while denying that children should suffer directly for

Carrie Buck's case was never about mental deficiency; she was persecuted for supposed sexual immorality and social deviance.

the crimes of their parents, nonetheless defended the banishment of a personally guiltless man whose father, grandfather, and great-grandfather had all been condemned to death.

It is, perhaps, merely coincidental that both Jehovah and Plato chose three generations as their criterion for establishing different forms of guilt by association. Yet we maintain a strong folk, or vernacular, tradition for viewing triple occurrences as minimal evidence of regularity. Bad things, we are told, come in threes. Two may represent an accidental association; three is a pattern. Perhaps, then, we should not wonder that our own century's most famous pronouncement of blood guilt employed the same criterion—Oliver Wendell Holmes's defense of compulsory sterilization in Virginia (Supreme Court decision of 1927 in *Buck v. Bell*): "three generations of imbeciles are enough."

Restrictions upon immigration, with national quotas set to discriminate against those deemed mentally unfit by early versions of IQ testing, marked the greatest triumph of the

American eugenics movement—the flawed hereditarian doctrine, so popular earlier in our century and by no means extinct today, that attempted to "improve" our human stock by preventing the propagation of those deemed biologically unfit and encouraging procreation among the supposedly worthy. But the movement to enact and enforce laws for compulsory "eugenic" sterilization had an impact and success scarcely less pronounced. If we could debar the shiftless and the stupid from our shores, we might also prevent the propagation of those similarly afflicted but already here.

The movement for compulsory sterilization began in earnest during the 1890s, abetted by two major factors—the rise of eugenics as an influential political movement and the perfection of safe and simple operations (vasectomy for men and salpingectomy, the cutting and tying of Fallopian tubes, for women) to replace castration and other socially unacceptable forms of mutilation. Indiana passed the first sterilization act based on eugenic principles in 1907 (a few states had previously mandated castration as a punitive measure for certain sexual crimes, although such laws were rarely enforced and usually overturned by judicial review). Like so many others to follow, it provided for sterilization of afflicted people residing in the state's "care," either as inmates of mental hospitals and homes for the feeble-minded or as inhabitants of prisons. Sterilization could be imposed upon those judged insane, idiotic, imbecilic, or moronic, and upon convicted rapists or criminals when recommended by a board of experts.

By the 1930s, more than thirty states had passed similar laws, often with an expanded list of so-called hereditary defects, including alcoholism and drug addiction in some states, and even blindness and deafness in others. These laws were continually challenged and rarely enforced in most states; only California and Virginia applied them zealously. By January 1935, some 20,000 forced "eugenic" sterilizations had been performed in the United States, nearly half in California.

No organization crusaded more vociferously and success-   8
fully for these laws than the Eugenics Record Office, the semi-
official arm and repository of data for the eugenics movement
in America. Harry Laughlin, superintendent of the Eugenics
Record Office, dedicated most of his career to a tireless campaign of writing and lobbying for eugenic sterilization. He
hoped, thereby, to eliminate in two generations the genes of
what he called the "submerged tenth"—"the most worthless
one-tenth of our present population." He proposed a "model
sterilization law" in 1922, designed

> *to prevent the procreation of persons socially inade-*
> *quate from defective inheritance, by authorizing*
> *and providing for eugenical sterilization of certain*
> *potential parents carrying degenerate hereditary*
> *qualities.*

This model bill became the prototype for most laws passed   9
in America, although few states cast their net as widely as
Laughlin advised. (Laughlin's categories encompassed "blind,
including those with seriously impaired vision; deaf, including those with seriously impaired hearing; and dependent, including orphans, ne'er-do-wells, the homeless, tramps, and
paupers.") Laughlin's suggestions were better heeded in
Nazi Germany, where his model act inspired the infamous
and stringently enforced *Erbgesundheitsrecht*, leading by the
eve of World War II to the sterilization of some 375,000 people, most for "congenital feeble-mindedness," but including
nearly 4,000 for blindness and deafness.

The campaign for forced eugenic sterilization in America   10
reached its climax and height of respectability in 1927, when
the Supreme Court, by an 8–1 vote, upheld the Virginia sterilization bill in *Buck v. Bell*. Oliver Wendell Holmes, then in
his mid-eighties and the most celebrated jurist in America,
wrote the majority opinion with his customary verve and
power of style. It included the notorious paragraph, with its
chilling tag line, cited ever since as the quintessential statement of eugenic principles. Remembering with pride his own

distant experiences as an infantryman in the Civil War, Holmes wrote:

> *We have seen more than once that the public welfare may call upon the best citizens for their lives. It would be strange if it could not call upon those who already sap the strength of the state for these lesser sacrifices. . . . It is better for all the world, if instead of waiting to execute degenerate offspring for crime, or to let them starve for their imbecility, society can prevent those who are manifestly unfit from continuing their kind. The principle that sustains compulsory vaccination is broad enough to cover cutting the Fallopian tubes. Three generations of imbeciles are enough.*

Who, then, were the famous "three generations of imbeciles," and why should they still compel our interest? 11

When the state of Virginia passed its compulsory sterilization law in 1924, Carrie Buck, an eighteen-year-old white woman, lived as an involuntary resident at the State Colony for Epileptics and Feeble-Minded. As the first person selected for sterilization under the new act, Carrie Buck became the focus for a constitutional challenge launched, in part, by conservative Virginia Christians who held, according to eugenical "modernists," antiquated views about individual preferences and "benevolent" state power. (Simplistic political labels do not apply in this case, and rarely in general for that matter. We usually regard eugenics as a conservative movement and its most vocal critics as members of the left. This alignment has generally held in our own decade. But eugenics, touted in its day as the latest in scientific modernism, attracted many liberals and numbered among its most vociferous critics groups often labeled as reactionary and antiscientific. If any political lesson emerges from these shifting allegiances, we might consider the true inalienability of certain human rights.) 12

But why was Carrie Buck in the State Colony and why was   13
she selected? Oliver Wendell Holmes upheld her choice as
judicious in the opening lines of his 1927 opinion:

> *Carrie Buck is a feeble-minded white woman who*
> *was committed to the State Colony. . . . She is the*
> *daughter of a feeble-minded mother in the same*
> *institution, and the mother of an illegitimate feeble-*
> *minded child.*

In short, inheritance stood as the crucial issue (indeed as   14
the driving force behind all eugenics). For if measured mental deficiency arose from malnourishment, either of body or
mind, and not from tainted genes, then how could sterilization be justified? If decent food, upbringing, medical care,
and education might make a worthy citizen of Carrie Buck's
daughter, how could the State of Virginia justify the severing
of Carrie's Fallopian tubes against her will? (Some forms of
mental deficiency are passed in inheritance in family lines, but
most are not—a scarcely surprising conclusion when we consider the thousand shocks that beset us all during our lives,
from abnormalities in embryonic growth to traumas of birth,
malnourishment, rejection, and poverty. In any case, no fair-
minded person today would credit Laughlin's social criteria
for the identification of hereditary deficiency—ne'er-do-wells,
the homeless, tramps, and paupers—although we shall soon
see that Carrie Buck was committed on these grounds.)

When Carrie Buck's case emerged as the crucial test of   15
Virginia's law, the chief honchos of eugenics understood that
the time had come to put up or shut up on the crucial issue
of inheritance. Thus, the Eugenics Record Office sent Arthur
H. Estabrook, their crack fieldworker, to Virginia for a
"scientific" study of the case. Harry Laughlin himself provided a deposition, and his brief for inheritance was presented at the local trial that affirmed Virginia's law and later
worked its way to the Supreme Court as *Buck v. Bell.*

Laughlin made two major points to the court. First, that   16
Carrie Buck and her mother, Emma Buck, were feeble-minded
by the Stanford-Binet test of IQ then in its own infancy. Carrie

scored a mental age of nine years, Emma of seven years and eleven months. (These figures ranked them technically as "imbeciles" by definitions of the day, hence Holmes's later choice of words—though his infamous line is often misquoted as "three generations of idiots." Imbeciles displayed a mental age of six to nine years; idiots performed worse, morons better, to round out the old nomenclature of mental deficiency.) Second, that most feeble-mindedness resides ineluctably in the genes, and that Carrie Buck surely belonged with this majority. Laughlin reported:

> *Generally, feeble-mindedness is caused by the inheritance of degenerate qualities; but sometimes it might be caused by environmental factors which are not hereditary. In the case given, the evidence points strongly toward the feeble-mindedness and moral delinquency of Carrie Buck being due, primarily, to inheritance and not to environment.*

Carrie Buck's daughter was then, and has always been, the pivotal figure of this painful case. I noted in beginning this essay that we tend (often at our peril) to regard two as potential accident and three as an established pattern. The supposed imbecility of Emma and Carrie might have been an unfortunate coincidence, but the diagnosis of similar deficiency for Vivian Buck (made by a social worker, as we shall see, when Vivian was but six months old) tipped the balance in Laughlin's favor and led Holmes to declare the Buck lineage inherently corrupt by deficient heredity. Vivian sealed the pattern—*three* generations of imbeciles are enough. Besides, had Carrie not given illegitimate birth to Vivian, the issue (in both senses) would never have emerged. 17

Oliver Wendell Holmes viewed his work with pride. The man so renowned for his principle of judicial restraint, who had proclaimed that freedom must not be curtailed without "clear and present danger"—without the equivalent of falsely yelling "fire" in a crowded theater—wrote of his judgment in *Buck v. Bell:* "I felt that I was getting near the first principle of real reform." 18

And so *Buck v. Bell* remained for fifty years, a footnote to   19
a moment of American history perhaps best forgotten. Then,
in 1980, it reemerged to prick our collective conscience, when
Dr. K. Ray Nelson, then director of the Lynchburg Hospital where Carrie Buck had been sterilized, researched the
records of his institution and discovered that more than
4,000 sterilizations had been performed, the last as late
as 1972. He also found Carrie Buck, alive and well near
Charlottesville, and her sister Doris, covertly sterilized under
the same law (she was told that her operation was for appendicitis), and now, with fierce dignity, dejected and bitter
because she had wanted a child more than anything else in
her life and had finally, in her old age, learned why she had
never conceived.

As scholars and reporters visited Carrie Buck and her   20
sister, what a few experts had known all along became abundantly clear to everyone. Carrie Buck was a woman of obviously normal intelligence. For example, Paul A. Lombardo of
the School of Law at the University of Virginia, and a leading
scholar of *Buck v. Bell,* wrote in a letter to me:

> *As for Carrie, when I met her she was reading news-*
> *papers daily and joining a more literate friend to*
> *assist at regular bouts with the crossword puzzles. She*
> *was not a sophisticated woman, and lacked social*
> *graces, but mental health professionals who exam-*
> *ined her in later life confirmed my impressions that*
> *she was neither mentally ill nor retarded.*

On what evidence, then, was Carrie Buck consigned to the   21
State Colony for Epileptics and Feeble-Minded on January
23, 1924? I have seen the text of her commitment hearing; it
is, to say the least, cursory and contradictory. Beyond the
bald and undocumented say-so of her foster parents, and her
own brief appearance before a commission of two doctors
and a justice of the peace, no evidence was presented. Even
the crude and early Stanford-Binet test, so fatally flawed as a
measure of innate worth (see my book *The Mismeasure of*

Man, although the evidence of Carrie's own case suffices) but at least clothed with the aura of quantitative respectability, had not yet been applied.

When we understand why Carrie Buck was committed in January 1924, we can finally comprehend the hidden meaning of her case and its message for us today. The silent key, again as from the first, is her daughter Vivian, born on March 28, 1924, and then but an evident bump on her belly. Carrie Buck was one of several illegitimate children borne by her mother, Emma. She grew up with foster parents, J. T. and Alice Dobbs, and continued to live with them as an adult, helping out with chores around the house. She was raped by a relative of her foster parents, then blamed for the resulting pregnancy. Almost surely, she was (as they used to say) committed to hide her shame (and her rapist's identity), not because enlightened science had just discovered her true mental status. In short, she was sent away to have her baby. Her case never was about mental deficiency; Carrie Buck was persecuted for supposed sexual immorality and social deviance. The annals of her trial and hearing reek with the contempt of the well-off and well-bred for poor people of "loose morals." Who really cared whether Vivian was a baby of normal intelligence; she was the illegitimate child of an illegitimate woman. Two generations of bastards are enough. Harry Laughlin began his "family history" of the Bucks by writing: "These people belong to the shiftless, ignorant and worthless class of anti-social whites of the South." 22

We know little of Emma Buck and her life, but we have no more reason to suspect her than her daughter Carrie of true mental deficiency. Their supposed deviance was social and sexual; the charge of imbecility was a cover-up, Mr. Justice Holmes notwithstanding. 23

We come then to the crux of the case, Carrie's daughter, Vivian. What evidence was ever adduced for her mental deficiency? This and only this: At the original trial in late 1924, when Vivian Buck was seven months old, a Miss Wilhelm, social worker for the Red Cross, appeared before the court. 24

She began by stating honestly the true reason for Carrie Buck's commitment:

> Mr. Dobbs, who had charge of the girl, had taken her when a small child, had reported to Miss Duke [the temporary secretary of Public Welfare for Albemarle County] that the girl was pregnant and that he wanted to have her committed somewhere— to have her sent to some institution.

Miss Wilhelm then rendered her judgment of Vivian Buck   25
by comparing her with the normal granddaughter of Mrs. Dobbs, born just three days earlier:

> It is difficult to judge probabilities of a child as young as that, but it seems to me not quite a normal baby. In its appearance—I should say that perhaps my knowledge of the mother may prejudice me in that regard, but I saw the child at the same time as Mrs. Dobbs' daughter's baby, which is only three days older than this one, and there is a very decided difference in the development of the babies. That was about two weeks ago. There is a look about it that is not quite normal, but just what it is, I can't tell.

This short testimony, and nothing else, formed all the   26
evidence for the crucial third generation of imbeciles. Cross-examination revealed that neither Vivian nor the Dobbs grandchild could walk or talk, and that "Mrs. Dobbs' daughter's baby is a very responsive baby. When you play with it or try to attract its attention—it is a baby that you can play with. The other baby is not. It seems very apathetic and not responsive." Miss Wilhelm then urged Carrie Buck's sterilization: "I think," she said, "it would at least prevent the propagation of her kind." Several years later, Miss Wilhelm denied that she had ever examined Vivian or deemed the child feeble-minded.

Unfortunately, Vivian died at age eight of "enteric colitis"   27
(as recorded on her death certificate), an ambiguous diagnosis

that could mean many things but may well indicate that she fell victim to one of the preventable childhood diseases of poverty (a grim reminder of the real subject in *Buck v. Bell*). She is therefore mute as a witness in our reassessment of her famous case.

When *Buck v. Bell* resurfaced in 1980, it immediately struck me that Vivian's case was crucial and that evidence for the mental status of a child who died at age eight might best be found in report cards. I have therefore been trying to track down Vivian Buck's school records for the past four years and have finally succeeded. (They were supplied to me by Dr. Paul A. Lombardo, who also sent other documents, including Miss Wilhelm's testimony, and spent several hours answering my questions by mail and Lord knows how much time playing successful detective *in re* Vivian's school records. I have never met Dr. Lombardo; he did all this work for kindness, collegiality, and love of the game of knowledge, not for expected reward or even requested acknowledgment. In a profession—academics—so often marred by pettiness and silly squabbling over meaningless priorities, this generosity must be recorded and celebrated as a sign of how things can and should be.)

Vivian Buck was adopted by the Dobbs family, who had raised (but later sent away) her mother, Carrie. As Vivian Alice Elaine Dobbs, she attended the Venable Public Elementary School of Charlottesville for four terms, from September 1930 until May 1932, a month before her death. She was a perfectly normal, quite average student, neither particularly outstanding nor much troubled. In those days before grade inflation, when C meant "good, 81–87" (as defined on her report card) rather than barely scraping by, Vivian Dobbs received A's and B's for deportment and C's for all academic subjects but mathematics (which was always difficult for her, and where she scored D) during her first term in Grade 1A, from September 1930 to January 1931. She improved during her second term in 1B, meriting an A in deportment, C in mathematics, and B in all other academic subjects; she was placed on the honor roll in April 1931. Promoted to 2A, she had trouble during the fall term of 1931, failing mathematics and spelling but receiving A in deportment, B in reading, and C in writing and English. She was "retained to 2A" for the next term—or "left back" as we used to say, and scarcely a sign of imbecility as I remember all my buddies who suffered a similar fate. In any case, she again did well in her final term, with B in deportment, reading, and spelling, and C in writing, English, and mathematics during her last month in school. This daughter of "lewd and immoral" women excelled in deportment and performed adequately, although not brilliantly, in her academic subjects.

In short, we can only agree with the conclusion that Dr. 30 Lombardo has reached in his research on *Buck v. Bell*—there were no imbeciles, not a one, among the three generations of Bucks. I don't know that such correction of cruel but forgotten errors of history counts for much, but I find it both symbolic and satisfying to learn that forced eugenic sterilization, a procedure of such dubious morality, earned its official justification (and won its most quoted line of rhetoric) on a patent falsehood.

Carrie Buck died last year. By a quirk of fate, and not by 31 memory or design, she was buried just a few steps from her only daughter's grave. In the umpteenth and ultimate verse of a favorite old ballad, a rose and a brier—the sweet and the bitter—emerge from the tombs of Barbara Allen and her lover, twining about each other in the union of death. May Carrie and Vivian, victims in different ways and in the flower of youth, rest together in peace.

For Study and Discussion

QUESTIONS ABOUT PURPOSE

1. Chief Justice Oliver Wendell Holmes is probably the most famous, most revered, and most frequently quoted of all Supreme Court justices. What does Gould accomplish by showing the role he played in the Carrie Buck decision?
2. What attitudes of the society in which Carrie Buck was reared does Gould want his readers to analyze and evaluate? Why?

QUESTIONS ABOUT AUDIENCE

1. What knowledge about the racial policies of the Nazi regime in Germany in the 1930s does Gould count on his readers having?
2. How does Gould connect the analysis of why Carrie Buck was sterilized to his readers' knowledge of contemporary social problems?

QUESTIONS ABOUT STRATEGIES

1. What evidence does Gould bring in to support his belief that Carrie Buck's treatment was motivated by prejudice and shame, not by concern over her mental abilities?
2. In what paragraphs do you notice Gould's own feelings surfacing? How do you think his showing those feelings affects the impact of the essay?

For Writing and Research

1. *Analyze* the way Gould uses historical information to demonstrate "guilt by genealogical association."
2. *Practice* by analyzing how the character virtues and flaws of your parents or grandparents have caused your character virtues and flaws.
3. *Argue* that the current immigration controversy has been caused by a desire to prevent the procreation of an "undesirable" population.
4. *Synthesize* the research on how nature (genes) and nurture (environment) affect character. Then use this evidence to support Gould's argument about the mistreatment of Carrie Buck's daughter.

TERRY McMILLAN

Terry McMillan was born in 1951 in Port Huron,
Michigan, and was educated at the University of
California at Berkeley and Columbia University.
She taught at the University of Wyoming and the
University of Arizona before the critical success of
her first novel, *Mama* (1987), and the controversy
surrounding her second novel, *Disappearing Acts*
(1989), encouraged her to devote her full attention to writing. Her third novel, *Waiting to Exhale*
(1992), a story of the romantic complications beset-
ting four contemporary African American women
friends, was adapted into an extremely popular
film. Her most recent work includes *How Stella
Got Her Groove Back* (1996) and *The Interrup-
tion of Everything* (2005). In "The Movie That
Changed My Life," reprinted from *The Movie That
Changed My Life* (1991), McMillan analyzes her
positive and negative reaction to watching *The
Wizard of Oz*.

The Movie That Changed
My Life

I GREW UP in a small industrial town in the thumb of   1
Michigan: Port Huron. We had barely gotten used to the
idea of color TV. I can guess how old I was when I first saw
The Wizard of Oz on TV because I remember the house we
lived in when I was still in elementary school. It was a huge,
drafty house that had a fireplace we never once lit. We lived
on two acres of land, and at the edge of the back yard was the
woods, which I always thought of as a forest. We had weep-
ing willow trees, plum and pear trees, and blackberry bushes.
We could not see into our neighbors' homes. Railroad tracks

were part of our front yard, and the house shook when a train passed—twice, sometimes three times a day. You couldn't hear the TV at all when it zoomed by, and I was often afraid that if it ever flew off the tracks, it would land on the sun porch, where we all watched TV. I often left the room during this time, but my younger sisters and brother thought I was just scared. I think I was in the third grade around this time.

It was a raggedy house which really should've been con- 2
demned, but we fixed it up and kept it clean. We had our German shepherd, Prince, who slept under the rickety steps to the side porch that were on the verge of collapsing but never did. I remember performing a ritual whenever *Oz* was coming on. I either baked cookies or cinnamon rolls or popped

---

The movie [The Wizard of Oz] *taught me
that it's okay to be an idealist, that you have
to imagine something better and go for it.*

---

popcorn while all five of us waited for Dorothy to spin from black and white on that dreary farm in Kansas to the luminous land of color of Oz.

My house was chaotic, especially with four sisters and 3
brothers and a mother who worked at a factory, and if I'm remembering correctly, my father was there for the first few years of the *Oz* (until he got tuberculosis and had to live in a sanitarium for a year). I do recall the noise and the fighting of my parents (not to mention my other relatives and neighbors). Violence was plentiful, and I wanted to go wherever Dorothy was going where she would not find trouble. To put it bluntly, I wanted to escape because I needed an escape.

I didn't know any happy people. Everyone I knew was 4
either angry or not satisfied. The only time they seemed to laugh was when they were drunk, and even that was short-lived. Most of the grown-ups I was in contact with lived their

lives as if it had all been a mistake, an accident, and they were paying dearly for it. It seemed as if they were always at someone else's mercy—women at the mercy of men (this prevailed in my hometown) and children at the mercy of frustrated parents. All I knew was that most of the grown-ups felt trapped, as if they were stuck in this town and no road would lead out. So many of them felt a sense of accomplishment just getting up in the morning and making it through another day. I overheard many a grown-up conversation, and they were never life-affirming: "Chile, if the Lord'll just give me the strength to make it through another week . . ."; "I just don't know how I'ma handle this, I can't take no more. . . ." I rarely knew what they were talking about, but even a fool could hear that it was some kind of drudgery. When I was a child, it became apparent to me that these grown-ups had no power over their lives, or, if they did, they were always at a loss as to how to exercise it. I did not want to grow up and have to depend on someone else for my happiness or be miserable or have to settle for whatever I was dished out—if I could help it. That much I knew already.

I remember being confused a lot. I could never understand   5
why no one had any energy to do anything that would make them feel good, besides drinking. Being happy was a transient and very temporary thing which was almost always offset by some kind of bullshit. I would, of course, learn much later in my own adult life that these things are called obstacles, barriers—or again, bullshit. When I started writing, I began referring to them as "knots." But life wasn't one long knot. It seemed to me it just required stamina and common sense and the wherewithal to know when a knot was before you and you had to dig deeper than you had in order to figure out how to untie it. It could be hard, but it was simple.

The initial thing I remember striking me about *Oz* was   6
how nasty Dorothy's Auntie Em talked to her and everybody on the farm. I was used to that authoritative tone of voice because my mother talked to us the same way. She never asked you to do anything; she gave you a command and never said "please," and, once you finished it, rarely said "thank you."

The tone of her voice was always hostile, and Auntie Em sounded just like my mother—bossy and domineering. They both ran the show, it seemed, and I think that because my mother was raising five children almost single-handedly, I must have had some inkling that being a woman didn't mean you had to be helpless. Auntie Em's husband was a wimp, and for once the tables were turned: he took orders from her! My mother and Auntie Em were proof to me that if you wanted to get things done you had to delegate authority and keep everyone apprised of the rules of the game as well as the consequences. In my house it was punishment—you were severely grounded. What little freedom we had was snatched away: As a child, I often felt helpless, powerless, because I had no control over my situation and couldn't tell my mother when I thought (or knew) she was wrong or being totally unfair, or when her behavior was inappropriate. I hated this feeling to no end, but what was worse was not being able to do anything about it except keep my mouth shut.

So I completely identified when no one had time to listen   7
to Dorothy. That dog's safety was important to her, but no one seemed to think that what Dorothy was saying could possibly be as urgent as the situation at hand. The bottom line was, it was urgent to her. When I was younger, I rarely had the opportunity to finish a sentence before my mother would cut me off or complete it for me, or, worse, give me something to do. She used to piss me off, and nowadays I catch myself—stop myself—from doing the same thing to my seven-year-old. Back then, it was as if what I had to say wasn't important or didn't warrant her undivided attention. So when Dorothy's Auntie Em dismisses her and tells her to find somewhere where she'll stay out of trouble, and little Dorothy starts thinking about if there in fact is such a place— one that is trouble free—I was right there with her, because I wanted to know, too.

I also didn't know or care that Judy Garland was supposed   8
to have been a child star, but when she sang "Somewhere Over the Rainbow," I *was* impressed. Impressed more by the song than by who was singing it. I mean, she wasn't exactly

Aretha Franklin or the Marvelettes or the Supremes, which was the only vocal music I was used to. As kids, we often laughed at white people singing on TV because their songs were always so corny and they just didn't sound anything like the soulful music we had in our house. Sometimes we would mimic people like Doris Day and Fred Astaire and laugh like crazy because they were always so damn happy while they sang and danced. We would also watch square-dancing when we wanted a real laugh and try to look under the women's dresses. What I hated more than anything was when in the middle of a movie the white people always had to start singing and dancing to get their point across. Later, I would hate it when black people would do the same thing—even though it was obvious to us that at least they had more rhythm and, most of the time, more range vocally.

We did skip through the house singing "We're off to see 9 the Wizard," but other than that, most of the songs in this movie are a blank, probably because I blanked them out. Where I lived, when you had something to say to someone, you didn't sing it, you told them, so the cumulative effect of the songs wore thin.

I was afraid for Dorothy when she decided to run away, 10 but at the same time I was glad. I couldn't much blame her— I mean, what kind of life did she have, from what I'd seen so far? She lived on an ugly farm out in the middle of nowhere with all these old people who did nothing but chores, chores, and more chores. Who did she have to play with besides that dog? And even though I lived in a house full of people, I knew how lonely Dorothy felt, or at least how isolated she must have felt. First of all, I was the oldest, and my sisters and brothers were ignorant and silly creatures who often bored me because they couldn't hold a decent conversation. I couldn't ask them questions, like: Why are we living in this dump? When is Mama going to get some more money? Why can't we go on vacations like other people? Like white peo-ple? Why does our car always break down? Why are we poor? Why doesn't Mama ever laugh? Why do we have to live in Port Huron? Isn't there someplace better than this we can go live? I remember thinking this kind of stuff in kindergarten, to be honest, because times were hard, but I'd saved twenty-five cents in my piggy bank for hotdog-and-chocolate-milk day at school, and on the morning I went to get it, my piggy bank was empty. My mother gave me some lame excuse as to why she had to spend it, but all I was thinking was that I would have to sit there (again) and watch the other children slurp their chocolate milk, and I could see the ketchup and mustard oozing out of the hot-dog bun that I wouldn't get to taste. I walked to school, and with the exception of walking to my father's funeral when I was sixteen, this was the longest walk of my entire life. My plaid dress was starched and my socks were white, my hair was braided and not a strand out of place; but I wanted to know why I had to feel this kind of humiliation when in fact I had saved the money for this very purpose. Why? By the time I got to school, I'd wiped my nose and dried my eyes and vowed not to let anyone know that I was even moved by this. It was no one's business why I couldn't eat my hot dog and chocolate milk, but the irony of it was that my teacher, Mrs. Johnson, must have sensed what had happened, and she bought my hot dog and chocolate milk for me that day. I can still remember feeling how unfair things can be, but how they somehow always turn out good. I guess seeing so much negativity had already started to turn me into an optimist.

I was a very busy child, because I was the oldest and had to see to it that my sisters and brother had their baths and did their homework; I combed my sisters' hair, and by fourth grade I had cooked my first Thanksgiving dinner. It was my responsibility to keep the house spotless so that when my mother came home from work it would pass her inspection, so I spent many an afternoon and Saturday morning mopping and waxing floors, cleaning ovens and refrigerators, grocery shopping, and by the time I was thirteen, I was paying bills for my mother and felt like an adult. I was also tired of it, sick of all the responsibility. So yes, I rooted for Dorothy when she and Toto were vamoosing, only I wanted to know: Where in the hell was she going? Where would I go if I were to run away? I had no idea because there was nowhere to go. What I did know was that one day I would go somewhere— which is why I think I watched so much TV. I was always on the lookout for Paradise, and I think I found it a few years later on "Adventures in Paradise," with Gardner McKay, and on "77 Sunset Strip." Palm trees and blue water and islands made quite an impression on a little girl from a flat, dull little depressing town in Michigan.

Professor Marvel really pissed me off, and I didn't believe   12 for a minute that that crystal ball was real, even before he started asking Dorothy all those questions, but I knew this man was going to be important, and I just couldn't figure out how. Dorothy was so gullible, I thought, and I knew this word because my mother used to always drill it in us that you should "never believe everything somebody tells you." So after Professor Marvel convinced Dorothy that her Auntie Em might be in trouble, and Dorothy scoops up Toto and runs back home, I was totally disappointed, because now I wasn't going to have an adventure. I was thinking I might actually learn how to escape drudgery by watching Dorothy do it successfully, but before she even gave herself the chance to discover for herself that she could make it, she was on her way back home. "Dummy" we all yelled on the sun porch. "Dodo brain!"

The storm. The tornado. Of course, now the entire set of   13 this film looks so phony it's ridiculous, but back then I knew the wind was a tornado because in Michigan we had the same kind of trapdoor underground shelter that Auntie Em had on the farm. I knew Dorothy was going to be locked out once Auntie Em and the workers locked the door, and I also knew she wasn't going to be heard when she knocked on it. This was drama at its best, even though I didn't know what drama was at the time.

In the house she goes, and I was frightened for her. I knew   14 that house was going to blow away, so when little Dorothy gets banged in the head by a window that flew out of its casement, I remember all of us screaming. We watched everybody fly by the window, including the wicked neighbor who turns out to be the Wicked Witch of the West, and I'm sure I probably substituted my mother for Auntie Em and fantasized that all of my siblings would fly away, too. They all got on my nerves because I could never find a quiet place in my house—no such thing as peace—and I was always being disturbed.

It wasn't so much that I had so much I wanted to do by myself, but I already knew that silence was a rare commodity, and when I managed to snatch a few minutes of it, I could daydream, pretend to be someone else somewhere else—and this was fun. But I couldn't do it if someone was bugging me. On days when my mother was at work, I would often send the kids outside to play and lock them out, just so I could have the house to myself for at least fifteen minutes. I loved pretending that none of them existed for a while, although after I finished with my fantasy world, it was reassuring to see them all there. I think I was grounded.

When Dorothy's house began to spin and spin and spin, I was curious as to where it was going to land. And to be honest, I didn't know little Dorothy was actually dreaming until she woke up and opened the door and everything was in color! It looked like Paradise to me. The foliage was almost an iridescent green, the water bluer than I'd ever seen in any of the lakes in Michigan. Of course, once I realized she was in fact dreaming, it occurred to me that this very well might be the only way to escape. To dream up another world. Create your own.

I had no clue that Dorothy was going to find trouble, though, even in her dreams. Hell, if I had dreamed up something like another world, it would've been a perfect one. I wouldn't have put myself in such a precarious situation. I'd have been able to go straight to the Wizard, no strings attached. First of all, that she walked was stupid to me; I would've asked one of those Munchkins for a ride. And I never bought into the idea of those slippers, but once I bought the whole idea, I accepted the fact that the girl was definitely lost and just wanted to get home. Personally, all I kept thinking was, if she could get rid of that Wicked Witch of the West, the Land of Oz wasn't such a bad place to be stuck in. It beat the farm in Kansas.

At the time, I truly wished I could spin away from my family and home and land someplace as beautiful and surreal as Oz—if only for a little while. All I wanted was to get a chance to see another side of the world, to be able to make comparisons, and then decide if it was worth coming back home. 18

What was really strange to me, after the Good Witch of the North tells Dorothy to just stay on the Yellow Brick Road to get to the Emerald City and find the Wizard so she can get home, was when Dorothy meets the Scarecrow, the Tin Man, and the Lion—all of whom were missing something I'd never even given any thought to. A brain? What did having one really mean? What would not having one mean? I had one, didn't I, because I did well in school. But because the Scarecrow couldn't make up his mind, thought of himself as a failure, it dawned on me that having a brain meant you had choices, you could make decisions and, as a result, make things happen. Yes, I thought, I had one, and I was going to use it. One day. And the Tin Man, who didn't have a heart. Not having one meant you were literally dead to me, and I never once thought of it as being the house of emotions (didn't know what emotions were), where feelings of jealousy, devotion, and sentiment lived. I'd never thought of what else a heart was good for except keeping you alive. But I did have feelings, because they were often hurt, and I was envious of the white girls at my school who wore mohair sweaters and box-pleat skirts, who went skiing and tobogganing and yachting and spent summers in Quebec. Why didn't white girls have to straighten their hair? Why didn't their parents beat each other up? Why were they always so goddamn happy? 19

And courage. Oh, that was a big one. What did having it and not having it mean? I found out that it meant having guts and being afraid but doing whatever it was you set out to do anyway. Without courage, you couldn't do much of anything. I liked courage and assumed I would acquire it 20 somehow. As a matter of fact, one day my mother *told* me to get her a cup of coffee, and even though my heart was pounding and I was afraid, I said to her pointblank, "Could you please say please?" She looked up at me out of the corner of her eye and said, "What?" So I repeated myself, feeling more powerful because she hadn't slapped me across the room already, and then something came over her and she looked at me and said, "Please." I smiled all the way to the kitchen, and from that point forward, I managed to get away with this kind of behavior until I left home when I was seventeen. My sisters and brother—to this day—don't know how I stand up to my mother, but I know. I decided not to be afraid or intimidated by her, and I wanted her to treat me like a friend, like a human being, instead of her slave.

I do believe that Oz also taught me much about friendship. I mean, the Tin Man, the Lion, and the Scarecrow hung in there for Dorothy, stuck their "necks" out and made sure she was protected, even risked their own "lives" for her. They told each other the truth. They trusted each other. All four of them had each other's best interests in mind. I believe it may have been a while before I actually felt this kind of sincerity in a friend, but really good friends aren't easy to come by, and when you find one, you hold on to them.

Okay. So Dorothy goes through hell before she gets back to Kansas. But the bottom line was, she made it. And what I remember feeling when she clicked those heels was that you have to have faith and be a believer, for real, or nothing will ever materialize. Simple as that. And not only in life but even in your dreams there's always going to be adversity, obstacles, knots, or some kind of bullshit you're going to have to deal with in order to get on with your life. Dorothy had a good heart and it was in the right place, which is why I suppose she won out over the evil witch. I've learned that one, too. That good *always* overcomes evil; maybe not immediately, but in the long run, it does. So I think I vowed when I was little to try to be a good person. An honest person. To care about others and not just myself. Not to be a selfish person, because my heart would be of no service if I used it only for myself.

And I had to have the courage to see other people and my-self as not being perfect (yes, I had a heart and a brain, but some other things would turn up missing, later), and I would have to learn to untie every knot that I encountered—some self-imposed, some not—in my life, and to believe that if I did the right things, I would never stray too far from my Yellow Brick Road.

I'm almost certain that I saw *Oz* annually for at least five or six years, but I don't remember how old I was when I stopped watching it. I do know that by the time my parents were divorced (I was thirteen), I couldn't sit through it again. I was a mature teen-ager and had finally reached the point where Dorothy got on my nerves. Singing, dancing, and skipping damn near everywhere was so corny and utterly sentimental that even the Yellow Brick Road became sicken-ing. I already knew what she was in for, and sometimes I rewrote the story in my head. I kept asking myself, what if she had just run away and kept going, maybe she would've ended up in Los Angeles with a promising singing career. What if it had turned out that she hadn't been dreaming, and the Wizard had given her an offer she couldn't refuse—say, for instance, he had asked her to stay on in the Emerald City, that she could visit the farm whenever she wanted to, but, get a clue, Dorothy, the Emerald City is what's happening; she could make new city friends and get a hobby and a boyfriend and free rent and never have to do chores . . .

I had to watch *The Wizard of Oz* again in order to write this, and my six-and-a-half-year-old son, Solomon, joined me. At first he kept asking me if something was wrong with the TV be-cause it wasn't in color, but as he watched, he became mesmer-ized by the story. He usually squirms or slides to the floor and under a table or just leaves the room if something on TV bores him, which it usually does, except if he's watching Nick-elodeon, a high-quality cable kiddie channel. His favorite shows, which he watches with real consistency, and, I think, actually goes through withdrawal if he can't get them for what-ever reason, are "Inspector Gadget," "Looney Tunes," and "Mr. Ed." "Make the Grade," which is sort of a junior-high

23

24

version of "Jeopardy," gives him some kind of thrill, even though he rarely knows any of the answers. And "Garfield" is a must on Saturday morning. There is hardly anything on TV that he watches that has any real, or at least plausible, drama to it, but you can't miss what you've never had.

The Wicked Witch intimidated the boy no end, and he   25
was afraid of her. The Wizard was also a problem. So I explained—no, I just told him pointblank—"Don't worry, she'll get it in the end, Solomon, because she's bad. And the Wizard's a fake, and he's trying to sound like a tough guy, but he's a wus." That offered him some consolation, and even when the Witch melted he kind of looked at me with those *Home Alone* eyes and asked "But where did she go, Mommy?" "She's history," I said. "Melted. Gone. Into the ground. Remember, this is pretend. It's not real. Real people don't melt. This is only TV," I said. And then he got that look in his eyes as if he'd remembered something.

Of course he had a nightmare that night and of course   26
there was a witch in it, because I had actually left the sofa a few times during this last viewing to smoke a few cigarettes (the memory bank is a powerful place—I still remembered many details), put the dishes in the dishwasher, make a few phone calls, water the plants. Solomon sang "We're off to see the Wizard" for the next few days because he said that was his favorite part, next to the Munchkins (who also showed up in his nightmare).

So, to tell the truth, I really didn't watch the whole movie   27
again. I just couldn't. Probably because about thirty or so years ago little Dorothy had made a lasting impression on me, and this viewing felt like overkill. You only have to tell me, show me, once in order for me to get it. But even still, the movie itself taught me a few things that I still find challenging. That it's okay to be an idealist, that you have to imagine something better and go for it. That you have to believe in *something,* and it's best to start with yourself and take it from there. At least give it a try. As corny as it may sound, sometimes I am afraid of what's around the corner, or what's not around the corner. But I look anyway. I believe that writing is

one of my "corners"—an intersection, really; and when I'm confused or reluctant to look back, deeper, or ahead, I create my own Emerald Cities and force myself to take longer looks, because it is one sure way that I'm able to see.

Of course, I've fallen, tumbled, and been thrown over all kinds of bumps on my road, but it still looks yellow, although every once in a while there's still a loose brick. For the most part, though, it seems paved. Perhaps because that's the way I want to see it.   28

For Study and Discussion

QUESTIONS ABOUT PURPOSE

1. In the process of showing why the movie was significant for her, what does McMillan reveal about herself?
2. What advantages does McMillan suggest that fantasy has for children? What effects might fantasies other than *The Wizard of Oz* have, perhaps books like C. S. Lewis's Narnia series or a movie like *Star Trek*?

QUESTIONS ABOUT AUDIENCE

1. How justified do you think McMillan is in assuming that her readers are very familiar with the movie *The Wizard of Oz*? What would be the effect if they're not familiar with the movie?
2. What personality traits and outlook on life do you think readers are likely to have who like this essay and find it persuasive? To what extent do you think you and your friends share those traits?

QUESTIONS ABOUT STRATEGIES

1. How does McMillan tie the attraction that the Oz movie has for her to conditions in her own life? How well does that strategy work?
2. How does McMillan fill in details of the movie for readers who may have forgotten or didn't know the story of *The Wizard of Oz*? How good a job does she do?

For Writing and Research

1. *Analyze* the strategies McMillan uses to connect the story of her own life with the story of *The Wizard of Oz*.

2. *Practice* by analyzing the effect a contemporary movie or television show has had on you and your circle of friends.

3. *Argue* that the "philosophy" of *The Wizard of Oz* has shaped the central values of American culture.

4. *Synthesize* information from the books about Oz by L. Frank Baum and Gregory Maguire and the Broadway musical *Wicked*. Then use this evidence to speculate on the effect of Dorothy's departure on Oz.

Arthur C. Clarke was born in 1917 in Somerset, England. He was interested in science at an early age, but his family could not afford to give him a formal university education. During World War II, he was a radar specialist with the Royal Air Force. Following the war he entered King's College, University of London, graduating with Honorary degrees in math and physics. His nonfiction publications include *Interplanetary Flight* (1950), *The Exploration of Space* (1951), and *The Making of a Moon* (1957), but his science fiction about space travel brought him fame. His many short stories are collected in such volumes as *The Other Side of the Story* (1958), *The Wind from the Sun* (1972), and *The Collected Stories of Arthur C. Clarke* (2001). His novels include *The Sounds of Mars* (1951), *A Fall of Moondust* (1961), and *Rendezvous with Rama* (1974), and his screenplay for Stanley Kubrik's *2001: A Space Odyssey* is considered a classic. In "The Star," reprinted from *The Nine Billion Names of God* (1955), a Jesuit astronomer tells of a space journey that challenges his faith in God.

The Star

IT IS THREE thousand light-years to the Vatican. Once, I believed that space could have no power over faith, just as I believed that the heavens declared the glory of God's handiwork. Now I have seen that handiwork, and my faith is sorely troubled. I stare at the crucifix that hangs on the cabin wall above the Mark VI Computer, and for the first time in my life I wonder if it is no more than an empty symbol.

I have told no one yet, but the truth cannot be concealed. 2
The facts are there for all to read, recorded on the countless
miles of magnetic tape and the thousands of photographs we
are carrying back to Earth. Other scientists can interpret
them as easily as I can, and I am not one who would condone
that tampering with the truth which often gave my order a
bad name in the olden days.

The crew were already sufficiently depressed: I wonder 3
how they will take this ultimate irony. Few of them have any
religious faith, yet they will not relish using this final weapon
in their campaign against me—that private, good-natured,
but fundamentally serious war which lasted all the way from
Earth. It amused them to have a Jesuit as chief astrophysicist:
Dr. Chandler, for instance, could never get over it. (Why are
medical men such notorious atheists?) Sometimes he would
meet me on the observation deck, where the lights are always
low so that the stars shine with undiminished glory. He
would come up to me in the gloom and stand staring out of
the great oval port, while the heavens crawled slowly around
us as the ship turned end over end with the residual spin we
had never bothered to correct.

"Well, Father," he would say at last, "it goes on forever 4
and forever, and perhaps *Something* made it. But how you
can believe that Something has a special interest in us and our
miserable little world—that just beats me." Then the argument would start, while the stars and nebulae would swing
around us in silent, endless arcs beyond the flawlessly clear
plastic of the observation port.

It was, I think, the apparent incongruity of my position 5
that caused most amusement to the crew. In vain I would
point to my three papers in the *Astrophysical Journal,* my five
in the *Monthly Notices of the Royal Astronomical Society.* I
would remind them that my order has long been famous for
its scientific works. We may be few now, but ever since the
eighteenth century we have made contributions to astronomy and geophysics out of all proportion to our numbers.
Will my report on the Phoenix Nebula end our thousand
years of history? It will end, I fear, much more than that.

I do not know who gave the nebula its name, which seems   6
to me a very bad one. If it contains a prophecy, it is one that
cannot be verified for several billion years. Even the word
"nebula" is misleading: this is a far smaller object than those
stupendous clouds of mist—the stuff of unborn stars—that
are scattered throughout the length of the Milky Way. On the
cosmic scale, indeed, the Phoenix Nebula is a tiny thing—a
tenuous shell of gas surrounding a single star.

Or what is left of a star . . .   7

The Rubens engraving of Loyola seems to mock me as it   8
hangs there above the spectrophotometer tracings. What
would *you*, Father, have made of this knowledge that has
come into my keeping, so far from the little world that was all
the Universe you knew? Would your faith have risen to the
challenge, as mine has failed to do?

You gaze into the distance, Father, but I have traveled a   9
distance beyond any that you could have imagined when you
founded our order a thousand years ago. No other survey
ship has been so far from Earth: we are at the very frontiers
of the explored Universe. We set out to reach the Phoenix
Nebula, we succeeded, and we are homeward bound with our
burden of knowledge. I wish I could lift that burden from my
shoulders, but I call to you in vain across the centuries and the
light-years that lie between us.

On the book you are holding the words are plain to read.   10
AD MAIOREM DEI GLORIAM, the message runs, but it is
a message I can no longer believe. Would you still believe it,
if you could see what we have found?

We knew, of course, what the Phoenix Nebula was. Every   11
year, in our Galaxy alone, more than a hundred stars explode,
blazing for a few hours or days with thousands of times their
normal brilliance before they sink back into death and obscu-
rity. Such are the ordinary novae—the commonplace disas-
ters of the Universe. I have recorded the spectrograms and
light curves of dozens since I started working at the Lunar
Observatory.

But three or four times in every thousand years occurs some-   12
thing beside which even a nova pales into total insignificance.

When a star becomes a *supernova,* it may for a little while 13
outshine all the massed suns of the Galaxy. The Chinese astronomers watched this happen in A.D. 1054, not knowing
what it was they saw. Five centuries later, in 1572, a supernova blazed in Cassiopeia so brilliantly that it was visible in
the daylight sky. There have been three more in the thousand
years that have passed since then.

Our mission was to visit the remnants of such a catastrophe, 14
to reconstruct the events that led up to it, and, if possible, to
learn its cause. We came slowly in through the concentric shells
of gas that had been blasted out six thousand years before, yet
were expanding still. They were immensely hot, radiating
even now with a fierce violet light, but were far too tenuous to
do us any damage. When the star had exploded, its outer layers had been driven upward with such speed that they had
escaped completely from its gravitational field. Now they
formed a hollow shell large enough to engulf a thousand solar
systems, and at its center burned the tiny, fantastic object
which the star had now become—a White Dwarf, smaller than
the Earth, yet weighing a million times as much.

The glowing gas shells were all around us, banishing the 15
normal night of interstellar space. We were flying into the
center of the cosmic bomb that had detonated millennia ago
and whose incandescent fragments were still hurtling apart.
The immense scale of the explosion, and the fact that the debris already covered a volume of space many billions of miles
across, robbed the scene of any visible movement. It would
take decades before the unaided eye could detect any motion
in these tortured wisps and eddies of gas, yet the sense of
turbulent expansion was overwhelming.

We had checked our primary drive hours before, and were 16
drifting slowly toward the fierce little star ahead. Once it had
been a sun like our own, but it had squandered in a few hours
the energy that should have kept it shining for a million years.
Now it was a shrunken miser, hoarding its resources as if trying to make amends for its prodigal youth.

No one seriously expected to find planets. If there had 17
been any before the explosion, they would have been boiled

into puffs of vapor, and their substance lost in the greater wreckage of the star itself. But we made the automatic search, as we always do when approaching an unknown sun, and presently we found a single small world circling the star at an immense distance. It must have been the Pluto of this vanished Solar System, orbiting on the frontiers of the night. Too far from the central sun ever to have known life, its remoteness had saved it from the fate of all its lost companions.

The passing fires had seared its rocks and burned away the   18
mantle of frozen gas that must have covered it in the days before the disaster. We landed, and we found the Vault.

Its builders had made sure that we should. The monolithic   19
marker that stood above the entrance was now a fused stump, but even the first long-range photographs told us that here was the work of intelligence. A little later we detected the continent-wide pattern of radioactivity that had been buried in the rock. Even if the pylon above the vault had been destroyed, this would have remained, an immovable and all but eternal beacon calling to the stars. Our ship fell toward this gigantic bull's-eye like an arrow into its target.

The pylon must have been a mile high when it was built,   20
but now it looked like a candle that had melted down into a puddle of wax. It took us a week to drill through the fused rock, since we did not have the proper tools for a task like this. We were astronomers, not archaeologists, but we could improvise. Our original purpose was forgotten: this lonely monument, reared with such labor at the greatest possible distance from the doomed sun, could have only one meaning. A civilization that knew it was about to die had made its last bid for immortality.

It will take us generations to examine all the treasures that   21
were placed in the Vault. They had plenty of time to prepare, for their sun must have given its first warnings many years before the final detonation. Everything that they wished to preserve, all the fruit of their genius, they brought here to this distant world in the days before the end, hoping that some other race would find it and that they would not be utterly forgotten. Would we have done as well, or would we

have been too lost in our own misery to give thought to a future we could never see or share?

If only they had had a little more time! They could travel freely enough between the planets of their own sun, but they had not yet learned to cross the interstellar gulfs, and the nearest Solar System was a hundred light-years away. Yet even had they possessed the secret of the Transfinite Drive, no more than a few millions could have been saved. Perhaps it was better thus. 22

Even if they had not been so disturbingly human as their sculpture shows, we could not have helped admiring them and grieving for their fate. They left thousands of visual records and the machines for projecting them, together with elaborate pictorial instructions from which it will not be difficult to learn their written language. We have examined many of these records, and brought to life for the first time in six thousand years the warmth and beauty of a civilization that in many ways must have been superior to our own. Perhaps they only showed us the best, and one can hardly blame them. But their worlds were very lovely, and their cities were built with a grace that matches anything of man's. We have watched them at work and play, and listened to their musical speech sounding across the centuries. One scene is still before my eyes—a group of children on a beach of strange blue sand, playing in the waves as children play on Earth. Curious whiplike trees line the shore, and some very large animal is wading in the shallows yet attracting no attention at all. 23

And sinking into the sea, still warm and friendly and life-giving, is the sun that will soon turn traitor and obliterate all this innocent happiness. 24

Perhaps if we had not been so far from home and so vulnerable to loneliness, we should not have been so deeply moved. Many of us had seen the ruins of ancient civilizations on other worlds, but they had never affected us so profoundly. This tragedy was unique. It is one thing for a race to fail and die, as nations and cultures have done on Earth. But to be destroyed so completely in the full flower of its achievement, leaving no survivors—how could that be reconciled with the mercy of God? 25

My colleagues have asked me that, and I have given what   26
answers I can. Perhaps you could have done better, Father
Loyola, but I have found nothing in the *Exercitia Spiritualia*
that helps me here. They were not an evil people: I do not
know what gods they worshiped, if indeed they worshiped
any. But I have looked back at them across the centuries,
and have watched while the loveliness they used their last
strength to preserve was brought forth again into the light of
their shrunken sun. They could have taught us much: why
were they destroyed?

I know the answers that my colleagues will give when they   27
get back to Earth. They will say that the Universe has no purpose and no plan, that since a hundred suns explode every
year in our Galaxy, at this very moment some race is dying in
the depths of space. Whether that race has done good or evil
during its lifetime will make no difference in the end: there is
no divine justice, for there is no God.

Yet, of course, what we have seen proves nothing of the   28
sort. Anyone who argues thus is being swayed by emotion,
not logic. God has no need to justify His actions to man. He
who built the Universe can destroy it when He chooses. It is
arrogance—it is perilously near blasphemy—for us to say
what He may or may not do.

This I could have accepted, hard though it is to look upon   29
whole worlds and peoples thrown into the furnace. But there
comes a point when even the deepest faith must falter, and
now, as I look at the calculations lying before me, I know I
have reached that point at last.

We could not tell, before we reached the nebula, how long   30
ago the explosion took place. Now, from the astronomical
evidence and the record in the rocks of that one surviving
planet, I have been able to date it very exactly. I know in what
year the light of this colossal conflagration reached our Earth.
I know how brilliantly the supernova whose corpse now
dwindles behind our speeding ship once shone in terrestrial
skies. I know how it must have blazed low in the east before
sunrise, like a beacon in that oriental dawn.

There can be no reasonable doubt: the ancient mystery is 31
solved at last. Yet, oh God, there were so many stars you
could have used. What was the need to give these people to
the fire, that the symbol of their passing might shine above
Bethlehem?

COMMENT ON "THE STAR"

The distressed narrator of this story is a Jesuit scientist who,
on the basis of evidence that he cannot refute professionally
or ethically, finds himself forced to acknowledge a scientific
discovery that he fears may destroy his religious faith, the
rock of his very existence. Two arguments are going on in
the story. The first is a vocal one between the Jesuit and the
crew, particularly a medical doctor, who represents the traditional scientific view that although there may be order in the
universe, there is no God who takes a special interest in the affairs of humans. The Jesuit represents the argument for faith
in God and His concern for humankind. The second argument is the silent one that the Jesuit astrophysicist has seen
building as his spaceship penetrated the outer reaches of
space to investigate the origins of the Phoenix Nebula. He
collects evidence from three sources: from the interstellar
space debris that testifies to the explosion of a supernova;
from irrefutable evidence left purposefully by a superior, cul-
tured civilization that flourished on a lost planet several thousand years before; and, finally, from the evidence that allows
him to calculate the date of the explosion that destroyed that
planet. When he puts all the pieces together, the Jesuit sees
the conclusion of the second argument. Ironically, it destroys
the first argument but almost destroys the Jesuit also. God
does indeed take special interest in the affairs of humans; the
proof is that the date of the supernova that destroyed the
beautiful lost civilization coincides precisely with the Star of
Bethlehem announcing the birth of Jesus.

PERSUASION
AND
ARGUMENT

Readers encounter persuasion and argument every day as writers try to persuade them to spend money, take action, support a cause, accept an opinion, or consider an idea. The starting point for persuasion and argument is an *assertion,* a statement of belief or a claim that the writer undertakes to explain and support. At one extreme, both the statement and the support may be highly emotional, depending heavily on biased language and strong appeals to feelings and instincts; this kind of writing is classified as *persuasion.* At the other extreme, the assertion and support may be strictly rational, depending on logical explanations and appeals to intelligence;

this kind of writing is classified as *argument*. Advertising and political writing cluster toward the persuasion end of the continuum, while scientific writing and grant proposals cluster toward the argument end.

Seldom, however, does persuasive writing appeal only to emotions, and seldom does argument rely entirely on reason. Rather, when people write to convince, they appeal to both emotions and intelligence, but they vary the balance of emotion and reason according to their audience and purpose.

Writing that is primarily rational is not necessarily better than writing that is primarily emotional. Some occasions call for appeals to pride and patriotism, for vivid metaphors that reach the senses, and for strong language that arouses the passions. This kind of writing is called *ceremonial discourse*. The audience already knows and probably agrees with what the writer (or speaker) is going to say, and they expect not intellectual stimulation, but emotional satisfaction and inspiration. Inaugural speeches, graduation addresses, and political speeches usually fit into this emotional category and are often successful precisely because they are emotional.

Most arguments, however, must be fairly rational if they are to convince critical readers, and those readers are justified in expecting writers to support major assertions with evidence and logic. Generally speaking, people who write effective arguments do what a good trial lawyer does: they present a case persuasively but give strong reasons to support their assertions. In the final analysis, the quality of any argument must be judged not by some absolute standard of rationality, but by how well it accomplished its intended purpose with its intended audience.

PURPOSE

Although you may think of disagreement when you hear the word *argument,* not all people who write arguments are trying to win a dispute. Instead, they may want to persuade people to *support a cause* or *make a commitment*. Political leaders and ministers frequently write for these purposes. Writers may also argue in order to get people to *take action* or to try to *change a situation.* Editorial writers, reformers, and political activists often have these purposes in mind.

Sometimes writers persuade in order to *change behavior or attitudes.* Someone advocating a new approach to child-rearing would have such a purpose, as would a person arguing against racial or sexual prejudice. Other writers argue to *refute a theory.* For example, feminist writers continually seek to disprove the belief that women are less talented and creative than men. Writers also use persuasive strategies to *arouse sympathies, to stimulate concern, to win agreement,* and *to provoke anger.* They may incorporate several of these purposes into one piece of writing.

AUDIENCE

More than any other kind of writing, persuasion and argument require writers to think about their audience. To choose effective rhetorical strategies, writers must have a clear sense of who may read their writing, what kinds of attitudes and biases those persons will bring to the reading, and what readers expect to get from an essay. Making such analysis of an audience may be difficult, and sometimes writers have to work by instinct rather than information. Usually, however, writers can assume that readers will fit into one of the following classes:

1. *Readers who already agree with the writer's ideas and are reading mainly for reinforcement or encouragement.* These readers do not expect a tightly reasoned and carefully structured argument; rather they want to see their position stated with vigor and conviction.
2. *Readers who are interested in and are inclined to agree with the issue the writer is discussing but want to know more.* Although they are interested in evidence that will help them make a decision, they do not expect a completely rational argument and will not object if the writer uses slanted language or emotional examples to strengthen a point.

3. *Readers who are neutral on an issue and want explanations and arguments based on evidence and logical reasoning before they make up their mind.* For these readers, a writer must make a carefully developed and factual argument, although the writer can also reinforce facts with opinions.

4. *Readers who are skeptical about an issue and will not take a stand until they hear both sides of an argument explained in complete detail.* They want data and documentation from someone who gives the impression that he or she is knowledgeable, capable, and balanced.

STRATEGIES

Collecting Evidence

To construct an argument you need to collect one or more of the following kinds of evidence: *facts, judgments,* and *testimony.*

Facts are a valuable ally in building an argument because they cannot be debated. It is a fact that the stock market crashed on October 29, 1929. It is a fact that at the close of the week of May 18, 2007, the Dow Jones Average reached a new high of 13,556.53. But not all facts are so clear cut, and some statements that look like facts may not be facts. A stock analyst who announces a company's projected earnings for the next five years is making an estimate, not a statement of fact.

Judgments are conclusions inferred from facts. Unlike opinions, judgments lend credibility to an argument because they result from careful reasoning. A doctor considering a patient's symptoms reaches a tentative diagnosis of either tuberculosis or a tumor. If the laboratory test eliminates tuberculosis, then the patient probably has a tumor that is either malignant or benign, questions that can be settled by surgery and further testing.

Testimony affirms or asserts facts. A person who has had direct experience (an *eyewitness*) or who has developed expertise in a subject (an *expert witness*) can provide testimony based on facts, judgment, or both. An eyewitness is asked to report facts, as when an observer reports seeing a man drown in a strong current. An expert witness is asked to study facts and render a judgment, as when a coroner reports that an autopsy has shown that the victim did not drown but died of a heart attack.

Both kinds of testimony can constitute powerful evidence. Eyewitness testimony provides authenticity. Expert testimony provides authority. Each has its limitations, however. An eyewitness is not always trustworthy; eyewitness testimony can be distorted by faulty observation or biased opinion. An expert witness is not infallible or always unbiased; expert testimony, though often difficult for the nonexpert to challenge, can be disputed by other experts employing a different method of investigation. Each type of testimony can be abused. An eyewitness account of an event may be convincing, but it should not be used to draw parallels to unrelated events. And an expert's credentials in one field, whatever eminence they convey, do not automatically carry over to other fields.

The best way to evaluate evidence in an argument is to determine if it is *pertinent, verifiable,* and *reliable.* A stock analyst who uses the success of the polio vaccine as a reason for investing in a drug company researching a vaccine for the common cold is not presenting evidence that is *pertinent* to the argument. A historian who claims that Amelia Earhart's flying ability was impaired by Alzheimer's disease is using an argument that is not *verifiable.* And an attorney who builds a case on the eyewitness testimony of a person who has been arrested several times for public intoxication is not using the most *reliable* evidence.

Arranging Evidence

After you have collected your evidence, you need to determine how to *arrange* it. Because every argument creates its own problems and possibilities, no one method of arrangement will always work best. Sometimes you may have to combine methods to make your case. To make an informed decision, you need to consider how you might adapt your evidence to one of the four common strategies: *induction, deduction, claims and warrants,* and *accommodation.*

Induction   *Induction,* often called the *scientific method,* begins by presenting specific evidence and then moves to a general conclusion. This arrangement reflects the history of your
investigation. You begin your research with a question you
want to answer. You then collect a cross-section of evidence
until a pattern emerges and you arrange your individual pieces
of evidence in a way that helps your readers see the pattern
you have discovered. You need not list all the false leads or
blind alleys you encountered along the way unless they
changed your perspective or confirmed your judgment. At
this point, you make what scientists call an *inductive leap:*
you determine that although you have not collected every
example, you have examined enough to risk proposing a
probable conclusion.

For example:

> Research question: Why is our company losing so
> many valuable data processors to other companies?
> Evidence:
>
> 1. Most data processors are women who have
>   preschool children. (Provide facts.)
> 2. A nearby day-care center used by employees
>   has closed because it lost federal funding.
>   (Provide facts.)
> 3. Other day-care centers in the area are incon-
>   venient and understaffed. (Provide testimony.)
> 4. Other companies provide on-site day care for
>   children of employees. (Provide facts.)
> 5. On-site day care is beneficial to the emotional
>   well-being of both preschool children and
>   their mothers because of the possibility of con-
>   tact during the workday.
>
> Conclusion: Therefore, our company needs to pro-
> vide on-site day care to retain valuable employees.

Deduction   *Deduction,* usually identified with classical reasoning, begins with a general statement or *major premise*
that when restricted by a *minor premise* leads to a specific

conclusion. Unlike induction, which in theory makes an assertion only in its conclusion, deduction does make initial assertions (based on evidence) from which a conclusion is derived. This strategy is called a *three-step syllogism:*

> Major premise: Retention of data processors who have preschool children is promoted by on-site day care.
> Minor premise: Our company wants to retain data processors who have preschool children.
> Conclusion: Our company should establish on-site day-care centers.

To gain your audience's acceptance of your major and minor premises you must support each assertion with specific evidence. Demonstrate that retaining data processors who have preschool children is promoted by on-site day-care centers and that "our company" wants to retain computer operators who have preschool children. If your readers accept your premises, then they are logically committed to accepting your conclusion.

Claims and Warrants   Claims and warrants—often called the *Toulmin argument* after Stephen Toulmin, the legal philosopher who analyzed the process and defined its terminology— argues from a general principle to a specific example, but it presents a more complex arrangement than a syllogism.

You begin by asserting a *claim* (or a general assertion about the argument you intend to make), then provide evidence to support your claim. The statement that links the claim to the evidence is called a *warrant.* In some arguments, the warrant is implied; in others, you need to state it directly. Additional parts of the claims and warrants strategy include *support* to strengthen your argument, *qualifiers* to modify or limit your claim, and *reservations* to point out instances in which your claim may not apply.

For example:

> Claim: Retention of data processors who have preschool children is promoted by on-site day-care centers.

Evidence:

1. Many of our data processors have preschool children.
2. These employees have difficulties arranging and paying for day-care services.
3. Mothers are more effective employees when they don't have to worry about their children.

Warrant: Our company should establish on-site day-care centers.

Support:

1. Competitors who provide on-site day care for their employees have a high retention rate.
2. Data processors at such companies have a lower absentee rate.
3. The cost of training new data processors is expensive.

Qualification: Some of our data processors do not have preschool children.

Reservation: Because our company wants to retain a qualified work force, we don't want to add expenses to the workplace that will penalize data processors who do not have children.

Claims and warrants is an effective arrangement because, like induction, it enables you to present evidence systematically, and, like induction, the inclusion of qualifiers and reservations suggests that you are considering your evidence objectively. But, like deduction, claims and warrants enables you to provide a clear and cogent link (warrant) between your general assertion (claim) and the data you have collected (evidence).

Accommodation **Accommodation,** sometimes called *nonthreatening argument,* arranges evidence so that all parties believe their position has received a fair hearing. Induction reveals how a chain of evidence leads to a conclusion. Deduction demonstrates why certain premises demand a single conclusion. Although both procedures work effectively in specific situations, they occasionally defeat your purpose. Readers may feel trapped by the relentless march of your argument; though unable to refute your logic, they are still unwilling to listen to reason. Accommodation takes your audience's hesitations into account. Instead of trying to win the argument, you try to improve communication and increase understanding.

To employ this strategy, begin by composing an objective description of the controversy:

> Women data processors who have preschool children are leaving the company.

Then draft a complete and accurate statement of the contending positions, supplying evidence that makes each position credible:

> Corporation board: We need a qualified work force, but we are not in business to provide social services. (Provide evidence.)
>
> Fellow workers (single, male, etc.): We understand their problem, but providing an on-site day-care center is giving expensive, preferential treatment to a small segment of the work force. (Provide evidence.)
>
> Competitors: We need better data processors if we are going to compete, and we will provide what is necessary to hire them. (Provide evidence.)

Next, show where and why you and the various parties agree:

> The corporation should not be in the day-care business; women data processors have the right to market their skills in a competitive market.

Then present your own argument explaining where it differs from other positions and why it deserves serious consideration:

> We have invested a large amount of money in training our work force; childcare is an appropriate investment in view of the long-term contribution these people will make to the corporation.

Finally, present a proposal that might resolve the issue in a way that recognizes the interests of all concerned:

> The corporation might help to fund the nearby day-care center that was previously supported by government money.

Monitoring the Appeals

In developing an argument, you must keep track of how you are using the three basic appeals of argument: the *emotional appeal*, the *ethical appeal*, and the *logical appeal*. These three appeals are rarely separate; they all weave in and out of virtually every argument. But to control their effects to your advantage, you must know when and why you are using them.

The Emotional Appeal   Readers feel as well as think, and to be thoroughly convinced, they must be emotionally as well as intellectually engaged by your argument. Some people think that the *emotional appeal* is suspect because it relies on the feelings, instincts, and opinions of readers. They connect it to the devious manipulations of advertising or politics. The emotional appeal is often used to stampede an audience into thoughtless action, but such abuses do not negate its value. The emotional appeal should never replace more rational appeal, but it can be an effective strategy for convincing your readers that they need to pay attention to your argument.

The greatest strength of the emotional appeal is also its greatest weakness. Dramatic examples, presented in concrete images and connotative language, personalize a problem and produce powerful emotions. Some examples produce predictable emotions: an abandoned puppy or a lonely old woman evokes pity; a senseless accident or recurring incompetence evokes anger; a smiling face or a heroic deed evokes delight. Some examples, however, produce unpredictable results, and their dramatic presentation often works against your purpose. It would be difficult to predict, for instance, how your readers would respond to the plight of an undocumented, immigrant working mother's need for health insurance. Some might pity her; others might disdain her illegal

status and her desire for federal funding from tax-paying citizens. Because controversial issues attract a range of passions,
use the emotional appeal with care.

All the writers in this chapter use emotional appeals, but
those who rely on it most heavily are Barbara Kingsolver, Barbara Dafoe Whitehead, H. L. Mencken, and Jonathan Swift.
All of them are writing on strongly emotional topics: Kingsolver and Whitehead on the family, Mencken on the death
penalty, and Swift on how to "solve" the "Irish problem."

The Ethical Appeal   The character (or *ethos*) of the writer—
not the writer's morality—is the basis of the *ethical appeal*. It
suggests that the writer is someone to be trusted, a claim that
emerges from a demonstration of competence as an authority
on the subject under discussion. Readers trust a writer who
has established a reputation for informed, reasonable, and
reliable writing about controversial subjects.

You can use the ethical appeal in your argument either by
citing authorities who have conducted thorough investigations of your subject or by following the example of authorities in your competent treatment of evidence. There are two
potential dangers with the ethical appeal. First, you cannot
win the trust of your readers by citing as an authority in one
field someone who is best known to be an authority in another field. Second, you cannot convince your readers that
you are knowledgeable if you present your argument exclusively in personal terms. Your own experience may allow you
to assemble detailed and powerful evidence. But to establish
your ethical appeal, you need to balance such evidence with
the experience of other authorities.

All the writers in this chapter rely on their ethical appeal, but
it works most effectively for writers such as Martin Luther King
Jr. and Henry David Thoreau, who have established themselves
as symbolic authorities on the issues of racism and civil disobedience. In a similar way, Rachael Carson has earned her ethical
appeal by her pioneering efforts on behalf of a safer and cleaner
environment. Joan Acocella and Harold Bloom's contending

arguments on the Harry Potter books each have strong ethical appeal: Acocella has clearly done her research on the myths and legends that underlie the books, and Bloom has a distinguished reputation as a literary critic.

The Logical Appeal   The rational strategies used to develop an argument constitute a *logical appeal*. Some people think that the forceful use of logic makes an argument absolutely true. But controversies contain many truths, no one of which can be graded simply true or false. By using the logical appeal, you acknowledge that arguments are conducted in a world of probability, not certainty. By offering a series of reasonable observations and conclusions, you establish the most reliable case.

The logical appeal is widely used and accepted in argument. Establishing the relationships that bind your evidence to your assertion engages your readers' reasoning power, and an appeal to their intelligence and common sense is likely to win their assent. But the logical appeal is not infallible. Its limit is in acknowledging limits: How much evidence is enough? There is no simple answer to this question. For example, the amount of evidence required to convince fellow workers that your company should provide on-site day care may not be sufficient to persuade the company's board of directors. On the other hand, too much evidence, however methodically analyzed, may win the argument but lose your audience. Without emotional or ethical appeal, your "reasonable" presentation may be put aside in favor of more urgent issues. Accurate and cogent reasoning is the basis for any sound argument, but the logical appeal, like the emotional and ethical appeals, must be monitored carefully to accomplish your purpose.

The essays in this chapter use a variety of evidence. But the arguments that use evidence to make the most logical appeals are those of Robert F. Kennedy Jr. and Francis Broadhurst. Although they disagree with each other about the economic and environmental value of placing windmills in Nantucket Sound, they present facts, judgment, and testimony to support their assertions.

PERSUASION AND ARGUMENT

Points to Remember

1. To argue well, you have to know your audience and your purpose. Do you understand your audience's interests, their backgrounds, and what questions they might have? Do you know what you want to accomplish with this particular group of readers? It's useful to write out the answers to both of these questions before you start.

2. Understand the three principal kinds of persuasive appeals.
   - *Appeal to reason.* Emphasizes logic, evidence, authority, cause and effect, precedent, and comparison and analogy.
   - *Appeal to emotion.* Emphasizes feelings, the senses, personal biases, connotative language, and images and metaphor.
   - *Appeal from integrity and character.* Emphasizes the writer's (ethos)—competence, experience, and reputation.

   The most persuasive writers usually combine elements from all three kinds of appeals.

3. Construct your arguments as a lawyer would construct a case to present to a jury: state your claim and back it up with evidence and reason, but, when appropriate, also use metaphor and connotation.

4. Always assume your audience is intelligent, if perhaps uninformed about some particulars. Be respectful; avoid a superior tone.

5. Argue responsibly.
   - Don't overstate your claim.
   - Don't oversimplify complex issues.
   - Support your claims with specific details and evidence.

FAMILY DINNERS:
A VISUAL ESSAY

Questions

1. How would you describe the way that the families are posed in each photograph?

2. What assumptions about culture, cuisine, and etiquette are represented in each photograph?

3. Three of the photographs depict sumptuous meals. One of them depicts a small meal. How does the small meal suggest a cultural stereotype? What other explanations can you suggest to interpret this picture?

In this public service advertisement created by the Leo Burnett advertising company, PALM, or Physicians Against Land Mines, presents its argument about the death, dismemberment, and disability caused by land mines. The text below Emina Uzicanin's missing leg describes how, as a child playing on the outskirts of Sarajevo, she stepped on a land mine. In addition to this emotional story, the text offers other compelling evidence: "every 22 minutes another civilian is killed or maimed by a land mine"; "there are over 60 million unexploded land mines in nearly 70 countries." Select another public service advertising campaign—such as those sponsored by MADD (Mothers Against Drunk Driving) or ADL (Anti-Defamation League)—and analyze the visual and textual features that make it a persuasive argument.

A Debate About Family

BARBARA KINGSOLVER

Barbara Kingsolver was born in Annapolis, Maryland, in 1955 and educated at DePauw University and the University of Arizona. She began her writing career as a technical writer in the office of arid studies, then began working as a freelance journalist before publishing her first novel, *The Bean Trees* (1988). Her other novels include *Animal Dreams* (1990), *The Poisonwood Bible* (1998), and *Prodigal Summer* (2000). She has published short stories in *Homeland and Other Stories* (1989) and essays in *High Tide in Tucson: Essays from Now or Never* (1995) and *Small Wonder* (2002) and a nonfiction narrative, *Animal, Vegetable, Miracle: A Year of Food Life* (2007). In "Stone Soup," reprinted from *High Tide in Tucson* (1995), Kingsolver argues that there is not necessarily one best model for a successful family.

Stone Soup

IN THE CATALOG of family values, where do we rank an occasion like this? A curly-haired boy who wanted to run before he walked, age seven now, a soccer player scoring a winning goal. He turns to the bleachers with his fists in the air and a smile wide as a gap-toothed galaxy. His own cheering section of grown-ups and kids all leap to their feet and hug each other, delirious with love for this boy. He's Andy, my best friend's son. The cheering section includes his mother and her friends, his brother, his father and stepmother, a stepbrother and stepsister, and a grandparent. Lucky is the child with this many relatives on hand to hail a proud accomplishment.

I'm there too, witnessing a family fortune. But in spite of myself, defensive words take shape in my head. I am thinking: I dare *anybody* to call this a broken home.

Families change, and remain the same. Why are our names for home so slow to catch up to the truth of where we live? 2

When I was a child, I had two parents who loved me without cease. One of them attended every excuse for attention I ever contrived, and the other made it to the ones with higher 3

> *Arguing about whether nontraditional families deserve pity or tolerance is a little like the medieval debate about left-handedness as a mark of the devil.*

production values, like piano recitals and appendicitis. So I was a lucky child too. I played with a set of paper dolls called "The Family of Dolls," four in number, who came with the factory-assigned names of Dad, Mom, Sis, and Junior. I think you know what they looked like, at least before I loved them to death and their heads fell off.

Now I've replaced the dolls with a life. I knit my days 4 around my daughter's survival and happiness, and am proud to say her head is still on. But we aren't the Family of Dolls. Maybe you're not, either. And if not, even though you are statistically no oddity, it's probably been suggested to you in a hundred ways that yours isn't exactly a real family, but an impostor family, a harbinger of cultural ruin, a slapdash substitute—something like counterfeit money. Here at the tail end of our century, most of us are up to our ears in the noisy business of trying to support and love a thing called family. But there's a current in the air with ferocious moral force that finds its way even into political campaigns, claiming there is only one right way to do it, the Way It Has Always Been.

In the face of a thriving, particolored world, this narrow 5
view is so pickled and absurd I'm astonished that it gets air-
play. And I'm astonished that it still stings.

Every parent has endured the arrogance of a child- 6
unfriendly grump sitting in judgment, explaining what those
kids of ours really need (for example, "a good licking"). If we're
polite, we move our crew to another bench in the park. If we're
forthright (as I am in my mind, only, for the rest of the day), we
fix them with a sweet imperious stare and say, "Come back and
let's talk about it after you've changed a thousand diapers."

But it's harder somehow to shrug off the Family-of-Dolls 7
Family Values crew when they judge (from their safe distance)
that divorced people, blended families, gay families, and single
parents are failures. That our children are at risk, and the
whole arrangement is messy and embarrassing. A marriage
that ends is not called "finished," it's called *failed*. The children of this family may have been born to a happy union, but
now they are called *the children of divorce*.

I had no idea how thoroughly these assumptions overlaid my 8
culture until I went through divorce myself. I wrote to a friend:
"This might be worse than being widowed. Overnight I've suffered the same losses—companionship, financial and practical
support, my identity as a wife and partner, the future I'd taken
for granted. I am lonely, grieving, and hard-pressed to take care
of my household alone. But instead of bringing casseroles, people are acting like I had a fit and broke up the family china."

Once upon a time I held these beliefs about divorce: that 9
everyone who does it could have chosen not to do it. That
it's a lazy way out of marital problems. That it selfishly puts
personal happiness ahead of family integrity. Now I tremble
for my ignorance. It's easy, in fortunate times, to forget about
the ambush that could leave your head reeling: serious mental or physical illness, death in the family, abandonment, financial calamity, humiliation, violence, despair.

I started out like any child, intent on being the Family of 10
Dolls. I set upon young womanhood believing in most of the
doctrines of my generation: I wore my skirts four inches above
the knee. I had the Barbie with her zebra-striped swimsuit and

a figure unlike anything found in nature. And I understood the Prince Charming Theory of Marriage, a quest for Mr. Right that ends smack dab where you find him. I did not completely understand that another whole story *begins* there, and no fairy tale prepared me for the combination of bad luck and persistent hope that would interrupt my dream and lead me to other arrangements. Like a cancer diagnosis, a dying marriage is a thing to fight, to deny, and finally, when there's no choice left, to dig in and survive. Casseroles would help. Likewise, I imagine it must be a painful reckoning in adolescence (or later on) to realize one's own true love will never look like the soft-focus fragrance ads because Prince Charming (surprise!) is a princess. Or vice versa. Or has skin the color your parents didn't want you messing with, except in the Crayola box.

It's awfully easy to hold in contempt the straw broken home, and that mythical category of persons who toss away nuclear family for the sheer fun of it. Even the legal terms we use have a suggestion of caprice. I resent the phrase "irreconcilable differences," which suggests a stubborn refusal to accept a spouse's little quirks. This is specious. Every happily married couple I know has loads of irreconcilable differences. Negotiating where to set the thermostat is not the point. A nonfunctioning marriage is a slow asphyxiation. It is waking up despised each morning, listening to the pulse of your own loneliness before the radio begins to blare its raucous gospel that you're nothing if you aren't loved. It is sharing your airless house with the threat of suicide or other kinds of violence, while the ghost that whispers, "Leave here and destroy your children," has passed over every door and nailed it shut. Disassembling a marriage in these circumstances is as much *fun* as amputating your own gangrenous leg. You do it, if you can, to save a life—or two, or more.

I know of no one who really went looking to hoe the harder row, especially the daunting one of single parenthood. Yet it seems to be the most American of customs to blame the burdened for their destiny. We'd like so desperately to believe in freedom and justice for all, we can hardly name that rogue bad luck, even when he's a close enough snake to bite us. In the wake of my divorce, some friends (even a few close ones) chose to vanish, rather than linger within striking distance of misfortune.

But most stuck around, bless their hearts, and if I'm any the 13 wiser for my trials, it's from having learned the worth of stead-fast friendship. And also, what not to say. The least helpful question is: "Did you want the divorce, or didn't you?" Did I want to keep that gangrenous leg, or not? How to explain, in a culture that venerates choice: two terrifying options are much worse than none at all. Give me any day the quick hand of cruel fate that will leave me scarred but blameless. As it was, I kept thinking of that wicked third-grade joke in which some boy comes up behind you and grabs your ear, starts in with a prolonged tug, and asks, "Do you want this ear any longer?"

Still, the friend who holds your hand and says the wrong 14 thing is made of dearer stuff than the one who stays away. And generally, through all of it, you live. My favorite fictional char-acter, Kate Vaiden (in the novel by Reynolds Price), advises: "Strength just comes in one brand—you stand up at sunrise and meet what they send you and keep your hair combed."

Once you've weathered the straits, you get to cross the 15 tricky juncture from casualty to survivor. If you're on your feet at the end of a year or two, and have begun putting to-gether a happy new existence, those friends who were kind enough to feel sorry for you when you needed it must now accept you back to the ranks of the living. If you're truly blessed, they will dance at your second wedding. Everybody else, for heaven's sake, should stop throwing stones.

Arguing about whether nontraditional families deserve 16 pity or tolerance is a little like the medieval debate about left-handedness as a mark of the devil. Divorce, remarriage, sin-gle parenthood, gay parents, and blended families simply are. They're facts of our time. Some of the reasons listed by soci-ologists for these family reconstructions are: the idea of mar-riage as a romantic partnership rather than a pragmatic one; a shift in women's expectations, from servility to self-respect and independence; and longevity (prior to antibiotics no marriage was expected to last many decades—in Colonial days the average couple lived to be married less than twelve years). Add to all this, our growing sense of entitlement to happiness and safety from abuse. Most would agree these are all good things. Yet their result—a culture in which serial monogamy and the consequent reshaping of families are the norm—gets diagnosed as "failing."

For many of us, once we have put ourselves Humpty-Dumpty-wise back together again, the main problem with our reorganized family is that other people think we have a problem. My daughter tells me the only time she's uncomfortable about being the child of divorced parents is when her friends say they feel sorry for her. It's a bizarre sympathy, given that half the kids in her school and nation are in the same boat, pursuing childish happiness with the same energy as their married-parent peers. When anyone asks how *she* feels about it, she spontaneously lists the benefits: our house is in the country and we have a dog, but she can go to her dad's neighborhood for the urban thrills of a pool and sidewalks for roller-skating. What's more, she has three sets of grandparents!

Why is it surprising that a child would revel in a widened family and the right to feel at home in more than one house? Isn't it the opposite that should worry us—a child with no home at all, or too few resources to feel safe? The child at risk is the one whose parents are too immature themselves to guide wisely; too diminished by poverty to nurture; too far from opportunity to offer hope. The number of children in the U.S. living in poverty at this moment is almost unfathomably large: twenty percent. There are families among us that need help all right, and by no means are they new on the landscape. The rate at which teenage girls had babies in 1957 (ninety-six per thousand) was twice what it is now. That remarkable statistic is ignored by the religious right—probably because the teen birth rate was cut in half mainly by legalized abortion. In fact, the policy gatekeepers who coined the phrase "family values" have steadfastly ignored the desperation of too-small families, and since 1979 have steadily reduced the amount of financial support available to a single parent. But, this camp's most outspoken attacks seem aimed at the notion of families getting too complex, with add-ons and extras such as a gay parent's partner, or a remarried mother's new husband and his children.

To judge a family's value by its tidy symmetry is to purchase   19
a book for its cover. There's no moral authority there. The famous family comprised of Dad, Mom, Sis, and Junior living as an isolated economic unit is not built on historical bedrock. In *The Way We Never Were,* Stephanie Coontz writes, "Whenever people propose that we go back to the traditional family, I always suggest that they pick a ballpark date for the family they have in mind." Colonial families were tidily disciplined, but their members (meaning everyone but infants) labored incessantly and died young. Then the Victorian family adopted a new division of labor, in which women's role was domestic and children were allowed time for study and play, but this was an upper-class construct supported by myriad slaves. Coontz writes, "For every nineteenth-century middle-class family that protected its wife and child within the family circle, there was an Irish or German girl scrubbing floors . . . a Welsh boy mining coal to keep the home-baked goodies warm, a black girl doing the family laundry, a black mother and child picking cotton to be made into clothes for the family, and a Jewish or an Italian daughter in a sweatshop making 'ladies' dresses or artificial flowers for the family to purchase."

The abolition of slavery brought slightly more democratic   20
arrangements, in which extended families were harnessed together in cottage industries; at the turn of the century came a steep rise in child labor in mines and sweatshops. Twenty percent of American children lived in orphanages at the time; their parents were not necessarily dead, but couldn't afford to keep them.

During the Depression and up to the end of World War II,   21
many millions of U.S. households were more multigenerational than nuclear. Women my grandmother's age were likely to live with a fluid assortment of elderly relatives, in-laws, siblings, and children. In many cases they spent virtually every waking hour working in the company of other women—a

companionable scenario in which it would be easier, I imagine, to tolerate an estranged or difficult spouse. I'm reluctant to idealize a life of so much hard work and so little spousal intimacy, but its advantage may have been resilience. A family so large and varied would not easily be brought down by a single blow: it could absorb a death, long illness, an abandonment here or there, and any number of irreconcilable differences.

The Family of Dolls came along midcentury as a great 22 American experiment. A booming economy required a mobile labor force and demanded that women surrender jobs to returning soldiers. Families came to be defined by a single breadwinner. They struck out for single-family homes at an earlier age than ever before, and in unprecedented numbers they raised children in suburban isolation. The nuclear family was launched to sink or swim.

More than a few sank. Social historians corroborate that 23 the suburban family of the postwar economic boom, which we have recently selected as our definition of "traditional," was no panacea. Twenty-five percent of Americans were poor in the mid-1950s, and as yet there were no food stamps. Sixty percent of the elderly lived on less than $1,000 a year, and most had no medical insurance. In the sequestered suburbs, alcoholism and sexual abuse of children were far more widespread than anyone imagined.

Expectations soared, and the economy sagged. It's hard to 24 depend on one other adult for everything, come what may. In the last three decades, that amorphous, adaptable structure we call "family" has been reshaped once more by economic tides. Compared with fifties families, mothers are far more likely now to be employed. We are statistically more likely to divorce, and to live in blended families or other extranuclear arrangements. We are also more likely to plan and space our children, and to rate our marriages as "happy." We are less likely to suffer abuse without recourse, or to stare out at our lives through a glaze of prescription tranquilizers. Our aged parents are less likely to be destitute, and we're half as likely to have a teenage daughter turn up a mother herself. All in all, I would say that if "intact" in modern family-values jargon means living quietly desperate in the bell jar, then hip-hip-hooray for "broken." A neat family model constructed to service the Baby Boom economy seems to be returning gradually to a grand, lumpy shape that human families apparently have tended toward since they first took root in the Olduvai Gorge. We're social animals, deeply fond of companionship, and children love best to run in packs. If there is a *normal* for humans, at all, I expect it looks like two or three Families of Dolls, connected variously by kinship and passion, shuffled like cards and strewn over several shoeboxes.

The sooner we can let go of the fairy tale of families functioning perfectly in isolation, the better we might embrace the relief of community. Even the admirable parents who've stayed married through thick and thin are very likely, at present, to incorporate other adults into their families—household help and baby-sitters if they can afford them, or neighbors and grandparents if they can't. For single parents, this support is the rock-bottom definition of family. And most parents who have split apart, however painfully, still manage to maintain family continuity for their children, creating in many cases a boisterous phenomenon that Constance Ahrons in her book *The Good Divorce* calls the "binuclear family." Call it what you will—when ex-spouses beat swords into plowshares and jump up and down at a soccer game together, it makes for happy kids. [25]

Cinderella, look, who needs her? All those evil stepsisters? That story always seemed like too much cotton-picking fuss over clothes. A childhood tale that fascinated me more was the one called "Stone Soup," and the gist of it is this: Once upon a time, a pair of beleaguered soldiers straggled home to a village empty-handed, in a land ruined by war. They were famished, but the villagers had so little they shouted evil words and slammed their doors. So the soldiers dragged out a big kettle, filled it with water, and put it on a fire to boil. They rolled a clean round stone into the pot, while the villagers peered through their curtains in amazement. [26]

"What kind of soup is that?" they hooted. [27]

"Stone soup," the soldiers replied. "Everybody can have some when it's done."   28

"Well, thanks," one matron grumbled, coming out with a shriveled carrot. "But it'd be better if you threw this in."   29

And so on, of course, a vegetable at a time, until the whole suspicious village managed to feed itself grandly.   30

Any family is a big empty pot, save for what gets thrown in. Each stew turns out different. Generosity, a resolve to turn bad luck into good, and respect for variety—these things will nourish a nation of children. Name-calling and suspicion will not. My soup contains a rock or two of hard times, and maybe yours does too. I expect it's a heck of a bouillabaise.   31

For Study and Discussion

QUESTIONS ABOUT PURPOSE

1. In paragraphs 19 through 23, Kingsolver gives several snapshots of what so-called traditional families have actually looked like for the past several decades. What do you think she hopes to accomplish with these accounts?
2. What new insights do you think Kingsolver wants her readers to have about the divorce process?

QUESTIONS ABOUT AUDIENCE

1. What experience with divorce, single parenthood, and the step-families created by second marriages do you think today's readers under forty are likely to have? How do those experiences affect the way they are likely to respond to an essay like this?
2. What details in the essay suggest that Kingsolver feels she is writing more for women than for men?

QUESTIONS ABOUT STRATEGIES

1. Kingsolver has published several successful novels, two of which—*The Bean Trees* and *Pigs in Heaven*—tell the story of a single mother who adopts and raises a child. What strategies do you see in this essay that you think might have come from her talent for writing fiction?

2. Kingsolver draws examples from two sources: from her own experience and observations and from historical examples from previous eras. What are the strengths of examples from each of these sources?

For Writing and Research

1. *Analyze* how Kingsolver uses historical evidence to challenge the myth of the "traditional family."
2. *Practice* by demonstrating how reconstructed families—like Kingsolver's—offer children more advantages than disadvantages.
3. *Argue* that the ideas of romantic love presented in the movies provide a distorted view of family values.
4. *Synthesize* some of the data presented in Stephanie Coontz's *The Way We Never Were* (1992). Then use this evidence to support the argument that the idea of a traditional family is a "nostalgia trap."

Barbara Dafoe Whitehead was born in Rochester, Minnesota, in 1944 and was educated at the University of Wisconsin and the University of Chicago. She has contributed articles to *Commonweal*, the *New York Times*, and the *Wall Street Journal*. Her most controversial article, "Dan Quayle Was Right," published in the *Atlantic*, refers to former vice president Dan Quayle's criticism of the television show *Murphy Brown* because its title character chose to have a baby without being married. She has also written another controversial article for the *Atlantic*, "The Failure of Sex Education." These articles have led to books such as *The Divorce Culture* (1997), *Goodbye to Girlhood: What's Troubling Girls and What We Can Do About It* (1999), and *Why There Are No Good Men Left: The Romantic Plight of the New Single Woman* (2003). In "Women and the Future of Fatherhood," reprinted from *The Wilson Quarterly* (1996), Whitehead argues that even the best mothers cannot be good fathers.

Women and the Future of Fatherhood

MUCH OF OUR contemporary debate over fatherhood is 1 governed by the assumption that men can solve the fatherhood problem on their own. The organizers of last year's Million Man March asked women to stay home, and the leaders of Promise Keepers and other grass-roots fatherhood movements whose members gather with considerably less fanfare simply do not admit women.

There is a cultural rationale for the exclusion of women. The 2 fatherhood movement sees the task of reinstating responsible fatherhood as an effort to alter today's norms of masculinity and correctly believes that such an effort cannot succeed unless it is voluntarily undertaken and supported by men. There is also a political rationale in defining fatherlessness as a men's issue. In the debate about marriage and parenthood, which women have dominated for at least 30 years, the fatherhood movement gives men a powerful collective voice and presence.

Yet however effective the grass-roots movement is at stirring 3 men's consciences and raising their consciousness, the fatherhood problem will not be solved by men alone. To be sure, by signaling their commitment to accepting responsibility for

---

[This] notion of marriage as a union of two sovereign selves may be inadequate to define a relationship that carries with it the obligations, duties, and sacrifices of parenthood.

---

the rearing of their children, men have taken the essential first step. But what has not yet been acknowledged is that the success of any effort to renew fatherhood as a social fact and a cultural norm also hinges on the attitudes and behavior of women. Men can't be fathers unless the mothers of their children allow it.

Merely to say this is to point to how thoroughly marital 4 disruption has weakened the bond between fathers and children. More than half of all American children are likely to spend at least part of their lives in one-parent homes. Since the vast majority of children in disrupted families live with their mothers, fathers do not share a home or a daily life with their children. It is much more difficult for men to make the kinds of small, routine, instrumental investments in their children that help forge a good relationship. It is hard to fix a flat bike tire or run a bath when you live in another neighborhood or another town. Many a father's instrumental contribution is reduced to the postal or electronic transmission of money, or, all too commonly, to nothing at all. Without regular contact with their children, men often make reduced emotional contributions as well. Fathers must struggle to sustain close emotional ties across time and space, to "be there" emotionally without being there physically. Some may pick up the phone, send a birthday card, or buy a present, but for many fathers, physical absence also becomes emotional absence.

Without marriage, men also lose access to the social and   5
emotional intelligence of women in building relationships. Wives teach men how to care for young children, and they also encourage children to love their fathers. Mothers who do not live with the father of their children are not as likely as married mothers to represent him in positive ways to the children; nor are the relatives who are most likely to have greatest contact with the children—the mother's parents, brothers, and sisters— likely to have a high opinion of the children's father. Many men are able to overcome such obstacles, but only with difficulty. In general, men need marriage in order to be good fathers.

If the future of fatherhood depends on marriage, how-   6
ever, its future is uncertain. Marriage depends on women as well as men, and women are less committed to marriage than ever before in the nation's history. In the past, women were economically dependent on marriage and assumed a disproportionately heavy responsibility for maintaining the bond, even if the underlying relationship was seriously or irretrievably damaged. In the last third of the 20th century, however, as women have gained more opportunities for paid work and the availability of child care has increased, they have become less dependent on marriage as an economic arrangement. Though it is not easy, it is possible for women to raise children on their own. This has made divorce far more attractive as a remedy for an unsatisfying marriage, and a growing number of women have availed themselves of the option.

Today, marriage and motherhood are coming apart. Re- 7
marriage and marriage rates are declining even as the rates of
divorce remain stuck at historic highs and childbearing outside marriage becomes more common. Many women see single motherhood as a choice and a right to be exercised if a
suitable husband does not come along in time.

The vision of the "first stage" feminism of the 1960s and 8
'70s, which held out the model of the career woman unfet-
tered by husband or children, has been accepted by women
only in part. Women want to be fettered by children, even to
the point of going through grueling infertility treatments or
artificial insemination to achieve motherhood. But they are
increasingly ambivalent about the ties that bind them to a
husband and about the necessity of marriage as a condition of
parenthood. In 1994, a National Opinion Research survey
asked a group of Americans. "Do you agree or disagree: one
parent can bring up a child as well as two parents together."
Women split 50/50 on the question; men disagreed by more
than two to one.

And indeed, women enjoy certain advantages over men in 9
a society marked by high and sustained levels of family
breakup. Women do not need marriage to maintain a close
bond to their children, and thus to experience the larger
sense of social and moral purpose that comes with raising
children. As the bearers and nurturers of children and (increasingly) as the sole breadwinners for families, women
continue to be engaged in personally rewarding and socially
valuable pursuits. They are able to demonstrate their feminine virtues outside marriage.

Men, by contrast, have no positive identity as fathers out- 10
side marriage. Indeed, the emblematic absent father today is
the infamous "deadbeat dad." In part, this is the result of
efforts to stigmatize irresponsible fathers who fail to pay al-
imony and child support. But this image also reflects the fact
that men are heavily dependent on the marriage partnership
to fulfill their role as fathers. Even those who keep up their
child support payments are deprived of the social importance and sense of larger purpose that comes from providing

for children and raising a family. And it is the rare father who can develop the qualities needed to meet the new cultural ideal of the involved and "nurturing" father without the help of a spouse.

These differences are reflected in a growing virtue gap. American popular culture today routinely recognizes and praises the achievements of single motherhood, while the widespread failure of men as fathers has resulted in a growing sense of cynicism and despair about men's capacity for virtuous conduct in family life. The enormously popular movie *Waiting to Exhale* captures the essence of this virtue gap with its portrait of steadfast mothers and deadbeat fathers, morally sleazy men and morally unassailable women. And women feel free to vent their anger and frustration with men in ways that would seem outrageous to women if the shoe were on the other foot. In *Operating Instructions* (1993), her memoir of single motherhood, Anne Lamott mordantly observes, "On bad days, I think straight white men are so poorly wired, so emotionally unenlightened and unconscious that you must approach each one as if he were some weird cross between a white supremacist and an incredibly depressing T. S. Eliot poem."

Women's weakening attachment to marriage should not be taken as a lack of interest in marriage or in a husband-wife partnership in child rearing. Rather, it is a sign of women's more exacting emotional standards for husbands and their growing insistence that men play a bigger part in caring for children and the household. Given their double responsibilities as breadwinners and mothers, many working wives find men's need for ego reinforcement and other forms of emotional and physical upkeep irksome and their failure to share housework and child care absolutely infuriating. (Surveys show that husbands perform only one-third of all household tasks even if their wives are working full-time.) Why should men be treated like babies? women complain. If men fail to meet their standards, many women are willing to do without them. Poet and polemicist Katha Pollitt captures the prevailing sentiment: "If single women can have sex, their own homes, the respect of friends and interesting work, they don't need to tell themselves that any marriage is better than none. Why not have a child on one's own? Children are a joy. Many men are not."

For all these reasons, it is important to see the fatherhood 13 problem as part of the larger cultural problem of the decline of marriage as a lasting relationship between men and women. The traditional bargain between men and women has broken down, and a new bargain has not yet been struck. It is impossible to predict what that bargain will look like—or whether there will even be one. However, it is possible to speculate about the talking points that might bring women to the bargaining table. First, a crucial proviso: there must be recognition of the changed social and economic status of women. Rightly or wrongly, many women fear that the fatherhood movement represents an effort to reinstate the status quo ante, to repeal the gains and achievements women have made over the past 30 years and return to the "separate spheres" domestic ideology that put men in the workplace and women in the home. Any effort to rethink marriage must accept the fact that women will continue to work outside the home.

Therefore, a new bargain must be struck over the division of 14 paid work and family work. This does not necessarily mean a 50/50 split in the work load every single day, but it does mean that men must make a more determined and conscientious effort to do more than one-third of the household chores. How each couple arrives at a sense of what is fair will vary, of course, but the goal is to establish some mutual understanding and commitment to an equitable division of tasks.

Another talking point may focus on the differences in the 15 expectations men and women have for marriage and intimacy. Americans have a "best friends" ideal for marriage that includes some desires that might in fact be more easily met by a best friend—someone who doesn't come with all the complicated entanglements of sharing a bed, a bank account, and a bathroom. Nonetheless, high expectations for emotional intimacy in marriage often are confounded by the very different understandings men and women have of intimacy. Much more than men, women seek intimacy and affection through talking and emotional disclosure. Men often prefer sex to talking, and physical disrobing to emotional disclosing. They tend to be less than fully committed to (their own) sexual fidelity, while women view fidelity as a crucial sign of commitment. These are differences that the sexes need to engage with mutual recognition and tolerance.

In renegotiating the marital bargain, it may also be useful to acknowledge the biosocial differences between mothers and fathers rather than to assume an androgynous model for the parental partnership. There can be a high degree of flexibility in parental roles, but men and women are not interchangeable "parental units," particularly in their children's early years. Rather than struggle to establish identical tracks in career and family lives, it may be more realistic to consider how children's needs and well-being might require patterns of paid work and child rearing that are different for mothers and fathers but are nevertheless equitable over the course of a lifetime.

16

Finally, it may be important to think and talk about marriage in another kind of language than the one that suffuses our current discourse on relationships. The secular language of "intimate relationships" is the language of politics and psychotherapy, and it focuses on individual rights and individual needs. It can be heard most clearly in the personal-ad columns, a kind of masked ball where optimists go in search of partners who respect their rights and meet their emotional needs. These are not unimportant in the achievement of the contemporary ideal of marriage, which emphasizes egalitarianism and emotional fulfillment. But this notion of marriage as a union of two sovereign selves may be inadequate to define a relationship that carries with it the obligations, duties, and sacrifices of parenthood. There has always been a tension between marriage as an intimate relationship between a man and a woman and marriage as an institutional arrangement for raising children, and though the language of individual rights plays a part in defining the former, it cannot fully describe the latter. The parental partnership requires some

17

language that acknowledges differences, mutuality, complementarity, and, more than anything else, altruism.

There is a potentially powerful incentive for women to respond to an effort to renegotiate the marriage bargain, and that has to do with their children. Women can be good mothers without being married. But especially with weakened communities that provide little support, children need levels of parental investment that cannot be supplied solely by a good mother, even if she has the best resources at her disposal. These needs are more likely to be met if the child has a father as well as a mother under the same roof. Simply put, even the best mothers cannot be good fathers.   18

For Study and Discussion

QUESTIONS ABOUT PURPOSE

1. What changes in women's behaviors and attitudes would Whitehead like to bring about?
2. What changes in men's behaviors and attitudes would Whitehead like to bring about?

QUESTIONS ABOUT AUDIENCE

1. Whom do you see as the principal audience that Whitehead hopes to reach with this essay, men or women? On what do you base your answer?
2. What differences in responses to this article would you expect from readers over forty and those under forty?

QUESTIONS ABOUT STRATEGIES

1. Whitehead's argument is built on strong statements like this: "Today, marriage and motherhood are coming apart," and "Men have no positive identity as fathers outside marriage." In light of your own observations about today's families, how credible do you find these statements? Why?
2. Although Whitehead is writing about a topic that often generates a great deal of emotion, she is careful not to sound angry or to blame anyone. How does her argument benefit from her maintaining this moderate tone?

For Writing and Research

1. *Analyze* the evidence Whitehead presents for why "men need marriage to become good fathers."
2. *Practice* by demonstrating why men and women need to "renegotiate the marriage bargain."
3. *Argue* that the media has stereotyped "steadfast mothers" and "deadbeat dads."
4. *Synthesize* the research that supports Katha Pollitt's argument that women don't need marriage to have children.

Argument Writing Assignment

Each person's definition of family is often dictated by personal experience. However, our contemporary society is redefining the concept of family as circumstances and need dictate. Therefore, the definition of family has become increasingly more fluid, although some people espouse the opinion that the definition of a family is restricted to a husband, wife, and children, *only*.

Read the two essays in "A Debate About Family" carefully. Then write an essay that defends or qualifies the claims of this student essay. Support your position with evidence from the text.

Student Writing

JURUBY MORENO
Redefining Family

The concept of family, in contemporary terms, spans beyond the context of the mid-twentieth century view of the traditional patriarch-dominated nuclear family. In present-day society, it is not uncommon to see a family that may include heretofore unlikely members, perhaps the absence of one of the basic members (mom, dad, or in some cases, both) or the integration of two or more families into one. Although there has been a shift in the accepted infrastructure of the family unit, the *qualities* that reflect a family have not changed at all over the years. The family, when we look beyond the surface of *who* comprises it, and pay closer attention to the function of the parts as a whole, is a group of two or more tightly knit individuals who may not be related but nevertheless provide emotional, moral, and physical support to one another toward the goal of each member's personal growth. Family is often judged on a visually discriminatory basis, but it derives its true value from the bond that is formed between the members within it. Therefore, the diversity of constituents does not necessarily affect the essence of family.

Barbara Kingsolver's "Stone Soup" defends the nontraditional families' capability of raising children in a healthy, nurturing environment while simultaneously exposing the conservative biases and prejudiced outlooks that still linger in this era against the non-nuclear family. Often, when a proponent of the traditional ways observes a child who is not under the watchful eye of two heterosexual parents, they become squeamish and judgmental at the mere sight, wrongly inferring that the child's psyche may have undergone (or eventually will undergo) some trauma as a result. It is argued that "little Timmy" and "small Joanne" need both Mommy and Daddy in order to indicate a healthy, successful household. Of course, this perspective can be considered valid only if the mother and father raise the child in a loving, harmonious environment that enables that child to thrive. So, what happens to the child in a dysfunctional traditional family where that is not the case?

The answer lies in embracing a new concept of family in a society with an inordinately high divorce rate and one in which increasingly more children are born to single parents. The dissolving of a marriage can be a long and painful process that may have wide-reaching effects on the spouses and thus their children, true enough, but over time, all people, especially children, generally learn to adapt to the situation. The alternatives should be explored for a child before we can rashly dismiss nontraditional families. The child must be given the opportunity to have a family in which to grow, even if the family in question may be considered broken or unusual. Otherwise, the sad possibility many children in our country face is of being trapped in one that does not provide the love, safety, and support they all desperately need. Kingsolver herself states, "Why is it surprising that a child would revel in a widened family and the right to feel at home in more than one house? Isn't it the opposite that should worry us—a child with no home at all, or too few resources to feel safe?" Instead of questioning and condemning those single, gay, or uncustomary parents for their relationship preferences or status, we should focus more on what resources and caring stability they have to offer for the child. Members of a nontraditional family who embody and live the values necessary to a child's healthy development should be recognized as a genuine family in equal standing with the traditional family.

The real harm that a child can suffer from living in a nontraditional family comes ironically from the conservative critics bringing it to that child's attention, as they are supposedly the saviors seeking to shelter the children from the awareness of that very sense of insecurity. This situation is evident even among school-aged children, as was the case for Kingsolver's daughter. "My daughter tells me the only time she's uncomfortable about being the child of divorced parents is when her friends say they feel sorry for her." Here is the evidence that children will consider their family situation normal regardless of the makeup of members if they feel love and support, unless a respected authority convinces them otherwise.

Divorce, common-law separations, and civil unions are common facets of modern day life, just as much so, if not more, than the traditional family. It seems ludicrous to see that such nontraditional families are treated like leprosy-infected people by some. Now is the time to rid ourselves of such an archaic mindset. The only evident and credible difference between nuclear families and nontraditional families is superficial and trite. Their sincere, well-meaning intentions are very much the same— to guide, and to provide wisdom and unceasing love to the children who are much too innocent to care about the irrelevant differences of the people supplying these essentials so long as they are tangibly loved. We could all learn a valuable lesson from the pure and nonjudgmental minds of these young people. In the end, children usually have the instinctual wisdom to know whether the adult members of their family have their welfare at heart, so that the external observers' concept of family is irrelevant. Simply, family, regardless of its constitution, is where there is love, nurturing, and security.

A Debate About Windmills

ROBERT F. KENNEDY JR.

Robert F. Kennedy Jr. was born in 1954 and was educated at Harvard University, the London School of Economics, and the University of Virginia Law School. In 1978 he published his first book, based on his Harvard senior thesis—a biography of Alabama federal judge Frank M. Johnson Jr., who opposed the segregation policies of Governor George Wallace. In recent years, Kennedy has become a strong advocate for environmental issues, cohosting *Ring of Fire* on Air American Radio, contributing articles to magazines such as *Sierra Magazine* and *Rolling Stone,* and teaching environmental law at Pace University. In 1997, together with John Cronin, he co-authored *The Riverkeepers: Two Activists Fight to Reclaim Our Environment as a Basic Human Right* and *Crimes Against Nature: How George W. Bush and His Corporate Pals Are Plundering the Country and Highjacking Our Democracy* (2004). In "An Ill Wind Off Cape Cod," an op-ed column reprinted from the *New York Times* (2005), Kennedy argues against Cape Wind's proposal to build giant windmills in Nantucket Sound.

An Ill Wind Off Cape Cod

A S AN ENVIRONMENTALIST, I support wind power, includ- 1 ing wind power on the high seas. I am also involved in siting wind farms in appropriate landscapes, of which there are many. But I do believe that some places should be off limits to any sort of industrial development. I wouldn't build a wind farm in Yosemite National Park. Nor would I build one on Nantucket Sound, which is exactly what the company Energy Management is trying to do with its Cape Wind project.

Environmental groups have been enticed by Cape Wind, but they should be wary of lending support to energy companies that are trying to privatize the commons—in this case 24 square miles of a heavily used waterway. And because offshore wind costs twice as much as gas-fired electricity and significantly more than onshore wind, the project is financially feasible only because the federal and state governments have promised $241 million in subsidies.   2

Cape Wind's proposal involves construction of 130 giant turbines whose windmill arms will reach 417 feet above the water and be visible for up to 26 miles. These turbines are less than six miles from shore and would be seen from Cape Cod,   3

Environmental groups have been enticed by Cape Wind, but they should be wary of lending support to energy companies that are trying to privatize the commons.

Martha's Vineyard and Nantucket. Hundreds of flashing lights to warn airplanes away from the turbines will steal the stars and nighttime views. The noise of the turbines will be audible onshore. A transformer substation rising 100 feet above the sound would house giant helicopter pads and 40,000 gallons of potentially hazardous oil.

According to the Massachusetts Historical Commission, the project will damage the views from 16 historic sites and lighthouses on the cape and nearby islands. The Humane Society estimates the whirling turbines could every year kill thousands of migrating songbirds and sea ducks.   4

Nantucket Sound is among the most densely traveled boating corridors in the Atlantic. The turbines will be perilously   5 close to the main navigation channels for cargo ships, ferries and fishing boats. The risk of collisions with the towers would increase during the fogs and storms for which the area is famous. That is why the Steamship Authority and HyLine Cruises, which transport millions of passengers to and from the cape and islands every year, oppose the project. Thousands of small businesses, including marina owners, hotels, motels, whale watching tours and charter fishing operations will also be hurt. The Beacon Hill Institute at Suffolk University in Boston estimates a loss of up to 2,533 jobs because of the loss of tourism—and over a billion dollars to the local economy.

Nantucket Sound is a critical fishing ground for the com-   6
mercial fishing families of Martha's Vineyard and Cape Cod. Hundreds of fishermen work Horseshoe Shoal, where the Cape Wind project would be built, and make half their annual income from the catch. The risks that their gear will become fouled in the spider web of cables between the 130 towers will largely preclude fishing in the area, destroying family-owned businesses that enrich the palate, economy and culture of Cape Cod.

Many environmental groups support the Cape Wind proj-   7
ect, and that's unfortunate because making enemies of fishermen and marina owners is bad environmental strategy in the long run. Cape Cod's traditional-gear commercial fishing families and its recreational anglers and marina owners have all been important allies for environmentalists in our battles for clean water.

There are those who argue that unlike our great Western   8
national parks, Cape Cod is far from pristine, and that Cape Wind's turbines won't be a significant blot. I invite these critics to see the pods of humpback, minke, pilot, finback and right whales off Nantucket, to marvel at the thousands of harbor and gray seals lolling on the bars off Monomoy and Horseshoe Shoal, to chase the dark clouds of terns and shorebirds descending over the thick menhaden schools exploding over acre-sized feeding frenzies of striped bass, bluefish and bonita.

I urge them to come diving on some of the hundreds of   9
historic wrecks in this "graveyard of the Atlantic," and to visit

the endless dune-covered beaches of Cape Cod, our fishing villages immersed in history and beauty, or to spend an afternoon netting blue crabs or mucking clams, quahogs and scallops by the bushel on tidal mud flats—some of the reasons my uncle, John F. Kennedy, authorized the creation of the Cape Cod National Seashore in 1961, and why Nantucket Sound is under consideration as a national marine sanctuary, a designation that would prohibit commercial electrical generation.

All of us need periodically to experience wilderness to renew   10
our spirits and reconnect ourselves to the common history of our nation, humanity and to God. The worst trap that environmentalists can fall into is the conviction that the only wilderness worth preserving is in the Rocky Mountains or Alaska. To the contrary, our most important wildernesses are those that are closest to our densest population centers, like Nantucket Sound.

There are many alternatives that would achieve the same   11
benefits as Cape Wind without destroying this national treasure. Deep water technology is rapidly evolving, promising huge bounties of wind energy with fewer environmental and economic consequences. Scotland is preparing to build wind turbines in the Moray Firth more than 12 miles offshore. Germany is considering placing turbines as far as 27 miles off its northern shores.

If Cape Wind were to place its project further offshore, it   12
could build not just 130, but thousands of windmills—where they can make a real difference in the battle against global warming without endangering the birds or impoverishing the experience of millions of tourists and residents and fishing families who rely on the sound's unspoiled bounties.

For Study and Discussion

QUESTIONS ABOUT PURPOSE

1. What is Kennedy's main argument against the building of the Cape Wind project?
2. What suggestions does he make that would allow the project to be built?

QUESTIONS ABOUT AUDIENCE

1. Why does Kennedy begin by telling his readers that he is an environmentalist who supports wind power?
2. How does his assertion that "all of us" need to experience wilderness establish a connection with his readers?

QUESTIONS ABOUT STRATEGIES

1. How does Kennedy use expert testimony from organizations such as the Massachusetts Historical Commission, the Humane Society, and the Beacon Hill Institute to support his argument?
2. How does he use his "invitations" to his critics to help explain what would be lost if the project were built?

For Writing and Research

1. *Analyze* the various kinds of evidence Kennedy uses to support his argument.
2. *Practice* by arguing for or against an environmental project proposed by your community.
3. *Argue* that wind power is not a reliable source of alternative energy.
4. *Synthesize* Kennedy's uncle John F. Kennedy's various activities to establish the Cape Cod National Seashore. Then use this information to explain Kennedy's position on Cape Wind.

FRANCIS BROADHURST

Francis Broadhurst was born in 1935 in Becket, Massachusetts, and was educated at the University of Massachusetts at Amherst. He has written for numerous newspapers in New England, such as the *Boston Herald* and the *Cape Cod Times*. He has also worked as the news editor for several New England radio stations, including WQRC radio, where he produced the *Broadhurst Report,* a daily commentary and news analysis program. In "Cape Wind Is Sound for the Sound," which appeared as an op-ed column in the *Cape Cod Times* (2006) and was also broadcast on Cape Cod's National Public Radio station, Broadhurst argues that the Cape Wind project presents no environmental dangers and promises valuable economic benefits.

Cape Wind Is Sound
for the Sound

C APE WIND IS the foundation for our renewable energy   1
future—an opportunity to put Massachusetts on the map as a clean energy leader while paving the way for other renewable energy projects. Cape Wind will provide the Cape and Islands with 75% of our energy needs. In conjunction with the future of offshore wind, it will reduce our dependence on foreign oil and slow global warming. Wind Power is a clean, renewable energy resource that does not pollute our air with dirty fossil fuel emissions that cause global warming. By reducing greenhouse gas emissions, properly sited wind farms will also help prevent bird populations from becoming extinct.

A recent study published in the journal *Nature* indicates   2
that 15–37 percent of all bird species could face extinction

due to global warming by the year 2050. Radar studies conducted by Denmark's National Environmental Research Institute indicate that wind farms have no adverse impact on bird populations, concluding that most bird species exhibit an avoidance reaction to wind turbines, thereby reducing the probability of a collision. Jack Clarke, director of public policy and government relations at the Massachusetts Audubon Society states that the Denmark studies are quite credible. Moreover, Mass. Audubon conducted their own study, concluding that roseate terns avoid Horseshoe Shoals completely. "If it looked like these birds were going to be further

---

Cape Wind is the gateway to our renewable energy future.

---

jeopardized in the northeast as a result of this project, then we would have some very, very serious concerns and strong doubts about whether it's a viable project, but we don't see that," Jack Clarke said in an interview with the PBS News Hour this fall.

Cape Wind will also bring significant economic benefits to 3 the local region by creating jobs, stimulating the local economy, and diversifying the region's energy sources. Renewable energy in Nantucket Sound will displace energy we currently generate using fossil fuels without any additional back-up power being required. Forty-five percent of Southeastern Massachusetts' generating capacity is oil-fired, which means Cape Wind will reduce our dependence on foreign oil. Further, in contrast to the skyrocketing energy prices we are currently experiencing, the cost of wind energy remains constant and brings a stabilizing influence to energy prices.

In light of the increasing costs of heating our homes this 4 winter, local residents would stand to benefit greatly from the Cape Wind Project through a fixed-price deal where electricity rates would remain the same. The Cape Light Compact could negotiate long-term contracts on behalf of the 197,000 Cape and Martha's Vineyard residents they supply. This would benefit local residents by providing a fixed-price electricity supply well into the future.

Cape Wind is a stepping-stone for deep-water technology 5 and this near-shore experience is essential to deep-water success. Currently, there are no deep-water wind turbines anywhere in the world. The purpose of the first proposed deepwater site, the Beatrice "demonstrator" project in Scotland, is to test new technology. Unlike the Cape Wind project, the Beatrice demonstrator is heavily subsidized, receiving almost $16 million for two turbines. Furthermore, the developer acknowledges that deep-water technology is not currently viable. The future of deep-water offshore wind energy is promising. The present viability of near-shore wind energy is real. The near-shore Cape Wind project can supply our short-term needs and lay the foundation for the coming of deep-water wind.

Cape Wind is the gateway to our renewable energy future. 6 The project has been undergoing an environmental review for four years, and no major flaws have been found. It is the right project, for the right place, at the right time.

For Study and Discussion

QUESTIONS ABOUT PURPOSE

1. How does Broadhurst's title suggest his position in the Cape Wind controversy?
2. What is the primary reason he supports the Cape Wind project?

QUESTIONS ABOUT AUDIENCE

1. How does Broadhurst use the pronoun *our* to establish a relationship with his readers?
2. How does he use the promise of "fixed-price electricity" to appeal to his readers?

QUESTIONS ABOUT STRATEGIES

1. How does Broadhurst use expert testimony from organizations such as the Audubon Society to support his argument?
2. How does he use the difference between deep-water and near-shore technology to advance his argument?

For Writing and Research

1. *Analyze* the way Broadhurst uses pronouns such as *our* to create a "band wagon" appeal (that is, "everybody agrees with us; you should, too").
2. *Practice* by using "accommodation" as a way to deal with an environmental controversy in which both sides can present reasonable arguments.
3. *Argue* that wind power is a reliable source of alternative energy.
4. *Synthesize* the research on "deep-water technology." Then use this information to argue that such technology is or is not a promising investment.

Synthesis Writing Assignment

In this era, we face the challenge of finding alternative energy sources to replace the dwindling oil supply. One of the sources that has received a great deal of attention is wind energy.

Read the two previous essays, study the map on page 426 and analyze the following student essay, Sean Tansley's "Wind Energy: An Effective Alternative?" Then, in an essay that synthesizes these sources for support, take a position that defends, challenges, or qualifies the claims that wind energy is an effective alternative energy source for the communities that surround Nantucket Sound.

This map illustrates a possible site for a wind farm off the coast of Massachusetts. Why is this site controversial? What other sites offer the possibility of a compromise for the contesting sides in this controversy?

Student Writing

SEAN TANSLEY
Wind Energy: An Effective Alternative?

We have reached a crucial point in relation to our consumption of the fossil fuel supply. That supply is finite and dwindling. More alarming, its production and use have already harmed our environment. For that reason, there has been increasing interest in effective energy alternatives such as wind power.

Scientists, economists, and environmentalists support the concept of wind energy because it is renewable, affordable, and clean. But harnessing wind energy is a complicated technology, and the most common form of that technology, a wind farm, needs to be constructed in a particular kind of environment. Without appropriate planning, the construction of a wind farm can create considerable public controversy. Such is the case with the wind farm proposed for Nantucket Sound, in the waters between the island of Nantucket and Cape Cod, Massachusetts.

In "An Ill Wind Off Cape Code," Robert F. Kennedy Jr., an environmentalist, supports the idea of wind power, but he objects to constructing a wind farm in Nantucket Sound because he believes that such a farm, complete with flashing lights, noisy turbines, and powerful transformers, will not only damage "the views from 16 historic sites," but also destroy the environment.

Kennedy also argues that placing giant windmills too close to shore will hurt small businesses, alter the tourist industry, and destroy commercial fishing. He estimates that such disruptions could cost thousands of jobs and billions of dollars. So although the proposed wind farm could provide a valuable source of energy Kennedy suggests that developers follow the planning model provided by Scotland and Germany and place the farm away from the shore, in the deep waters of the Atlantic Ocean. (See map on page 426.)

By contrast, journalist Francis Broadhurst, in "Cape Wind Is Sound for the Sound," cites research that argues that the proposed near-shore location will not have any adverse impact on the environment. Additionally, he makes a compelling case that the wind farm will "bring significant economic benefits to the local region."

Broadhurst acknowledges the eventual value of the deep-water alternative but argues that the current technology needs further research and development. He prefers to construct a near-shore wind farm not only because it can "supply our short term needs . . . , but also lay the foundation for the coming deep-water wind."

This debate over the Nantucket Wind Farm illustrates the problem we face when we try to find an immediate fix for a problem as complicated as the energy crisis. Each side believes in the ultimate goal—to find an effective alternative to fossil fuels. Each side presents a reasonable and powerful argument in favor of a particular strategy—to construct wind farms. But when it comes to making a decision—placing the wind farm in Nantucket Sound—the two sides disagree about basic premises: will the near-shore farm destroy or protect the environment, will the near-shore farm disrupt or develop the economy, and is the deep-water proposal a real or simply a "promising" alternative?

A controversy is a controversy because it is controversial. That is, there may be no way to resolve the conflict between the opposing arguments, the contending research about environmental and economic effects, and the different forecasts about the status of deep-water technology.

Because we need to find a solution to the problems created by fossil fuel, we feel compelled to act—to escape the endless debates about which alternative is the most effective. We feel like we need to act now if we are to protect the environment and improve the economy. Perhaps we can choose the alternative that contains the least risk. But even that strategy may not work. Despite Broadhurst's assurances, the near-shore alternative risks damaging the environment and disrupting the economy. And despite Kennedy's assurances, deep-water technology may not work—and it may have environmental and economic consequences that have not been thoroughly researched.

So perhaps the best way out of this trap is not to act—just yet. We need to study the deep-water alternatives being constructed in Scotland and Germany to determine if they work effectively. If they do, then the most effective alternative is to place the wind farm in deep water, where it will provide the most energy and do the least harm.

A Debate About Harry Potter

JOAN ACOCELLA

Joan Acocella was born in 1945 in San Francisco and was educated at the University of California at Berkeley and Rutgers University. She began her writing career as a dance critic for *Dance Magazine,* the *New York Daily News,* and the *Wall Street Journal* before joining the staff of the *New Yorker.* Her books include *Mark Morris* (1993), *Creating Hysteria: Women and Multiple Personality Disorder* (1999), *Willa Cather and the Politics of Criticism* (2000), and *Twenty-Eight Artists and Two Saints* (2007). In "Under the Spell," reprinted from the *New Yorker* (2000), Acocella argues that the appeal of the Harry Potter books lies in their willingness to raise complicated moral questions.

Under the Spell

NOT SINCE Y2K have we seen a fuss like the one over "Harry Potter and the Goblet of Fire," the fourth volume in J. K. Rowling's series about a junior wizard. Biggest advance order ever (including Amazon.com's three hundred and fifty thousand), biggest first printing ever (three million eight hundred thousand copies in this country alone), biggest takeover, ever, of the *Times* best-seller list by a single writer, let alone a children's writer. As "The Goblet of Fire" was being printed, the three preceding volumes were all still in the ranking—a circumstance that resulted, last Sunday, in the creation of a separate, children's best-seller list, just what we didn't need. Prior to publication, the book was shrouded in ultra-tight, press-inflaming secrecy. There were no copies for reviewers, or for anyone, before publication day, July 8th. Many stores stayed open late on July 7th—indeed, threw Harry Potter parties—and started ringing up the sales at a minute after midnight. I myself went to Books of Wonder, on West Eighteenth Street, and stood in line for two hours with a lot of excited children and bleary-eyed parents as a Harry Potter lookalike, presumably associated with the store, cruised the sidewalk, distributing press-on lightning-bolt

---

The subject of the Harry Potter series is power, an important matter for children, since they have so little of it.

---

tattoos and fake cheer. Around 1:45 A.M., I made it to the front of the line and was allowed to buy "The Goblet of Fire." After all that, I would love to tell you that the book is a big nothing. In fact, it's wonderful, just like its predecessors.

Part of the secret of Rowling's success is her utter tradi- 2 tionalism. The Potter story is a fairy tale, plus a bildungsroman, plus a murder mystery, plus a cosmic war of good and evil, and there's almost no classic in any of those genres that doesn't reverberate between the lines of Harry's saga. The Arthurian legend, the Superman comics, "Star Wars," "Cinderella," "The Lord of the Rings," the "Chronicles of Narnia," "The Adventures of Sherlock Holmes," Genesis, Exodus, the Divine Comedy, "Paradise Lost"—they're all there. The Gothic paraphernalia, too: turreted castles, purloined letters, surprise visitors arriving in the dark of night, backed by forked lightning. If you take a look at Vladimir Propp's 1928 book "Morphology of the Folk Tale," which lists just about every convention ever used in fairy tales, you can check off, one by one, the devices that Rowling has unabashedly picked up. At the beginning of the story, Propp says, the villain harms someone in the hero's family. (The evil wizard Voldemort murdered Harry's good-wizard parents when the boy was a year old, and tried to kill him, too.) The hero is branded. (Voldemort's attack left Harry with a scar in the shape of a lightning bolt on his forehead.) The hero is banished. (Harry is forced to go live with his loathsome aunt and uncle, the Dursleys.) The hero is released. (Harry is finally informed that he is a wizard, and goes off to live at Hogwarts School of Witchcraft and Wizardry.) The hero must survive ordeals, seek things, acquire a wise helper, all of which Harry does. The villain must change form and leave bloody trails; Voldemort obliges. According to Propp, a fairy tale is supposed to end with the hero's marriage, but Rowling may break ranks here. She has said that the series will be seven novels long, one for each of Harry's years at Hogwarts. He started there at age eleven, so he will be seventeen when we say goodbye to him. In the line in front of Books of Wonder, there was heated speculation as to who is going to end up as Harry's girl. (I say Ginny Weasley.) I doubt we'll have a wedding, though. Seventeen's a little young.

So Rowling's books are chock-a-block with archetypes,   3 and she doesn't just use them; she glories in them, plays with them, postmodernly. At the Dursleys' house, Harry lives in a cupboard under the stairs, with spiders. Rowling is also a great showoff when it comes to surprise endings, and this, I think, is actually a fault of the books, or of the last two. The dénouements last for pages and pages, as red herrings are eliminated, false identities cleared up, friends unmasked as foes, and vice versa. Not only is this too complicated, the surprises are too surprising. How can Sirius Black, who has been stalking Harry throughout "The Prisoner of Azkaban," turn out to be a good guy—indeed, the boy's godfather? How can Scabbers, whom we have known and loved for three volumes as a dusty, useless little rat, snoozing in the sun, emerge at the end of that book as a deep-dyed villain in disguise? It seems to invalidate all our prior experience of the series. Not to speak of the sheer confusion. Faced with the equally counterintuitive revelations at the end of "The Goblet of Fire,"

Harry thinks, "It made no sense . . . no sense at all." I agree with him, but apparently we're in a minority.

Rowling has said that she has no trouble at all thinking her- 4
self back to age eleven, and the novels show it. There are toilet jokes, booger jokes. There is a ball game, Quidditch—with
four kinds of players (all flying on brooms) and three kinds of
balls—that sounds as though it were made up by a clever
eleven-year-old. And the books are filled with children's problems. Do you have bad dreams? Did you find your Christmas
presents rather a letdown? Do you hate the new baby in your
house? Do you wish you had different parents? Is there something weird that lives under your bed and makes noises at
night? If so, Joanne Rowling is thinking about you. Best of all
is her treatment of the social nightmares of the schoolyard:
cliques, bullying, ostracism, kids who like to remind you that
your family doesn't have much money. Such problems are
perhaps more pressing in the English boarding school, on
which Hogwarts is modelled. (Last year, in the *Times Book
Review*, Pico Iyer claimed that Hogwarts was a near-exact
replica of Eton, where he did his time.) But the situation
clearly rings a bell with Rowling's American readers, too.

More, even, than the Potter books' sensitivity to preteen 5
terrors, it is their wised-upness, their lack of sentimentality,
that must appeal to Rowling's audience. However much they
have to do with goodness, these are not prissy books. Harry
lies to adults again and again. He also hates certain people,
and Rowling hates them, too. Uncle Vernon Dursley is not
only cruel; he spits when he talks. Harry says the Dursleys
wish him dead, and he's right. As for the forces of good, they
are often well out of reach. In "The Sorcerer's Stone" there is
a heart-stopping scene in which Harry comes upon a mirror,
the so-called Mirror of Erised, and sees his dead parents in it.
His father waves at him; his mother weeps and smiles. Reading this, you think, Oh, good, thank God—Harry's not really
alone, not really an orphan. Yes, he's being hunted down by a
remorseless villain—in each of the books, Voldemort pursues
him—but his parents' spirits are there to protect him. Then

Dumbledore, Hogwarts's wise headmaster, appears and tells Harry that the Mirror of Erised shows us not what is but what we desire. (Read "Erised" backward.) Harry is alone.

The great beauty of the Potter books is their wealth of imagination, their sheer, shining fullness. Rowling has said that the idea for the series came to her on a train trip from Manchester to London in 1990, and that, even before she started writing the first volume, she spent years just working out the details of Harry's world. We reap the harvest: the inventory of magical treats (Ice Mice, Jelly Slugs, Fizzing Whizbees—levitating sherbet balls) in the wizard candy store; the wide range of offerings (Dungbombs, Hiccup Sweets, Nose-Biting Teacups) in the wizard joke store. Hogwarts is a grand, creepy castle, a thousand years old, with more dungeons and secret passages than you can shake a stick at. There are a hundred and forty-two staircases, some of which go to different places on different days of the week. There are suits of armor that sing carols at Christmastime, and get the words wrong. There are poltergeists—Peeves, for example, who busies himself jamming gum into keyholes. We also get ghosts, notably Nearly Headless Nick, whose executioner didn't quite finish the job, so that Nick's head hangs by an "inch or so of ghostly skin and muscle"—it keeps flopping over his ruff—thus, to his grief, excluding him from participating in the Headless Hunt, which is confined to the thoroughly decapitated.

The Hogwarts staff is a display case all its own: Mad-Eye Moody, the professor of Defense Against the Dark Arts, who, apart from his ocular problems, has a chunk of his nose missing and a wooden leg ending in a clawed foot; Rubeus Hagrid, the gentle-giant gamekeeper, with his pet, Norbert, a baby dragon, whom he feeds a bucket of brandy mixed with chicken blood every half hour. Norbert isn't the only monster. There are also centaurs, basilisks, and hippogriffs, together with hinkypunks, boggarts, and, my favorites, the grindylows. Harry encounters his first grindylow in a tank in a professor's office: "A sickly green creature with sharp little horns had its face pressed against the glass, . . . flexing its long spindly fingers." (Later, the grindylow shakes its fist at him.) To deal with such encounters, and other life events, the students must learn many spells: "Expelliarmus," to get rid of something; "Waddiwasi," to extract gum from keyholes; "Peskipiksi Pesternomi," to make pixies leave you alone. Hogwarts is a whole, bursting world.

Most of Rowling's characters are types, and excellent as such, but some rise to a richness beyond the reach of British central casting. Voldemort, for example. When he failed to kill the infant Harry, Voldemort was disempowered, and it is in this weakened state that we first encounter him in "The Goblet of Fire." But he isn't just weak. He is—grotesquely, disgustingly, terrifyingly—a *baby:* "hairless and scaly-looking, a dark, raw, reddish black. Its arms and legs were thin and feeble, and its face—no child alive ever had a face like that— flat and snakelike, with gleaming red eyes." Soon—as soon as he is immersed in a potion made from Harry's blood and some- one else's hacked-off hand and various other ingredients— he becomes his adult self again, which is not so handsome either, but that first sight of him, that little red thing, swad- dled in blankets, is a triumph of horror fiction.

It's horror with a difference, though. Rowling's favorite writer, she has told interviewers, is Jane Austen. She also loves Dickens. And it is in their bailiwick—English morals- and-manners realism, the world of Pip and Miss Bates, of money and position and trying to keep your head up if you have neither—that she scores her greatest victories. A nice ex- ample is the scene, in "The Sorcerer's Stone," where Harry and Ron meet for the first time, on the train that is taking them, as entering students, to Hogwarts. Each is handi- capped. Harry, though he is famous throughout the wizard world (because, as an infant, he repelled Voldemort's attack), and though he has a pile of gold left to him by his parents, is without family and utterly ignorant of wizardry. Ron comes from a long line of wizards, and he has family galore, but that is his problem: five older brothers, no position. He is always dressed in hand-me-downs; his mother always forgets what kind of sandwich he likes; he has no spending money.

Together, in the train compartment, the two boys comfort
and help each other. Harry shares the wizard candies he buys
from the vender (he can afford them); Ron explains the wizard trading cards that come with the candies (he understands
them). Harry gives Ron prestige; Ron gives Harry a sense of
belonging. All this is done very Englishly, very subtly, in small
gestures, but in the end each boy, because of the other,
arrives at Hogwarts slightly better armed against the harshness of the world.

   The subject of the Harry Potter series is power, an important   10
matter for children, since they have so little of it. How does one
acquire power? How can it be used well, and ill? Does ultimate
power lie with the good? (In other words, is there a God?) If so,
why is there so much cruelty around? These are questions that
Milton, among others, addressed before Rowling, and she is
not ashamed to follow in their wake. Voldemort is an avatar of
Milton's Lucifer; Dumbledore of Milton's God, who so mysteriously permits evil in the world.

   Each of the novels approaches the problem from a different   11
angle. The first, "Harry Potter and the Sorcerer's Stone," is
heroic. We meet our champion; he is a child; we watch
him grow into competence and faith. The second volume,
"Harry Potter and the Chamber of Secrets," is quite different:
secular, topical, political. Sexism is not a major problem at
Hogwarts. The school is coed. Several of the Quidditch
champions are girls. Harry's friend Hermione, the know-it-all
girl, the hand-up-in-class girl—Rowling has said she based the
character on herself as a child—is not forced to go through
the Katharine Hepburn treatment (take off her glasses, unpin
her hair) before she becomes likable. But racism *is* a problem
at Hogwarts. Yes, the student body includes Cho Chang and
Parvati Patil and Dean Thomas, who has dreadlocks. (Rowling
forgot about a few other groups, though. I would not have
minded if the evil Professor Snape had not had a hook nose,
greasy black hair, and sallow skin—standard features of the ra-
pacious Jew—or if the chief villain of "The Sorcerer's Stone"
had not worn a purple turban, been prone to faint and weep,

and had the name Quirrell, which is rather close to "queer.")
But the wizard world is in the grip of an overarching race
war, a campaign to rid wizardry of those with Muggle, or
non-wizard, blood. This ethnic-cleansing campaign, led by
Voldemort, is the subject of "The Chamber of Secrets." It fails,
but only for the time being. We will hear about it again.

The strangest volume is the third, "Harry Potter and the 12
Prisoner of Azkaban," the psychological installment, featur-
ing a pack of demons—operating at Voldemort's bidding—
who are the most frightening monsters in the series so far.
These are the Dementors: huge, cloaked, faceless creatures,
with rotting hands, who, if they get you, clamp their jaws on
your mouth and suck out of you every thought of happiness.
The Dementors represent depression. Actually, if I'm not
mistaken, they represent a specific, British theory of depression—John Bowlby's theory that loss of a parent in early
childhood is a major risk factor for that disorder. At age one,
Harry lost both his parents. (I don't know much about
Rowling's childhood, but she has told interviewers that she
suffered a period of depression as an adult, and had to get
professional help.) In any case, the Dementors are after
Harry, and he escapes them only with the help of a teacher
named Lupin. To Lupin alone can he fully confide his fears,
and Lupin's teachings are the closest thing, in the Potter series, to overt psychological counselling of child readers. At
the end of "The Prisoner of Azkaban," this nice man turns
out to be a werewolf (Rowling's antisentimentality again),
but he's a good werewolf.

The new book, "Harry Potter and the Goblet of Fire," is 13
the central pillar of the projected series of seven and is thus a
transitional volume. It introduces many new subjects, notably sex. (Harry is fourteen now, and mightily taken with
Cho Chang.) Also, the politics become more ambitious.
Rowling now asks her readers to consider the cynicism of government officials, the injustice of the law courts, the vagaries
of international relations, the mendacity of the press, even
the psychology of slavery. ("They're *happy*," Ron's brother
says of the house-elves. Hermione does not agree.) This is a

great, toppling heap of subjects, and Rowling takes seven hundred and thirty-four pages to deal with them. (Has there ever before been a children's story seven hundred and thirty-four pages long? What confidence!) Where the prior volumes moved like lightning, here the pace is slower, the energy more dispersed. At the same time, the tone becomes more grim. Voldemort has been restored to power. Things will now become harder for Harry, and for all the wizard world. Dumbledore says so.

There is much for Rowling to resolve in the remaining volumes, above all the question about power—is it reconcilable with goodness?—that she poses in the first four books. Already in "The Sorcerer's Stone," Quirrell says, "There is no good and evil, there is only power, and those too weak to seek it." As Harry has grown, he has become more powerful and ambitious and, at the same time, more virtuous. In "The Goblet of Fire," as in all the books, there is a big contest, which Harry longs to win. The contest is in three parts, and in each part, lest we miss the point, Rowling shows Harry handicapping himself, hurting his chances of victory, out of concern for others. He wins, but how will he do, thus compromised by altruism, in future contests? Remember: Voldemort is back.

Even more interesting, however, is a strange matter— something about the *kinship* of good and evil—that Rowling has been hinting at since the beginning of the series. Harry and Voldemort have a lot in common. Both have Muggle blood; both are orphans. Their wands contain feathers from the same phoenix. When they met in armed combat in "The Goblet of Fire," their wands, as they touch, produce a single stream of light, which binds them together. There is some connection between these two. (Shades of "Star Wars.") I don't know what Rowling has in mind here. Maybe it's the Miltonic idea of evil as merely good perverted. Or maybe not.

But that is the main virtue of these books, their philosophical seriousness. Rowling is a good psychotherapist, and she teaches excellent morals. (Those parents who have objected to the Potter series on the ground that it promotes unchristian values should give it another read.) She also spins a good yarn. Undoubtedly, it is Voldemort and the Dementors and the grindylows that have gotten these books translated into forty languages and won them sales, *before* "The Goblet of Fire," of more than thirty million copies. But her great glory, and the thing that may place her in the pantheon, is that she asks her preteen readers to face the hardest questions of life, and does not shy away from the possibility that the answers may be sad: that loss may be permanent, evil ever-present, good exhaustible. In an odd, quiet moment in "The Goblet of Fire," Harry stands alone in Hogwarts's Owlery, gazing out into the twilight. He sees his friend Hagrid digging in the earth. Is Hagrid burying something? Or looking for something? Harry doesn't know, and for once he doesn't investigate. He seems tired. He just stays there, watching Hagrid, until he can see him no more, whereupon the owls in the Owlery awaken and swoosh past him, "into the night." In this volume, some darkness has fallen. With the light—the next three books—new griefs will surely come.

For Study and Discussion

QUESTIONS ABOUT PURPOSE

1. Although the Harry Potter books are written for children, this serious review of them was written for the *New Yorker*, a magazine for sophisticated, well-educated readers. Why do you think Acocella chose them for her audience?
2. Why does Acocella trace the traditions, from the King Arthur legends to *Star Wars*, that underlie the books, giving references that range from the Bible and literary classics to comic books?

QUESTIONS ABOUT AUDIENCE

1. Educators know that young boys are a notoriously difficult audience for writers to reach, but both boys and girls are reading Harry Potter in record numbers. How does Acocella explain this wide appeal?
2. Who besides the readers of the Potter books themselves might be interested in learning more about this publishing phenomenon?

QUESTIONS ABOUT STRATEGIES

1. Acocella goes into great detail to show the lurid and gory details of the Potter stories. How does she engage her readers with these descriptions?
2. How does Acocella present herself in this essay? How does she establish her credentials to analyze the traditions and legends that are so important to the Potter series?

For Writing and Research

1. *Analyze* how Acocella uses the expert testimony of Vladimir Propp's book *Morphology of the Folk Tale* to support her argument that the Harry Potter books have "classic reverberations."
2. *Practice* by writing an argument supporting the literary value of a film sequence such as "Spiderman."
3. *Argue* that power and goodness are or are not compatible.
4. *Synthesize* the evidence from the last three volumes of the series that supports Acocella's argument about the kinship of good and evil.

HAROLD BLOOM

Harold Bloom was born in 1930 in New York and was educated at Cornell University and Yale University. In his distinguished teaching career, he has taught literature at Yale, Cornell, Harvard, and New York University. A staunch defender of the Western literary tradition, his numerous critical books include *The Anxiety of Influence: A Theory of Poetry* (1973), *A Map of Misreading* (1975), *The Breaking of Vessels* (1982), *The Western Canon: The Books and School of the Ages* (1994), and most recently *Hamlet: Poem Unlimited* (2003). In "Can 35 Million Book Buyers Be Wrong? Yes," reprinted from the *Wall Street Journal* (2000), Bloom argues that the Harry Potter books are inferior to classic children's books.

Can 35 Million Book Buyers Be Wrong? Yes.

TAKING ARMS AGAINST Harry Potter, at this moment, is to emulate Hamlet taking arms against a sea of troubles. By opposing the sea, you won't end it. The Harry Potter epiphenomenon will go on, doubtless for some time, as J. R. R. Tolkien did, and then wane. 1

The official newspaper of our dominant counter-culture, the *New York Times,* has been startled by the Potter books into establishing a new policy for its not very literate book review. Rather than crowd out the Grishams, Clancys, Crichtons, Kings and other vastly popular prose fictions on its fiction bestseller list, the Potter volumes will now lead a separate children's list. J. K. Rowling, the chronicler of Harry Potter, thus has an unusual distinction: She has changed the policy of the policy-maker. 2

IMAGINATIVE VISION

I read new children's literature, when I can find some of any 3
value, but had not tried Rowling until now. I have just concluded the 300 pages of the first book in the series, "Harry
Potter and the Sorcerer's Stone," purportedly the best of the
lot. Though the book is not well written, that is not in itself
a crucial liability. It is much better to see the movie, "The
Wizard of Oz," than to read the book upon which it was
based, but even the book possessed an authentic imaginative

---

*Hogwarts enchants many of Harry's fans,
perhaps because it is much livelier than the
schools they attend, but it seems to me an
academy more tiresome than grotesque.*

---

vision. "Harry Potter and the Sorcerer's Stone" does not, so
that one needs to look elsewhere for the book's (and its se-
quels') remarkable success. Such speculation should follow
an account of how and why Harry Potter asks to be read.

The ultimate model for Harry Potter is "Tom Brown's 4
School Days" by Thomas Hughes, published in 1857. The
book depicts the Rugby School presided over by the formidable Thomas Arnold, remembered now primarily as the father
of Matthew Arnold, the Victorian critic-poet. But Hughes's
book, still quite readable, was realism, not fantasy. Rowling
has taken "Tom Brown's School Days" and re-seen it in the
magical mirror of Tolkien. The resultant blend of a schoolboy
ethos with a liberation from the constraints of reality-testing
may read oddly to me, but is exactly what millions of children
and their parents desire and welcome at this time.

In what follows, I may at times indicate some of the inad- 5
equacies of "Harry Potter." But I will keep in mind that a
host are reading it who simply will not read superior fare,
such as Kenneth Grahame's "The Wind in the Willows" or

the "Alice" books of Lewis Carroll. Is it better that they read Rowling than not read at all? Will they advance from Rowling to more difficult pleasures?

Rowling presents two Englands, mundane and magical, divided not by social classes, but by the distinction between the "perfectly normal" (mean and selfish) and the adherents of sorcery. The sorcerers indeed seem as middle-class as the Muggles, the name the witches and wizards give to the common sort, since those addicted to magic send their sons and daughters off to Hogwarts, a Rugby School where only witchcraft and wizardry are taught. Hogwarts is presided over by Albus Dumbledore as Headmaster, he being Rowling's version of Tolkien's Gandalf. The young future sorcerers are just like any other budding Britons, only more so, sports and food being primary preoccupations. (Sex barely enters into Rowling's cosmos, at least in the first volume.)   6

Harry Potter, now the hero of so many millions of children and adults, is raised by dreadful Muggle relatives after his sorcerer parents are murdered by the wicked Voldemort, a wizard gone trollish and, finally, post-human. Precisely why poor Harry is handed over by the sorcerer elders to his piggish aunt and uncle is never clarified by Rowling, but it is a nice touch, suggesting again how conventional the alternative Britain truly is. They consign their potential hero-wizard to his nasty blood-kin, rather than let him be reared by amiable warlocks and witches, who would know him for one of their own.   7

The child Harry thus suffers the hateful ill treatment of the Dursleys, Muggles of the most Muggleworthy sort, and of their sadistic son, his cousin Dudley. For some early pages we might be in Ken Russell's film of "Tommy," the rock-opera by The Who, except that the prematurely wise Harry is much healthier than Tommy. A born survivor, Harry holds on until the sorcerers rescue him and send him off to Hogwarts, to enter upon the glory of his schooldays.   8

Hogwarts enchants many of Harry's fans, perhaps because it is much livelier than the schools they attend, but it seems to me an academy more tiresome than grotesque. When the future witches and wizards of Great Britain are not studying   9 how to cast a spell, they preoccupy themselves with bizarre intramural sports. It is rather a relief when Harry heroically suffers the ordeal of a confrontation with Voldemort, which the youth handles admirably.

One can reasonably doubt that "Harry Potter and the Sorcerer's Stone" is going to prove a classic of children's literature, but Rowling, whatever the aesthetic weakness of her work, is at least a millennial index to our popular culture. So huge an audience gives her importance akin to rock stars, movie idols, TV anchors, and successful politicians. Her prose style, heavy on cliché, makes no demands upon her readers. In an arbitrarily chosen single page—page 4—of the first Harry Potter book, I count seven clichés, all of the "stretch his legs" variety. 10

How to read "Harry Potter and the Sorcerer's Stone"? Why, very quickly, to begin with, perhaps also to make an end. Why read it? Presumably, if you cannot be persuaded to read anything better, Rowling will have to do. Is there any redeeming educational use to Rowling? Is there any to Stephen King? Why read, if what you read will not enrich mind or spirit or personality? For all I know, the actual wizards and witches of Britain, or of America, may provide an alternative culture for more people than is commonly realized. 11

Perhaps Rowling appeals to millions of reader non-readers because they sense her wistful sincerity, and want to join her world, imaginary or not. She feeds a vast hunger for unreality: can that be bad? At least her fans are momentarily emancipated from their screens, and so may not forget wholly the sensation of turning the pages of a book, any book. 12

INTELLIGENT CHILDREN

And yet I feel a discomfort with the Harry Potter mania, and I hope that my discontent is not merely a highbrow snobbery, or a nostalgia for a more literate fantasy to beguile (shall we say) intelligent children of all ages. Can more than 35 million book buyers, and their offspring, be wrong? Yes, they 13 have been, and will continue to be so for as long as they persevere with Potter.

A vast concourse of inadequate works, for adults and for children, crams the dustbins of the ages. At a time when public judgment is no better and no worse than what is proclaimed by the ideological cheerleaders who have so destroyed humanistic study, anything goes. The cultural critics will, soon enough, introduce Harry Potter into their college curriculum, and the *New York Times* will go on celebrating another confirmation of the dumbing-down it leads and exemplifies.   14

For Study and Discussion

QUESTIONS ABOUT PURPOSE

1. What do you think an eminent professor of Bloom's standing hopes to accomplish by taking time to read a popular children's book and then give it—and the *New York Times*—such a scathing review?
2. What kind of reading do you think Bloom would recommend as literature that would, as he says, "enrich the mind or spirit or personality"?

QUESTIONS ABOUT AUDIENCE

1. Bloom published this essay in the *Wall Street Journal.* How does he anticipate the knowledge and interests of his readers, who are predominantly business executives and people involved in the world of finance?
2. On the other hand, why might the readers of the *Wall Street Journal* be intrigued by the Harry Potter books?

QUESTIONS ABOUT STRATEGIES

1. What persona do you think Bloom wants to present to his readers? How does his first sentence contribute to that persona?
2. Why does he liken Harry's creator, J. K. Rowling, to the "rock stars, movie idols, TV anchors, and successful politicians" of the millennium? What's his point?

For Writing and Research

1. *Analyze* the evidence Bloom uses to support his criticism of the first Harry Potter book.

2. *Practice* by arguing that the movie version of a children's tale—*The Wizard of Oz, Stuart Little, Cinderella*—is better than the book.

3. *Argue* that Bloom's examples of "superior fare"—*The Wind in the Willows* or the "Alice" books—is really highbrow nostalgia rather than effective criticism.

4. *Synthesize* the evidence Bloom cites from the books by Thomas Hughes and J. R. R. Tolkien. Then use this information to argue that Rowling's indebtedness to these authors illustrates her imaginative use of classics.

Classical Arguments

MARTIN LUTHER KING JR.

Martin Luther King Jr. (1929–1968) was born in Atlanta, Georgia, and was educated at Morehouse College, Crozer Theological Seminary, and Boston University. Ordained a Baptist minister in his father's church in 1947, King soon became involved in civil rights activities in the South. In 1957 he founded the Southern Christian Leadership Conference and established himself as America's most prominent spokesman for nonviolent racial integration. In 1963 he was named *Time* magazine's Man of the Year; in 1964 he was given the Nobel Peace Prize. In 1968 he was assassinated in Memphis, Tennessee. His writing includes *Letter from Birmingham Jail* (1963), *Why We Can't Wait* (1964), and *Where Do We Go from Here: Chaos or Community?* (1967). "I Have a Dream" is the famous speech King delivered at the Lincoln Memorial at the end of the March on Washington in 1963 to commemorate the one hundredth anniversary of the Emancipation Proclamation. King argues that realization of the dream of freedom for all American citizens is long overdue.

I Have a Dream

FIVE SCORE YEARS ago, a great American, in whose symbolic shadow we stand, signed the Emancipation Proclamation. This momentous decree came as a great beacon light of hope to millions of Negro slaves who had been seared in the flames of withering injustice. It came as a joyous daybreak to end the long night of captivity.

But one hundred years later, we must face the tragic fact that the Negro is still not free. One hundred years later, the life of the Negro is still sadly crippled by the manacles of segregation and the chains of discrimination. One hundred years later, the Negro lives on a lonely island of poverty in the midst of a vast ocean of material prosperity. One hundred years later, the Negro is still languishing in the corners of American society and finds himself an exile in his own land. So we have come here today to dramatize an appalling condition.

In a sense we have come to our nation's Capitol to cash a check. When the architects of our republic wrote the magnificent words of the Constitution and the Declaration of

---

There will be neither rest nor tranquility in America until the Negro is granted his citizenship rights.

Independence, they were signing a promissory note to which every American was to fall heir. This note was a promise that all men would be guaranteed the unalienable rights of life, liberty, and the pursuit of happiness.

It is obvious today that America has defaulted on this promissory note insofar as her citizens of color are concerned. Instead of honoring this sacred obligation, America has given the Negro people a bad check; a check which has come back marked "insufficient funds." But we refuse to believe that the bank of justice is bankrupt. We refuse to believe that there are insufficient funds in the great vaults of opportunity of this nation. So we have come to cash this check—a check that will give us upon demand the riches of freedom and the security of justice. We have also come to this hallowed spot to remind America of the fierce urgency of *now*. This is no time to engage in the luxury of cooling off or to take the tranquilizing drug of gradualism. *Now* is the time to make real the promises of Democracy. *Now* is the time to rise from the dark and desolate valley of segregation to the sunlit path of racial justice. *Now* is the time to open the doors of opportunity to all of God's children. *Now* is the time to lift our nation from the quicksands of racial injustice to the solid rock of brotherhood.

It would be fatal for the nation to overlook the urgency of the moment and to underestimate the determination of the Negro. This sweltering summer of the Negro's legitimate discontent will not pass until there is an invigorating autumn of freedom and equality. 1963 is not an end, but a beginning. Those who hope that the Negro needed to blow off steam and will now be content will have a rude awakening if the nation returns to business as usual. There will be neither rest nor tranquility in America until the Negro is granted his citizenship rights. The whirlwinds of revolt will continue to shake the foundations of our nation until the bright day of justice emerges.

But there is something I must say to my people who stand on the warm threshold which leads into the palace of justice. In the process of gaining our rightful place we must not be guilty of wrongful deeds. Let us not seek to satisfy our thirst for freedom by drinking from the cup of bitterness and hatred. We must forever conduct our struggle on the high plane of dignity and discipline. We must not allow our creative protest to degenerate into physical violence. Again and again we must rise to the majestic heights of meeting physical force with soul force. The marvelous new militancy which has engulfed the Negro community must not lead us to a distrust of all white people, for many of our white brothers, as evidenced by their presence here today, have come to realize that their destiny is tied up with our destiny and their freedom is inextricably bound to our freedom. We cannot walk alone.

And as we walk, we must make the pledge that we shall march ahead. We cannot turn back. There are those who are asking the devotees of civil rights, "When will you be satisfied?" We can never be satisfied as long as the Negro is the victim of the unspeakable horrors of police brutality. We can never be satisfied as long as our bodies, heavy with the fatigue of travel, cannot gain lodging in the motels of the highways and the hotels of the cities. We cannot be satisfied as long as the Negro's basic mobility is from a smaller ghetto to a larger one. We can never be satisfied as long as a Negro in Mississippi cannot vote and a Negro in New York believes he has nothing for which to vote. No, no, we are not satisfied, and we will not be satisfied until justice rolls down like waters and righteousness like a mighty stream.

I am not unmindful that some of you have come here out of great trials and tribulations. Some of you have come fresh from narrow jail cells. Some of you have come from areas where your quest for freedom left you battered by the storms of persecution and staggered by the winds of police brutality. You have been the veterans of creative suffering. Continue to work with the faith that unearned suffering is redemptive. 8

Go back to Mississippi, go back to Alabama, go back to South Carolina, go back to Georgia, go back to Louisiana, go back to the slums and ghettoes of our northern cities, knowing that somehow this situation can and will be changed. Let us not wallow in the valley of despair. 9

I say to you today, my friends, that in spite of the difficulties and frustrations of the moment I still have a dream. It is a dream deeply rooted in the American dream. 10

I have a dream that one day this nation will rise up and live out the true meaning of its creed: "We hold these truths to be self-evident; that all men are created equal." 11

I have a dream that one day on the red hills of Georgia the sons of former slaves and the sons of former slaveowners will be able to sit down together at the table of brotherhood. 12

I have a dream that the state of Mississippi, a desert state sweltering with the heat of injustice and oppression, will be transformed into an oasis of freedom and justice. 13

I have a dream that my four little children will one day live in a nation where they will not be judged by the color of their skin but by the content of their character. 14

I have a dream today. 15

I have a dream that the state of Alabama, whose governor's lips are presently dripping with the words of interposition and nullification, will be transformed into a situation where little black boys and black girls will be able to join hands with little white boys and white girls and walk together as sisters and brothers. 16

I have a dream today. 17

I have a dream that one day every valley shall be exalted, every hill and mountain shall be made low, the rough places will be made plain, and the crooked places will be made straight, and the glory of the Lord shall be revealed, and all flesh shall see it together. 18

This is our hope. This is the faith with which I return to the South. With this faith we will be able to hew out of the mountain of despair a stone of hope. With this faith we will be able to transform the jangling discords of our nation into a beautiful symphony of brotherhood. With this faith we will be able to work together, to pray together, to struggle together, to go to jail together, to stand up for freedom together, knowing that we will be free one day. 19

This will be the day when all of God's children will be able to sing with new meaning. 20

> My country, 'tis of thee
> Sweet land of liberty,
>   Of thee I sing:
> Land where my fathers died,
> Land of the pilgrims' pride,
> From every mountainside
>   Let freedom ring.

And if America is to be a great nation this must become true. So let freedom ring from the prodigious hilltops of New Hampshire. Let freedom ring from the mighty mountains of New York. Let freedom ring from the heightening Alleghenies of Pennsylvania! 21

Let freedom ring from the snowcapped Rockies of Colorado! 22

Let freedom ring from the curvaceous peaks of California!   23

But not only that; let freedom ring from Stone Mountain   24
of Georgia!

Let freedom ring from Lookout Mountain of Tennessee!   25

Let freedom ring from every hill and molehill of Mississippi.   26
From every mountainside, let freedom ring.

When we let freedom ring, when we let it ring from every   27
village and every hamlet, from every state and every city, we
will be able to speed up that day when all of God's children,
black men and white men, Jews and Gentiles, Protestants and
Catholics, will be able to join hands and sing in the words of
the old Negro spiritual, "Free at last! free at last! thank God
almighty, we are free at last!"

For Study and Discussion

QUESTIONS ABOUT PURPOSE

1. King has at least two strong messages. One message is local and
   immediate; the other one is national and long range. How
   would you summarize those two messages?
2. How does King use his speech to reinforce his belief in nonvi-
   olence as the appropriate tool in the struggle for civil rights?

QUESTIONS ABOUT AUDIENCE

1. King gave this speech to a huge live audience that had come to
   Washington for a march for freedom and civil rights. How much
   larger is the national audience he is addressing, and why is that
   audience also important?
2. This speech is one of the most widely anthologized of modern
   speeches. What audiences does it continue to appeal to and why?

QUESTIONS ABOUT STRATEGIES

1. How does King draw on metaphor to engage his listeners' feelings of injustice and give them hope for a new day?
2. In what way do King's talents as a minister serve his purposes in
   the speech?

For Writing and Research

1. *Analyze* the economic metaphors King uses throughout his speech.
2. *Practice* by persuading a group of your fellow students that it is the "content of their character" that is the measure of their success.
3. *Argue* that much of King's dream has or has not come true since he gave this speech over forty years ago.
4. *Synthesize* the arguments about race in Booker T. Washington's "Atlanta Exhibition Address" and W. E. B. Dubois's "The Niagara Movement Manifesto." Then trace the development of race relations in the United States.

Rachel Carson (1907–1964) was born in Spring-field, Pennsylvania, and was educated at Pennsylvania College for Women and Johns Hopkins University. After graduation she taught for several years in the zoology department of the University of Maryland before accepting a position as aquatic biologist with the United States Bureau of Fisheries (now the Fish and Wildlife Service). She worked at the bureau for over fifteen years, rising to the position of editor-in-chief of publications. Throughout her period of government service Carson wrote about various aspects of her work for both popular audiences (*Under the Sea-Wind: A Naturalist's Picture of Ocean Life*, 1941) and scientific audiences (*Fish and Shellfish of the Middle Atlantic Coast*, 1945). With the publication of *The Sea Around Us* (1951), which won the National Book Award, she was able to resign her editorial position and devote full time to her writing. Her books include *The Edge of the Sea* (1955), *Silent Spring* (1962), and *The Sense of Wonder* (1965). *Silent Spring*, certainly Carson's most influential book, was the first major attack on the harmful use of pesticides. In "The Obligation to Endure," reprinted from *Silent Spring*, Carson's argument that the imprudent use of chemicals in the environment threatens our ability to endure seems even more compelling.

The Obligation to Endure

THE HISTORY OF life on earth has been a history of inter- 1
action between living things and their surroundings. To a large extent, the physical form and the habits of the earth's vegetation and its animal life have been molded by the

environment. Considering the whole span of earthly time, the opposite effect, in which life actually modifies its surroundings, has been relatively slight. Only within the moment of time represented by the present century has one species—man—acquired significant power to alter the nature of his world.

During the past quarter century this power has not only increased to one of disturbing magnitude but it has changed in character. The most alarming of all man's assaults upon the environment is the contamination of air, earth, rivers, and sea with dangerous and even lethal materials. This pollution is for the most part irrecoverable; the chain of evil it initiates not only in the world that must support life but in living tissues is for the most part irreversible. In this now universal contamination of the environment, chemicals are the sinister and little-recognized partners of radiation in changing the very nature of the world—the very nature of its life. Strontium 90, released through nuclear explosions into the air, comes to earth in rain or drifts down as fallout, lodges in soil, enters into the grass or corn or wheat grown there, and in time takes up its abode in the bones of a human being, there to remain until his death. Similarly, chemicals sprayed on croplands or forests or gardens lie long in soil, entering into living organisms, passing from one to another in a chain of poisoning and death. Or they pass mysteriously by underground streams until they emerge and through the alchemy of air and sunlight, combine into new forms that kill vegetation, sicken cattle, and work unknown harm on those who drink from once pure wells. As Albert Schweitzer has said, "Man can hardly even recognize the devils of his own creation."

It took hundreds of millions of years to produce the life that now inhabits the earth—eons of time in which that developing and evolving and diversifying life reached a state of adjustment and balance with its surroundings. The environment, rigorously shaping and directing the life it supported, contained elements that were hostile as well as supporting. Certain rocks gave out dangerous radiation; even within the light of the sun, from which all life draws its energy, there were short-wave radiations with power to injure. Given time—time not in years but in millennia—life adjusts, and a balance has been reached. For time is the essential ingredient; but in the modern world there is no time.

The rapidity of change and the speed with which new situa-   4
tions are created follow the impetuous and heedless pace of man rather than the deliberate pace of nature. Radiation is no longer merely the background radiation of rocks, the bombardment of cosmic rays, the ultraviolet of the sun that have existed before there was any life on earth; radiation is now the unnatural creation of man's tampering with the atom. The chemicals to which life is asked to make its adjustment are no longer merely the calcium and silica and copper and all the rest of the minerals washed out of the rocks and carried in rivers to the sea; they are the synthetic creations of man's inventive mind, brewed in his laboratories, and having no counterparts, in nature.

To adjust to these chemicals would require time on the scale   5
that is nature's; it would require not merely the years of a man's life but the life of generations. And even this, were it by some miracle possible, would be futile, for the new chemicals come from our laboratories in an endless stream; almost five hundred annually find their way into actual use in the United States alone. The figure is staggering and its implications are not easily grasped—500 new chemicals to which the bodies of men and animals are required somehow to adapt each year, chemicals totally outside the limits of biologic experience.

Among them are many that are used in man's war against   6
nature. Since the mid-1940's over 200 basic chemicals have been created for use in killing insects, weeds, rodents, and other organisms described in the modern vernacular as "pests"; and they are sold under several thousand different brand names.

These sprays, dusts, and aerosols are now applied almost   7
universally to farms, gardens, forests, and homes—nonselective chemicals that have the power to kill every insect, the "good" and the "bad," to still the song of birds and the leaping of fish in the streams, to coat the leaves with a deadly film, and to linger on in soil—all this though the intended target may be only a few weeds or insects. Can anyone believe it is possible to lay down such a barrage of poisons on the surface

of the earth without making it unfit for all life? They should not be called "insecticides," but "biocides."

The whole process of spraying seems caught up in an end- 8 less spiral. Since DDT was released for civilian use, a process of escalation has been going on in which ever more toxic materials must be found. This has happened because insects, in a triumphant vindication of Darwin's principle of the survival of the fittest, have evolved super races immune to the particular insecticide used, hence a deadlier one has always to be developed—and then a deadlier one than that. It has happened also because, for reasons to be described later, destructive insects often undergo a "flareback," or resurgence, after spraying in numbers greater than before. Thus the chemical war is never won, and all life is caught in its violent crossfire.

Along with the possibility of the extinction of mankind by 9 nuclear war, the central problem of our age has therefore become the contamination of man's total environment with such substances of incredible potential for harm—substances that accumulate in the tissues of plants and animals and even penetrate the germ cells to shatter or alter the very material of heredity upon which the shape of the future depends.

Some would-be architects of our future look toward a time 10 when it will be possible to alter the human germ plasm by design. But we may easily be doing so now by inadvertence, for many chemicals, like radiation, bring about gene mutations. It is ironic to think that man might determine his own future by something so seemingly trivial as the choice of an insect spray.

All this has been risked—for what? Future historians may 11 well be amazed by our distorted sense of proportion. How could intelligent beings seek to control a few unwanted species by a method that contaminated the entire environment and brought the threat of disease and death even to their own kind? Yet this is precisely what we have done. We have done it, moreover, for reasons that collapse the moment we examine them. We are told that the enormous and expanding use of pesticides is necessary to maintain farm production. Yet is our real problem not one of *overproduction?* Our farms, despite measures to remove acreages from production and to pay farmers *not* to produce, have yielded such a staggering excess of crops that the American taxpayer in 1962 is paying out more than one billion dollars a year as the total carrying cost of the surplus-food storage program. And is the situation helped when one branch of the Agriculture Department tries to reduce production while another states, as it did in 1958, "It is believed generally that reduction of crop acreages under provisions of the Soil Bank will stimulate interest in use of chemicals to obtain maximum production on the land retained in crops."

All this is not to say there is no insect problem and no need of control. I am saying, rather, that control must be geared to realities, not to mythical situations, and that the methods employed must be such that they do not destroy us along with the insects.   12

The problem whose attempted solution has brought such a train of disaster in its wake is an accompaniment of our modern way of life. Long before the age of man, insects inhabited the earth—a group of extraordinarily varied and adaptable beings. Over the course of time since man's advent, a small percentage of the more than half a million species of insects have come into conflict with human welfare in two principal ways: as competitors for the food supply and as carriers of human disease.   13

Disease-carrying insects become important where human beings are crowded together, especially under conditions where sanitation is poor, as in time of natural disaster or war or in situations of extreme poverty and deprivation. Then control of some sort becomes necessary. It is a sobering fact, however, as we shall presently see, that the method of massive chemical control has had only limited success, and also threatens to worsen the very conditions it is intended to curb.   14

Under primitive agricultural conditions the farmer had few insect problems. These arose with the intensification of agriculture—the devotion of immense acreages to a single crop. Such a system set the stage for explosive increases in specific insect populations. Single-crop farming does not take advantage of the principles by which nature works; it is agriculture as an engineer might conceive it to be. Nature has introduced great   15 variety into the landscape, but man has displayed a passion for simplifying it. Thus he undoes the built-in checks and balances by which nature holds the species within bounds. One important natural check is a limit on the amount of suitable habitat for each species. Obviously then, an insect that lives on wheat can build up its population to much higher levels on a farm devoted to wheat than on one in which wheat is intermingled with other crops to which the insect is not adapted.

The same thing happens in other situations. A generation or more ago, the towns of large areas of the United States lined their streets with the noble elm tree. Now the beauty they hopefully created is threatened with complete destruction as disease sweeps through the elms carried by a beetle that would have only limited chance to build up large populations and to spread from tree to tree if the elms were only occasional trees in a richly diversified planting. 16

Another factor in the modern insect problem is one that must be viewed against a background of geologic and human history: the spreading of thousands of different kinds of organisms from their native homes to invade new territories. This worldwide migration has been studied and graphically described by the British ecologist Charles Elton in his recent book *The Ecology of Invasions.* During the Cretaceous Period, some hundred million years ago, flooding seas cut many land bridges between continents and living things found themselves confined in what Elton calls "colossal separate nature reserves." There, isolated from others of their kind, they developed many new species. When some of the land masses were joined again, about 15 million years ago, these species began to move out into new territories—a movement that is not only still in progress but is now receiving considerable assistance from man. 17

The importation of plants is the primary agent in the modern spread of species, for animals have almost invariably gone along with the plants, quarantine being a comparatively recent and not completely effective innovation. The United States Office of Plant Introduction alone has introduced almost 200,000 species and varieties of plants from all over the world. Nearly half of the 180 or so major insect enemies of 18 plants in the United States are accidental imports from abroad, and most of them have come as hitchhikers on plants.

In new territory, out of reach of the restraining hand of [19] the natural enemies that kept down its numbers in its native land, an invading plant or animal is able to become enormously abundant. Thus it is no accident that our most troublesome insects are introduced species.

These invasions, both the naturally occurring and those [20] dependent on human assistance, are likely to continue indefinitely. Quarantine and massive chemical campaigns are only extremely expensive ways of buying time. We are faced, according to Dr. Elton, "with a life-and-death need not just to find new technological means of suppressing this plant or that animal"; instead we need the basic knowledge of animal populations and their relations to their surroundings that will "promote an even balance and damp down the explosive power of outbreaks and new invasions."

Much of the necessary knowledge is now available but we [21] do not use it. We train ecologists in our universities and even employ them in our governmental agencies but we seldom take their advice. We allow the chemical death rain to fall as though there were no alternative, whereas in fact there are many, and our ingenuity could soon discover many more if given opportunity.

Have we fallen into a mesmerized state that makes us ac- [22] cept as inevitable that which is inferior or detrimental as though having lost the will or the vision to demand that which is good? Such thinking, in the words of the ecologist Paul Shepard, "idealizes life with only its head out of water, inches above the limits of toleration of the corruption of its own environment . . . Why should we tolerate a diet of weak poisons, a home in insipid surroundings, a circle of acquaintances who are not quite our enemies, the noise of motors with just enough relief to prevent insanity? Who would want to live in a world which is just not quite fatal?"

Yet such a world is pressed upon us. The crusade to create a [23] chemically sterile, insect-free world seems to have engendered a fanatic zeal on the part of many specialists and most of the so-called control agencies. On every hand there is evidence that those engaged in spraying operations exercise a ruthless power. "The regulatory entomologists . . . function as prosecutor, judge and jury, tax assessor and collector and sheriff to enforce their own orders," said Connecticut entomologist Neely Turner. The most flagrant abuses go unchecked in both state and federal agencies.

It is not my contention that chemical insecticides must never 24 be used. I do contend that we have put poisonous and biologically potent chemicals indiscriminately into the hands of persons largely or wholly ignorant of their potentials for harm. We have subjected enormous numbers of people to contact with these poisons, without their consent and often without their knowledge. If the Bill of Rights contains no guarantee that a citizen shall be secure against lethal poisons distributed either by private individuals or by public officials, it is surely only because our forefathers, despite their considerable wisdom and foresight, could conceive of no such problem.

I contend, furthermore, that we have allowed these chemicals to be used with little or no advance investigation of their 25 effect on soil, water, wildlife, and man himself. Future generations are unlikely to condone our lack of prudent concern for the integrity of the natural world that supports all life.

There is still very limited awareness of the nature of the 26 threat. This is an era of specialists, each of whom sees his own problem and is unaware of or intolerant of the larger frame into which it fits. It is also an era dominated by industry, in which the right to make a dollar at whatever cost is seldom challenged. When the public protests, confronted with some obvious evidence of damaging results of pesticide applications, it is fed little tranquilizing pills of half truth. We urgently need an end to these false assurances, to the sugar coating of unpalatable facts. It is the public that is being asked to assume the risks that the insect controllers calculate. The public must decide whether it wishes to continue on the present road, and it can do so only when in full possession of the facts. In the words of Jean Rostand, "The obligation to endure gives us the right to know."

For Study and Discussion

QUESTIONS ABOUT PURPOSE

1. What is Carson's primary purpose in this essay? How does the essay's title help establish that purpose?
2. How does Carson want us to rearrange our priorities?

QUESTIONS ABOUT AUDIENCE

1. What assumptions does Carson make about the identity of her readers? How does she use the pronoun *we*—as in "we have done it, moreover, for reasons that collapse the moment we examine them"—to identify those readers?
2. If Carson is addressing readers who would have the power to impose strict controls on pesticides, what objections from them would she have to anticipate when she planned her essay? Would the essay be effective with that audience? Why?

QUESTIONS ABOUT STRATEGIES

1. How does Carson's use of historical perspective at the beginning (and in several other sections) of her essay help establish the rationality of her argument?
2. How does her citation of facts about the creation of new chemicals, the escalation of immunity, and the cost of overproduction lend authority to her case?

For Writing and Research

1. *Analyze* Carson's assumptions about the "thing" that has been chiefly responsible for the contamination of our world.
2. *Practice* by arguing for some specific action that would help clean up our environment.
3. *Argue* that the chemicals used by agrobusiness have improved or contaminated our food supply.
4. *Synthesize* some of the major arguments about the environment that have been made since Carson's argument—for example, Al Gore's Oscar-winning documentary *An Inconvenient Truth*. Then argue that we have or have not made progress in our attempt to solve our environmental problems.

H. L. MENCKEN

H(enry) L(ouis) Mencken (1880–1956) was born in Baltimore, Maryland. After graduating from Brooklyn Polytechnic Institute at the age of sixteen, he decided to forego a college education for a plan of private study and a career in journalism. He joined the *Baltimore Morning Herald* as a reporter and later worked for the Sun Syndicate. Although he maintained his contact with these Baltimore papers throughout his career, he became engaged in many other publishing projects—as literary advisor to Alfred A. Knopf, as coeditor with George Jean Nathan of *The Smart Set,* and then, several years later, as cofounder (with Nathan) of *The American Mercury.* Mencken's own writing ranges from informative cultural history (*The American Language,* 1919) to outrageous iconoclasm (the essays that filled six volumes aptly titled *Prejudices,* 1919–1927) to several volumes of engaging autobiography. Although critics in his time considered him a radical, contemporary readers find most of his opinions conservative. In "The Penalty of Death," taken from the anthology *A Mencken Chrestomathy* (1949), Mencken tries to refute the two common arguments against capital punishment by arguing that the execution of criminals satisfies the basic human need for revenge.

The Penalty of Death

O F THE ARGUMENTS against capital punishment that   1
issue from uplifters, two are commonly heard most often, to wit:

1. That hanging a man (or frying him or gassing him) is a dreadful business, degrading to those who have to do it and revolting to those who have to witness it.

2. That it is useless, for it does not deter others from the same crime.

The first of these arguments, it seems to me, is plainly too weak to need serious refutation. All it says, in brief, is that the work of the hangman is unpleasant. Granted. But suppose it is? It may be quite necessary to society for all that. There are, indeed, many other jobs that are unpleasant, and yet no one thinks of abolishing them—that of the plumber, that of the soldier, that of the garbage-man, that of the priest hearing confessions, that of the sand-hog, and so on. Moreover, what evidence is there that any actual hangman complains of his work? I have heard none. On the contrary, I have known many who delighted in their ancient art, and practised it proudly.

In the second argument of the abolitionists there is rather more force, but even here, I believe, the ground under them is shaky. Their fundamental error consists in assuming that the whole aim of punishing criminals is to deter other (potential) criminals—that we hang or electrocute A simply in order to so alarm B that he will not kill C. This, I believe, is an assumption which confuses a part with the whole. Deterrence, obviously, is *one* of the aims of punishment, but it is surely not the only one. On the contrary, there are at least half a dozen, and some are probably quite as important. At least one of them, practically considered, is *more* important. Commonly, it is described as revenge, but revenge is really not the word for it. I borrow a better term from the late Aristotle: *katharsis. Katharsis,* so used, means a salubrious discharge of emotions, a healthy letting off of steam. A school-boy, disliking his teacher, deposits a tack upon the pedagogical chair; the teacher jumps and the boy laughs. This is *katharsis.* What I contend is that one of the prime objects of all judicial punishments is to afford the same grateful relief (*a*) to the immediate victims of the criminal punished, and (*b*) to the general body of moral and timorous men.

These persons, and particularly the first group, are concerned only indirectly with deterring other criminals. The thing they crave primarily is the satisfaction of seeing the criminal actually before them suffer as he made them suffer. What they want is the peace of mind that goes with the feeling that accounts are squared. Until they get that satisfaction they are in a state of emotional tension, and hence unhappy. The instant they get it they are comfortable. I do not argue that this yearning is noble; I simply argue that it is almost universal among human beings. In the face of injuries that are unimportant and can be borne without damage it may yield to higher impulses; that is to say, it may yield to what is called Christian charity. But when the injury is serious Christianity is adjourned, and even saints reach for their sidearms. It is plainly asking too much of human nature to expect it to conquer so natural an impulse. A keeps a store and has a bookkeeper, B. B. steals $700, employs it in playing at dice or bingo, and is cleaned out. What is A to do? Let B go? If he does so he will be unable to sleep at night. The sense of injury, of injustice, of frustration will haunt him like pruritus. So he turns B over to the police, and they hustle B to prison. Thereafter A can sleep. More, he has pleasant dreams. He pictures B chained to the wall of a dungeon a hundred feet underground, devoured by rats and scorpions. It is so agreeable that it makes him forget his $700. He has got his *katharsis*.

The same thing precisely takes place on a larger scale when   5 there is a crime which destroys a whole community's sense of security. Every law-abiding citizen feels menaced and frustrated until the criminals have been struck down—until the communal capacity to get even with them, and more than even, has been dramatically demonstrated. Here, manifestly, the business of deterring others is no more than an afterthought. The main thing is to destroy the concrete scoundrels whose act has alarmed everyone, and thus made everyone unhappy. Until they are brought to book that unhappiness continues; when the law has been executed upon them there is a sigh of relief. In other words, there is *katharsis*.

I know of no public demand for the death penalty for   6 ordinary crimes, even for ordinary homicides. Its infliction would shock all men of normal decency of feeling. But for crimes involving the deliberate and inexcusable taking of human life, by men openly defiant of all civilized order—for such crimes it seems, to nine men out of ten, a just and proper punishment. Any lesser penalty leaves them feeling that the criminal has got the better of society—that he is free to add insult to injury by laughing. That feeling can be dissipated only by a recourse to *katharsis,* the invention of the aforesaid Aristotle. It is more effectively and economically achieved, as human nature now is, by wafting the criminal to realms of bliss.

The real objection to capital punishment doesn't lie   7
against the actual extermination of the condemned, but against our brutal American habit of putting it off so long. After all, every one of us must die soon or late, and a murderer, it must be assumed, is one who makes that sad fact the cornerstone of his metaphysic. But it is one thing to die, and quite another thing to lie for long months and even years under the shadow of death. No sane man would choose such a finish. All of us, despite the Prayer Book, long for a swift and unexpected end. Unhappily, a murderer, under the irrational American system, is tortured for what, to him, must seem a whole series of eternities. For months on end he sits in prison while his lawyers carry on their idiotic buffoonery with writs, injunctions, mandamuses, and appeals. In order to get his money (or that of his friends) they have to feed him with hope. Now and then, by the imbecility of a judge or some trick of juridic science, they actually justify it. But let us say that, his money all gone, they finally throw up their hands. Their client is now ready for the rope or the chair. But he must still wait for months before it fetches him.

That wait, I believe, is horribly cruel. I have seen more   8
than one man sitting in the death-house, and I don't want to see any more. Worse, it is wholly useless. Why should he wait at all? Why not hang him the day after the last court dissipates his last hope? Why torture him as not even cannibals would torture their victims? The common answer is that he must have time to make his peace with God. But how long does that take? It may be accomplished, I believe, in two hours quite as comfortably as in two years. There are, indeed, no temporal limitations upon God. He could forgive a whole herd of murderers in a millionth of a second. More, it has been done.

For Study and Discussion

QUESTIONS ABOUT PURPOSE

1. What statements in Mencken's essay are probably meant to shock some of his readers?
2. Does Mencken intend to make a logical appeal? If so, in what ways?

QUESTIONS ABOUT AUDIENCE

1. In what ways do you think contemporary readers' attitudes about the death penalty might be different from those of readers in the 1920s, when this essay was first published? In what ways might they not have changed?
2. To what emotions in his audience is Mencken trying to appeal?

QUESTIONS ABOUT STRATEGIES

1. Why does Mencken start by giving two arguments *against* his thesis?
2. Why does Mencken start paragraph 6 with three qualifying sentences?

For Writing and Research

1. *Analyze* what is fact, judgment, eyewitness, and expert testimony in Mencken's essay.
2. *Practice* by citing the facts, judgments, and testimony that lead you to support or reject capital punishment.
3. *Argue* that Mencken's tone and language encourage you to accept or reject his argument.
4. *Synthesize* the impact of DNA research on several capital punishment cases. Then argue that this new scientific research supports or undercuts public opinion on execution.

Jonathan Swift (1667–1745) was born in Dublin, Ireland, and was educated at Trinity College, Dublin. When his cousin, John Dryden, told him he would never be a poet, Swift reluctantly decided on a career in the church. He earned his M.A. at Oxford, was ordained an Anglican priest, and was assigned a parish in Kilroot, Ireland. Swift soon resigned his position and began traveling to England to negotiate church business, to participate in political activities, and to plead for a special church assignment in London. He was forced to settle for a minor appointment, deanship of St. Patrick's Cathedral in Dublin. As demonstrated in his best-known book, *Gulliver's Travels* (1726), Swift's real gift as a writer is as a satirist. His other writing includes attacks on the corruption in religion and learning (*A Tale of a Tub,* 1704; *The Battle of the Books,* 1704) and this preposterous parody of a solution to the difficulties between Ireland and England— "A Modest Proposal" (1729).

A Modest Proposal
For Preventing the Children of Ireland from Being a Burden to Their Parents or Country; and for Making Them Beneficial to the Publick

I T IS A melancholly Object to those, who walk through the great Town or travel in the Country; when they see the Streets, the Roads and Cabbin-doors crowded with Beggars of the Female Sex, followed by three, four, or six Children all in Rags, and importuning every Passenger for an Alms. These

Mothers, instead of being able to work for their honest Livelyhood, are forced to employ all their Time in stroling to beg
Sustenance for their helpless Infants; who, as they grow up,
either turn Thieves for want of Work; or leave their dear Native Country, to fight for the Pretender in Spain, or sell themselves to the Barbadoes.

I think it is agreed by all Parties, that this prodigious num-   2
ber of Children in the Arms, or on the Backs, or at the Heels
of their Mothers, and frequently of their Fathers, is in the present deplorable state of the Kingdom, a very great additional
Grievance; and therefore, whoever could find out a fair, cheap,
and easy Method of making these Children sound and useful
Members of the Commonwealth, would deserve so well of
the Publick, as to have his Statue set up for a Preserver of the
Nation.

But my Intention is very far from being confined to pro-   3
vide only for the Children of professed Beggars: It is of a
much greater Extent, and shall take in the whole Number of
Infants at a certain Age, who are born of Parents in effect as
little able to support them, as those who demand our Charity in the Streets.

As to my own Part, having turned my Thoughts, for many   4
Years, upon this important Subject, and maturely weighed
the several Schemes of other Projectors, I have always found
them grossly mistaken in their Computation. It is true, a
Child, just dropt from its Dam, may be supported by her
Milk, for a Solar Year with little other Nourishment; at most
not above the Value of two Shillings; which the Mother may
certainly get, or the Value in Scraps, by her lawful Occupa-
tion of Begging: and it is exactly at one Year old that I propose to provide for them in such a manner, as, instead of
being a Charge upon their Parents or the Parish, or wanting
Food and Raiment for the rest of their Lives; they shall, on
the contrary, contribute to the Feeding and partly to the
Cloathing, of many Thousands.

There is likewise another great Advantage in my Scheme,   5
that it will prevent those voluntary Abortions and that horrid
practice of Women murdering their Bastard Children, alas!

too frequent among us; Sacrificing the poor innocent Babes, I doubt, more to avoid the Expence than the Shame; which would move Tears and Pity in the most Savage and inhuman breast.

The number of Souls in Ireland being usually reckoned 6 one Million and a half; of these I calculate there may be about Two hundred Thousand Couple whose Wives are Breeders; from which number I subtract thirty Thousand Couples, who are able to maintain their own Children, although I apprehend there cannot be so many under the present Distresses of the Kingdom; but this being granted there will remain an Hundred and Seventy Thousand Breeders. I again Subtract Fifty Thousand, for those Women who miscarry, or whose Children die by Accident, or Disease, within the Year. There only remain an Hundred and Twenty Thousand Children of poor Parents, annually born: The Question therefore is, How this Number shall be reared, and provided for? Which, as I have already said, under the present Situation of Affairs, is utterly impossible, by all the Methods hitherto proposed: For we can neither employ them in Handicraft or Agriculture; we neither build Houses, (I mean in the Country) nor cultivate Land: They can very seldom pick up a Livelyhood by Stealing until they arrive at six Years old; except where they are of towardly Parts; although, I confess, they learn the Rudiments much earlier; during which Time, they can, however be properly looked upon only as Probationers; as I have been informed by a principal Gentleman in the Country of Cavan, who protested to me, that he never knew above one or two Instances under the Age of six, even in a part of the Kingdom so renowned for the quickest Proficiency in that Art.

I am assured by our Merchants, that a Boy or a Girl before 7 twelve Years old, is no saleable Commodity; and even when they come to this Age, they will not yield above Three Pounds, or Three Pounds and half a Crown at most, on the Exchange; which cannot turn to Account either to the Parents or the Kingdom; the Charge of Nutriment and Rags, having been at least four Times that Value.

I shall now therefore humbly propose my own Thoughts; 8
which I hope will not be liable to the least Objection.

I have been assured by a very knowing American of my 9
Acquaintance in London, that a young healthy Child, well
nursed is, at a Year old, a most delicious, nourishing and
wholesome Food, whether Stewed, Roasted, Baked, or Boiled;
and I make no doubt that it will equally serve in a Fricasie,
or Ragoust.

I do therefore humbly offer it to publick Consideration, 10
that of the Hundred and Twenty Thousand Children, already computed, Twenty thousand may be reserved for
Breed; whereof only one Fourth Part to be Males; which is
more than we allow to Sheep, black Cattle, or Swine; and my
Reason is, that these Children are seldom the Fruits of Marriage, a Circumstance not much regarded by our Savages;
therefore, one Male will be sufficient to serve four Females.
That the remaining Hundred thousand, may, at a Year old
be offered in Sale to the Persons of Quality and Fortune,
through the Kingdom; always advising the Mother to let
them suck plentifully in the last Month, so as to render them
plump, and fat for a good Table. A Child will make two
Dishes at an Entertainment for Friends; and when the Family
dines alone, the fore or hind Quarter will make a reasonable
Dish; and seasoned with a little Pepper or Salt, will be very
good Boiled on the fourth Day, especially in Winter.

I have reckoned upon a Medium, that a Child just born 11
will weigh Twelve Pounds; and in a solar Year, if tolerably
nursed, increaseth to 28 Pounds.

I grant this Food will be somewhat dear, and therefore 12
very proper for Landlords; who, as they have already de-
voured most of the Parents, seem to have the best Title to the
Children.

Infant's Flesh will be in Season throughout the Year; but 13
more plentiful in March, and a little before and after for we are
told by a grave Author an eminent French Physician, that Fish
being a prolifick Dyet, there are more Children born in
Roman Catholick Countries about Nine Months after Lent,
than at any other Season: Therefore reckoning a Year after

Lent, the Markets will be more glutted than usual; because the Number of Popish Infants, is, at least, three to one in this Kingdom; and therefore it will have one other Collateral advantage; by lessening the Number of Papists among us.

I have already computed the Charge of nursing a Beggar's 14 Child (in which List I reckon all Cottagers, Labourers, and Four fifths of the Farmers) to be about two Shillings per Annum, Rags included; and I believe no Gentleman would repine to give Ten Shillings for the Carcase of a good fat Child; which, as I have said, will make four Dishes of excellent nutritive meat, when he hath only some particular Friend, or his own Family, to dine with him. Thus the Squire will learn to be a good Landlord, and grow popular among his Tenants; the Mother will have Eight Shillings net Profit, and be fit for Work till she produce another Child.

Those who are more thrifty (as I must confess the Times 15 require) may flay the Carcase; the Skin of which artificially dressed, will make admirable Gloves for Ladies, and Summer Boots for fine Gentlemen.

As to our City of Dublin; Shambles may be appointed for 16 this Purpose, in the most convenient Parts of it, and Butchers we may be assured will not be wanting; although I rather recommend buying the Children alive, and dressing them hot from the Knife, as we do roasting Pigs.

A very worthy Person, a true Lover of his Country, and 17 whose Virtues I highly esteem, was lately pleased, in discoursing on this Matter, to offer a Refinement upon my Scheme. He said, that many Gentlemen of this Kingdom, having of late destroyed their Deer; he conceived that the Want of Venison might be well supplied by the Bodies of young Lads and Maidens, not exceeding fourteen Years of Age, nor under twelve; so great a Number of both Sexes in every County being ready to Starve, for want of Work and Service: And these to be disposed of by their Parents, if alive, or otherwise by their nearest Relations. But with due Deference to so excellent a Friend, and so deserving a Patriot, I cannot be altogether in his Sentiments. For as to the Males, my American Acquaintance assured me from frequent Experience, that their Flesh was generally tough and lean, like that of our School-boys, by continual Exercise, and their Taste disagreeable; and to fatten them would not answer the Charge. Then, as to the Females, it would, I think, with humble Submission, be a Loss to the Publick, because they soon would become Breeders themselves: And besides it is not improbable, that some scrupulous People might be apt to censure such a Practice, (although indeed very unjustly) as a little bordering upon Cruelty; which, I confess, hath always been with me the strongest Objection against any Project, how well soever intended.

But in order to justify my Friend; he confessed, that this [18] Expedient was put into his Head by the famous Salmanaazor, a Native of the Island Formosa, who came from Hence to London, above twenty Years ago, and in Conversation told my Friend, that in his Country, when any young Person happened to be put to Death, the executioner sold the Carcase to Persons of Quality, as a prime Dainty, and that, in his Time, the Body of a plump Girl of fifteen, who was crucified for an Attempt to poison the emperor, was sold to his Imperial Majesty's prime Minister of State, and other great Mandarins of the Court, in Joints from the Gibbet, at Four hundred Crowns. Neither indeed can I deny, that if the same Use were made of several plump young girls in this Town, who, without one single Groat to their Fortunes, cannot stir Abroad without a Chair, and appear at the Play-house, and Assemblies in foreign fineries, which they never will pay for; the Kingdom would not be the worse.

Some Persons of a desponding Spirit are in great Concern [19] about that vast Number of poor People, who are Aged, Diseased, or Maimed; and I have been desired to imploy my Thoughts what Course may be taken, to ease the Nation of so grievous an Incumbrance. But I am not in the least Pain upon that Matter; because it is very well known, that they are every Day dying, and rotting, by Cold and Famine, and Filth, and Vermin, as fast as can be reasonably expected. And as to the younger Labourers, they are now in almost as hopeful a Condition: They cannot get Work, and consequently pine away for Want of Nourishment to a Degree, that if at any Time they are accidentally hired to common Labour, they have not Strength to perform it; and thus the Country, and themselves, are in a fair Way of being delivered from the Evils to come.

I have too long digressed; and therefore shall return to my [20] Subject. I think the Advantages by the Proposal which I have made are obvious, and many, as well as of the highest Importance.

For First, as I have already observed, it would greatly lessen [21] the Number of Papists, with whom we are Yearly overrun; being the principal Breeders of the Nation, as well as our most dangerous Enemies; and who stay at home on Purpose, with a Design to deliver the Kingdom to the Pretender; hoping to take their Advantage by the Absence of so many good Protestants, who have chosen rather to leave their Country, than stay at home, and pay Tithes against their Conscience, to an idolatrous Episcopal Curate.

Secondly, The poorer Tenants will have something valu- [22] able of their own, which, by Law, may be made liable to Distress, and help to pay their Landlord's Rent; their Corn and Cattle being already seized, and Money a Thing unknown.

Thirdly, Whereas the Maintenance of an Hundred Thou- [23] sand Children, from two Years old, and upwards, cannot be computed at less than ten Shillings a Piece per Annum, the Nation's Stock will be thereby encreased Fifty Thousand Pounds per Annum; besides the Profit of a new Dish, introduced to the Tables of all Gentlemen of Fortune in the Kingdom, who have any Refinement in Taste; and the Money will circulate among ourselves, the Goods being entirely of our own Growth and Manufacture.

Fourthly, The constant Breeders, besides the Gain of Eight [24] Shillings Sterling per Annum, by the Sale of their Children, will be rid of the Charge of maintaining them after the first Year.

Fifthly, This Food would likewise bring great Custom to [25] Taverns, where the Vintners will certainly be so prudent, as to procure the best Receipts for dressing it to perfection; and consequently, have their Houses frequented by all the fine Gentlemen, who justly value themselves upon their Knowledge in good Eating; and a skilful Cook, who understands how to oblige his Guests, will contrive to make it as expensive as they please.

Sixthly, This would be a great Inducement to Marriage, which all wise Nations have either encouraged by Rewards, or enforced by Laws and Penalties. It would encrease the Care and Tenderness of Mothers towards their Children, when they were sure of a Settlement for Life, to the poor Babes, provided in some Sort by the Publick, to their annual Profit instead of Expence. We should soon see an honest Emulation among the married Women, which of them could bring the fattest Child to the Market. Men would become as fond of their Wives, during the Time of their Pregnancy, as they are now of their Mares in Foal, their Cows in Calf, or Sows when they are ready to farrow; nor offer to beat or kick them, (as is too frequent a Practice) for fear of a Miscarriage.   26

Many other Advantages might be enumerated. For instance, the Addition of some Thousand Carcases in our Exportation of barrel'd Beef: The Propagation of Swine's Flesh, and Improvement in the Art of making good Bacon; so much wanted among us by the great Destruction of Pigs, too frequent at our Tables, and are no way comparable in Taste, or Magnificence, to a well-grown, fat yearling Child; which, roasted whole, will make a considerable Figure at a Lord Mayor's Feast, or any other publick Entertainment. But this, and many others, I omit; being studious of Brevity.   27

Supposing that one Thousand Families in this City, would be constant Customers for Infants Flesh, besides others who might have it at merry Meetings, particularly Weddings and Christenings; I compute that Dublin would take off, annually, about Twenty Thousand Carcasses; and the rest of the Kingdom (where probably they will be sold somewhat cheaper) the remaining Eighty Thousand.   28

I can think of no one Objection, that will possibly be raised against this Proposal; unless it should be urged, that the Number of People will be thereby much lessened in the   29

Kingdom. This I freely own; and it was indeed one principal Design in offering it to the World. I desire the Reader will observe, that I calculate my Remedy for this one individual Kingdom of Ireland, and for no other that ever was, is, or, I think, ever can be upon Earth. Therefore, let no man talk to me of other Expedients: Of taxing our Absentees at five Shillings a Pound: Of using neither Cloaths, nor Household Furniture, except what is of our own Growth and Manufacture: Of utterly rejecting the Materials and Instruments that promote foreign Luxury: Of curing the Expensiveness of Pride, Vanity, Idleness, and Gaming in our Women: Of introducing a Vein of Parsimony, Prudence and Temperance: Of learning to love our Country, wherein we differ even from Laplanders, and the Inhabitants of Topinamboo: Of quitting our Animosities and Factions; nor act any longer like the Jews, who were murdering one another at the very Moment their City was taken: Of being a little cautious not to sell our Country and Consciences for nothing: Of teaching Landlords to have, at least, one Degree of Mercy towards their Tenants. Lastly, of Putting a Spirit of Honesty, Industry, and Skill into our Shopkeepers; who, if a Resolution could now be taken to buy only our native Goods, would immediately unite to cheat and exact upon us in the Price, the Measure, and the Goodness; nor could ever yet be brought to make one fair Proposal of just Dealing, though often and earnestly invited to it.

Therefore I repeat, let no Man talk to me of these and the like Expedients; till he hath, at least, a Glimpse of Hope, that there will ever be some hearty and sincere Attempt to put them in Practice. 30

But, as to my self; having been wearied out for many Years with offering vain, idle, visionary Thoughts; and at length utterly despairing of Success, I fortunately fell upon this Proposal; which, as it is wholly new, so it hath something solid and real, of no Expense and little Trouble, full in our own Power; and whereby we can incur no Danger in disobliging England: For this Kind of Commodity will not bear Exportation; the Flesh being of too tender a Consistence, to admit a 31 long Continuance in Salt; although, perhaps, I could name a Country, which would be glad to eat up our whole Nation without it.

After all, I am not so violently bent upon my own Opin- 32 ion, as to reject any Offer, proposed by wise Men, which shall be found equally innocent, cheap, easy, and effectual. But before something of that Kind shall be advanced in Contradiction to my Scheme, and offering a better; I desire the Author, or Authors, will be pleased maturely to consider two Points. First, As Things now stand, how they will be able to find Food and Raiment, for a Hundred Thousand useless Mouths and Backs? And Secondly, There being a round Million of Creatures in human Figure, throughout this Kingdom; whose whole Subsistence, put into a common Stock, would leave them in Debt two Millions of Pounds Sterling; adding those, who are Beggars by Profession, to the Bulk of Farmers, Cottagers and Labourers, with their Wives and Children, who are Beggars in Effect; I desire those Politicians, who dislike my Overture, and may perhaps be so bold to attempt an Answer, that they will first ask the Parents of these Mortals, Whether they would not at this Day think it a great Happiness to have been sold for Food at a Year old, in the Manner I prescribe; and thereby have avoided such a perpetual Scene of Misfortunes, as they have since gone through; by the Oppression of Landlords; the impossibility of paying Rent, without Money or Trade; the Want of common Sustenance, with neither House nor Cloaths, to cover them from the Inclemencies of the Weather; and the most inevitable Prospect of intailing the like, or greater Miseries upon their Breed for ever.

I profess, in the Sincerity of my Heart, that I have not the 33 least personal Interest, in endeavouring to promote this necessary Work, having no other Motive than the publick Good of my Country, by advancing our Trade providing for Infants, relieving the Poor, and giving some Pleasure to the Rich. I have no Children, by which I can propose to get a single Penny; the youngest being nine Years Old and my Wife past Child-bearing.

For Study and Discussion

QUESTIONS ABOUT PURPOSE

1. What social problem does Swift attempt to solve with his "modest proposal"?
2. What "collateral advantage" does he see in adapting his scheme?

QUESTIONS ABOUT AUDIENCE

1. What assumptions does Swift make about his audience when he asserts—in paragraph 2—that "it is agreed by all Parties"?
2. What does he assume about his readers' reaction to his assertion that his proposal "will not be liable to the least Objection"?

QUESTIONS ABOUT STRATEGIES

1. How does Swift manipulate facts and testimony to construct his argument?
2. How does his summary suggest that he is attempting an appeal to "logic"?

For Writing and Research

1. *Analyze* how Swift uses numbers to support his proposal.
2. *Practice* by constructing your own "modest proposal" to solve a major social problem.
3. *Argue* that Swift's satire helped or hurt his readers' sympathy for the Irish people.
4. *Synthesize* the various attempts to solve the conflict between the English and the Irish. Then argue that the current agreement does or does not offer a solution to "the troubles."

Henry David Thoreau (1817–1862) was born in Concord, Massachusetts, and was educated at Harvard University. After a brief teaching assignment, he and his brother, John, established a private academy. But John's death ended Thoreau's interest in formal teaching. He lived for several years with the Emerson family, serving as a handyman and as an editorial assistant at the Transcendentalist journal, *The Dial*. For two years Thoreau lived in a one-room hut on Walden Pond, where he stored up experiences for his masterpiece, *Walden: or, Life in the Woods* (1854). His other major books, dealing with his experiences in nature, include *A Week on the Concord and Merrimack Rivers* (1849), *The Maine Woods* (1864), *Cape Cod* (1865), and *A Yankee in Canada* (1866). "Resistance to Civil Government," later titled "Civil Disobedience" (1849), was prompted by Thoreau's decision to go to jail rather than pay his poll tax to a government that supported slavery. In this essay, he argues for civil disobedience, a position later adapted by Mahatma Gandhi in colonial India and Martin Luther King Jr. in the segregated American South.

Resistance to Civil Government

I HEARTILY ACCEPT the motto, —"That government is best which governs least;" and I should like to see it acted up to more rapidly and systematically. Carried out, it finally amounts to this, which also I believe,—"That government is best which governs not at all;" and when men are prepared   1 for it, that will be the kind of government which they will have. Government is at best but an expedient; but most governments are usually, and all governments are sometimes, inexpedient. The objections which have been brought against a standing army, and they are many and weighty, and deserve to prevail, may also at last be brought against a standing government. The standing army is only an arm of the standing government. The government itself, which is only the mode which the people have chosen to execute their will, is equally liable to be abused and perverted before the people can act through it. Witness the present Mexican war, the work of comparatively a few individuals using the standing government as their tool; for, in the outset, the people would not have consented to this measure.

This American government,—what is it but a tradition, 2 though a recent one, endeavoring to transmit itself unimpaired to posterity, but each instant losing some of its integrity? It has not the vitality and force of a single living man; for a single man can bend it to his will. It is a sort of wooden gun to the people themselves; and, if ever they should use it in earnest as a real one against each other, it will surely split. But it is not the less necessary for this; for the people must have some complicated machinery or other, and hear its din, to satisfy that idea of government which they have. Governments show thus how successfully men can be imposed on, even impose on themselves, for their own advantage. It is excellent, we must all allow; yet this government never of itself furthered any enterprise, but by the alacrity with which it got out of its way. *It* does not keep the country free. *It* does not settle the West. *It* does not educate. The character inherent in the American people has done all that has been accomplished; and it would have done somewhat more, if the government had not sometimes got in its way. For government is an expedient by which men would fain succeed in letting one another alone; and, as has been said, when it is most expedient, the governed are most let alone by it. Trade and commerce, if they were not made of India rubber, would never manage to bounce over the obstacles which legislators are continually putting in their way; and, if one were to judge these men wholly by the effects of their actions, and not partly by their intentions, they would deserve to be classed and punished with those mischievous persons who put obstructions on the railroads.

But, to speak practically and as a citizen, unlike those who call themselves no-government men, I ask for, not at once no government, but *at once* a better government. Let every man make known what kind of government would command his respect, and that will be one step toward obtaining it. 3

After all, the practical reason why, when the power is once in the hands of the people, a majority are permitted, and for a long period continue, to rule, is not because they are most likely to be in the right, nor because this seems fairest to the minority, but because they are physically the strongest. But a government in which the majority rule in all cases cannot be based on justice, even as far as men understand it. Can there not be a government in which majorities do not virtually decide right and wrong, but conscience?—in which majorities decide only those questions to which the rule of expediency is applicable? Must the citizen ever for a moment, or in the least degree, resign his conscience to the legislator? Why has every man a conscience, then? I think that we should be men first, and subjects afterward. It is not desirable to cultivate a respect for the law, so much as for the right. The only obligation which I have a right to assume, is to do at any time what I think right. It is truly enough said, that a corporation has no conscience; but a corporation of conscientious men is a corporation *with* a conscience. Law never made men a whit more just; and, by means of their respect for it, even the well-disposed are daily made the agents of injustice. A common and natural result of an undue respect for law is, that you may see a file of soldiers, colonel, captain, corporal, privates, powder-monkeys and all, marching in admirable order over hill and dale to the wars, against their wills, aye, against their common sense and consciences, which makes it very steep marching indeed, and produces a palpitation of the heart. They have no doubt that it is a damnable business in which 4 they are concerned; they are all peaceably inclined. Now, what are they? Men at all? or small moveable forts and magazines, at the service of some unscrupulous man in power? Visit the Navy Yard and behold a marine, such a man as an American government can make, or such as it can make a man with its black arts, a mere shadow and reminiscence of humanity, a man laid out alive and standing, and already, as one may say, buried under arms with funeral accompaniments, though it may be

> "Not a drum was heard, not a funeral note,
>   As his corse to the rampart we hurried;
> Not a soldier discharged his farewell shot
>   O'er the grave where our hero we buried."

The mass of men serve the State thus, not as men mainly,   5
but as machines, with their bodies. They are the standing army, and the militia, jailers, constables, *posse comitatus*, &c. In most cases there is no free exercise whatever of the judgment or of the moral sense; but they put themselves on a level with wood and earth and stones; and wooden men can perhaps be manu- factured that will serve the purpose as well. Such command no more respect than men of straw, or a lump of dirt. They have the same sort of worth only as horses and dogs. Yet such as these even are commonly esteemed good citizens. Others, as most legislators, politicians, lawyers, ministers, and office- holders, serve the State chiefly with their heads; and, as they rarely make any moral distinctions, they are as likely to serve the devil, without intending it, as God. A very few, as heroes, patriots, martyrs, reformers in the great sense, and *men*, serve the State with their consciences also, and so necessarily resist it for the most part; and they are commonly treated by it as ene- mies. A wise man will only be useful as a man, and will not sub- mit to be "clay," and "stop a hole to keep the wind away," but leave that office to his dust at least:—

> "I am too high-born to be propertied,
> To be a secondary at control,
> Or useful serving-man and instrument
> To any sovereign state throughout the world."

He who gives himself entirely to his fellow-men appears to   6
them useless and selfish; but he who gives himself partially to
them is pronounced a benefactor and philanthropist.

How does it become a man to behave toward this American   7
government to-day? I answer that he cannot without disgrace
be associated with it. I cannot for an instant recognize that
political organization as *my* government which is the *slave's*
government also.

All men recognize the right of revolution; that is, the right   8
to refuse allegiance to and to resist the government, when its
tyranny or its inefficiency are great and unendurable. But almost all say that such is not the case now. But such was the
case, they think, in the Revolution of '75. If one were to tell
me that this was a bad government because it taxed certain
foreign commodities brought to its ports, it is most probable
that I should not make an ado about it, for I can do without
them: all machines have their friction; and possibly this does
enough good to counterbalance the evil. At any rate, it is a
great evil to make a stir about it. But when the friction comes
to have its machine, and oppression and robbery are organized, I say, let us not have such a machine any longer. In other
words, when a sixth of the population of a nation which has
undertaken to be the refuge of liberty are slaves, and a whole
country is unjustly overrun and conquered by a foreign army,
and subjected to military law, I think that it is not too soon for
honest men to rebel and revolutionize. What makes this duty
the more urgent is the fact, that the country so overrun is not
our own, but ours is the invading army.

Paley, a common authority with many on moral questions,   9
in his chapter on the "Duty of Submission to Civil Government," resolves all civil obligation into expediency; and
he proceeds to say, "that so long as the interest of the whole
society requires it, that is, so long as the established government cannot be resisted or changed without public inconve-
niency, it is the will of God that the established government
be obeyed, and no longer."—"This principle being admitted,
the justice of every particular case of resistance is reduced to
a computation of the quantity of the danger and grievance on
the one side, and of the probability and expense of redressing

it on the other." Of this, he says, every man shall judge for
himself. But Paley appears never to have contemplated those
cases to which the rule of expediency does not apply, in
which a people, as well as an individual, must do justice, cost
what it may. If I have unjustly wrested a plank from a drowning man, I must restore it to him though I drown myself.
This, according to Paley, would be inconvenient. But he that
would save his life, in such a case, shall lose it. This people
must cease to hold slaves, and to make war on Mexico, though
it cost them their existence as a people.

In their practice, nations agree with Paley; but does any   10
one think that Massachusetts does exactly what is right at the
present crisis?

> "A drab of state, a cloth-o'-silver slut,
> To have her train borne up, and her soul trail in the dirt."

Practically speaking, the opponents to a reform in Massachusetts are not a hundred thousand politicians at the South, but
a hundred thousand merchants and farmers here, who are
more interested in commerce and agriculture than they are in
humanity, and are not prepared to do justice to the slave and
to Mexico, *cost what it may*. I quarrel not with far-off foes,
but with those who, near at home, co-operate with, and do
the bidding of those far away, and without whom the latter
would be harmless. We are accustomed to say, that the mass
of men are unprepared; but improvement is slow, because the
few are not materially wiser or better than the many. It is not
so important that many should be as good as you, as that
there be some absolute goodness somewhere; for that will
leaven the whole lump. There are thousands who are *in opinion* opposed to slavery and to the war, who yet in effect do
nothing to put an end to them; who, esteeming themselves
children of Washington and Franklin, sit down with their
hands in their pockets, and say that they know not what
to do, and do nothing; who even postpone the question of
freedom to the question of free-trade, and quietly read the

prices-current along with the latest advices from Mexico, after dinner, and, it may be, fall asleep over them both. What is the price-current of an honest man and patriot to-day? They hesitate, and they regret, and sometimes they petition; but they do nothing in earnest and with effect. They will wait, well disposed, for others to remedy the evil, that they may no longer have it to regret. At most, they give only a cheap vote, and a feeble countenance and God-speed, to the right, as it goes by them. There are nine hundred and ninety-nine patrons of virtue to one virtuous man; but it is easier to deal with the real possessor of a thing than with the temporary guardian of it.

All voting is a sort of gaming, like chequers or backgammon, with a slight moral tinge to it, a playing with right and wrong, with moral questions; and betting naturally accompanies it. The character of the voters is not staked. I cast my vote, perchance, as I think right; but I am not vitally concerned that that right should prevail. I am willing to leave it to the majority. Its obligation, therefore, never exceeds that of expediency. Even voting *for the right* is *doing* nothing for it. It is only expressing to men feebly your desire that it should prevail. A wise man will not leave the right to the mercy of chance, nor wish it to prevail through the power of the majority. There is but little virtue in the action of masses of men. When the majority shall at length vote for the abolition of slavery, it will be because they are indifferent to slavery, or because there is but little slavery left to be abolished by their vote. *They* will then be the only slaves. Only *his* vote can hasten the abolition of slavery who asserts his own freedom by his vote. 11

I hear of a convention to be held at Baltimore, or elsewhere, for the selection of a candidate for the Presidency, made up chiefly of editors, and men who are politicians by profession; but I think, what is it to any independent, intelligent, and respectable man what decision they may come to, shall we not have the advantage of his wisdom and honesty, nevertheless? Can we not count upon some independent votes? Are there not many individuals in the country who do 12 not attend conventions? But no: I find that the respectable man, so called, has immediately drifted from his position, and despairs of his country, when his country has more reason to despair of him. He forthwith adopts one of the candidates thus selected as the only *available* one, thus proving that he is himself *available* for any purposes of the demagogue. His vote is of no more worth than that of any unprincipled foreigner or hireling native, who may have been bought. Oh for a man who is a *man*, and, as my neighbor says, has a bone in his back which you cannot pass your hand through! Our statistics are at fault: the population has been returned too large. How many *men* are there to a square thousand miles in this country? Hardly one. Does not America offer any inducement for men to settle here? The American has dwindled into an Odd Fellow,—one who may be known by the development of his organ of gregariousness, and a manifest lack of intellect and cheerful self-reliance; whose first and chief concern, on coming into the world, is to see that the alms-houses are in good repair; and, before yet he has lawfully donned the virile garb, to collect a fund for the support of the widows and orphans that may be; who, in short, ventures to live only by the aid of the mutual insurance company, which has promised to bury him decently.

It is not a man's duty, as a matter of course, to devote himself to the eradication of any, even the most enormous wrong; he may still properly have other concerns to engage him; but it is his duty, at least, to wash his hands of it, and, if he gives it no thought longer, not to give it practically his support. If I devote myself to other pursuits and contemplations, I must first see, at least, that I do not pursue them sitting upon another man's shoulders. I must get off him first, that he may pursue his contemplations too. See what gross inconsistency is tolerated. I have heard some of my townsmen say, "I should like to have them order me out to help put down an insurrection of the slaves, or to march to Mexico,—see if I would go;" and yet these very men have each, directly by their allegiance, and so indirectly, at least, by their money, furnished a substitute. The soldier is applauded who refuses to serve in an unjust war by

13

those who do not refuse to sustain the unjust government which makes the war; is applauded by those whose own act and authority he disregards and sets at nought; as if the State were penitent to that degree that it hired one to scourge it while it sinned, but not to that degree that it left off sinning for a moment. Thus, under the name of order and civil government, we are all made at last to pay homage to and support our own meanness. After the first blush of sin, comes its indifference; and from immoral it becomes, as it were, *un*moral, and not quite unnecessary to that life which we have made.

The broadest and most prevalent error requires the most   14
disinterested virtue to sustain it. The slight reproach to which the virtue of patriotism is commonly liable, the noble are most likely to incur. Those who, while they disapprove of the character and measures of a government, yield to it their allegiance and support, are undoubtedly its most conscientious supporters, and so frequently the most serious obstacles to reform. Some are petitioning the State to dissolve the Union, to disregard the requisitions of the President. Why do they not dissolve it themselves,—the union between themselves and the State,—and refuse to pay their quota into its treasury? Do not they stand in the same relation to the State, that the State does to the Union? And have not the same reasons prevented the State from resisting the Union, which have prevented them from resisting the State?

How can a man be satisfied to entertain an opinion merely,   15
and enjoy *it*? Is there any enjoyment in it, if his opinion is that he is aggrieved? If you are cheated out of a single dollar by your neighbor, you do not rest satisfied with knowing that you are cheated, or with saying that you are cheated, or even with petitioning him to pay you your due; but you take effectual steps at once to obtain the full amount, and see that you are never cheated again. Action from principle,—the perception and the performance of right,—changes things and relations; it is essentially revolutionary, and does not consist wholly with any thing which was. It not only divides states and churches, it divides families; aye, it divides the *individual,* separating the diabolical in him from the divine.

Unjust laws exist: shall we be content to obey them, or
shall we endeavor to amend them, and obey them until we
have succeeded, or shall we transgress them at once? Men
generally, under such a government as this, think that they
ought to wait until they have persuaded the majority to alter
them. They think that, if they should resist, the remedy
would be worse than the evil. But it is the fault of the government itself that the remedy *is* worse than the evil. *It* makes it
worse. Why is it not more apt to anticipate and provide for
reform? Why does it not cherish its wise minority? Why does
it cry and resist before it is hurt? Why does it not encourage
its citizens to be on the alert to point out its faults, and *do*
better than it would have them? Why does it always crucify
Christ, and excommunicate Copernicus and Luther, and pronounce Washington and Franklin rebels?

One would think, that a deliberate and practical denial
of its authority was the only offence never contemplated by
government; else, why has it not assigned its definite, its
suitable and proportionate penalty? If a man who has no
property refuses but once to earn nine shillings for the State,
he is put in prison for a period unlimited by any law that I
know, and determined only by the discretion of those who
placed him there; but if he should steal ninety times nine
shillings from the State, he is soon permitted to go at large
again.

If the injustice is part of the necessary friction of the machine of government, let it go, let it go: perchance it will wear
smooth,—certainly the machine will wear out. If the injustice
has a spring, or a pulley, or a rope, or a crank, exclusively for
itself, then perhaps you may consider whether the remedy
will not be worse than the evil; but if it is of such a nature that
it requires you to be the agent of injustice to another, then, I
say, break the law. Let your life be a counter friction to stop
the machine. What I have to do is to see, at any rate, that I do
not lend myself to the wrong which I condemn.

As for adopting the ways which the State has provided
for remedying the evil, I know not of such ways. They take
too much time, and a man's life will be gone. I have other

affairs to attend to. I came into this world, not chiefly to make this a good place to live in, but to live in it, be it good or bad. A man has not every thing to do, but something; and because he cannot do *every thing*, it is not necessary that he should do *something* wrong. It is not my business to be petitioning the governor or the legislature any more than it is theirs to petition me; and, if they should not hear my petition, what should I do then? But in this case the State has provided no way: its very Constitution is the evil. This may seem to be harsh and stubborn and unconciliatory; but it is to treat with the utmost kindness and consideration the only spirit that can appreciate or deserves it. So is all change for the better, like birth and death which convulse the body.

I do not hesitate to say, that those who call themselves 20 abolitionists should at once effectually withdraw their support, both in person and property, from the government of Massachusetts, and not wait till they constitute a majority of one, before they suffer the right to prevail through them. I think that it is enough if they have God on their side, without waiting for that other one. Moreover, any man more right than his neighbors, constitutes a majority of one already.

I meet this American government, or its representative the 21 State government, directly, and face to face, once a year, no more, in the person of its tax-gatherer; this is the only mode in which a man situated as I am necessarily meets it; and it then says distinctly, Recognize me; and the simplest, the most effectual, and, in the present posture of affairs, the indispensablest mode of treating with it on this head, of expressing your little satisfaction with and love for it, is to deny it then. My civil neighbor, the tax-gatherer, is the very man I have to deal with,—for it is, after all, with men and not with parchment that I quarrel,—and he has voluntarily chosen to be an agent of the government. How shall he ever know well what he is and does as an officer of the government, or as a man, until he is obliged to consider whether he shall treat me, his neighbor, for whom he has respect, as a neighbor and well-disposed man, or as a maniac and disturber of the peace, and see if he can get over this obstruction to his neighborliness without a ruder and more impetuous thought or speech corresponding with his action? I know this well, that if one thousand, if one hundred, if ten men whom I could name,—if ten *honest* men only,—aye, if *one* HONEST man, in this State of Massachusetts, *ceasing to hold slaves,* were actually to withdraw from this copartnership, and be locked up in the county jail therefor, it would be the abolition of slavery in America. For it matters not how small the beginning may seem to be: what is once well done is done for ever. But we love better to talk about it: that we say is our mission. Reform keeps many scores of newspapers in its service, but not one man. If my esteemed neighbor, the State's ambassador, who will devote his days to the settlement of the question of human rights in the Council Chamber, instead of being threatened with the prisons of Carolina, were to sit down the prisoner of Massachusetts, that State which is so anxious to foist the sin of slavery upon her sister,—though at present she can discover only an act of inhospitality to be the ground of a quarrel with her,— the Legislature would not wholly waive the subject the following winter.

Under a government which imprisons any unjustly, the 22
true place for a just man is also a prison. The proper place to-day, the only place which Massachusetts has provided for her freer and less desponding spirits, is in her prisons, to be put out and locked out of the State by her own act, as they have already put themselves out by their principles. It is there that the fugitive slave, and the Mexican prisoner on parole, and the Indian come to plead the wrongs of his race, should find them; on that separate, but more free and honorable ground, where the State places those who are not *with* her but *against* her,—the only house in a slave-state in which a free man can abide with honor. If any think that their influence would be lost there, and their voices no longer afflict the ear of the State, that they would not be as an enemy within its walls, they do not know by how much truth is stronger than error, nor how much more eloquently and effectively he can combat injustice who has experienced a little in his own

person. Cast your whole vote, not a strip of paper merely, but your whole influence. A minority is powerless while it conforms to the majority; it is not even a minority then; but it is irresistible when it clogs by its whole weight. If the alternative is to keep all just men in prison, or give up war and slavery, the State will not hesitate which to choose. If a thousand men were not to pay their tax-bills this year, that would not be a violent and bloody measure, as it would be to pay them, and enable the State to commit violence and shed innocent blood. This is, in fact, the definition of a peaceable revolution, if any such is possible. If the tax-gatherer, or any other public officer, asks me, as one has done, "But what shall I do?" my answer is, "If you really wish to do any thing, resign your office." When the subject has refused allegiance, and the officer has resigned his office, then the revolution is accomplished. But even suppose blood should flow. Is there not a sort of blood shed when the conscience is wounded? Through this wound a man's real manhood and immortality flow out, and he bleeds to an everlasting death. I see this blood flowing now.

I have contemplated the imprisonment of the offender, 23 rather than the seizure of his goods,—though both will serve the same purpose,—because they who assert the purest right, and consequently are most dangerous to a corrupt State, commonly have not spent much time in accumulating property. To such the State renders comparatively small service, and a slight tax is wont to appear exorbitant, particularly if they are obliged to earn it by special labor with their hands. If there were one who lived wholly without the use of money, the State itself would hesitate to demand it of him. But the rich man—not to make any invidious comparison—is always sold to the institution which makes him rich. Absolutely speaking, the more money, the less virtue; for money comes between a man and his objects, and obtains them for him; and it was certainly no great virtue to obtain it. It puts to rest many questions which he would otherwise be taxed to answer; while the only new question which it puts is the hard but superfluous one, how to spend it. Thus his moral ground is taken from under his feet. The opportunities of living are diminished in proportion as what are called the "means" are increased. The best thing a man can do for his culture when he is rich is to endeavour to carry out those schemes which he entertained when he was poor. Christ answered the Herodians according to their condition. "Show me the tribute-money," said he;—and one took a penny out of his pocket;—If you use money which has the image of Cæsar on it, and which he has made current and valuable, that is, *if you are men of the State,* and gladly enjoy the advantages of Cæsar's government, then pay him back some of his own when he demands it; "Render therefore to Cæsar that which is Cæsar's, and to God those things which are God's,"— leaving them no wiser than before as to which was which; for they did not wish to know.

When I converse with the freest of my neighbors, I perceive that, whatever they may say about the magnitude and seriousness of the question, and their regard for the public tranquillity, the long and the short of the matter is, that they cannot spare the protection of the existing government, and they dread the consequences of disobedience to it to their property and families. For my own part, I should not like to think that I ever rely on the protection of the State. But, if I deny the authority of the State when it presents its tax-bill, it will soon take and waste all my property, and so harass me and my children without end. This is hard. This makes it impossible for a man to live honestly and at the same time comfortably in outward respects. It will not be worth the while to accumulate property; that would be sure to go again. You must hire or squat somewhere, and raise but a small crop, and eat that soon. You must live within yourself, and depend upon yourself, always tucked up and ready for a start, and not have many affairs. A man may grow rich in Turkey even, if he will be in all respects a good subject of the Turkish government. Confucius said,—"If a State is governed by the principles of reason, poverty and misery are subjects of shame; if a State is not governed by the principles of reason, riches and honors are the subjects of shame." No: until I

24

want the protection of Massachusetts to be extended to me in some distant southern port, where my liberty is endangered, or until I am bent solely on building up an estate at home by peaceful enterprise, I can afford to refuse allegiance to Massachusetts, and her right to my property and life. It costs me less in every sense to incur the penalty of disobedience to the State, than it would to obey. I should feel as if I were worth less in that case.

Some years ago, the State met me in behalf of the church, and commanded me to pay a certain sum toward the support of a clergyman whose preaching my father attended, but never I myself. "Pay it," it said, "or be locked up in the jail." I declined to pay. But, unfortunately, another man saw fit to pay it. I did not see why the schoolmaster should be taxed to support the priest, and not the priest the schoolmaster; for I was not the State's schoolmaster, but I supported myself by voluntary subscription. I did not see why the lyceum should not present its tax-bill, and have the State to back its demand, as well as the church. However, at the request of the selectmen, I condescended to make some such statement as this in writing:—"Know all men by these presents, that I, Henry Thoreau, do not wish to be regarded as a member of any incorporated society which I have not joined." This I gave to the town-clerk; and he has it. The State, having thus learned that I did not wish to be regarded as a member of that church, has never made a like demand on me since; though it said that it must adhere to its original presumption that time. If I had known how to name them, I should then have signed off in detail from all the societies which I never signed on to; but I did not know where to find a complete list.

I have paid no poll-tax for six years. I was put into a jail once on this account, for one night; and, as I stood considering the walls of solid stone, two or three feet thick, the door of wood and iron, a foot thick, and the iron grating which strained the light, I could not help being struck with the foolishness of that institution which treated me as if I were mere flesh and blood and bones, to be locked up.

I wondered that it should have concluded at length that this was the best use it could put me to, and had never thought to avail itself of my services in some way. I saw that, if there was a wall of stone between me and my townsmen, there was a still more difficult one to climb or break through, before they could get to be as free as I was. I did not for a moment feel confined, and the walls seemed a great waste of stone and mortar. I felt as if I alone of all my townsmen had paid my tax. They plainly did not know how to treat me, but behaved like persons who are underbred. In every threat and in every compliment there was a blunder; for they thought that my chief desire was to stand the other side of that stone wall. I could not but smile to see how industriously they locked the door on my meditations, which followed them out again without let or hinderance, and *they* were really all that was dangerous. As they could not reach me, they had resolved to punish my body; just as boys, if they cannot come at some person against whom they have a spite, will abuse his dog. I saw that the State was half-witted, that it was timid as a lone woman with her silver spoons, and that it did not know its friends from its foes, and I lost all my remaining respect for it, and pitied it.

Thus the State never intentionally confronts a man's sense, intellectual or moral, but only his body, his senses. It is not armed with superior wit or honesty, but with superior physical strength. I was not born to be forced. I will breathe after my own fashion. Let us see who is the strongest. What force has a multitude? They only can force me who obey a higher law than I. They force me to become like themselves. I do not hear of *men* being *forced* to live this way or that by masses of men. What sort of life were that to live? When I meet a government which says to me, "Your money or your life," why should I be in haste to give it my money? It may be in a great strait, and not know what to do: I cannot help that. It must help itself; do as I do. It is not worth the while to snivel about it. I am not responsible for the successful working of the machinery of society. I am not the son of the engineer. I perceive that, when an acorn and a chestnut fall side by side, the one does not remain inert to make way for the other, but both obey their own laws, and spring and grow and flourish as best they can, till one, perchance, overshadows and destroys the other. If a plant connot live according to its nature, it dies; and so a man.

The night in prison was novel and interesting enough. The prisoners in their shirt-sleeves were enjoying a chat and the evening air in the door-way, when I entered. But the jailer said, "Come, boys, it is time to lock up;" and so they dispersed, and I heard the sound of their steps returning into the hollow apartments. My room-mate was introduced to me by the jailer, as "a first-rate fellow and a clever man." When the door was locked, he showed me where to hang my hat, and how he managed matters there. The rooms were whitewashed once a month; and this one, at least, was the whitest, most simply furnished, and probably the neatest apartment in the town. He naturally wanted to know where I came from, and what brought me there; and, when I had told him, I asked him in my turn how he came there, presuming him to be an honest man, of course; and, as the world goes, I believe he was. "Why," said he, "they accuse me of burning a barn; but I never did it." As near as I could discover, he had probably gone to bed in a barn when drunk, and smoked his pipe there; and so a barn was burnt. He had the reputation of being a clever man, had been there some three months waiting for his trial to come on, and would have to wait as much longer; but he was quite domesticated and contented, since he got his board for nothing, and thought that he was well treated.

He occupied one window, and I the other; and I saw, that if one stayed there long, his principal business would be to look out the window. I had soon read all the tracts that were left there, and examined where former prisoners had broken out, and where a grate had been sawed off, and heard the history of the various occupants of that room; for I found that even here there was a history and a gossip which never circulated beyond the walls of the jail. Probably this is the only house in the town where verses are composed, which are

28

29

afterward printed in a circular form, but not published. I was
shown quite a long list of verses which were composed by
some young men who had been detected in an attempt to escape, who avenged themselves by singing them.

I pumped my fellow-prisoner as dry as I could, for fear I   30
should never see him again; but at length he showed me
which was my bed, and left me to blow out the lamp.

It was like travelling into a far country, such as I had never   31
expected to behold, to lie there for one night. It seemed to
me that I never had heard the town-clock strike before, nor
the evening sounds of the village; for we slept with the windows open, which were inside the grating. It was to see my
native village in the light of the middle ages, and our Concord
was turned into a Rhine stream, and visions of knights and
castles passed before me. They were the voices of old burghers
that I heard in the streets. I was an involuntary spectator and
auditor of whatever was done and said in the kitchen of the
adjacent village-inn,—a wholly new and rare experience to me.
It was a closer view of my native town. I was fairly inside of it.
I never had seen its institutions before. This is one of its peculiar institutions; for it is a shire town. I began to comprehend
what its inhabitants were about.

In the morning, our breakfasts were put through the hole   32
in the door, in small oblong-square tin pans, made to fit, and
holding a pint of chocolate, with brown bread, and an iron
spoon. When they called for the vessels again, I was green
enough to return what bread I had left; but my comrade
seized it, and said that I should lay that up for lunch or dinner. Soon after, he was let out to work at haying in a neighboring field, whither he went every day, and would not be
back till noon; so he bade me good-day, saying that he
doubted if he should see me again.

When I came out of prison,—for some one interfered, and   33
paid the tax,—I did not perceive that great changes had taken
place on the common, such as he observed who went in a
youth, and emerged a tottering and gray-headed man; and yet
a change had to my eyes come over the scene,—the town, and
State, and country,—greater than any that mere time could

effect. I saw yet more distinctly the State in which I lived. I saw to what extent the people among whom I lived could be trusted as good neighbors and friends; that their friendship was for summer weather only; that they did not greatly purpose to do right; that they were a distinct race from me by their prejudices and superstitions, as the Chinamen and Malays are; that, in their sacrifices to humanity, they ran no risks, not even to their property; that, after all, they were not so noble but they treated the thief as he had treated them, and hoped, by a certain outward observance and a few prayers, and by walking in a particular straight though useless path from time to time, to save their souls. This may be to judge my neighbors harshly; for I believe that most of them are not aware that they have such an institution as the jail in their village.

It was formerly the custom in our village, when a poor   34 debtor came out of jail, for his acquaintances to salute him, looking through their fingers, which were crossed to represent the grating of a jail window, "How do ye do?" My neighbors did not thus salute me, but first looked at me, and then at one another, as if I had returned from a long journey. I was put into jail as I was going to the shoemaker's to get a shoe which was mended. When I was let out the next morning, I proceeded to finish my errand, and, having put on my mended shoe, joined a huckleberry party, who were impatient to put themselves under my conduct; and in half an hour,—for the horse was soon tackled,—was in the midst of a huckleberry field, on one of our highest hills, two miles off; and then the State was nowhere to be seen.

This is the whole history of "My Prisons."   35

I have never declined paying the highway tax, because I am   36 as desirous of being a good neighbor as I am of being a bad subject; and, as for supporting schools, I am doing my part to educate my fellow-countrymen now. It is for no particular item in the tax-bill that I refuse to pay it. I simply wish to refuse allegiance to the State, to withdraw and stand aloof from it effectually. I do not care to trace the course of my dollar, if I could, till it buys a man, or a musket to shoot one with,—the dollar is innocent,—but I am concerned to trace the effects of my allegiance. In fact, I quietly declare war with the State, after my fashion, though I will still make what use and get what advantage of her I can, as is usual in such cases.

If others pay the tax which is demanded of me, from a 37 sympathy with the State, they do but what they have already done in their own case, or rather they abet injustice to a greater extent than the State requires. If they pay the tax from a mistaken interest in the individual taxed, to save his property or prevent his going to jail, it is because they have not considered wisely how far they let their private feelings interfere with the public good.

This, then, is my position at present. But one cannot be 38 too much on his guard in such a case, lest his action be biassed by obstinacy, or an undue regard for the opinions of men. Let him see that he does only what belongs to himself and to the hour.

I think sometimes, Why, this people mean well; they are 39 only ignorant; they would do better if they knew how: why give your neighbors this pain to treat you as they are not inclined to? But I think, again, this is no reason why I should do as they do, or permit others to suffer much greater pain of a different kind. Again, I sometimes say to myself, When many millions of men, without heat, without ill-will, without personal feeling of any kind, demand of you a few shillings only, without the possibility, such is their constitution, of retracting or altering their present demand, and without the possibility, on your side, of appeal to any other millions, why expose yourself to this overwhelming brute force? You do not resist cold and hunger, the winds and the waves, thus obstinately; you quietly submit to a thousand similar necessities. You do not put your head into the fire. But just in proportion as I regard this as not wholly a brute force, but partly a human force, and consider that I have relations to those millions as to so many millions of men, and not of mere brute or inanimate things, I see that appeal is possible, first and instantaneously, from them to the Maker of them, and, secondly, from them to themselves. But, if I put my head deliberately into the fire, there is no appeal to fire or to the Maker of fire, and I have only myself to blame. If I could convince myself that I have any right to be satisfied with men as they are, and to treat them accordingly, and not according, in some respects, to my requisitions and expectations of what they and I ought to be, then, like a good Mussulman and fatalist, I should endeavor to be satisfied with things as they are, and say it is the will of God. And, above all, there is this difference between resisting this and a purely brute or natural force, that I can resist this with some effect; but I cannot expect, like Orpheus, to change the nature of the rocks and trees and beasts.

I do not wish to quarrel with any man or nation. I do not wish to split hairs, to make fine distinctions, or set myself up as better than my neighbors. I seek rather, I may say, even an excuse for conforming to the laws of the land. I am but too ready to conform to them. Indeed I have reason to suspect myself on this head; and each year, as the tax-gatherer comes round, I find myself disposed to review the acts and position of the general and state governments, and the spirit of the people, to discover a pretext for conformity. I believe that the State will soon be able to take all my work of this sort out of my hands, and then I shall be no better a patriot than my fellow-countrymen. Seen from a lower point of view, the Constitution, with all its faults, is very good; the law and the courts are very respectable; even this State and this American government are, in many respects, very admirable and rare things, to be thankful for, such as a great many have described them; but seen from a point of view a little higher, they are what I have described them; seen from a higher still, and the highest, who shall say what they are, or that they are worth looking at or thinking of at all?

However, the government does not concern me much, and I shall bestow the fewest possible thoughts on it. It is not many moments that I live under a government, even in this world. If a man is thought-free, fancy-free, imagination-free, that which *is not* never for a long time appearing *to be* to him, unwise rulers or reformers cannot fatally interrupt him.

I know that most men think differently from myself; but those whose lives are by profession devoted to the study of

these or kindred subjects, content me as little as any. States-
men and legislators, standing so completely within the institution, never distinctly and nakedly behold it. They speak of
moving society, but have no resting-place without it. They
may be men of a certain experience and discrimination, and
have no doubt invented ingenious and even useful systems,
for which we sincerely thank them; but all their wit and usefulness lie within certain not very wide limits. They are wont
to forget that the world is not governed by policy and expediency. Webster never goes behind government, and so cannot
speak with authority about it. His words are wisdom to those
legislators who contemplate no essential reform in the existing government; but for thinkers, and those who legislate for
all time, he never once glances at the subject. I know of those
whose serene and wise speculations on this theme would soon
reveal the limits of his mind's range and hospitality. Yet, compared with the cheap professions of most reformers, and the
still cheaper wisdom and eloquence of politicians in general,
his are almost the only sensible and valuable words, and we
thank Heaven for him. Comparatively, he is always strong,
original, and, above all, practical. Still his quality is not wisdom,
but prudence. The lawyer's truth is not Truth, but consistency, or a consistent expediency. Truth is always in harmony
with herself, and is not concerned chiefly to reveal the justice
that may consist with wrong-doing. He well deserves to be
called, as he has been called, the Defender of the Constitution. There are really no blows to be given by him but defensive ones. He is not a leader, but a follower. His leaders are
the men of '87. "I have never made an effort," he says, "and
never propose to make an effort; I have never countenanced
an effort, and never mean to countenance an effort, to disturb
the arrangement as originally made, by which the various
States came into the Union." Still thinking of the sanction
which the Constitution gives to slavery, he says, "Because it
was a part of the original compact,—let it stand." Notwithstanding his special acuteness and ability, he is unable to take
a fact out of its merely political relations, and behold it as it
lies absolutely to be disposed of by the intellect,—what, for

instance, it behoves a man to do here in America to-day with regard to slavery, but ventures, or is driven, to make some such desperate answer as the following, while professing to speak absolutely, and as a private man,—from which what new and singular code of social duties might be inferred—"The manner," says he, "in which the governments of those States where slavery exists are to regulate it, is for their own consideration, under their responsibility to their constituents, to the general laws of propriety, humanity, and justice, and to God. Associations formed elsewhere, springing from a feeling of humanity, or any other cause, have nothing whatever to do with it. They have never received any encouragement from me, and they never will."

They who know of no purer sources of truth, who have 43 traced up its stream no higher, stand, and wisely stand, by the Bible and the Constitution, and drink at it there with reverence and humility; but they who behold where it comes trickling into this lake or that pool, gird up their loins once more, and continue their pilgrimage toward its fountain-head.

No man with a genius for legislation has appeared in 44 America. They are rare in the history of the world. There are orators, politicians, and eloquent men, by the thousand; but the speaker has not yet opened his mouth to speak, who is capable of settling the much-vexed questions of the day. We love eloquence for its own sake, and not for any truth which it may utter, or any heroism it may inspire. Our legislators have not yet learned the comparative value of free-trade and of freedom, of union, and of rectitude, to a nation. They have no genius or talent for comparatively humble questions of taxation and finance, commerce and manufactures and agriculture. If we were left solely to the wordy wit of legislators in Congress for our guidance, uncorrected by the seasonable experience and the effectual complaints of the people, America would not long retain her rank among the nations. For eighteen hundred years, though perchance I have no right to say it, the New Testament has been written; yet where is the legislator who has wisdom and practical talent enough to avail himself of the light which it sheds on the science of legislation?

The authority of government, even such as I am willing to   45
submit to,—for I will cheerfully obey those who know and can
do better than I, and in many things even those who neither
know nor can do so well,—is still an impure one: to be strictly
just, it must have the sanction and consent of the governed.
It can have no pure right over my person and property but
what I concede to it. The progress from an absolute to a limited monarchy, from a limited monarchy to a democracy, is a
progress toward a true respect for the individual. Is a democracy, such as we know it, the last improvement possible in
government? Is it not possible to take a step further towards
recognizing and organizing the rights of man? There will never
be a really free and enlightened State, until the State comes to
recognize the individual as a higher and independent power,
from which all its own power and authority are derived, and
treats him accordingly. I please myself with imagining a State at
last which can afford to be just to all men, and to treat the individual with respect as a neighbor; which even would not think
it inconsistent with its own repose, if a few were to live aloof
from it, not meddling with it, nor embraced by it, who fulfilled
all the duties of neighbors and fellow-men. A State which bore
this kind of fruit, and suffered it to drop off as fast as it ripened,
would prepare the way for a still more perfect and glorious
State, which also I have imagined, but not yet anywhere seen.

For Study and Discussion

QUESTIONS ABOUT PURPOSE

1. What is the major premise Thoreau asserts in the first paragraph
   of his argument?
2. How do unjust laws justify his assertion to break the law?

QUESTIONS ABOUT AUDIENCE

1. How does Thoreau address those who are "in opinion" opposed
   to slavery and the war?
2. How does he address his neighbors who believe in obedience to
   the state?

QUESTIONS ABOUT STRATEGIES

1. How does Thoreau use the examples of slavery and the Mexican war to make his case against the government?
2. How does he use his night in jail to explain his changed attitude toward the State?

For Writing and Research

1. *Analyze* Thoreau's argument about the right of the government to govern his life.
2. *Practice* by constructing an argument that explains why you disobeyed a rule or custom.
3. *Argue* the case for Thoreau's neighbors who believe in the value of government to protect the commonwealth.
4. *Synthesize* the state of public opinion in Thoreau's community about the legality of slavery or the Mexican war. Then use this evidence to construct an argument about the limited value of majority rule.

KURT VONNEGUT JR.

Kurt Vonnegut Jr. (1922–2007) was born in Indianapolis, Indiana, and attended Cornell University where he studied biochemistry before being drafted into the infantry in World War II. Vonnegut was captured by the Germans at the Battle of the Bulge and sent to Dresden, where he worked in the underground meat locker of a slaughterhouse. He miraculously survived the Allied firebombing of Dresden and, following the war, returned to the United States to study anthropology at the University of Chicago and to work for a local news bureau. In 1947 Vonnegut accepted a position writing publicity for the General Electric Research Laboratory in Schenectady, New York, but left the company in 1950 to work on his own writing. His first three novels—*Player Piano* (1952), a satire on the tyrannies of corporate automation; *The Sirens of Titan* (1959), a science-fiction comedy on the themes of free will and determination; and *Cat's Cradle* (1963), a science fantasy on the amorality of atomic scientists—established Vonnegut's reputation as a writer who could blend humor with serious insights into the human experience. His most successful novel, *Slaughterhouse-Five, or the Children's Crusade* (1969), is based on his wartime experiences in Dresden. His other works include *God Bless You, Mr. Rosewater* (1966), *Breakfast of Champions* (1973), *Jailbird* (1979), *Palm Sunday* (1981), *Galapagos* (1985), *Hocus Pocus* (1990), and *Timequake* (1997). His best-known short stories are collected in *Canary in the Cat House* (1961) and *Welcome to the Monkey House* (1968). "Harrison Bergeron," reprinted from the latter collection, is the story of the apparatus that a future society must create to make everyone equal.

Harrison Bergeron

THE YEAR WAS 2081, and everybody was finally equal. They weren't only equal before God and the law. They were equal every which way. Nobody was smarter than anybody else. Nobody was better looking than anybody else. Nobody was stronger or quicker than anybody else. All this equality was due to the 211th, 212th, and 213th Amendments to the Constitution, and to the unceasing vigilance of agents of the United States Handicapper General.

Some things about living still weren't quite right, though. April, for instance, still drove people crazy by not being springtime. And it was in that clammy month that the H-G men took George and Hazel Bergeron's fourteen-year-old son, Harrison, away.

It was tragic, all right, but George and Hazel couldn't think about it very hard. Hazel had a perfectly average intelligence, which meant she couldn't think about anything except in short bursts. And George, while his intelligence was way above normal, had a little mental handicap radio in his ear. He was required by law to wear it at all times. It was tuned to a government transmitter. Every twenty seconds or so, the transmitter would send out some sharp noise to keep people like George from taking unfair advantage of their brains.

George and Hazel were watching television. There were tears on Hazel's cheeks, but she'd forgotten for the moment what they were about.

On the television screen were ballerinas.

A buzzer sounded in George's head. His thoughts fled in panic, like bandits from a burglar alarm.

"That was a real pretty dance, that dance they just did," said Hazel.

"Huh?" said George.

"That dance—it was nice," said Hazel.

"Yup," said George. He tried to think a little about the ballerinas. They weren't really very good—no better than anybody else would have been, anyway. They were burdened

with sashweights and bags of birdshot, and their faces were
masked, so that no one, seeing a free and graceful gesture or
a pretty face, would feel like something the cat drug in.
George was toying with the vague notion that maybe dancers
shouldn't be handicapped. But he didn't get very far with it
before another noise in his ear radio scattered his thoughts.

George winced. So did two of the eight ballerinas.   11

Hazel saw him wince. Having no mental handicap herself,   12
she had to ask George what the latest sound had been.

"Sounded like somebody hitting a milk bottle with a ball   13
peen hammer," said George.

"I'd think it would be real interesting, hearing all the differ-   14
ent sounds," said Hazel, a little envious. "All the things they
think up."

"Um," said George.   15

"Only, if I was Handicapper General, you know what I   16
would do?" said Hazel. Hazel, as a matter of fact, bore a
strong resemblance to the Handicapper General, a woman
named Diana Moon Glampers. "If I was Diana Moon Glampers," said Hazel, "I'd have chimes on Sunday—just chimes.
Kind of in honor of religion."

"I could think, if it was just chimes," said George.   17

"Well—maybe make 'em real loud," said Hazel. "I think   18
I'd make a good Handicapper General."

"Good as anybody else," said George.   19

"Who knows better'n I do what normal is?" said Hazel.   20

"Right," said George. He began to think glimmeringly   21
about his abnormal son who was now in jail, about Harrison,
but a twenty-one-gun salute in his head stopped that.

"Boy!" said Hazel, "that was a doozy, wasn't it?"   22

It was such a doozy that George was white and trembling, and   23
tears stood on the rims of his red eyes. Two of the eight ballerinas had collapsed on the studio floor, were holding their temples.

"All of a sudden you look so tired," said Hazel. "Why   24
don't you stretch out on the sofa, so's you can rest your handicap bag on the pillows, honeybunch." She was referring to
the forty-seven pounds of birdshot in a canvas bag, which was
padlocked around George's neck. "Go on and rest the bag for

a little while," she said. "I don't care if you're not equal to me for a while."

George weighed the bag with his hands. "I don't mind it," 25 he said. "I don't notice it any more. It's just a part of me."

"You been so tired lately—kind of wore out," said Hazel. 26 "If there was just some way we could make a little hole in the bottom of the bag, and just take out a few of them lead balls. Just a few."

"Two years in prison and two thousand dollars fine for every 27 ball I took out," said George. "I don't call that a bargain."

"If you could just take a few out when you came home 28 from work," said Hazel. "I mean—you don't compete with anybody around here. You just set around."

"If I tried to get away with it," said George, "then other 29 people'd get away with it—and pretty soon we'd be right back to the dark ages again, with everybody competing against everybody else. You wouldn't like that, would you?"

"I'd hate it," said Hazel. 30

"There you are," said George. "The minute people start 31 cheating on laws, what do you think happens to society?"

If Hazel hadn't been able to come up with an answer to 32 this question, George couldn't have supplied one. A siren was going off in his head.

"Reckon it'd fall all apart," said Hazel. 33

"What would?" said George blankly. 34

"Society," said Hazel uncertainly. "Wasn't that what you 35 just said?"

"Who knows?" said George. 36

The television program was suddenly interrupted for a 37 news bulletin. It wasn't clear at first as to what the bulletin was about, since the announcer, like all announcers, had a se-rious speech impediment. For about half a minute, and in a state of high excitement, the announcer tried to say, "Ladies and gentlemen—"

He finally gave up, handed the bulletin to a ballerina to read. 38

"That's all right—" Hazel said to the announcer, "he tried. 39 That's the big thing. He tried to do the best he could with what God gave him. He should get a nice raise for trying so hard."

"Ladies and gentlemen—" said the ballerina, reading the   40
bulletin. She must have been extraordinarily beautiful, because the mask she wore was hideous. And it was easy to
see that she was the strongest and most graceful of all the
dancers, for her handicap bags were as big as those worn by
two-hundred-pound men.

And she had to apologize at once for her voice, which was   41
a very unfair voice for a woman to use. Her voice was a warm,
luminous, timeless melody. "Excuse me—" she said, and she
began again, making her voice absolutely uncompetitive.

"Harrison Bergeron, age fourteen," she said in a grackle   42
squawk, "has just escaped from jail, where he was held on
suspicion of plotting to overthrow the government. He is a
genius and an athlete, is under-handicapped, and should be
regarded as extremely dangerous."

A police photograph of Harrison Bergeron was flashed on   43
the screen upside down, then sideways, upside down again,
then right side up. The picture showed the full length of
Harrison against a background calibrated in feet and inches.
He was exactly seven feet tall.

The rest of Harrison's appearance was Halloween and hard-   44
ware. Nobody had ever borne heavier handicaps. He had out-
grown hindrances faster than the H-G men could think them
up. Instead of a little ear radio for a mental handicap, he wore
a tremendous pair of earphones, and spectacles with thick wavy
lenses. The spectacles were intended to make him not only half
blind, but to give him whanging headaches besides.

Scrap metal was hung all over him. Ordinarily, there was a   45
certain symmetry, a military neatness to the handicaps issued
to strong people, but Harrison looked like a walking junk-
yard. In the race of life, Harrison carried three hundred
pounds.

And to offset his good looks, the H-G men required that   46
he wear at all times a red rubber ball for a nose, keep his eye-
brows shaved off, and cover his even white teeth with black
caps at snaggle-tooth random.

"If you see this boy," said the ballerina, "do not—I repeat,   47
do not—try to reason with him."

There was the shriek of a door being torn from its hinges.   48

Screams and barking cries of consternation came from   49
the television set. The photograph of Harrison Bergeron on the
screen jumped again and again, as though dancing to the tune
of an earthquake.

George Bergeron correctly identified the earthquake, and   50
well he might have—for many was the time his own home
had danced to the same crashing tune. "My God—" said
George, "that must be Harrison!"

The realization was blasted from his mind instantly by the   51
sound of an automobile collision in his head.

When George could open his eyes again, the photograph   52
of Harrison was gone. A living, breathing Harrison filled the
screen.

Clanking, clownish, and huge, Harrison stood in the center   53
of the studio. The knob of the uprooted studio door was still
in his hand. Ballerinas, technicians, musicians, and announcers
cowered on their knees before him, expecting to die.

"I am the Emperor!" cried Harrison. "Do you hear? I am   54
the Emperor! Everybody must do what I say at once!" He
stamped his foot and the studio shook.

"Even as I stand here—" he bellowed, "crippled, hobbled,   55
sickened—I am a greater ruler than any man who ever lived!
Now watch me become what I *can* become!"

Harrison tore the straps of his handicap harness like wet   56
tissue paper, tore straps guaranteed to support five thousand
pounds.

Harrison's scrap-iron handicaps crashed to the floor.   57

Harrison thrust his thumbs under the bars of the padlock that   58
secured his head harness. The bar snapped like celery. Harrison
smashed his headphones and spectacles against the wall.

He flung away his rubber-ball nose, revealed a man that   59
would have awed Thor, the god of thunder.

"I shall now select my Empress!" he said, looking down   60
on the cowering people. "Let the first woman who dares rise
to her feet claim her mate and her throne!"

A moment passed, and then a ballerina arose, swaying like   61
a willow.

Harrison plucked the mental handicap from her ear, 62
snapped off her physical handicaps with marvelous delicacy.
Last of all, he removed her mask.

She was blindingly beautiful.

"Now——" said Harrison, taking her hand, "shall we show 63
the people the meaning of the word dance? Music!" he 64
commanded.

The musicians scrambled back into their chairs, and 65
Harrison stripped them of their handicaps, too. "Play your
best," he told them, "and I'll make you barons and dukes
and earls."

The music began. It was normal at first—cheap, silly, false. 66
But Harrison snatched two musicians from their chairs,
waved them like batons as he sang the music as he wanted it
played. He slammed them back into their chairs.

The music began again and was much improved. 67

Harrison and his Empress merely listened to the music for 68
a while—listened gravely, as though synchronizing their
heartbeats with it.

They shifted their weights to their toes. 69

Harrison placed his big hands on the girl's tiny waist, letting 70
her sense the weightlessness that would soon be hers.

And then, in an explosion of joy and grace, into the air 71
they sprang!

Not only were the laws of the land abandoned, but the law 72
of gravity and the laws of motion as well.

They reeled, whirled, swiveled, flounced, capered, gam- 73
boled, and spun.

They leaped like deer on the moon. 74

The studio ceiling was thirty feet high, but each leap 75
brought the dancers nearer to it.

It became their obvious intention to kiss the ceiling. 76

They kissed it. 77

And then, neutralizing gravity with love and pure will, 78
they remained suspended in air inches below the ceiling, and
they kissed each other for a long, long time.

It was then that Diana Moon Glampers, the Handicapper 79
General, came into the studio with a double-barreled ten-gauge

shotgun. She fired twice, and the Emperor and the Empress were dead before they hit the floor.

Diana Moon Glampers loaded the gun again. She aimed it at the musicians and told them they had ten seconds to get their handicaps back on. 80

It was then that the Bergerons' television tube burned out. 81

Hazel turned to comment about the blackout to George. But George had gone out into the kitchen for a can of beer. 82

George came back in with the beer, paused while a handicap signal shook him up. And then he sat down again. "You been crying?" he said to Hazel. 83

"Yup," she said. 84

"What about?" he said. 85

"I forgot," she said. "Something real sad on television." 86

"What was it?" he said. 87

"It's all kind of mixed up in my mind," said Hazel. 88

"Forget sad things," said George. 89

"I always do," said Hazel. 90

"That's my girl," said George. He winced. There was the sound of a rivetting gun in his head. 91

"Gee—I could tell that one was a doozy," said Hazel. 92

"You can say that again," said George. 93

"Gee—" said Hazel, "I could tell that one was a doozy." 94

COMMENT ON "HARRISON BERGERON"

Known for his offbeat and sometimes bizarre vision of reality, Kurt Vonnegut Jr. has created in "Harrison Bergeron" a science fiction story full of black humor and grotesque details. The society he creates in the story is reminiscent of the society pictured in Orwell's *1984*, totally controlled by a government that invades and interferes in every facet of its citizens' lives. In a travesty of the famous declaration that "All men are created equal," the government has set out to legislate equality. Vonnegut portrays the results of such legislation in macabre images of people forced to carry weighted bags to reduce their strength, wear grotesque masks to conceal their beauty, and suffer implants in their brain to disrupt their thinking. When a fourteen-year-old boy, Harrison Bergeron, shows signs of excellence, he is first arrested, then ruthlessly destroyed when he throws off his restraints and literally rises to the top.

Underneath the farce, Vonnegut has created a tragic picture of a culture so obsessed with equality that people must be leveled by decree. Mediocrity reigns; any sign of excellence or superiority threatens law and order and must be suppressed immediately. Ultimately, of course, such a society will perish because it will kill its talent and stagnate.

Vonnegut wrote this story in 1961, after the repressive Stalinist regime that wiped out thousands of leaders and intellectuals in Russia; it precedes by a few years the disastrous era of Mao's Red Guards in China, when hundreds of thousands of intellectuals and artists were killed or imprisoned in the name of equality. Is Vonnegut commenting on the leveling tendencies of these totalitarian societies? Or does he see such excesses reflected in our own society? No one knows, but it's the genius of artists to prod us to think about such concerns.

USING
AND
DOCUMENTING
SOURCES

The essays in *The Riverside Reader* are sources. Many of the writing assignments at the end of each chapter ask you to *analyze* these sources or to use them to support your own ideas. Most academic writing asks you to use sources—from books, journals, magazines, newspapers, and the Internet—to augment and advance the ideas in your writing. Every time you cite a source, or use it in some way, you must *document*

it. The student research paper at the end of this chapter uses MLA style to cite print and electronic sources.

This chapter explains the style recommended by the Modern Language Association (MLA) for documenting sources in research papers. It also analyzes some of the implications of MLA style for your research and composing. More detailed information is given in the *MLA Handbook* and the *MLA Style Manual.**

MLA style has three major features:

- All sources cited in a paper are listed in a section entitled **Works Cited,** which is located at the end of the paper.
- Material borrowed from another source is documented within the text by a brief parenthetical reference that directs readers to the full citation in the list of works cited.
- Numbered footnotes or endnotes are used to present two types of supplementary information: (1) commentary or explanation that the text cannot accommodate and (2) bibliographical notes that contain several source citations.

Preparing the List of Works Cited

In an academic paper that follows MLA style, the list of works cited is the only place where readers will find complete information about the sources you have cited. For that reason, your list must be thorough and accurate.

The list of works cited appears at the end of your paper and, as its title suggests, lists only the works you have cited in your paper. Occasionally, your instructor may ask you to prepare a list of works consulted. That list would include not only the sources you cite but also the sources you consulted

---

*Joseph Gibaldi, *MLA Handbook for Writers of Research Papers,* 6th ed. (New York: MLA, 2003). Joseph Gibaldi, *MLA Style Manual and Guide to Scholarly Publishing,* 2d ed. (New York: MLA, 1998).

as you conducted your research. In either case, MLA prefers Works Cited or Works Consulted to the more limited heading Bibliography (literally, "description of books") because those headings are more likely to accommodate the variety of sources—articles, films, Internet sources—that writers may cite in a research paper.

To prepare the list of works cited, follow these general guidelines:

1. Paginate the Works Cited section as a continuation of your text. If the conclusion of your paper appears on page 8, begin your list on page 9 (unless there is an intervening page of endnotes).
2. Double-space between successive lines of an entry and between entries.
3. Begin the first line of an entry flush left, and indent successive lines one-half inch or five spaces.
4. List entries in alphabetical order according to the last name of the author.
5. If you are listing more than one work by the same author, alphabetize the works according to title (excluding the articles, *a, an,* and *the*). Instead of repeating the author's name, type *three* hyphens and a period, and then give the title.
6. Underline the titles of works published as independent units: books, plays, long poems, pamphlets, periodicals, films. Do not underline article titles.
7. Although you do not need to underline the spaces between words, a continuous line is easier to type and guarantees that all features of the title are underlined. Type a continuous line under titles unless you are instructed to do otherwise.
8. If you are citing a book whose title includes the title of another book, underline the main title, but do not underline the other title (for example, A Casebook on Ralph Ellison's Invisible Man).
9. Use quotation marks to indicate titles of short works, such as articles, that appear in larger works (for example,

"Minutes of Glory." African Short Stories). Also use quotation marks for song titles and for titles of unpublished works, including dissertations, lectures, and speeches.

10. Use arabic numerals except with names of monarchs (Elizabeth II) and except for the preliminary pages of a work (ii–xix), which are traditionally numbered with roman numerals.

11. Use lowercase abbreviations to identify the parts of a work (for example, *vol.* for *volume*), a named translator (*trans.*), and a named editor (*ed.*). However, when these designations follow a period, they should be capitalized (for example, Woolf, Virginia. A Writer's Diary. Ed. Leonard Woolf).

12. Whenever possible, use appropriate shortened forms for the publisher's name (*Random* instead of *Random House*).

13. Separate author, title, and publication information with a period followed by one space.

14. Use a colon and one space to separate the volume number and year of a periodical from the page numbers (for example, Trimmer, Joseph. "Memoryscape: Jean Shepherd's Midwest." Old Northwest 2 (1976): 357-69).

15. Treat inclusive page numbers in text citations and in the list of works cited as follows: 67–68, 102–03, 237–42, 389–421.

In addition to these guidelines, MLA recommends procedures for documenting an extensive variety of sources, including electronic sources and non-print materials such as films and television programs. The following models illustrate sources most commonly cited.

Sample Entries: Books

When citing books, provide the following general categories of information:

Author's last name, first name. Book Title. Additional information.

  City of publication: Publisher, publication date.

Entries illustrating variations on this basic format appear below and are numbered to facilitate reference.

A BOOK BY ONE AUTHOR

1. Light, Richard J. Making the Most of College: Students Speak Their Minds. Cambridge: Harvard UP, 2001.

TWO OR MORE BOOKS BY THE SAME AUTHOR

2. Rose, Mike. Lives on the Boundary: The Struggles and Achievements of America's Underprepared. New York: Free, 1989.

3. ---. The Mind at Work: Valuing the Intelligence of the American Worker. New York: Viking, 2004.

A BOOK BY TWO OR THREE AUTHORS

4. Wynn, Charles M., and Arthur Wiggins. Quantum Leaps in the Wrong Direction: Where Real Science Ends . . . and Pseudoscience Begins. Washington: National Academy, 2001.

5. Peel, Robin, Annette Patterson, and Jeanne Gerlach. Questions of English: Ethics, Aesthetics, Rhetoric and the Formation of the Subject in England, Australia, and the United States. London: Routledge, 2000.

A BOOK BY FOUR OR MORE AUTHORS

6. Lassiter, Luke Eric, et al. The Other Side of Middletown: Exploring Muncie's African American Community. Walnut Creek, CA: AltaMira, 2004.

A BOOK BY A CORPORATE AUTHOR

7. National Geographic Society. Cradle and Crucible: History and Faith in the Middle East. Washington: National Geographic, 2002.

A BOOK BY AN ANONYMOUS AUTHOR

8.   Literary Market Place 2001: The Dictionary of the American
     Book Publishing Industry. New Providence, NJ: Bowker,
     2000.

A BOOK WITH AN EDITOR

9.   Jackson, Kenneth T., ed. The Encyclopedia of New York City.
     New Haven: Yale UP, 1995.

A BOOK WITH AN AUTHOR AND AN EDITOR

10. Toomer, Jean. Cane: Ed. Darwin T. Turner. New York: Norton,
     1988.

A BOOK WITH A PUBLISHER'S IMPRINT

11. Hillenbrand, Laura. Seabiscuit: An American Legend. New
     York: Ballantine-Random, 2001.

AN ANTHOLOGY OR COMPILATION

12. Smith, Barbara Leigh, and John McCann, eds. Reinventing
     Ourselves: Interdisciplinary Education, Collaborative
     Learning, and Experimentation in Higher Education.
     Bolton, MA: Anker, 2001.

A WORK IN AN ANTHOLOGY

13. Peterson, Rai. "My Tribe Outside the Global Village." Visual
     Media and the Humanities: A Pedagogy of Representation.
     Ed. Kecia Driver McBride. Knoxville: U of Tennessee P, 2004.

AN INTRODUCTION, PREFACE, FOREWORD, OR AFTERWORD

14. Shulman, Lee S. Foreword. Disciplinary Styles in the Scholar-
     ship of Teaching and Learning. Eds. Mary Taylor Huber

and Sherwyn P. Morreale. Washington: American Assn. of Higher Educ., 2002.

A MULTIVOLUME WORK

15. Blotner, Joseph. Faulkner: A Biography. 2 vols. New York: Random, 1974.

AN EDITION OTHER THAN THE FIRST

16. Chaucer, Geoffrey. The Riverside Chaucer. 3rd ed. Ed. Larry D. Benson. Boston: Houghton, 1987.

A BOOK IN A SERIES

17. Eggers, Dave, ed. The Best American Nonrequired Reading, 2004. The Best American Series. Boston: Houghton, 2004.

A REPUBLISHED BOOK

18. Malamud, Bernard. The Natural. 1952. New York: Avon, 1980.

A SIGNED ARTICLE IN A REFERENCE BOOK

19. Tobias, Richard. "Thurber, James." Encyclopedia Americana. 2002 ed.

AN UNSIGNED ARTICLE IN A REFERENCE BOOK

20. "Tharp, Twyla." Who's Who of American Women. 17th ed. 1991–92.

A GOVERNMENT DOCUMENT

21. National Commission on Terrorist Attacks upon the United States. The 9/11 Commission Report: Final Report of the

National Commission on Terrorists Attacks upon the
United States. Washington: GPO, 2004.

PUBLISHED PROCEEDINGS OF A CONFERENCE

22. Sass, Steven A., and Robert K. Triest. Social Security Reform:
Conference Proceedings: Links to Saving, Investment and
Growth. Boston: Fed. Reserve Bank of Boston, 1997.

A TRANSLATION

23. Giroud, Françoise. Marie Curie: A Life. Trans. Lydia Davis.
New York: Holmes, 1986.

A BOOK WITH A TITLE IN ITS TITLE

24. Habich, Robert D. Transcendentalism and the Western
Messenger: A History of the Magazine and Its Contributors,
1835–1841. Rutherford: Fairleigh Dickinson UP, 1985.

A BOOK PUBLISHED BEFORE 1900

25. Field, Kate. The History of Bell's Telephone. London, 1878.

AN UNPUBLISHED DISSERTATION

26. Geissinger, Shirley Burry. "Openness versus Secrecy in
Adoptive Parenthood." Diss. U of North Carolina at
Greensboro, 1984.

A PUBLISHED DISSERTATION

27. Schottler, Beverly A. A Handbook for Dealing with Plagiarism
in Public Schools. Diss. Kansas State U, 2003. Ann Arbor:
UMI, 2004. AAT 3113929.

Sample Entries: Articles in Periodicals

When citing articles in periodicals, provide the following general categories of information:

Author's last name, first name. "Article title." Periodical Title

Date: inclusive pages.

Entries illustrating variations on this basic format appear below and are numbered to facilitate reference.

A SIGNED ARTICLE FROM A DAILY NEWSPAPER

28. Glanz, James. "Iraqi Insurgents Step Up Attacks after Elections." New York Times 13 Feb. 2005, late ed.; Al.

AN UNSIGNED ARTICLE FROM A DAILY NEWSPAPER

29. "Sunnis Worry of Future in New Shiite-run Iraq." Chicago Tribune 13 Feb. 2005, sec. 1: 16+.

AN ARTICLE FROM A MONTHLY OR BIMONTHLY MAGAZINE

30. Fallows, James. "Success without Victory." Atlantic Monthly Jan.–Feb. 2005: 80–90.

AN ARTICLE FROM A WEEKLY OR BIWEEKLY MAGAZINE

31. Mayer, Jane. "Outsourcing Torture." New Yorker 14–21 Feb. 2005: 106–23.

AN ARTICLE IN A JOURNAL WITH CONTINUOUS PAGINATION

32. Flower, Linda. "Intercultural Inquiry and the Transformation of Service." College English 65 (2002): 181–201.

AN ARTICLE IN A JOURNAL THAT NUMBERS PAGES IN EACH ISSUE SEPARATELY

33. Madden, Thomas F. "Revisiting the Crusades." <u>Wilson Quarterly</u> 26.4 (2002): 100–03.

AN EDITORIAL

34. "Poverty and Health" Editorial. <u>Washington Post</u> 31 Aug. 2004: A20.

A REVIEW

35. Nathan, Daniel A. "Of Grades and Glory: Rethinking Intercollegiate Athletics." Rev. of <u>The Game of Life: College Sports and Educational Values</u>, by James L. Shulman and William G. Bowen. <u>American Quarterly</u> 54.1 (2002): 139–47.

AN ARTICLE WHOSE TITLE CONTAINS A QUOTATION OR A TITLE WITHIN QUOTATION MARKS

36. DeCuir, Andre L. "Italy, England and the Female Artist in George Eliot's 'Mr. Gilfil's Love-Story'" <u>Studies in Short Fiction</u> 29 (1992): 67–75.

AN ABSTRACT FROM *DISSERTATION ABSTRACTS* OR *DISSERTATION ABSTRACTS INTERNATIONAL*

37. Creek, Mardena Bridges. "Myth, Wound, Accommodation: American Literary Responses to the War in Vietnam." <u>DAI</u> 43 (1982): 3539A.

Sample Entries: Miscellaneous Print and Nonprint Sources

FILMS; RADIO AND TELEVISION PROGRAMS

38. <u>Chicago</u>. Dir. Rob Marshall. With Renée Zellweger, Catherine Zeta-Jones, Richard Gere. Miramax, 2002.

39. "New York, New York (1944–1951)." <u>Leonard Bernstein—An American Life</u>. Prods. Steve Rowland and Larry Abrams. NPR. WBST, Muncie. 18 Jan. 2005.

40. "Seeds of Destruction." <u>Slavery and the Making of America</u>. Prod. Clara Gazit. PBS. WNET, New York. 16 Feb. 2005.

PERFORMANCES

41. <u>The Producers</u>. By Mel Brooks. Dir. Susan Stroman. With Nathan Lane and Matthew Broderick. St. James Theater, New York. 8 Oct. 2002.

42. Spano, Robert, cond. <u>Wagner, Mendelssohn, Wyner and Haydn</u>. Concert. Boston Symphony Orch. Symphony Hall, Boston. 17 Feb. 2005.

RECORDINGS

If you are not referring to an audio recording on a CD, then add the medium before the manufacturer.

43. Mozart, Wolfgang A. <u>Cosi Fan Tutte</u>. Record. With Kiri Te Kanawa, Frederica von Stade, David Rendall, and Philippe Huttenlochen. Cond. Alain Lombard. Strasbourg Philharmonic Orch. LP. RCA, 1978.

44. Jones, Norah. <u>Come Away with Me</u>. Blue Note, 2002.

WORKS OF ART

45. Botticelli, Sandro, Giuliano de' Medici. Samuel H. Kress
    Collection. National Gallery of Art, Washington.

46. Rodin, Auguste. The Gates of Hell. Rodin Museum, Paris.

INTERVIEWS

47. Ellison, Ralph. "Indivisible Man." Interview. By James Alan
    McPherson. Atlantic Dec. 1970: 45–60.

48. Martone, Michael. Telephone interview. 6 Jan. 2005.

49. Patterson, Annette. E-mail interview. 16 Feb. 2005.

MAPS AND CHARTS

50. Wine Country Map. Map. Napa Valley: Wine Zone, 2004.

CARTOONS AND ADVERTISEMENTS

51. Lynch, Mike. Cartoon. Chronicle Review 18 Feb. 2005: B17.

52. Lufthansa. Advertisement. New Yorker 11 Oct. 2004: 27.

LECTURES, SPEECHES, AND ADDRESSES

53. Paglia, Camille. "Art and Poetry v. Hollywood and Media."
    92nd Street YMCA, New York. 28 Mar. 2005.

54. Scholes, Robert. "The Presidential Address." MLA Conven-
    tion. Philadelphia. 29 Dec. 2004.

PUBLISHED AND UNPUBLISHED LETTERS

55. Fitzgerald, F. Scott. "To Ernest Hemingway." 1 June 1934.
    The Letters of F. Scott Fitzgerald. Ed. Andrew Turnbull.
    New York: Scribner's, 1963, 308–10.

56. Stowe, Harriet Beecher. Letter to George Eliot. 25 May 1869.
    Berg Collection. New York Public Lib., New York.

Sample Entries: Electronic Publications

MLA style for electronic sources resembles the MLA format for books and periodicals in most respects except for the inclusion of the user's date of access and the electronic address. Because many electronic documents are periodically updated, you need to supply the date of access—that is, the date you viewed the document. The date of access should be placed immediately *before* the electronic address. The electronic address, or URL (uniform resource locator), may have more information than you need—that is, the URL may be so long and complex that it invites transcription errors.

Enclose the URL in angle brackets. For lengthy or complex URLs, give enough information about the path so that a reader can locate the exact page to which you are referring from the search page of the site or database. If you need to break a URL at the end of a line, do so only after a slash and do not add punctuation or hyphens that are not in the original URL. *Note*: MLA suggests placing angle brackets <> at the beginning and at the end of the electronic address. However, many software systems read these signs as instructions to convert the address into color.

When citing information from an electronic source, provide the following general categories of information:

Author's last name, first name. "Article title" or Book title.

Publication information for any printed version. Or subject

line of forum or discussion grown. Indication of online posting

or home page. Title of Electronic Journal. Date of electronic

publication. Page numbers or the numbers of paragraphs or

sections. Name of institution or organization sponsoring

website. Date of success to the source <URL>.

The best way to confirm the accuracy of your electronic citations is to click on the "Frequently Asked Questions" link in the MLA Style section of the MLA website (<http://www.mla.org>).

A PROFESSIONAL SITE

57. MLA Style. 10 Jan. 2005. Modern Language Association.
17 Feb. 2005 <http://www.mla.org>.

A HOME PAGE FOR A COURSE

58. Papper, Carole Clark, Writing technologies. Course home
page. Jan. 2005–May 2005. Dept. of English, Ball State U.
17 Feb. 2005 <http://www.bsu.edu/web/cpapper/692>.

A PERSONAL SITE

59. Hawisher, Gail. Home page. U of Illinois, Urbana-Champaign.
26 Mar. 2003 <http://www.english.uiuc.edu/facpages/
Hawisher. htm>.

AN ONLINE BOOK

60. Anderson, Sherwood. Winesburg, Ohio. 1919. Bartleby.com:
Great Books Online. 1999. 17 Feb. 2005
<http://www.bartleby.com/156/index.html>.

AN ONLINE POEM

61. Roethke, Theodore. "My Papa's Waltz." Favorite Poem Project.
5 May 2003 <http://www.favoritepoem.org/poems/
roethke/waltz/html>.

AN ARTICLE IN A SCHOLARLY JOURNAL

62. Butler, Darrell L., and Martin Sellbom. "Barriers to Adopting
Technology for Teaching and Learning." Educause Quarterly 25.2 (2002): 22–28. Educause. 17 Feb. 2005
<http://www.educause.edu/ir/library/pdf/eqm0223.pdf>.

AN ARTICLE IN A REFERENCE DATABASE

63. "Women in American History." Britannica Online. Vers. 98.1.1, Nov. 1997. Encyclopedia Britannica. 10 Jan. 2005 <http://www.eb.com>.

AN ARTICLE IN A MAGAZINE

64. Glasser, Ronald J. "We Are Not Immune." Harper's Oct. 2004. 12 Dec. 2004 <http://www.harpers.org/WeAreNotImmune. html>.

A REVIEW

65. Chabon, Michael. "Inventing Sherlock Holmes." Rev. of The New Annotated Sherlock Holmes, Vols. 1 and 2, by Sir Arthur Conan Doyle. Ed. Leslie S. Klinger. New York Review of Books.. 10 Feb. 2005. 17 Feb. 2005 <http://www.nybooks.com/articles/17718>.

A POSTING TO A DISCUSSION GROUP

66. Inman, James. "Re: Technologist. "Online posting. 24 Sept. 1997. Alliance for Computers in Writing. 27 Feb. 2005 <acw-l@unicorn.acs.ttu.edu>.

A PERSONAL E-MAIL MESSAGE

67. Johnson, Alfred B. "Audio Interactive Awards." E-mail to James W. Miles. 14 Feb. 2005.

CD-ROM: PERIODICAL PUBLICATION WITH PRINTED SOURCE OR PRINTED ANALOGUE

68. West, Cornel. "The Dilemma of the Black Intellectual." Critical Quarterly 29 (1987): 39–52. MLA International Bibliography. CD-ROM. SilverPlatter. Feb. 1995.

CD-ROM: NONPERIODICAL PUBLICATION

69. "Entropy." The Oxford English Dictionary. 2nd ed. CD-ROM.

   Oxford, Eng.: Oxford UP, 1992.

CD-ROM: A WORK IN MORE THAN ONE ELECTRONIC MEDIUM

70. Mozart. CD-ROM, laser disk. Union City, CA: Ebook, 1992.

Implications for Your Research and Composing

MLA style emphasizes the importance of following the procedures for planning and writing the research paper outlined in any standard writing textbook. In particular, MLA style requires you to devote considerable attention to certain steps in your research and composing.

Evaluating Sources

As you begin collecting sources to advance your research, evaluate them according to the following criteria.

1. **A source should be relevant.** Ask yourself: Does the content of this source apply directly to the topic of the paper? Whether a particular source is relevant is not always apparent. When you begin your research, your lack of perspective on your subject may make every source seem potentially relevant. Titles of sources may be misleading or vague, prompting you to examine a source unrelated to your subject or to dismiss a source as too theoretical or general when it actually could give you vital perspective on your subject. The status of your sources may also change as you restrict and define your subject. A source that seemed irrelevant yesterday may appear more pertinent today.

2. **A source should be authoritative.** Ask yourself: Does the author of a particular source have the necessary expertise or experience to speak authoritatively about the subject of your paper? Most print sources enable you to judge the credentials and bias of the author. You can usually judge the authority of a book or an article because the book has been reviewed by knowledgeable persons or the article has been evaluated by the journal's editorial board. But you have no way to evaluate the authority of many electronic sources. A source that you assume is authoritative may have been posted by a hacker or by someone who wishes to further his or her own agenda.

3. **A source must be current.** Ask yourself: Is this source current? You don't want to cite a twenty-year-old source if you are writing about the latest cures for cancer. However, you may want to use that same twenty-year-old source if you are writing about the history of cancer therapy. Writers often cite standard print sources to establish the reliability of their arguments. Then they will cite recent electronic sources to address issues that have arisen since the print sources were originally published. Keep in mind that electronic sources are not necessarily the most current since many print sources are now posted on the Internet. To make sure that your sources are reliable and current, you may need to mix print and electronic sources.

4. **A source should be comprehensive.** Ask yourself: Does this source cover all the major issues that I need to discuss in my paper? Some sources will focus on an extremely narrow aspect of your subject; others will cover every feature and many related, or unrelated, topics as well. Begin reading the most comprehensive first because it will cover the essential information in the more specialized sources and give you the related subtopics within your subject. Most books, for example, are comprehensive sources whereas most websites provide only "bits" of information.

5. **A source should be stable.** Ask yourself: If I use this source, will my readers be able to locate it if they want to read more about the topic of my paper? You want to cite sources that provide the best and most stable information on your topic. There is nothing more stable than a book. Even if a library does not own a book or if a book goes out of print, librarians can find a copy for your readers through interlibrary loan. The same is true for most articles. But electronic sources are not stable. The source you stumble on today may not be there tomorrow. Your readers will not be able to find it because it may have been renamed, reclassified, or often simply deleted. If your readers want to check your sources, you should cite sources they can find.

6. **A source should provide links.** Ask yourself: Does this source help me locate other sources? The best sources lead to other sources, which can further your research. The subject headings on a source provide an excellent system for linking up with other sources. Annotated bibliographies not only link you to other sources but also provide you with an assessment of their value. Of course, the chief advantage of the Internet and its various search engines is that they allow you to link up with thousands of sources by simply pointing and clicking. If your source provides such links, your readers can use them to trace the research that informs the source and the way you have used it to broaden and deepen the research in your paper.

Compiling Source Information

Once you have located sources that you suspect will prove useful, fill out a source card or create a computer file for each item. List the source in the appropriate format (use the formats shown in the guidelines for preparing the list of works cited, pages 514–528). To guarantee that each card or file is complete and accurate, take your information directly from the source rather than from the card or online catalog or a bibliographical index. Your collection of cards or files will help you keep track of your sources throughout your research. Alphabetizing the cards or files will enable you to prepare a provisional list of works cited.

The provisional list must be in place *before* you begin writing your paper. You may expand or refine the list as you write, but to document each source in your text, you first need to know its correct citation. Thus, although Works Cited will be the last section of your paper, you must prepare it first.

Taking Notes

Note-taking demands that you read, select, interpret, and evaluate the information that will form the substance of your paper. After you have returned material to the library or turned off your computer, your notes will be the only record of your research. If you have taken notes carelessly, you will be in trouble when you try to use them in your paper. Many students inadvertently plagiarize because they are working from inaccurate note cards. (See "Avoiding Plagiarism," pages 535–537.)

If you are relying on your computer to create source files, you may also commit plagiarism by falling into the "copy-paste trap." The most efficient way to work with electronic sources is to **copy** important passages from online sources and then **paste** them into your research files. But this quick and easy way of saving information can also get you into a lot of trouble. If you simply "save" the material you have found without identifying it as a quotation and identifying its source, you may later assume that you composed the sentences that you see pasted in your file and present them as your own writing. (See "Avoiding Plagiarism," pages 535–537.)

As you select information from a source, use one of three methods to record it: **quoting, summarizing,** or **paraphrasing.**

Quoting sources   Although quoting an author's text word for word is the easiest way to record information, use this method selectively and quote only the passages that deal directly with your subject in memorable language. When you copy a quotation onto a note card or paste it into a file, place quotation marks at the beginning and the end of the passage. If you decide to omit part of the passage, use ellipsis points to indicate that you have omitted words from the original source. To indicate an omission from the middle of a sentence, use three periods (. . .) and leave a space before and after each period. To indicate the omission of the end of a sentence or of more than one sentence, use three spaced periods following the sentence period (. . . .).

To move a quotation from your notes to your paper, making it fit smoothly into the flow of your text, use one of the following methods.

1. Work the quoted passage into the syntax of your sentence.

Morrison points out that social context prevented the authors of slave narratives "from dwelling too long or too carefully on the more sordid details of their experience" (109).

2. Introduce the quoted passage with a sentence and a colon.

Commentators have tried to account for the decorum of most slave narratives by discussing social context: "popular taste discouraged the writers from dwelling too long or too carefully on the more sordid details of their experience" (Morrison 109).

3. Set off the quoted passage with an introductory sentence followed by a colon.

This method is reserved for long quotations (four or more lines of prose; three or more lines of poetry). Double-space the quotation, and indent it one inch (ten spaces) from the left margin. Because this special placement identifies the passage as a quotation, do not enclose it within quotation marks. Notice that the final period goes *before* rather than *after* the parenthetical reference. Leave one space after the final period. If the long quotation extends to two or more paragraphs, then indent the first line of these additional paragraphs one-quarter inch (three spaces).

Toni Morrison, in "The Site of Memory," explains how social context shaped slave narratives:

> No slave society in the history of the world wrote more—or more thoughtfully—about its own enslavement. The milieu, however, dictated the purpose and the style. The narratives are instructive, moral and obviously representative. Some of them are patterned after the sentimental novel that was in vogue at the time. But whatever the level of eloquence or the form, popular taste discouraged the writers from dwelling too long or too carefully on the more sordid details of their experience. (109)

Summarizing and paraphrasing sources   Summarizing and paraphrasing an author's text are the most efficient ways to record information. The terms *summary* and *paraphrase* are often used interchangeably to describe a brief restatement of the author's ideas in your own words, but they may be used more precisely to designate different procedures.

- A *summary* condenses the content of a lengthy passage. When you write a summary, you reformulate the main idea and outline the main points that support it.
- A *paraphrase* restates the content of a short passage. When you paraphrase, you reconstruct the passage phrase by phrase, recasting the author's words in your own.

A summary or a paraphrase is intended as a complete and objective presentation of an author's ideas, so be careful not to distort the original passage by omitting major points or by adding your own opinion. Because the words of a summary or a paraphrase are yours, they are not enclosed by quotation marks. But because the ideas you are restating came from someone else, you need to cite the source in your notes and in your text. (See "Avoiding Plagiarism," pages 535–537.)

The following examples illustrate two common methods of introducing a summary or a paraphrase into your paper.

Summary of a long quotation Often, the best way to proceed is to name the author of a source in the body of your sentence and place the page numbers in parentheses. This procedure informs your reader that you are about to quote or paraphrase. It also gives you an opportunity to state the credentials of the authority you are citing.

Award-winning novelist Toni Morrison argues that although slaves wrote many powerful narratives, the context of their enslavement prevented them from telling the whole truth about their lives (109).

Paraphrase of a short quotation You may decide to vary the pattern of documentation by presenting the information from a source and placing the author's name and page numbers in parentheses at the end of the sentence. This method is particularly useful if you have already established the identity of your source in a previous sentence and now want to develop the author's ideas in some detail without having to clutter your sentences with constant references to his or her name.

Slave narratives sometimes imitated the popular fiction of their era (Morrison 109).

Works Cited

Morrison, Toni. "The Site of Memory." Inventing the Truth: The

Art and Craft of Memoir. Ed. William Zinsser. Boston:

Houghton, 1987. 101–24.

Avoiding Plagiarism

Plagiarism is theft. It is using someone else's words or ideas without giving proper credit—or without giving any credit at all—to the writer of the original. Whether plagiarism is intentional or unintentional, it is a serious offense that your instructor and school will deal with severely. You can avoid plagiarism by adhering scrupulously to the following advice.

1. Document your sources whenever you
    - Use a direct quotation
    - Copy a table, chart, or other diagram
    - Construct a table from data provided by others
    - Summarize or paraphrase a passage in your own words
    - Present specific examples, figures, or factual information that you have taken from a specific source and used to explain or support your judgments
2. Take notes carefully, making sure that you identify quotations in your note cards or electronic files. Also, be sure to identify a passage in your notes that is a summary or paraphrase. (See "Taking Notes," pages 531–534.)
3. Formulate and develop your own ideas, using your sources to support rather than replace your own work.

The following excerpt is from Robert Hughes's *The Fatal Shore,* an account of the founding of Australia. The first two examples (Versions A and B) illustrate how students committed plagiarism by trying to use this source in their text. The last example (Version C) illustrates how a student avoided plagiarism by carefully citing and documenting the source.

Original version

Transportation did not stop crime in England or even slow it down. The "criminal class" was not eliminated by transportation, and could not be, because transportation did not deal with the causes of crime.

Version A

Transportation did not stop crime in England or even slow it down. Criminals were not eliminated by transportation because transportation did not deal with the causes of crime.

Version A is plagiarism. Because the writer of Version A does not indicate in the text or in a parenthetical reference that the words and ideas belong to Hughes, her readers will believe the words are hers. She has stolen the words and ideas and has attempted to cover the theft by changing or omitting an occasional word.

Version B

Robert Hughes points out that transportation did not stop crime in England or even slow it down. The criminal class was not eliminated by transportation, and could not be, because transportation did not deal with the causes of crime (168).

Version B is also plagiarism, even though the writer acknowledges his source and documents the passage with a parenthetical reference. He has worked from careless notes and has misunderstood the difference between quoting and paraphrasing. He has copied the original word for word yet has supplied no quotation marks to indicate the extent of the borrowing. As written and documented, the passage masquerades as a paraphrase when in fact it is a direct quotation.

Version C

Hughes argues that transporting criminals from England to Australia "did not stop crime. . . . The 'criminal class' was not eliminated by transportation, and could not be, because transportation did not deal with the causes of crime" (168).

Version C is one satisfactory way of handling this source material. The writer has identified her source at the beginning of the sentence, letting readers know who is being quoted. She then explains the concept of transportation in her own words, placing within quotation marks the parts of the original she wants to quote and using ellipsis points to delete the parts she wants to omit. She provides a parenthetical reference to the page number in the source listed in Works Cited.

Works Cited

Hughes, Robert. The Fatal Shore. New York: Knopf, 1987.

Sample Outline and Research Paper

The author of the following research paper used many features of MLA style to document her paper. Adhering to MLA style, she did not include a title page with her outline or her paper. Instead, she typed her name, her instructor's name, the course title, and the date on separate lines (double-spacing between lines) at the upper left margin. Then, after double-spacing again, she typed the title of her paper, double-spaced, and started the first line of her text. On page 1 and successive pages, she typed her last name and the page number in the upper right-hand corner, as recommended by MLA.

Ashley Keith

Mr. Johnson

English 104

12 December 2006

Video Games Redefining Education

Thesis: While video games should not replace books completely, they can be a useful way of enriching what students learn in class.

I. Parents worry that playing video games damages health.

   A. Parents are concerned about a lack of exercise.

   B. Like any activity, playing video games must be balanced with other pursuits.

   C. The video game industry has begun to create innovative solutions.

II. Parents worry about violent video games.

   A. Violent video games can make children more aggressive.

   B. The same kind of violence exists in other forms of media.

   C. Parents should have the responsibility of monitoring which games their children play.

   D. Not all video games are violent; some can affect the brain in a positive manner.

III. Parents are concerned that playing video games distracts their children from doing their schoolwork.

   A. School is not as engaging as the games.

   B. Children learn while playing video games.

   C. The problem is how to integrate the necessary lessons into the fun context of a game.

IV. Video games enhance children's ability to focus and learn.

   A. Video games engage children with complex systems.

       B. In a recent study, students playing simulation video games gained a deeper understanding of World War II.

   V. What makes a game compelling to learn?

       A. The learning must be a tool to reach the goal.

       B. Games offer a challenge to be overcome as the incentive for learning.

       C. Games have an element of urgency.

  VI. The content of what children learn is important.

       A. Children learn about financial transactions and costumer satisfaction in games.

       B. Video games help players to think and act in a calculated manner.

       C. Video games teach players to cope with complex systems.

       D. Children can apply what they learn in video games to real-life situations.

 VII. Books are still essential to learning.

       A. Good readers draw on their experience, knowledge, and vocabulary to understand.

       B. Reading comprehension is used to gauge students' overall knowledge.

       C. The valuable information collected in books over centuries cannot be replaced.

       D. Video games should be used as supplementary learning tools.

VIII. Making fun and educational video games is a difficult task.

       A. Game designers and educators are not the same, so there is a gap between fun and information.

       B. Game designers and educators need to learn to work together and respect the differences of perspective.

       C. Both groups need to respect the challenge of creating a game.

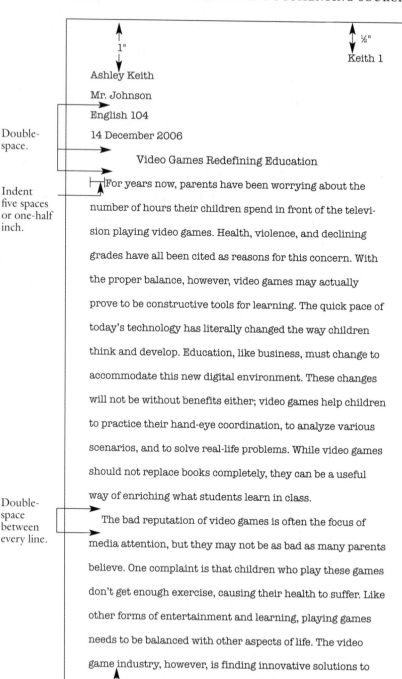

Ashley Keith

Mr. Johnson

English 104

14 December 2006

Video Games Redefining Education

For years now, parents have been worrying about the number of hours their children spend in front of the television playing video games. Health, violence, and declining grades have all been cited as reasons for this concern. With the proper balance, however, video games may actually prove to be constructive tools for learning. The quick pace of today's technology has literally changed the way children think and develop. Education, like business, must change to accommodate this new digital environment. These changes will not be without benefits either; video games help children to practice their hand-eye coordination, to analyze various scenarios, and to solve real-life problems. While video games should not replace books completely, they can be a useful way of enriching what students learn in class.

The bad reputation of video games is often the focus of media attention, but they may not be as bad as many parents believe. One complaint is that children who play these games don't get enough exercise, causing their health to suffer. Like other forms of entertainment and learning, playing games needs to be balanced with other aspects of life. The video game industry, however, is finding innovative solutions to

Margin annotations:

Double-space.

Indent five spaces or one-half inch.

Double-space between every line.

1"

½"

1"

Keith 2

this problem. The new Nintendo Wii console, for instance,
has a wireless controller that detects motion to function.
What does this mean when applied to a game? The player
will take an active role using real-life motions to create results within the virtual world on the screen in front of them.
Another example would be the popular game *Dance, Dance
Revolution (DDR)* which also engages players by getting
them to move. In this game, players quickly shift their feet in
an attempt to follow the dance cues on the screen.

Violence is often another concern of parents. The anxiety is
understandable considering the unfavorable press the issue
has received. In fact, Dr. Vincent Mathews, a radiology professor at Indiana University, reports, "It has been demonstrated
that violent video games can affect brain physiology and the
way the brain functions" (qtd. In "Video Game Violence"). Dr.
Mathews has also testified that video games "could potentially
lead someone to be more aggressive" (qtd. In Toppo, "Violent
Play"). However, the same kind of violence can be found in
other forms of media, including books and movies. If parents
are truly concerned about their child's welfare and behavior,
they should have the responsibility of monitoring which
games their children are allowed to play. Furthermore, video
games have just as much potential to affect the brain in a positive manner. The content of a video game is not always
violent, but the effects of playing can be just as profound.

Quotation: Quote embedded within electronic source.

Quotation: Quote embedded within source from newspaper.

Keith 3

Parents also express concern that video games may be distracting their child from school and, therefore, causing the child's grades to suffer. The problem is that school is not as engaging as the games. Children learn while playing games, though, so the real dilemma then is how to teach them what they need to learn in the fun context of a video game.

Quotation: Quotation from book.

Video games can actually enhance children's ability to focus and learn. Marc Prensky, author of *"Don't Bother Me Mom—I'm Learning,"* points out that

Long quotation: Quotation of more than four lines is set off from the text and is *not* placed within quotation marks. Indent ten spaces or one inch.

> digital technology has been an integral part of our children's lives since birth, and an important result is that they think and process information in fundamentally different ways. . . . These differences go much further and deeper than most parents and educators realize, likely affecting the organization of kids' brains. (28)

Documentation: The parenthetical reference to a block quotation *follows* the final mark of punctuation.

Growing up in this digital environment has allowed children to be faster, more connected, and better able to manage time and tasks. They, therefore, want "immediate response to their each and every action" (Prensky 36). Video games provide players with this immediate feedback in a world of continual action and change. In school, children are forced to slow down and focus on one subject at a time. Their minds are trained to be fast and efficient, and education is just not keeping up. Similarly, Greg Toppo

Keith 4

reports in USA Today that quality learning can result from

playing video games:

> History teacher David McDivitt wanted to find out
>
> whether video games could teach. So he asked 64
>
> sophomores at Oak Hill High School in Converse, Ind.,
>
> last spring to trade in their textbooks for a week and
>
> play a World War II simulation game instead. Another
>
> 45 stuck with the books. At week's end, he tested both
>
> groups and found that the gamers had learned more
>
> about the war and its geography—and wrote more so-
>
> phisticated essays. (D10).

So what makes a game so compelling to learn? According

Dr. James Gee, a professor from the University of Wisconsin

at Madison, learning must be a tool to reach the goal and not

the goal itself (Gee). Currently, the goal for learning is to re-

ceive an A, but in a game the goal is a challenge to be over-

come. This challenge also gives the student some kind of plot

that adds an element of urgency that normal lessons lack. If

children want a more demanding incentive for their educa-

tion, they should be given that opportunity.

The content of what children are learning is also impor-

tant. In his most recent book, Marc Prensky relates stories of

four children under the age of eight who have learned the

concepts of building costs, costumer service, city planning,

and net worth from playing video games such as *The Sims*

Long quotation: Cites author to establish identity and reliability of source.

Paraphrase: Author identified and para- phrased in sentence. Source identified in parentheses.

Keith 5

and *Roller Coaster Tycoon* (9, 10). These are just a few specific examples of how children are able to learn complex concepts at an early age by experiencing reality-based processes in the form of a game. Dr. James Gee also helps to identify some of the principles through which children learn when playing video games. In an interview with Alexis Johnson, Dr. Gee demonstrates how taking on a role within a game can help players to think and act in a particular and calculated manner: "You take on some identity you don't have and you try to grow into that identity" (Gee). Dr. Gee also points out that players develop skills for coping with complex systems while playing. These skills apply to life situations where people interact with each other and their envornment (Gee).

Despite all that video games have to offer, books are still essential in the classroom. Traditionally, books have been the main tool for learning. According to the United States' National Institute for Literacy (NIFL), good readers use "their experiences and knowledge of the world, their knowledge of vocabulary and language structure, and their knowledge of reading strategies . . . to get the most out of it" (2). This helps students to build valuable skills that can be applied in other areas as well. Reading comprehension is also essential for gauging a student's knowledge. All standardized tests require students to be able to read in order to figure out what the problem is and how to solve it. Besides, replacing all of the

Documentation: Cite electronic source.

Keith 6

information that has accumulated in books over the centuries would be impossible. Books provide for a well-rounded education, but video games have the potential to be helpful supplements to the curriculum. Educators want to engage their pupils, and video games may provide the necessary means of doing that.

While game designers continually attempt to make educational games fun, it is not always an easy task because designers are not usually teachers. Thus, there is a gap between fun and information that becomes very difficult to bridge. Fortugno and Zimmerman point out that they have often

> seen educators entering into game development that
> are content to transfer the style of games onto educa-
> tional tasks without understanding the *substance* of
> what makes a game work. And without these funda-
> mentals, the end experience can be dead in the water.

Game designers, likewise, do not understand the principles of learning. In order to develop fun and educational games, teachers and designers must work together and respect the expertise the other has to offer. Above all, they must both remember to respect the challenge (Fortugno and Zimmerman).

Video games, like other forms of media, have a great deal to offer. The effects of playing games can be either negative or positive depending on how the medium is utilized, but this is also the same for books and movies. Video games should

Quotation: Introduction of quote from electronic source explains authority of authors and purpose of quote.

Keith 7

also be used to enrich learning; they cannot replace all of the
valuable information learned from books, but they can make
learning fun and demonstrate a practical application for
newly-acquired knowledge. As technology advances, so must
education.

½"

1"

Works Cited

Double-space

Sample entry: An electronic source by two authors

Fortugno, Nick, and Eric Zimmerman. "Soapbox: Learning to

Play to Learn—Lessons in Educational Game Design."

Gamasutra.com. 5 April 2005. Gamasutra. 12 Dec.

2006. <http://www.gamasutra.com/features/

20050405/zimmerman_01.shtml>.

Gee, James. "The Learning Game—Researchers Study Video

Gaming Principles That Apply to Education." Interview.

By Alexis Johnson. Wisconsin Technology Network

21 Sept. 2003.

Indent five spaces

Prensky, Marc. "Don't Bother Me Mom—I'm Learning!"

St. Paul, MN: Paragon House, 2006.

Sample entry: A book by one author

Toppo, Greg. "Games Take on Books: An Educator's Experi-

ment Supports Teaching Potential." USA Today 30 Nov.

2006, D10.

Toppo, Greg. "Violent Play Rewires Brain." USA Today 30

Nov. 2006. D10.

Sample entry: An article by one author

United States. National Institute for Literacy. Put Reading

First: The Research Building Blocks for Teaching

Children to Read. Sept. 2001. 13 Dec. 2006

<http://www.nifl.gov/partnershipforreading/

publications/reading_first1text.html>.

Sample entry: Electronic source

"Video Game Violence Goes Straight to Kids' Heads."

Forbes.com. 28 Nov. 2006. Forbes. 12 Dec. 2006

<http://www.forbes.com/forbeslife/health/feeds/hscout/

2006/11/28/hscout536261.html>.

Date of access

Date of publication

RHETORICAL GLOSSARY

abstract terms   Terms that refer to qualities or characteristics we can conceive of mentally but cannot see, touch, or hear—for example, *bravery, laziness, perseverance*. Writers often illustrate such terms with examples to help readers grasp their significance. See also **concrete terms**.

accommodation   Sometimes called "nonthreatening argument." The arrangement of evidence in such a way that all parties believe their position has received a fair hearing.

active reading   A manner of reading in which one reads intently and consciously, simultaneously reading for meaning and being aware of one's responses to content and style. An active reader often reads with a pencil and ruler in hand, underlining important phrases or sentences and writing notes in the margin.

allusion   Reference to a person, event, or story familiar to the reader and that will enrich the writer's meaning because it draws on shared knowledge with the reader.

analogy   Comparison between two things or concepts that share certain characteristics although in most ways they are not similar.

analysis   Process that divides something into its parts to understand the whole more clearly.

annotate   To make notes or comments about a piece of writing.

appeals   Strategies used in persuasion and argument. Although most arguments combine different kinds of appeals, many rely on one dominant appeal to make a compelling case.

emotional appeal   Strategy that appeals to feelings, relying heavily on figurative language and provocative imagery to persuade readers.

ethical appeal   Strategy that appeals to the character (or *ethos*) of the writer, relying on the writer's reputation and competence to persuade readers.

logical appeal   Strategy that appeals to reason, relying on factual evidence, expert testimony, and logic to persuade readers.

argument   A piece of writing or an oral presentation in which an author or speaker seeks to persuade an audience to accept a proposition or an opinion by giving reasons and evidence. An argument does not necessarily involve controversy or anger; often it is simply a statement that presents a claim or a particular point of view.

assumption   Something taken for granted, presumed to be true without need for further explanation or proof. Writers usually make the assumption that their readers have certain knowledge and experiences that they can count on as they present their arguments.

audience   The readers for whom a piece of writing is intended. That audience may be close or distant, a small group or a large number, popular or specialized. Professional writers nearly always tailor their writing toward a particular audience about whom they know a good deal—for example, the readers of the *New York Times* or *Parade*—and they adapt their vocabulary and style to suit that audience.

audience analysis   Questions that help identify writer's audience: (1) Who am I writing for? (2) What do they expect of me? (3) What knowledge do they already have? (4) What kind of evidence and strategies are they most likely to respond to?

brainstorming   A way of generating ideas and material for writing by thinking about a topic intently and jotting down random thoughts as they occur to you without regard to whether they seem immediately useful and relevant.

cause and effect   A mode of writing that explains or persuades by analyzing cause-and-effect relationships.

central pattern   The dominant mode of exposition in an essay. Most writers use more than one expository pattern when they construct an essay.

ceremonial discourse   An argument, usually presented orally on special occasions, that appeals to the audience's pride, loyalty, and compassion.

claims and warrants   Often called the Toulmin argument after Stephen Toulmin, the legal philosopher who analyzed and defined its terminology. A method of arranging evidence in an argument that begins by asserting a *claim* (or general assertion), then presents evidence to support that claim and provides a *warrant* (or justification) that links the claim to the evidence.

classification and division   A method of organizing an explanation or argument by dividing a topic into distinct parts or classes and discussing the characteristics of those classes.

comparison and contrast   A popular and convenient way of organizing an essay or article to highlight important ways in which two things or processes can be similar yet different.

concept   A broad intellectual notion that captures the essential nature of an idea, system, or process—for example, the concept of affirmative action or the concept of intellectual property.

conclusion   The final paragraph or section of an essay that brings the argument or explanation to appropriate closure and leaves the reader feeling that the author has dealt with all the issues or questions he or she has raised. Good conclusions are challenging to write, and writers sometimes go through several drafts before they are satisfied.

concrete terms   Terms that refer to something specific and tangible that can be perceived through the senses—for example, *rocky, sizzling, bright yellow.* See also **abstract terms**.

connotation   The added psychological and emotional associations that certain words and phrases carry in addition to their simple meaning. For instance, words like *liberty* and *individualism* carry heavily positive connotations in our culture; they may carry negative connotations in a culture that puts great value on tradition and discipline.

critical reading   Questioning and analyzing content while reading in order to judge the truth, merit, and general quality of an essay or article. A critical reader might ask, "What is the source of the author's information?" "What evidence does he cite in support of his claim?" or "What organization or special interest might she be affiliated with?"

deduction   Usually identified with classical reasoning, or the *syllogism.* A method of arranging evidence that begins with a *major premise,* is restricted by a *minor premise,* and ends with a *conclusion.*

definition   A type of essay that identifies and gives the qualities of a person, object, institution, pattern of behavior, or political theory in a way that highlights its special characteristics. Authors often use definition in combination with description or comparison to make their point.

denotation   The specific, exact meaning of a word, independent of its emotional associations.

description   A kind of factual writing that aims to help the reader visualize and grasp the essential nature of an object, an action, a scene, or a person by giving details that reveal the special characteristics of that person or scene. Most skilled professional writers are good at choosing particular details that give color and interest.

diction   The selection of words to form a desired effect. To achieve this effect, writers consider words from various levels of usage—*popular, learned, colloquial,* and *slang*—and vary words that have appropriate *denotations* and *connotations.*

discovery draft   The first draft of an essay. In a discovery draft, writers expect to discover something new about their purpose, audience, and strategies.

division and classification   See **Classification and Division**.

documentation   A system used for giving readers information about where the writer found the sources he or she used in an academic or research paper or a technical report. Writers document their sources by inserting footnotes, endnotes, or in-text citations so a reader who wants to know more about the topic can easily find the article or book the author is citing or track down other related articles by the same author. The most common system writers use for documentation in academic papers in writing classes is Modern Language Association (MLA) style.

draft   A preliminary version of a piece of writing that enables the author to get started and develop an idea as he or she writes. Authors often write and revise several drafts before they are satisfied with a piece of writing.

editing   Small-scale changes in a piece of writing that is close to being complete. Editing may involve changing some word choices, checking for correct spelling and punctuation, eliminating repetition, rearranging sentences or paragraphs, and generally polishing a manuscript into final form before submitting it to an instructor or editor.

essay   An article or short nonfiction composition that focuses on a specific topic or theme. An essay is generally analytical, speculative, or interpretive. Thus a news story would not be an essay, but an opinion piece could be.

evidence   Specific kinds of information that support the claims of an argument. The most common forms of evidence are:

facts   Specific, detailed evidence—often reported in numbers—that is difficult to refute.

judgments   Conclusions that are inferred from facts. Judgments lend credibility to an argument because they result from careful reasoning.

testimony   Statements that affirm or assert facts. *Eyewitness testimony* enables a person who has had direct experience with an event to report what he or she saw. *Expert witness testimony* enables a recognized authority on a subject to present facts and judgments.

example   A specific incident, object, or anecdote used to illustrate and support a claim or expand on an assertion or generalization. Skillful writers know that readers expect and need examples to clarify a statement, develop a thesis sentence, or support an opening assertion.

figurative language   Language that uses vivid and sometimes fanciful comparisons to enliven and enrich prose. Such language often takes the form of metaphors that explain an unfamiliar thing or process by comparing it to a familiar thing.

focus   As a verb, to concentrate or emphasize; as a noun, the point of concentration or emphasis. Skillful writers know how to focus their writing on a single central idea or point; they have learned to "write more about less," to narrow their topic down to one that they can explore fully and enrich with details.

free-writing   A way to generate ideas for an essay or article by writing down whatever comes into mind about a topic, without concern for organization or style. In free-writing, work quickly to capture ideas. Don't stop to consider whether a phrase or sentence is pertinent or useful—just get it down. After you accumulate a substantial amount of material, you can comb through it to find a starting point for your first draft.

generalization   A broad statement that makes a general claim or an assertion without giving specific details or supporting evidence. Writers often begin an essay with a generalization, then use the next sentences and paragraphs to give details and information that expand on and support the generalization.

headnote A short introductory note before a piece of writing. For example, before each essay in *The Riverside Reader* is a headnote about its author. Its purpose is to give you enough information about the author's age, cultural heritage, and education to put him or her in some cultural context and to give you a few other pertinent facts, such as what else he has written or where she has published other articles.

hypothesis A statement, created during *planning,* of a possible or working purpose for your writing.

image In writing, an impression or visual effect created by an author through the skillful use of language that appeals to the senses of sight and sound.

logic An intellectual system or process that uses reason and evidence to arrive at conclusions. Often writers construct a logical framework for their arguments, setting up cause-and-effect relationships or establishing a chain of reasoning, but also embellish the logic with some figurative and emotional language.

metaphor See **Figurative Language**.

mode A style or pattern of writing or discourse that has certain features that characterize it and make it distinctive. The essays in *The Riverside Reader* are classified according to their mode: narration and description, process analysis, division and classification, definition, cause and effect, persuasion and argument, and so on. Often a writer combines two or three modes in an essay or article but emphasizes one dominant mode.

narration A mode of nonfiction writing that develops an idea or makes a point by telling a story or anecdote. The major strategy for fiction.

pace The rate at which an essay or article moves. Writers can create different paces through word choice, sentence length, and the selection of verbs.

paraphrase A passage that briefly restates in the writer's own words the content of a passage written by someone else in such a way that it retains the original meaning.

persuasion The process of using language to get readers to accept opinions, beliefs, or points of view. The essays in the Persuasion and Argument section of *The Riverside Reader* are the most strongly persuasive, but in an important sense, most essays tend to be persuasive.

plagiarism Using someone else's words or ideas without giving proper credit to the original author. Having another person write something that you turn in for credit—for instance, a term paper taken from the Internet or a commercial source—also constitutes plagiarism and can bring serious consequences.

planning The first stage in the writing purpose. A series of strategies designed to find and formulate information in writing. See **brainstorming** and **freewriting**.

plot The chain of events that develops a story; through it a writer puts characters into a set of circumstances, describes their behavior, and shows the consequences that ensue.

point of view The angle or perspective from which a story or account is told. An account in which the narrator uses "I" and gives an account of an event as it appeared to him or her is called *first-person* point of view. When the narrator recounts an incident as a detached but fully informed observer, he or she is using the *third-person omniscient* point of view.

purpose The goal of an author in a piece of writing. An author may wish to inform, to persuade, to explain, to support an assertion, or to entertain. Sometimes an author combines two or more of these purposes, but usually the author has a primary goal, one that should be evident to the reader.

quotation A passage that gives the actual words a speaker or writer has used in an article, book, speech, or conversation. Authors often use quotations to support their arguments. Such passages must always appear in quotation marks in academic papers or, indeed, in any writing done by a responsible author. Writers who fail to give proper credit for a quotation risk losing the respect of their readers or, in college, of getting disciplined for plagiarism. You'll find the proper format for citing quotations in the Documentation section of *The Riverside Reader*.

refute To counteract an argument or seek to disprove a claim or proposition.

response A reader's reaction to what he or she reads. Readers can respond in different ways—analytically, critically, emotionally, or approvingly—but in nearly every case, that response will come from their own experiences and background: what they know, where they grew up, what kind of culture they lived in, and so on. Readers look at an essay through the lens shaped by their own lives, and that lens affects what they see.

revising Making substantial changes in a written draft, changes that may involve narrowing the topic, adding or deleting material, rearranging sections, or rewriting the introduction or conclusion. Don't look at revising as a process of correcting a draft; rather, you develop your essay by the process of revising and often can clarify and strengthen your ideas by the process. Many writers revise an essay through three or four drafts.

strategy The means or tactic a writer uses to achieve his or her purpose. In the essays in *The Riverside Reader*, authors use various strategies: narration and description, comparison and contrast, process analysis, cause and effect, and so on.

summary A passage that condenses the ideas and content of a long passage in a few sentences or paragraphs; a summary should be objective and accurate.

synthesis Essay that requires writers to incorporate sources, including images, to support an argument. Synthesis essays require the writer to synthesize or integrate these varied sources, particularly to evaluate, cite, and utilize the source material effectively. These researched synthesis essays help writers formulate informed arguments, as well as remind them that they must consider various interpretations to analyze, reflect upon, and write about a given topic.

testimony Evidence offered in support of a claim or assertion. The term suggests factual statements given by experts or taken from sources such as historical or government records or from statistical data. Eyewitness accounts are frequently used as testimony.

thesis sentence   A comprehensive sentence, usually coming in the first paragraph or so of an essay, that summarizes and previews the main idea the author is going to develop in the essay.

tone   The emotional attitude toward their topic that authors convey in their writing. They create tone through the choices they make of words—particularly verbs—of sentence and paragraph length, of styles—formal or informal—and with the kinds of images and figurative language they use.

visual texts   Texts that provide a pictorial method for displaying information. These representational graphics can add visual interest to your subject, illustrate complicated ideas with shapes and images, and provide powerful and dramatic evidence to support your purpose. The most common types of visual texts are:

bar graphs   The comparison of numerical data through vertical or horizontal bars.

diagrams   The use of line drawings to outline, label, and identify various parts of an object, structure, or process.

flow charts   The use of line drawings and text to illustrate the interaction and movement among various parts of an object, structure, or process.

line graphs   The comparison of numerical data through lines that portray trends over time.

maps   The representation of the features of an area by illustrating their form, size, and relationships.

pie charts   The representation of the subdivisions of a subject as pieces of a pie designed to represent percentages. Taken together, these individual percentages add up to 100 percent.

works cited   The list of references and sources that appears at the end of an academic paper or report that uses Modern Language Association (MLA) style and gives the readers enough information about those sources to enable them to evaluate them or use them for further research.

writing process   The steps used in creating a piece of writing. While there is no single writing process that works for every writer or every writing task, writing specialists have found certain patterns when they analyze how most writers seem to work. They agree that productive writers tend to work through a series of steps in the process of creating an essay or article.

Stage 1: Planning. The process of discovering one's topic and generating material. Typical activities are reading and researching, brainstorming, freewriting, talking with fellow writers, and making rough preliminary outlines.

Stage 2: Drafting. Writing a first version of the paper that puts down ideas in some organized form. Many writers continue to generate ideas as they write and often write two or three drafts before they complete one they think is fairly satisfactory.

Stage 3: Revising and rewriting. Reviewing the completed first draft and making substantial changes, perhaps by narrowing the focus, reorganizing, adding and deleting material, or writing a new introduction or conclusion.

Stage 4: Editing, polishing, and proofreading. Making minor word changes, polishing style, and checking for spelling and typographical errors.

writing situation   The context in which a piece of writing is created. Every piece of writing, from business memos to inaugural speeches, is created within some context. Its components are (1) the writer, (2) the topic, (3) the audience, and (4) the purpose. To figure out what your writing situation is for any particular assignment, ask yourself,

- What is my persona or role in this situation?
- What do I want to say?
- To whom am I writing?
- What is my purpose?

By working out an answer to each of these questions before you begin to write, you'll have a good start on turning out a focused and effective product.

ACKNOWLEDGMENTS

JOAN ACOCELLA   "Under the Spell," from *The New Yorker*, July 31, 2000. Reprinted by permission of the author.

MAYA ANGELOU   "My Name is Margaret", copyright © 1969 and renewed 1997 by Maya Angelou, from *I Know Why the Caged Bird Sings* by Maya Angelou. Used by permission of Random House, Inc.

JAMES H. AUSTIN   "Four Kinds of Chance". From *Saturday Review/World*, November 2, 1974. Reprinted by permission of the author.

RUSSELL BAKER   "The Plot Against People," *New York Times*, June 18, 1968. © 1968, The New York Times. Reprinted by permission.

HAROLD BLOOM   "Can 35 Million Books Buyers Be Wrong? Yes" from *The Wall Street Journal*, July 11, 2000. Reprinted by permission of the author.

LAURA BOHANNON   "Shakespeare in the Bush" by Laura Bohannan, from *Ants, Indians, and Little Dinosaurs*, ed. by A. Ternes (Charles Scribner's Sons, 1975). Reprinted by permission of Dennis Bohannan.

FRANCIS BROADHURST   "Cape Wind is Sound for Sound," broadcast February 17, 2006, WCAL. Reprinted by permission.

RACHEL L. CARSON   "The Obligation to Endure", from *Silent Spring*. Copyright © 1962 by Rachel L. Carson. Copyright © renewed 1990 by Roger Christie. Reprinted by permission of Houghton Mifflin Company. All rights reserved.

BRUCE CATTON   "Grant and Lee: A Study in Contrasts" is reprinted from *The American Story*, edited by Earl Schenck Miers. Copyright © 1956 Broadcast Music, Inc. Reprinted by permission.

ARTHUR C. CLARKE   "The Star" from *Nine Billion Names of God* (Harcourt, 1955). Reprinted by permission of the author and the author's agents, Scovil Chichak Galen Literary Agency, Inc.

JUDITH ORTIZ COFER   "The Myth of the Latin Woman: I Just Met a Girl Named Maria" from *The Latin Deli*. Reprinted by permission of The University of Georgia Press.

JOAN DIDION   "In Bed" from *The White Album* by Joan Didion. Copyright © 1979 by Joan Didion. Reprinted by permission of Farrar, Straus and Giroux, LLC.

GRETEL EHRLICH   "Rules of the Game: Rodeo", from *The Solace of Open Spaces* by Gretel Ehrlich, copyright © 1985 by Gretel Ehrlich. Used by permission of Viking Penguin, a division of Penguin Group (USA) Inc.

LARS EIGHNER   "My Daily Dives into the Dumpster" from *Travels with Lisbeth* by Lars Eighner. Copyright © 1993 by the authors and reprinted by permission of St. Martin's Press, LLC.

LOREN EISELEY   "How Flowers Changed the World", from *The Immense Journey* by Loren Eiseley, copyright 1946, 1950, 1951, 1953, 1955, 1956, 1957 by Loren Eiseley. Used by permission of Random House, Inc.

EDWARD M. FORSTER   "My Wood" from *Abinger Harvest*, copyright 1936 and renewed 1964 by Edward M. Forster, reprinted by permission of Harcourt, Inc.

NIKKI GIOVANNI   "Campus Racism 101" from *Racism 101* by Nikki Giovanni. Copyright © 1994 by Nikki Giovanni. Reprinted by permission of HarperCollins Publishers.

ELLEN GOODMAN   "The Chem 20 Factor." Reprinted with the permission of Simon & Schuster Adult Publishing Group, from *Close to Home* by Ellen Goodman. Copyright © 1979 by The Washington Post Company. All rights reserved.

STEPHEN JAY GOULD   "Carrie Buck's Daughter", from *The Flamingo's Smile: Reflections in Natural History* by Stephen Jay Gould. Copyright © 1985 by Stephen Jay Gould. Used by permission of W.W. Norton & Company, Inc.

EDWARD HOAGLAND   "In the Toils of the Law" by Edward Hoagland. From *Walking the Dead Diamond River*. Published by The Lyons Press. Copyright © 1972, 1973, 1993 by Edward Hoagland. Reprinted by permission of Lescher & Lescher, Ltd. All rights reserved.

ROBERT F. KENNEDY JR.   "An Ill Wind Off Cape Cod", *New York Times*, September 16, 2005. © 2005, The New York Times. Reprinted by permission.

JAMAICA KINCAID   "Girl" from *At the Bottom of the River* by Jamaica Kincaid. Copyright © 1983 by Jamaica Kincaid. Reprinted by permission of Farrar, Straus and Giroux, LLC.

MARTIN LUTHER KING JR.   Excerpt from "Letter from Birmingham Jail" is reprinted by arrangement with The Heirs to the Estate of Martin Luther King Jr., c/o Writers House as agent for the proprietor New York, NY. Copyright 1963 Martin Luther King Jr.; copyright renewed 1991 Coretta Scott King.

BARBARA KINGSOLVER   "Stone Soup" from *High Tide in Tucson: Essays from Now or Never* by Barbara Kingsolver. Copyright © 1995 by Barbara Kingsolver. Reprinted by permission of HarperCollins Publishers.

BARRY LOPEZ "The Raven" from *Desert Notes*. Reprinted by permission of Sll/sterling Lord Literistic, Inc. Copyright 1976 by Barry Lopez.

TERRY McMILLAN "The Movie that Changed My Life" from *The Movie that Changed My Life*, edited by David Rosenberg, 1991, Penguin Putnam. Reprinted by permission of The Friedrich Agency.

H. L. MENCKEN "The Penalty of Death", from *A Mencken Chrestomathy* by H. L. Mencken, copyright 1916, 1918, 1919, 1920, 1921, 1922, 1924, 1926, 1927, 1929, 1932, 1934, 1942, 1949 by Alfred A. Knopf, a division of Random House, Inc. Used by permission of Alfred A. Knopf, a division of Random House.

N. SCOTT MOMADAY "The Way to Rainy Mountain," from *The Way to Rainy Mountain*, 1969. Reprinted by permission of the University of New Mexico Press.

GLORIA NAYLOR "A Word's Meaning Can Depend on Who Says It," *New York Times Magazine*, February 20, 1986. Reprinted by permission of Sll/Sterling Lord Literistic, Inc. Copyright © 1986 by Gloria Naylor.

FLANNERY O'CONNOR "Revelation" from *The Complete Stories* by Flannery O'Connor. Copyright © 1971 by the Estate of Mary Flannery O'Connor. Reprinted by permission of Farrar, Straus and Giroux, LLC.

GEORGE ORWELL "Politics and the English Language" by George Orwell, copyright 1946 by Sonia Brownell Orwell and renewed 1974 by Sonia Orwell, reprinted from *Shooting an Elephant and Other Essays* by permission of Harcourt, Inc.

KATHERINE ANNE PORTER "The Jilting of Granny Weatherall" from *Flowering Judas and Other Stories*, copyright 1930 and renewed 1958 by Katherine Anne Porter, reprinted by permission of Harcourt, Inc.

RAINER MARIA RILKE "Anistrophes", translated by Stephen Mitchell, "Tenth Elegy", translated by Stephen Mitchell, from *The Selected Poetry of Rainer Maria Rilke* by Rainer Maria Rilke, translated by Stephen Mitchell, copyright © 1982 by Stephen Mitchell. Used by permission.

RICHARD RODRIGUEZ "Growing Up Old in Los Angeles." Copyright 1997 U.S. News & World Report, L.P. Reprinted with permission.

RICHARD SELZER "The Knife" from *Mortal Lessons: Notes on the Art of Surgery* by Richard Selzer. Copyright © 1974, 1975, 1976, 1987 by Richard Selzer. Reprinted by permission of Georges Borchardt, Inc., on behalf of the author.

SUSAN SONTAG "Beauty," from *Daedalus*, Fall 2005. Copyright © 2005 The Estate of Susan Sontag, reprinted with the permission of the Wylie Agency Inc.

DEBORAH TANNEN "Rapport-Talk and Report-Talk" from *You Just Don't Understand* by Deborah Tannen. Copyright © 1990 by Deborah Tannen. Reprinted by permission of HarperCollins Publishers.

LEWIS THOMAS "The Technology of Medicine", copyright © 1971 by The Massachusetts Medical Society, from *The Lives of a Cell* by Lewis Thomas. Used by permission of Viking Penguin, a division of Penguin Group (USA) Inc.

INDEX